THE DAWN OF THE REFORMATION

THE DAWN
OF THE
REFORMATION

Essays in Late Medieval
and Early Reformation Thought

by
Heiko A. Oberman

WILLIAM B. EERDMANS PUBLISHING COMPANY
GRAND RAPIDS, MICHIGAN

First Published 1986
Reprinted 1992

Library of Congress Cataloging-in-Publication Data

Oberman, Heiko Augustinus
The dawn of the Reformation: essays in
late medieval and early Reformation thought/
Heiko Augustinus Oberman
p. cm.
Originally published: Edinburgh: T&T Clark, c 1986
Includes bibliographical references and index.
ISBN 0-8028-0655-4 (pbk.)
1. Reformation.   2. Religious thought—Middle Ages, 600–1500.
I. Title.
[BR309.0255 1992]
270.6—dc20   92-5204 CIP

Typeset by Print Origination, Liverpool
Printed in Great Britain by St Edmundsbury Press Ltd, Suffolk

ILLUSTRISSIMAE UNIVERSITATIS ABERDONENSIS COETUI
INCLITTISSIMO MAGISTRORUM QUORUM SANO VOTO
AC MATURA DELIBERATIONE GRADUM DOCTORIS
HONORIS CAUSA SACRAE THEOLOGIAE
MIHI INDIGNO ADJUDICATUM EST
HOC OPUSCULUM GRATO PROFUNDOQUE ANIMO DEVOTISSME DEDICO

PREFACE

This volume brings together articles which were written over a twenty-five year period and published variously in faraway and seemingly unrelated places: Harvard and Tubingen, Potchefstroom and Edinburgh. Yet there is a common and central theme: each of these articles testifies to the need and value of placing the Reformation movement in its medieval context and bridging the ideological gaps between late medieval, Renaissance and Reformation studies.

The first six chapters are dedicated to the emergence of the young Luther and his reformation programme. In a sense, the title of the collection itself constitutes a programme insofar as it confronts the romantic vision of a Luther who suddenly appears as a solitary shining morning star, out of the blue skies: the 'Dawn' calls attention to that period of adumbration and clarification in which the Wittenberg reformer was hindered and helped, enriched and infuriated, shaped and sharpened by the conflicting claims of mysticism, Augustinianism, nominalism and renaissance humanism. The impact upon Luther of these philological, spiritual and philosophical traditions must be closely scrutinized in terms of his own response to them; but they have also to be understood in their own right in order to discern what is silently ignored or rejected, and so to delineate the dimensions of what is new and original in early Reformation thought.

The second half of this volume expands the focus from Luther to the broader spectrum of events which mark the Reformation era: the Peasant War and the Copernican Revolution, the beginning of the Counter-reformation and the reform initiated by the Council of Trent – all of these reflected in John Calvin's catholic breadth of intellectual concern.

Both the medieval and the modern 'contexts' remind us also that the treasures of this heritage are contained 'in earthen vessels'.

Heiko A. Oberman
Tucson, Arizona
April 6, 1986

TABLE OF CONTENTS

I

FOURTEENTH-CENTURY RELIGIOUS THOUGHT: A PREMATURE PROFILE

1. INTRODUCTION

THE most telling critique leveled against Arnold Toynbee did not deal with his presentation of the facts or even with his theory of challenge and response, but with his assumption that "civilization" may be regarded and used as a historical entity. Artificial categories allow too much leeway for the historical imagination – a consideration that counts heavily against the treatment of such an external entity as that arbitrary quantity of time we call a century. The word "centuria", meaning a hundred years, belongs neither to the classical nor to the medieval Latin vocabulary. We owe it, as Denis Hay put it, "along with many other useful expressions, to the inventive genius of the humanist pedants of the Renaissance."[1]

Yet, *vestigia terrent*! Whatever else humanist historians achieved, their interpretation of the so-called "Middle Ages" does not encourage us to follow them here. The legitimation for turning nevertheless – from time to time – to such a comprehensive theme lies rather in the need to counterbalance the atomizing tendencies of our specialized inquiries, which afford a scholarly shelter against critique while obscuring the coordinates and shape of the puzzle.

I intend to use this clash of interests to my advantage by showing the pregnant plurality of fourteenth-century thought without yielding to the temptation to enforce patterns upon the material. Even when we limit our purview to Europe and the Western tradition, we shall – among other concerns – have to be sensitive to geographical diversity. Above all, we shall have to take into account the fact that, to put it somewhat forcefully, whereas one part of Europe has barely landed in the thirteenth, another seems already poised to enter the fifteenth century. Admittedly, the wealth of the material accords me a freedom of choice determined to a greater

---

[1] *Europe in the Fourteenth and Fifteenth Centuries* (New York, 1966), p. x.

1

degree by the necessity of limitation than by the standards of comprehensiveness.

The subtitle "A Premature Profile" is my own choice and points in a very different direction. A sketch of the fourteenth century not only must do justice to the pluriformity of receding and emerging trends but also must contend with a major drawback in our own perspective, in so far as that perspective has been determined by preceding scholarship, particularly by that of the first half of this century. This is the time at which such giants as Martin Grabmann and Etienne Gilson ruled the field through their accurate critical editions, their impressive interpretations, and their numerous well-trained students. Before going on to explain how the word "drawback" can be associated with these two names – symbolizing a number of others – I must not neglect to say that our present work in the field of the medieval history of ideas in many respects draws upon their heritage.

Yet, however extensive the scope of their work has been, ranging as it does from Augustine to Descartes, and from the very beginning of scholasticism until "the end of the journey," even so the central core of their research was the thirteenth century and the central point of reference St. Thomas Aquinas. Consequently, the fourteenth century tended to be treated in terms of the reception of Thomas's system and evaluated on the basis of its relation to Thomism. The commemorations of 1274 were internationally dedicated to St. Thomas, and little attention was paid to the fact that 1974 was also the septcentenary of the death of St. Bonaventure. For the fourteenth century, however, St. Bonaventure and the Franciscan tradition prove to be the main source of inspiration, so much so that when the later Middle Ages are viewed as a whole, they can be called the Franciscan Middle Ages.

Some half a century ago the learned Father Mandonnet wrote in commemoration of the canonization of Thomas in 1323, describing the climate of thought at that time: "L'oeuvre philosophique et théologique de Thomas d'Aquin s'est deja universellement impose au monde intellectuel."[2] I have only to mention Robert Kilwardby, Durandus de St. Porciano, Robert Holcot, and William Crathorn to bring to remembrance that this "universal acceptance" of Thomas does not even apply to the Dominican order. Furthermore, the names of Duns Scotus and William of Occam represent formidable alternatives within scholasticism in general. I say formidable advisedly. Representatives of "the Thomist point of view" are inclined, with

---

[2]*Mélanges Thomistes* (Paris, 1923), p. 4.

Gilson, to regard the fourteenth century as intellectually "the end of the journey." As Armand Maurer put it, the period is one of "disunion and disintegration," reflected in its "tendency toward division and decline"[3] – as if unity had preceded it ... and dissolution were its hallmark!

Finally, it would be a mistake to identify the universities with Mandonnet's "monde intellectuel." The increasing subordination of the monastic and cathedral schools to the university-related *studia* is indeed noticeable; yet the *translatio studii* from the monastic schools of the eleventh century to the new universities was far from complete. The earlier study of the *sacra pagina* was never completely replaced by what Grabmann called "the scholastic method"; alongside this "the symbolic method,"[4] which looked for harmonies, names and numbers, was kept alive and revitalized in ever-changing coalitions with a whole range of methods varying from typology to cabbalistic exegesis. In the intellectual world outside the university-related *studia*, Bernard of Clairvaux, the Victorines, and above all Bonaventure determine the questions asked as well as the answers given.

We have only just begun to discover and analyze the sources and resources of this world of thought, so that an assessment at this point is perforce premature and provisional. Yet we know enough to state that a monograph on our topic would have to include at least the following chapters in order to deal with even the major issues and trends:

The Myth of the Thomist Phalanx
The Franciscan Hegemony
The Augustinian Renaissance
The Coming of the Third Age
High Mysticism and the Beginnings of the *Devotio moderna*

Rather than pursuing only one of these topics it might well be more useful to advance a few theses on each of these themes.

---

[3]*Medieval Philosophy* (New York, 1962), p. 265. It is not completely clear whether it is appropriate to refer here to Gordon Leff, *The Dissolution of the Medieval Outlook: An Essay on Intellectual and Spiritual Change in the Fourteenth Century* (New York, 1976). The title hearkens back to the period in the author's literary career prior to his *William of Ockham: The Metamorphosis of Scholastic Discourse* (Manchester, 1975). The old skins are filled with new wine when "dissolution" is defined as "removing the old categories and with them the old certainties. The Christian assumptions remained unimpaired but they were being put to a new meaning ..." (*The Dissolution*, p. 91). On the other hand, Leff observes with reference to Ockham: "... his was a system to end system. He succeeded only too well" (ibid.).

[4]Thus designated by Horst Dieter Rauh, *Das Bild des Antichrist im Mittelalter. Von Tyconius zum deutschen Symbolismus* (Münster, 1973).

2. THE MYTH OF THE THOMIST PHALANX

We have already taken issue with a Thomistic stacking of the cards in the fourteenth century. The extent to which the thesis of Thomist supremacy has affected our perspective on the period appears from the fact that André Chastel in his excellent book on Italian art discerns Thomas's principle of individuation to be operative in Giotto's work as a whole and particularly in his presentation of the individuality of each person.[5] However, since the uniqueness of each individual being is a typical Franciscan theme and since throughout his life (the Bardi Chapel in St. Croce dates from 1320) Giotto was fascinated by St. Francis, Chastel's thesis may well leave the impression of being farfetched. In their interpretation of French Gothic cathedrals local art historians show Chastel to be no exception – the Thomist myth tends to lend rhythm to their eloquence.

The stature of St. Thomas is not to be denied. The transcription and discussion of his works play a significant role in the universities and in the Dominican *studia*, particularly south of the Alps. In his *Le Thomisme et la pensée italienne de la Renaissance*[6] Paul Oskar Kristeller has traced the inspiration derived by Renaissance philosophers from St. Thomas. And in the middle of the fifteenth century there is a short revival of Thomas in Cologne around Heinrich of Gorcum. Yet as Weiler has shown, even before the Reuchlin affair and the *Letters of Obscure Men* checked the ascent of Thomism, the highly technical "schoolish" form of Thomism did not give it much of a chance in an age looking increasingly for the virtues of *simplicitas* and *eloquentia*.[7]

Telling changes had already taken place in the fourteenth century. It has been argued that "the early Thomistic school"[8] retained the original impetus of Thomas to a remarkable extent. But it did so under adverse circumstances and only by paying a high price. We referred to the opposition within the order by Kilwardby and Durandus. In a period of twenty-five years the Dominican General Chapter had to repeat its support of Thomas four times before the injunction to teach Thomas "singulariter" began to be heeded. The fruit of these decrees is the *lectura thomasina*, the commentary on the *Sentences* of Lombard according to the young Thomas.[9]

---

[5]*L'Art italien*, 2 vols. (Paris, 1956), 1:148.

[6](Montreal and Paris, 1967).

[7]Anton G. Weiler, *Heinrich von Gorkum (†1431): Seine Stellung in der Philosophie und der Theologie des Spätmittelalters* (Hilversum, 1962), p. 302. Cf. "Auch das fünfzehnte Jahrhundert gehörte nicht dem hl. Thomas" (ibid., p. 303).

[8]Frederick J. Roensch, *Early Thomistic School* (Dubuque, Iowa, 1964).

[9]Josef Koch, *Kleine Schriften*, 2 vols. (Rome, 1973), 2:134.

By the early twenties the opposition from outside the order had become so forceful that the early disciples earned for themselves the name *defensores*. The *Correctorium* of William de la Mare, a selection of 230 errors of Aquinas, was rapidly transcribed and is extant today in numerous copies. Josef Koch has pointed out that the most vocal among the *defensores*, Peter de Palude, is not conspicious for a strikingly profound mastery of Thomas's world of thought.[10] Since the points attacked were *capita selecta* particularly pertaining to metaphysical issues, the *defensores* transmitted a metaphysical Thomas, without paying equal attention to Thomas as the interpreter of the Fathers and of the Scriptures.

In this way the caricature of an Aristotelian, anti-Augustinian Thomas could take hold. Furthermore, the *lectura thomasina* encouraged a stress on the young Thomas of the *Sentences* commentary rather than on the mature Thomas of the *Summa theologiae*. At least until Capreolus (†1444) in the middle of the fifteenth century, it was the young Thomas which determined the profile of the total Thomas. The implications of this may be gleaned from the fact that whereas the young Thomas shows semi-Pelagian inclinations in the central doctrine of justification, the mature Thomas of the *Summa* teaches unambiguously Augustine's justification *sola gratia*.

To conclude this section, when we speak about the emergence of Thomism we have to be very clear in our minds that Thomism stands for a particular type of interpretation of Thomas and not for the thought of Aquinas himself. Of more immediate significance, however, is the fact that the transformation of Thomas's thought in the hands of the *defensores* could not yield a solid phalanx of school loyalty in the order itself. What is more, the metaphysical *Doctor Communis* presented by his defenders may well explain why Aquinas failed to appeal to philosophers and theologians well into the fifteenth century.

3. THE FRANCISCAN HEGEMONY

First among the adverse circumstances for the organic development of Thomism are the anti-Averroist condemnations of 1270 and 1277. Although Latin Averroism made a major comeback in the fifteenth century, it would not have been necessary to mention here this rich and adaptable current of thought were it not for the fact that it became a significant factor in evoking the Franciscan alternative.

Research on Averroism is presently moving on such a broad front that a

---

[10]Ibid.

sketch of its profile would require an extensive weighing of hypotheses, but the far-reaching importance of the Parisian condemnation of Averroism has long been recognized. First of all, it put extra pressure on the *defensores* to clear Thomas of the charge of Averroist tendencies. More important, however, is the resulting frequent appeal to the Parisian ruling that no theology should be taught in the philosophical faculty. Consequently, the study of the authentic Aristotle could be pursued with force – but without the forced effort to baptize the Stagirite. However much Thomas had advanced the cause of Aristotelian studies, his had been a synthesis of Aristotle, as the chief witness for natural reason, with the supernatural truth of faith. Duns Scotus, and even more boldly Occam and the Nominalists, took great pride in presenting a purer, more scholarly interpretation of Aristotle. In short, the pagan Aristotle was discovered and allowed to speak for himself, often proving himself to be too self-willed for theological usage or exploitation.

However, the main effect of the concern with Averroism was the widespread and profoundly Franciscan reaction of aversion and suspicion over against a metaphysically fool-proof causal system which embraces the whole chain of being, including God as first and final cause. Initially, the chain of being itself was not called into question, but rather the resulting close association of God and necessity. Hence, a theology which could render an account of God as a freewilling person could count on a sympathetic hearing.

This intellectual climate proved to be propitious for the new trend which we call "the Franciscan alternative." In so far as it drew on the Augustinian concept of *promissio*, this alternative was by no means new but only newly emphasized. Initiating and underlying all of history, this *promissio* is God's reliable commitment, often referred to as *foedus* or *pactum*. This commitment is, as it were, the very riverbed whence springs the whole history of salvation, preceding, connecting, and underlying both Creation and Redemption. Hence we can best designate it as metahistorical. The extent to which this *metahistorical* conception deviates from the *metaphysical* ontology of Thomas can be gauged in many areas of theology, ranging all the way from predestination to redemption and justification.

Indeed, these two conceptions are *totaliter aliter*. Whereas in Thomas' metaphysical ontology the natural and supernatural realms are organically joined by the *Being* of God in whom we participate by reason and faith, the metahistorical alternative retraces nature and supernature, creation and redemption, to the *Person* of God, and points to God's will as – to use air traffic terminology – the "ceiling" of theology. His eternal decree of self-commitment has established the limits of theology which to surpass is to trespass, yielding sheer speculation.

It is this development which makes the use of the dialectics of the *potentia absoluta* and the *potentia ordinata* so significant. The *potentia ordinata* means here the domain of theology, properly finding its subject matter in the revealed will of God, in what God actually decided to do in creation and redemption. *Potentia absoluta* marks the realm where speculative reason is no longer guided by faith. It is the domain of God's unlimited freedom abstracted from his commitments *de potentia ordinata*. To look for the demarcation line between *potentia absoluta* and *potentia ordinata* becomes a second habit for all those who reject the axioms of the Thomistic metaphysical ontology. The insistence on the *potentia ordinata* as the basis of theology proper by no means implies a *sola scriptura* principle; rather, it points to the *sources* of revelation, as testified to in Scripture, the Fathers and the doctrinal decisions of the Church.

The Nominalists proudly regarded themselves as the more consistent adherents of this metahistorical conception of theology.[11] Admittedly, just as they could gratefully accept the moral theology of Thomas, so could they praise Scotus for having seen the dangers of metaphysical ontology. But on a number of points they charged Duns with having overstepped the boundaries of theology by a speculative penetration of the inner being of God. The suspicion of speculation and the programmatic call for an affective theology in its place will have to concern us again in the last section. It should here be emphasized that this anti-speculatism should not be confused

---

[11]In the last ten years significant advances have been made in the characterisation of single fourteenth-century authors. Special attention has been given to the Parisian Statutes of September 25, 1339 ("quod doctrina Okanica non dogmatizetur") and of December 29, 1340 ("modicam habent de nominibus sollicitudinem"). Cf. Ruprecht Paqué, *Das Pariser Nominalistenstatut: Zur Entstehung des Realitätsbegriffs der neuzeitlichen Naturwissenschaft*, Quellen und Studien zur Geschichte der Philosophie 14 (Berlin, 1970), pp. 306, 8–13. It has become clear that when "Nominalism" is reduced to epistemology and within that field is further restricted to the thesis that universals are mere "nomina" we are left with a so subtly differentiated series of individual thinkers that we lose sight of the lines of communication between them. From the perspective of the fifteenth century, however, Occam, Gregory of Rimini, Buridan, d'Ailly, Marsilius of Inghen, Adam Dorp, Albert of Saxony, Gabriel Biel, and others form one Nominalistic school. Cf. the French royal decrees of March 1, 1474, and April 30, 1481. See Augustin Renaudet, *Préréforme et humanisme à Paris pendant les premières guerres d'Italie (1494–1517)*, 2nd ed. (Paris, 1953), pp. 92–94. Whilst acknowledging the peril of an "anachronism" which would apply categories of some 150 years later, I suggest that the Franciscan hegemony of the fourteenth century allowed those domestic discords to gain a prominence which seen from the perspective of a century and a half later, when the coalition of emergent Thomism and Scotism became a force to be reckoned with, were to prove less divisive and of secondary significance. Hence the common shape of Nominalism is not created but formulated by the *via moderna* of the fifteenth-century universities. I trace this fifteenth/sixteenth-century perspective in *Werden und Wertung der Reformation. Vom Wegestreit zum Glaubenskampf* (Tübingen, 1977), pp. 28–55.

with anti-intellectualism or intellectual tiredness. Rather, it is the Franciscan alternative presented with such vigor, force, and conviction that it determines the mind and heart of a whole epoch. This anti-speculative, affective thrust seems to me to explain the Franciscan hegemony in the fourteenth century as well as during a large part of the fifteenth and sixteenth centuries. As a matter of fact, Franciscan thought dominated medieval intellectual history from Duns Scotus through the Great Schism, not losing much of its momentum in northern Europe until the Erasmians and reformers first dwarfed the differences between the "schools" and then evoked a new longing for a comprehensive system of thought.

4. The Augustinian Renaissance

There is no period in the history of medieval thought which could not be presented as a new phase in the appropriation of the heritage of St. Augustine. Yet in the third decade of the fourteenth century we encounter a revival of Augustine which may well lay claim to the much abused designation Renaissance. Its chief characteristic is that Augustine was no longer presented as only one of the four Church Fathers, but rather as the authoritative and definitive interpreter of the one *Evangelium* located in the Scriptures. In an extensive scholarly history reaching from Werner to Stange, Müller, van Rhijn, and Stakemeier, a third school, alongside the Thomist and Franciscan traditions, has been construed which is claimed to include also Martin Luther. As Hubert Jedin has clearly seen,[12] many key sources require critical editions before such far-reaching conclusions can be drawn. However, the first phase of this "Augustinian" school in the fourteenth century can now be reconstructed. We are dealing here with what one must call academic Augustinianism. But it is more than just that. I believe that we should avoid the designation "Augustinian revival," because of its emotional overtones. "Augustinian Renaissance" is perhaps more appropriate, since in ways yet to be traced with precision its two major representatives, Thomas Bradwardine and Gregory of Rimini, are affiliated with the beginnings of Renaissance humanism.

Thomas Bradwardine, archbishop of Canterbury, before falling victim to the devastating plague in 1349, was associated during his London period with the sodality around the bibliophile Richard de Bury. His major theological

---

[12]See my "'Tuus sum, salvum me fac'. Augustinréveil zwischen Renaissance und Reformation," in *Scientia Augustiniana: Studien über Augustinus, den Augustinismus und den Augustinerorden. Festschrift Adolar Zumkeller OSA*, ed. C. P. Mayer and W. Eckermann (Würzburg, 1975), pp. 349–394, 349, nn. 1 and 2.

work, *De Causa Dei contra Pelagium*, presents a *summa augustiniana* based to a large extent on Augustine who is for him the *Doctor Catholicus*.[13] His scholastic authorities range from Anselm and Bernard to Thomas and Scotus, but time and again he returns to the conviction that where these have come to valid conclusions they have drawn their wisdom from St. Augustine. As an outstanding member of the Merton School, this comprehensive savant also stands in the vanguard of progress in the history of science. As John Murdoch has shown, in Merton under Bradwardine's aegis "Calculatores" initiated the new math of the fourteenth century.[14] This not only created a scientific language but also allowed for a theoretical differentiation between physics and metaphysics, which was to furnish the springboard for advances in the Nominalists' theory of experimentation in the following decades.

In her precise and delightful *English Friars and Antiquity in the Early Fourteenth Century*,[15] Beryl Smalley tentatively proposes the term "proto-humanism" to describe the classicizing tendencies of a group of English clerics. Bradwardine is entitled to a worthy place in this circle in view of his extensive use of classical authors, particularly of the Latin poets Virgil and Ovid. We have learned to be cautious with the use of the term "humanism," and it should not be overlooked that Bradwardine respects Ovid explicitly not as a source of delight (*voluptas*), but as a source of truth (*auctoritas*).[16] By this very token, however, Ovid forms for him a link in that chain of truth, of the *sapientes* or *prisci theologi* reaching back via Hermes Trismegistos to Enoch, which was to play such a significant role in Renaissance thought. Paul Kristeller has pointed to the significance of Thomas and Thomism in the circle around Ficino.[17] On an earlier occasion I have pointed to the parallels between nominalist anthropology and aspects of Italian humanism.[18] The discovery of St. Augustine as the *Doctor Catholicus* and as the interpreter of

---

[13]*Thomae Bradwardini Archepiscopi olim Cantuariensis, De Causa Dei contra Pelagium et de virtute causarum ad suos Mertonenses Libri Tres* 3.52, ed. H. Savilius (London, 1618; repr. Frankfurt, 1964), fol. 855B.

[14]Besides Thomas Bradwardine the Mertonian "calculatores" comprise John Dumbleton, William Heytesbury, and Richard Swineshead. See further the article by Edith Sylla, "Medieval Quantifications of Qualities: The 'Merton School'," *Archive for History of Exact Science* 8 (1971), 9–39, 24, n. 43.

[15]*English Friars and Antiquity in the Early Fourteenth Century* (Oxford, 1960).

[16]*De Causa Dei* 1.1, fol. 73D.

[17]*Le Thomisme*, p. 96 f. Cf. *Renaissance Philosophy and the Mediaeval Tradition* (Latrobe, Pa., 1966), p. 40 f.

[18]Cf. my "Some Notes on the Theology of Nominalism with Attention to its Relation to the Renaissance," *Harvard Theological Review* 53 (1960), 47–77. See especially Charles Trinkaus, "Erasmus, Augustine, and the Nominalists," *Archiv für Reformationsgeschichte* 67 (1976), 5–32.

Christian experience is yet a third reminder of the continuity between medieval and Renaissance thought.

For Bradwardine the focal point of his theological work was the thesis "sola fide sine operibus praecedentibus fit homo iustus,"[19] which on the basis of Augustine he defended against the modern Pelagians. Exactly the same applies to Gregory of Rimini. Gregory's emphasis on the overriding authority of Augustine is so striking that one would have surmised Bradwardinian influence even if there had not been solid evidence: Gregory's *Lectura in primo et secundo sententiarum* carries three explicit references to *De Causa Dei*.[20] Nevertheless, Gregory's system of thought is so clearly all of one piece and makes such a different use of St. Augustine that we have to assume two simultaneous and independent recoveries of the heritage of St. Augustine. They were different, and their impact was to be different. In the theological domain Bradwardine's influence remained limited; admittedly, Wyclif made good use of him and soon copies of Bradwardiniana were available in Paris and Vienna. Nonetheless, at the beginning of the sixteenth century Johannes Eck reported that his search for a copy of Bradwardine's works was in vain.[21] Gregory's impact, on the other hand, can be traced through to the sixteenth century and it played a significant role during the Leipzig Disputation between Eck and Luther in 1519.[22]

A number of reasons may explain this difference in influence: the

---

[19]*De Causa Dei* 1.43. fol. 394B.

[20]Damasus Trapp has called attention to an entry ("Inceptus est [Secundus Gregorii] 17. Maii 1342") which establishes that the date of completion hitherto assumed (1344) applies to the *final* "publishable" (or rather "published") form of the manuscript, complete with tabulae and tituli: "... Gregory was 'Sententiarius dispositus ad legendum' in Paris from 1341–42; he became 'Baccalareus actu legens' in 1342." "Gregory of Rimini: Manuscripts, Editions and Additions," *Augustiniana* 8 (1958), 425–443; 425 f. At least a major part of *De Causa Dei* must have been written at Oxford before 1335, the date of Bradwardine's move to London: "Quicquid nunc scribo Oxoniae . . ." *De Causa Dei* 2.22, fol. 559B. For the respective dating of these main works of Bradwardine and Gregory of Rimini see William J. Courtenay, "John of Mirecourt and Gregory of Rimini on Whether God can Undo the Past," *Recherches de Théologie ancienne et médiévale* 39 (1972), 224–256, and 40 (1973), 147–174, 150, 157; idem, "Some Notes on Robert of Halifax, O.F.M.," *Franciscan Studies* 33 (1973), 135–142, 139; idem, "Alexander Langely, O.F.M.," *Manuscripta* 18 (1974), 96–104, 100, n. 16; idem, *Adam Wodeham: An Introduction to His Life and Writings*, Studies in Medieval and Reformation Thought 21 (Leiden, 1977), p. 117 f. My earlier arguments for the priority of Bradwardine remain uncontested: *Archbishop Thomas Bradwardine, a Fourteenth Century Augustinian: A study of His Theology in Its Historical Context* (Utrecht, 1958), p. 214.

[21]"Tuus sum, salvum me fac'," p. 355, n. 30.

[22]*Gregorii Ariminensis super primum et secundum Sententiarum* (Venice, 1522; repr. St. Bonaventure, 1955), II d 26, 27, 28 q 1 art. 3; fol. 92 P. Cited by Leif Grane, "Gregor von Rimini und Luthers Leipziger Disputation," *Studia Theologica* 22 (1968), 29–49, 36.

increasing isolation of Oxford during the period of the Hundred Years' War, the generation gap caused by one of the most devastating waves of the Black Death, and the disadvantages of a secular cleric without benefit of support from a monastic order were all important. But the decisive factor, it seems to me, is the fact that Bradwardine tried to argue the case of God's primacy and the prevenience of his grace on the basis of a causal metaphysics in keeping with the old way, the *via antiqua*, as the university statutes of the fifteenth century would classify this tradition. Gregory of Rimini, on the other hand, succeeded in matching this central Augustinian theme with the achievements of the *via moderna*.

Hitherto it has been assumed that Gregory was a Nominalist in his philosophy and an Augustinian in his theology. The Tübingen edition of his *Lectura* has now made sufficient progress for us to see more clearly that Gregory was a Nominalist in his theology as well as in his philosophy, and at the same time in both an Augustinian. His two central points of reference, the Scriptures in matters of faith and experience in the evaluation of time and space, are so coordinated that no trace of what has been called the epistemological skepticism of the *moderni* is left. At the same time their Pelagian tendencies in the realm of faith are eradicated. In this way Gregory could become the founder of the *Schola moderna Augustiniana* within his order and could incorporate as a cornerstone the *experientia* which would continue to be the central theme of that century.

The evidence does not yet allow us to draw a firm line from this Augustinian Renaissance to that Renaissance Augustinianism which has recently been described so well by William Bouwsma.[23] But, whereas we mentioned as a possibility Bradwardine's connection with proto-humanism in England, we have even stronger indications of Gregory's involvement with early Italian humanism. The unprecedented precision with which Gregory quotes his Augustine and his ability to unmask pseudo-Augustinian writings are matched and reflected by the *Milleloquium Divi Augustini* produced in his immediate environment by a task force of Augustinians under the direction of Bartholomew of Urbino (†1350). Containing more than 15,000 quotations from Augustine, with an elaborate index, this precious tool is introduced and recommended by Petrarch, and it may help to explain the authentic flavor of Petrarch's colloquies with an Augustine

---

[23]"The Two Faces of Humanism. Stoicism and Augustinianism in Renaissance Thought" in: *Itinerarium italicum: The Profile of the Italian Renaissance in the Mirror of its European Transformations, Dedicated to Paul Oskar Kristeller*, ed. H.A Oberman and T. A. Brady, Jr., Studies in Medieval and Reformation Thought 14 (Leiden, 1975), pp. 3–60.

who had shortly before played only a marginal role in Dante's *Divina Commedia*.[24]

5. THE COMING OF THE THIRD AGE

We now turn to an issue that took on overriding institutional importance on the eve of and during the Western Schism. The Franciscan alternative was operative not only in the area of metahistorical conceptions but also in the sensitive realm of ecclesiology. If the fifteenth century was the age of conciliarism and the quest for corporate structures of checks and balances, the fourteenth century was the climax of claims for the See of St. Peter. We can observe this first of all in *Unam Sanctam* (1302) with its doctrine of papal supremacy in Church and world that ushered in the Avignon exile. In retrospect, of perhaps even more lasting importance is the contribution made by the Franciscan theologian Peter John Olivi. Although he died in 1298 his influence reaches well into the fourteenth century.

Olivi's interpretation of the *suprema potestas* has drawn special attention ever since Brian Tierney in his *Origins of Papal Infallibility*[25] pointed to Olivi's *Quaestio de infallibilitate Romani Pontificis*. In this context, I cannot pursue the resulting debate about Tierney's thesis and the various reactions by Offler, Congar, and Kempf, and most aggressively by Bäumer.[26] Seldom have the different approaches of historians and dogmatic theologians in interpreting texts become so explicit. For my part I must concede the weight of Tierney's historical arguments; I cannot accept Congar's claim that the texts concerned must be read "dans le dynamisme des idées exprimées,"[27] when this means that later interpretations are read back into the earlier sources.

It is the fourteenth-century impact of Olivi that is important for us here. As becomes clear on the basis of Olivi's *Commentary on the Apocalypse* – edited by Warren Lewis and now in the course of being printed by the Franciscan Fathers in Grottaferrata – Olivi was aware of the fact that he was living on the eve of the coming of the Third Age, of the final *translatio ecclesiae* when the

---

[24]Cf. Kaspar Elm, "Mendikanten und Humanisten im Florenz des Tre- und Quattrocento. Zum Problem der Legitimierung humanistischer Studien in den Bettelorden," in *Die Humanisten in ihrer politischen und sozialen Umwelt*, ed. O. Herding and R. Stupperich (Boppard, 1976), pp. 51–85.

[25]*Origins of Papal Infallibility, 1150–1350: A Study of the Concepts of Infallibility, Sovereignty and Tradition in the Middle Ages*. Studies in the History of Christian Thought 6 (Leiden, 1972).

[26]Cf. my survey article "'Et tibi dabo claves regni caelorum.' Kirche und Konzil von Augustin bis Luther. Tendenzen und Ergebnisse, II," *Nederlands Theologisch Tijdschrift* 29 (1975), 97–118, 113 f.

[27]See Congar's review in *Revue d'histoire ecclésiastique* 68 (1973), 162–167, 166.

hierarchy of the Church will be replaced by the elect: "transferetur propter eius adulteria ad electos."[28] Accordingly Olivi was not interested in papal infallibility as such, but rather in holding out this high doctrine of the papacy as a standard for all to see – to see and to know that the Third Age will have come as soon as a pope no longer lives up to this high set of qualifications. In 1326 Pope John XXII condemned this treatise as heretical, but in the eighty years before conciliarism temporarily canalized and contained the spiritualist threat to the established Church, a papal condemnation was no match for the attractions of these explicitly Joachite ideas.[29] Instead, Pope John's condemnation must itself have seemed to be evidence of the coming of the Third Age.

The rapid spread of these ideas, traceable to northern France and Britain, is shown by the intensity of calculations concerning the end of the world and its initiation by the coming of the Antichrist. "Calculatores" is therefore not only the proper designation for the new mathematicians of the Merton School, but also for those who investigated the timetable of the Last Things, the *eschata*.[30] Arnaldo of Villanova calculated the end for c. 1366 and received a sympathetic hearing from the Dominican John of Quidort.[31] Many other dates were circulated before the academic reaction finally made itself felt. Guido Terrena regarded these calculations as sheer speculation – "fictio et vana ... curiosa est"[32] – and Nicholas of Lyra represented the case of scholarly exegesis when in 1310 he concisely declared: "simpliciter dico quod nescio."[33]

In 1313 the chancellor of the University of Oxford, Henry of Harclay, showed how history had already taken care of most of these prognostications: time has shown them to be sheer fantasy – "experientia temporum," or as he writes on a preceding page "experimento temporis" – "iam apparent falsa."[34] These "calculatores" are frequently referred to as "speculatores," designated as such in a positive sense on the basis of Jeremiah 6.17. This para-academic and at once para-ecclesial tradition of "speculators" is still sufficiently alive in the early sixteenth century to be a

---

[28]*Lectura super Apocalipsim* cap. 3:1, ed. W. Lewis, p. 246 (MS).

[29]Cf. the amazing statement by Gordon Leff: "The role of the Holy Spirit so important to Joachim, was not mentioned." *Heresy in the Later Middle Ages*, 2 vols. (Manchester, 1967), 1:125.

[30]Cf. Franz Pelster, "Die Quaestio Heinrichs von Harclay über die zweite Ankunft Christi *per la storia della pietà* 1 (Rome, 1951), 26–81, 31, 78, line 21.

[31]Ibid., p. 12, line 7.

[32]Ibid., p. 45.

[33]Ibid., p. 44.

[34]Ibid., p. 57, line 35; p. 56, line 35.

decisive factor in forming the thought of Thomas Müntzer, whose death in 1525 marks in this respect the end of an era. Choosing the preceding passage from the same chapter of Jeremiah as the climax of his 95 Theses – pax, pax, et non est pax – Martin Luther had learned to distinguish between experience and experiment well enough to side with the critics of the "speculators."

Guido's evaluation – vana curiosa est – is representative of a major concern in the later Middle Ages. His summary warning against vain speculation and metaphysical penetration of the realm not revealed to men – i.e., that of the *potentia absoluta* – finds an echo reaching from the earliest Nominalists to the representatives of the *Devotio moderna* and recurs in a poem by Pico recently discovered by Paul Oskar Kristeller. For Pico it is clear that the *sapiens*, the wise man, abstains from speculation about what lies beyond revelation and experience; he abstains from the concern, as Pico put it, "abstrusas rerum cognoscere causas."[35]

Two points seem to me characteristic of fourteenth-century eschatology, which in the history of thought is often synonymous with reform ideology. First, the expectation of the Third Age did not imply the pursuit of the millennium but rather the pursuit of holiness which is to bring about reform and, as the radical Franciscans felt, will soon bring to its close the era of the prelates. Second, exactly the same terminology that was used in the late fifteenth and early sixteenth centuries to discuss the certitude of salvation was applied in the fourteenth to the coming of the Antichrist. Some held that no knowledge of the time of his coming is possible, some that conjectures are permissible, and others that absolute certitude is both possible *and* the mark of the true Christian. The terminology applied to formulate – and rebuke – the chief issue of Reformation theology is derived from the earlier search for the supra-individual end not of life but of time, the time of the Antichrist and the coming of the Third Age.[36]

6. HIGH MYSTICISM AND THE BEGINNINGS OF THE *DEVOTIO MODERNA*

This daring picture would be too incomplete if we did not add two more

---

[35]*Giovanni Pico della Mirandola and his Sources* (Florence, 1965), p. 91.

[36]The conjunction of the indicated anti-speculative tendency – with its residual Aristotle-critique – and eschatological speculation is admirably documented by the "time test" which Henry of Harclay quotes from Alexander Neckam's *De naturis rerum:* "... Aristoteles philosophus viam universe carnis ingressurus precepit, [ut] omnia prescripta sua, que erant maxime subtilitatis, ponerentur in sepulcro secum, ne utilitati posteritatis sue deservirent, et ipse dum vixit locum sepulcro manu ita munivit, ut nullus usque huc ibi accedere potuit. Tamen locus iste, ut dicit, cedet Antichrito, cum venerit." F. Pelster, "Die Quaestio Heinrichs von Harclay," p. 77. lines 7–11.

lines characteristic of fourteenth-century piety.

In the North the high mysticism of Eckhardt, Suso, and Ruysbroeck evoked a reaction in the form of the *Devotio moderna*. The anti-speculative tendencies we have previously noted were accompanied by an emphasis on *simplicitas* in thought and life, a virtue basic to the *Devotio moderna*. Geert Groote was very much aware of the precarious position of his lay *fratres*, who programmatically did not want to take vows. Not as a later compromise, but from the very beginning, he planned the Windesheim congregation in order to establish the non-separatist intentions of the *Devotio moderna*. Yet suspicion remained, and has influenced research ever since, but owing to Post's basic work the full orthodoxy of the *Devotio moderna* can no longer be doubted.[37]

Towards the end of the century speculation met firm opposition in these three areas: Thomism in theology; the "calculatores" or "speculatores" in the field of history with their forecasts of the Antichrist; and finally speculative mysticism. Neither scepticism, nor fideism, nor tiredness is the appropriate designation for the fourteenth-century rejection of speculation. Operative behind and within the fourteenth-century rejection of speculation was a new conception of Christian thought and an alternative ideal of Christian life endowed with its own vigor and inventiveness in uncovering new dimensions in human experience, intuition, and affections. It involved a quest for an *Aggiornamento* of intellectual and spiritual life, and in this sense deserves the epithet "moderna." When this is not clearly seen we are bound to be led to such erroneous assumptions as that quattrocento humanist thought forms an erratic "modern" bloc in a "medieval" century.

Finally, the vitality of this alternative can be deduced from a theme which at first glance would not seem to be very promising, namely that of death. Since the middle of the century we find a reorientation within a widespread genre of literature, the *ars moriendi*, which not only provides a mirror for the dying at that time, but also for the historian alive today. While Johan Huizinga has described the late medieval preoccupation with death, Alberto Tenenti has helped us to see – in his *Il Senso della morte e l'amore della vita nel Rinascimento*[38] – that since about the middle of the century the view of death was determined by a new lust for life.

---

[37] *The Modern Devotion: Confrontation with Reformation and Humanism,* Studies in Medieval and Reformation Thought 3 (Leiden, 1968), p. 66.

[38] *Il Senso della morte e l'amore della vita nel Rinascimento* (Turin, 1957), p. 80. Cf. Rainer Rudolf, *Ars moriendi: Von der Kunst des heilsamen Lebens und Sterbens* (Cologne, 1957). For the parallel developments in the visual arts cf. Albert Czogalla, "David und Ganymedes," in *Festschrift für Georg Scheja*, ed. A. Leuteritz et al. (Sigmaringen, 1975), pp. 119–127, 121 f.

It is interesting to note that this not only applies to the Italian sources with which Tenenti deals, but also to the broad tradition derived from Suso in the North. Central to both was the "mito della gloria,"[39] the effort to prolong life by establishing one's fame and achieving a name which will survive death. Concomitantly, the shortness of life was no longer a point of consolation but of horror. Yet not only time itself, but also the physical dimension of existence took on a new importance. Youth was praised and the individuality of each man was emphasised. Perhaps we can best put it this way: Just as the horror of death reflected a new *amor vitae*, so the *ars bene moriendi* became an inverted *ars bene vivendi*.

7. EPILOGUE

All of this is the fourteenth century: *Via moderna* and *ars moriendi moderna*; "calculatores" in the new science and in the computation of the end of the world; the critique of St. Thomas and the emergence of the Franciscan metahistorical alternative; the recovery of the authentic Augustine and the flowering of a new Pelagianism; high mysticism and *Devotio moderna*, as well as radically diverging views of the Church and of the papacy. The historian must respect this plurality of phenomena and trends and withstand the temptation to present a coherent pattern. It is clear, however, that fourteenth-century thought can no longer be described only in terms of philosophy and academic theology, as we have been inclined to do. Lay thought and lay piety now begin to occupy the center of the stage.

The warning against *vana curiositas* and academic speculation gave weight and new authority to *experientia* – the experience of man and nature, of history and society, of daily life – which would soon put the validity of tradition to the test. Something new was afoot, and not only south of the Alps. As the entry for the year 1328, the *Chronikon Spanheimense* reports: "At this time the citizens were a constant threat to peace whereas the priests fought for freedom!"[40] Outside the monastic walls exactly the opposite must have seemed to be the case: peace and concord were no longer to be left to the care of those under vows ruling a Church in exile, soon to be torn by schism. The general tendency was to bring the *ecclesia universalis* of the Creed within the reach of daily experience in the form of learned sodalities and lay fraternities. In the course of the century institutions and ideas had been developed which could now prove their viability.

---

[39]A. Tenenti, *Il Senso della morta*, p. 48.
[40]*Chronikon Spanheimense*, ed. Carl Velten (Bad Kreuznach, 1969), p. 86.

The road to Reformation of Church, university, and society at large did not yet seem to require a break with the past. What is new, I suggest, is that mixture of *simplicitas* and *experientia* which was to provide the fifteenth century at once with the moral targets for reform and the conceptual tools for the new sciences. But looking beyond the fifteenth century we discern its most lasting contribution to the European heritage in the precious antidote to vain speculation so elusively called "common sense."

II

THE SHAPE OF LATE MEDIEVAL THOUGHT:
THE BIRTHPANGS OF THE MODERN ERA

1. THREE ASSUMPTIONS

1. Our very project of investigating the shape of late medieval thought –
even before it is under way – implies a number of disputable assumptions.

In the first place, what is implied is not merely an open question but rather
a quest for the beginning of the modern era. Usually an inordinate amount of
historical arrogance underlies such an investigation, since it assumes more or
less explicitly that the merits of an epoch can be measured by its degree of
proximity to our own era. It is not difficult to be sympathetic with those
who are unwilling to regard such a quest as part of genuine historical
research; though perhaps no longer put in that form, "each epoch is
immediate to God," and should therefore be described in its own terms.

Yet we recall two significant debates. The one, dealing with the
modernity of the Reformation, centered around the thesis of Troeltsch, who
opposed Holl and his disciples in arguing for the basically medieval basis and
horizon of Luther and the German Reformation. Thus Troeltsch claimed to
have established the non-modernity of the Reformation movement.[1] The
second debate is of more recent vintage and concerned with the Italian
Renaissance. Hans Baron in a paper read for the American Historical
Association in 1941 opposed the thesis of C.H. McIlwain, the authority on
medieval constitutional history, that the twelfth century Renaissance
"seems to be on the whole more significant in a perspective of the whole of
history, than the later development to which we usually attach the word
"Renaissance." Baron argued for the "modern" face and the
"precursorship" of Renaissance Italy in the field of political ideas and came

---

[1]Ernst Troeltsch, "Renaissance und Reformation", *Gesammelte Schriften*, IV (Tübingen, 1925),
pp. 261–296. Salient portions have been translated into English by Lewis W. Spitz in *The
Reformation – Material or Spiritual?* (Boston, 1962), 17–27. Cf. Gerhard Ebeling. "Luther und der
Anbruch der Neuzeit", *Zeitschrift für Theologie und Kirche*, 69 (1972), 185–213; 192–200.

close to the Burckhardtian thesis, which presents the Renaissance as the first-born among the sons of modern Europe.[2]

It should be granted that these debates revealed as much about the debators as about the periods in question. It should also be granted, however, that this – in the eyes of skeptics – idle game is of the very essence of the historical venture: the trek into the past, the move *ad fontes* serves the reflection upon oneself and one's society in providing a critical freedom over and against the tyranny of the *Zeitgeist*. Hence, to pose our question is at once a luxury *and* a necessity, not unlike the true double rating of historical research as such. By "luxury" I mean that vital dimension of our work not determined by the impatient, ever-shifting claims of relevance, that playsome freedom of the *homo ludens* who so – and only so – chances upon new horizons of understanding. By necessity I mean the dialectics of precision through details and perspective through distance, that distance which allows for the historian to function as the *homo quaerens intellectum*. Hence we pose our question not out of a presumptuous identification of modernity and utopia, but out of the need for perspective in order to interpret the past to the present.

2. In the second place, our question implies that there is good reason to look at the later Middle Ages for the beginnings of a new era. Admittedly we no longer assume a tripartite view of history with its periodisation of antiquity, Middle Ages and modern times. Furthermore, we distinguish today at least pre-modern, modern, and contemporary history, where the age of the Enlightenment seems to dwarf all preceding factors of change. Yet on the penalty of introducing an Olympic family of *dei ex machina*, we are well-advised to accept the Joachite cradle-view of history, according to which each period gives birth to the next in such a way that its birthpangs will precede its coming of age, *n'en déplaise* Collingwood,[3] as the best theory to

---

[2]Hans Baron, "Toward a More Positive Evaluation of the Fifteenth Century Renaissance", *Journal of the History of Ideas*, 4 (1943), 22–49. Cf. Karl Dannenfeldt, *The Renaissance, Medieval or Modern?* (Boston, 1959), 35–48; 64–75. Cf. Wallace K. Ferguson, *The Renaissance in Historical Thought. Five Centuries of Interpretation* (Boston, 1948), 195–252: The Burckhardtian Tradition in the Interpretation of the Italian Renaissance; 290–328: Reaction against the Burckhardtian Tradition; 329–385: The Revolt of the Medievalists.

[3]After introducing Joachim as illustration Collingwood – as it may seem, most reasonably – formulates the general rule: "Eschatology is always an intrusive element in history. The historian's business is to know the past, not to know the future . . ." R.G. Collingwood, *The Idea of History* (Oxford, 1949; New York, 1965[3]), 54. If we replace "eschatology" with futurology, Collingwood's thesis is no longer *luce clarius*! At least the historian cannot deny sharing responsibility for knowing the present – which in the newly developing field of futurology encompasses the future.

date which takes fully into account the coexistence of continuity and discontinuity.

For the later Middle Ages, which we – at this point arbitrarily – set for the two centuries, ranging from about 1350–1550,[4] the cradle-theory is of particular relevance, because this period has long been regarded as an age of regression, throwing its dark shadows well into the centuries to follow. Efforts to rectify the view of the *decline* and the *waning* of the Middle Ages with that of the *harvest* may well have helped to establish a more positive understanding; at the same time, it could be taken to stress continuity at the expense of discontinuity. In keeping with the positive implications of the harvest image but as a necessary extension, we shall deal today with a few aspects of the initiation of a new season, not looking for causes but for prototypes of modern ways of life and thought.

3. A third preliminary observation leads us to a point of special concern to me. Our question assumes that it is possible to trace the shape of late medieval thought. One should be skeptical *vis-à-vis* such a claim. If we have learned one thing in the last twenty years of research, then it is to enlarge our awareness of geographical and sociological as well as religious diversification. This lesson is clearly reflected in the trend away from pan-European and national to regional and local history. Granted that the shape of late medieval thought is an abstraction for the purpose of communication, with this expression we have, nevertheless, a very concrete goal in mind: namely, to present it as the common field of all those who are involved in the pursuit of the late medieval history of ideas, be it through late medieval scholastic, Renaissance, or Reformation research. The separation of these fields, often with their own chairs, their own journals and learned societies, has made for study in depth and detail, which should be gratefully acknowledged. This separation has also had the effect that equal mastery in all three fields has, by necessity, become rare if not impossible. Yet the establishment of such a tripartite approach allows for – and *de facto* encourages – *a priori* assumptions of differences which obscure and preclude a wholsesome vision of the whole period in its common features, and may lead us therefore to overlook characteristics of each. No question taxes so much the quest for the unity of our epoch as the question of modernity. It tends to

---

[4] I cannot argue here for this form of periodisation. An excellent recent survey by Josef Engel comes to another conclusion, but notices more generally "die Tendenz zur Vorverlegung der Neuzeit" in manuals and especially in monographic literature. "Von der spätmittelalterlichen respublica Christiana zum Mächte-Europa der Neuzeit", in Theodor Schieder, ed., *Handbuch der europäischen Geschichte*, III: *Die Entstehung des neuzeitlichen Europa* (Stuttgart, 1971), 1–443; 11.

bring out both the centripetal forces of the time and the often confessionally charged passion or else the cool *Vorverständnis* of the investigators.

2. THE MANY FACES OF CRISIS

We want to direct our attention to one central aspect of late medieval thought, under which other trends can be subsumed, which at the same time provides us with one of the clearest prototypes of modernity. By this I mean the closing of the gap between the sacred and the profane, looked at from the perspective of late medieval, Renaissance and Reformation studies.

The most obvious and pervasive factor in our period is the phenomenon of crisis. There exists a consensus on the significance, although not on the exact effects of the Black Death, which reached its high-point in England around 1349. Preceded by an extended food crisis on the continent, we notice in its wake both a relatively moderate acceleration of urbanization and a strikingly rapid expansion of existing urban centers. Whether the agrarian crisis is to be regarded as cause or effect, is a separate question: the deflation of wheat prices and the decline in agrarian self-sufficiency led to a dramatic trek to the cities, which left behind ghost villages and whole ghost areas, for Germany so carefully charted by Wilhelm Abel.[5] From around 1450 until *circa* 1520 the wheat prices reached an unprecedented drop simultaneously in England, France, Germany and Austria. The agrarian crisis did not only affect the lower aristocracy and the payroll agrarian workers. It also hit the town communities in thrusting upon them a fast-growing urban proletariat which did not find – and was not granted! – access to the guilds or representation in the city government. The monetary crisis is clearly reflected in the increasing protest against the threat to existing reliable value systems and against the arbitrary manipulation of coinage values.

I am rather inclined to associate the effects of the new money-economy with the subsequent but equally upsetting legal crisis implied in the growing impact and usage of Roman law based on the dogma of private property with its confiscatory exploitation of the distinction between *proprietas* and *possessio*. Both developments were not only a threat to valuables and *securities*, but also to values and *security*.

The *usus pauper* of the radical Franciscans had been able to provide for a moral response as the courageous free choice for what the fate of the

---

[5]Wilhelm Abel, "Landwirtschaft 1350–1550", in H. Aubin and W. Zorn, eds., *Handbuch der deutschen Wirtschafts-und Sozialgeschichte*, I (Stuttgart, 1971), 302; cf. p. 308. Cf. W. Abel, *Geschichte der deutschen Landwirtschaft vom frühen Mittelalter bis zum 19. Jahrhundert*, in G. Franz, ed., *Deutsche Agrargeschichte*, II (Stuttgart, 1967²), 128ff.

socio-economic forces had decreed. Yet after the condemnation of the apostolic ideal of poverty by Pope John XXII in 1323 the Church had deprived itself of a possible answer to the challenge of the times. Nevertheless, the Franciscan friars established themselves as the pastors to the plebeian city population; to the lower strata in society they related more readily than the other two mendicant orders, the scholarly Dominicans and the establishment-favored Augustinians. The reason can be found in their non-violent revolutionary eschatology, their tendency towards anti-intellectualism and the psychological rather than metaphysical basis of their theology in pulpit and confessional. Their more moderate revolutionary eschatology was based on the expectation of the seventh *status ecclesiae*, when friars would replace the prelates, all Jews would be converted, and peace would reign. The extreme interpretation led – since the condemnation of Olivi, the great theoretician of the Spirituals – an underground existence and had to find other forms of expression.

It is not surprising that the Franciscans proved to be in tune with the *Zeitgeist*; so much so that for two centuries late medieval spirituality, piety and theology outside the university halls can be said to have been dominated by them. The Thomistic revival in Cologne set off the Pfefferkorn affair, was ridiculed and then contained by the "Letters of Obscure Men," until it could find more receptive soil in what from the point of view of administration can be considered the first modern state, absolutist Spain.

The context in which the unsettling effects of all these crisis factors could have their full impact is, however, the ecclesiastical crisis. I regard it as a major breakthrough, that during the last international, largely Marxist, Colloquium organized by the Czechoslovakian Academy of Arts and Sciences at Smolenice in September 1969, we were able to agree that the economic crisis was not the cause, but rather an aspect of the late medieval crisis issuing from the Western Schism.[6] The Western Schism, with its concatenation of abortive solutions from Pisa and Constance to Basel, including the seemingly reassuring achievement of union with the Eastern Church at Florence, called the sacred basis of existence into question to an extent hitherto unknown. The confusion of consciences and the political strife resulting from the claims of – at times – three obediences with their own fiscal and administrative legislation are too well-known to be enlarged upon.

---

[6]The leading paper at this conference, by Frantisek Graus, is now available in English: "The Crisis of the Middle Ages and the Hussites", in Steven E. Ozment, ed., *The Reformation in Medieval Perspective* (Chicago, 1971), 76–103.

Less well-known is the role which – again – the Franciscan order played in the debate around the thesis *ubi papa, ibi ecclesia* at the heart of the curialist-conciliarist struggle. In a book recently published, Brian Tierney analyzes the emergence of the dogma of infallibility.[7] He calls for a revision of the dogmatic constitution of the First Vatican Council – at which papal, universal, *ex cathedra*, decrees were declared irreformable *ex sese, non autem ex consensu ecclesiae*. Tierney does so on the basis of the discovery that the matrix of this dogma is to be found among the adherents of the extreme heretical wing of the Franciscan Order at the beginning of the fourteenth century, namely with Petrus Olivi. Hence infallibility proved to have been launched by an accused heretic without support from the earlier tradition. The impressive array of arguments and convincing documentation of Tierney interests us here less than retracing one part of his argument by taking a closer look at the texture of Olivi's intentions in his *Quaestio de infallibilitate Romani Pontificis*.[8] It seems to me that Tierney has not only rightly pointed to the significance of this text, but also appropriately read it in the light of Olivi's later Apocalypse commentary. Yet his conclusions as to Olivi's intentions are too juridically conceived when Olivi's "new theory of papal infallibility" is seen as "designed to limit the power of future popes,"[9] – rather, I read Olivi as contending that the emerging New Age is not to be a future of popes at all.

As a matter of fact, Olivi refers to the Apocalypse to declare that the Western Church, and particularly the First See, has been given the primacy by God himself. In passing he allows a glance at occidental feelings of superiority, providing God with a valid reason for his choice: as appears from the historical sources, "tota gens orientalis semper fuit prona ad hereses et scissuras, gens vero latina semper inventa est simplicior et stabilior in fide."[10] We find a forewarning not to simplify Olivi when we look at the text referred to (Apoc. 17, 18) in his own commentary on the Apocalypse. In this comprehensive, partly futurological, elaboration of Joachite ideas Olivi identifies Rome with Babylon. True enough, this identification applies only to the last stage of history, but Olivi knows that he lives on the edge of at once the most modern and the last times, the *novissimi*, when the succession of Christ will be transferred to the sons of St. Francis. In this light, we have to read his conclusions. The pope is inerrant and his decrees are irreformable

[7]Brian Tierney, *Origins of Papal Infallibility 1150–1350* (Leiden, 1972).
[8]Michele Maccarone, ed., *Rivista di Storia della Chiesa in Italia*, 3 (1949), 325–343.
[9]Tierney, *op. cit.*, 130.
[10]Maccarone, *ed. cit.*, 337, 27–29.

– "nec papa nec sedes romana potest in fide pertinaciter errare." Yet when he is pope "secundum solam apparentiam," when he is not *verus papa*, then he has no jurisdictional authority at all, "quia omnis fidelis est maior eo."[11]

I do not believe that another Franciscan who wrote less than half a century later, William of Ockham, deviated theoretically from this defender of *this* infallibility of the *papa verus*; though we do not find the characteristic Olivian dimension of eschatology, which is not easily stripped away without changing the whole texture of thought, nevertheless, in his assessment of the pope, Ockham does declare the heretical pope deposed *ipso facto*, just as Olivi; and he comes to the same conclusion that "omnis fidelis est maior eo."[12] But instead of Olivi's looking toward the coming of the Third Age, Ockham looks to the convening of a General Council: if a heretical pope is deposed *ipso facto*, such is the case, because all heresies have been unmasked as such by General Councils.[13] Olivi's eschatological fervor has found in Ockham a more juridically oriented expression, where the millennial dream of the *ecclesia spiritualis* has been remoulded into a reform program for the *ecclesia universalis*. These two examples suffice to show the range of variants within one and the same tradition which shaped the mood of the times. It provided particularly a ferment of crisis for a society based on "eternal" institutions, which now increasingly were surmised to be "temporal" and perhaps even dated.

In the particular case of Olivi, the epithets and powers of the pope can be so highly exalted, because the great shift is imminent. The moment is near at which the final demarcation line between Rome and Babylon will be drawn: a pope who does not live up to the high qualities of his office proves to be a pseudo-pope, a pope "quoad solam apparentiam", in appearance only. What first seems to be the highest elevation of papal office, is a test of orthodoxy which soon is to unmask the antichrist. The eyes of all true believers are on the pope: once he does err, we have entered the most modern era, the time of the last things. Though Tierney is right in pointing to Olivi for the origins of infallibility in the sense of doctrinal

[11]*Ibid.*, 342, 38f.; 343, 8f.

[12]*Compendium Errorum Joannis XXII*, obiectio cavillosa 3, ratio 1 in Guilelmus de Occam. *Opera plurima* (Lyon, 1494–96; reprint Farnborough 1952), II, fol. BB 5ra. See further Arthur S. McGrade, *The Political Thought of William of Ockham: Personal and Institutional Principles* (Cambridge, 1973), Chapters II–III.

[13]"... papa hereticus incidit in antiquam heresim per generale concilium damnatam ... quia omnis heresis est explicite per generalia concilia iam condemnata." *Dialogus de imperio et pontificia potestate*, lb. VI, c. 73 in Occam, *ed. cit.*, I, fol. 88rb.

irreversibility,[14] we sense here a completely different climate of expectation than in 1870.

Such precarious claims and "faint praise" influenced the climate and set the stage on which the drama of the Western Schism is enacted. Its full implications are not immediately realized. At first, during the Pisan Council, such sober *grandseigneurs* as Gerson and d'Ailly thought they could avert disaster with common sense and decent diplomacy. At the opening of the Council of Constance, however, we find d'Ailly openly quoting and defending Joachim of Flora, and Jean Gerson looking for ever more radical solutions.

It may be too dramatic to call the later Middle Ages the Age of Crisis, because crisis is the turmoil caused by the passing away of one world of values and the painful birth of a new one, and this is no prerogative of any single era. Yet there have been few times when the awareness of crisis has reached and encompassed all social classes, and pervaded – though admittedly with *Phasenverschiebung* – such extensive areas of Western Europe.

3. THE SEARCH FOR NEW SECURITY

With his categories, Paul Tillich would have described this era as in search for new symbols of security. Exactly in this way has the former Marxist, Frantisek Graus, pointed to the Hussite revolution as the crisis, not of the monetary system, not a feudal or political crisis but as the crisis of symbols of security; he thus explained the Hussite concern with the sacraments.

In this section, I should like to pursue the late medieval effort to deal with one central aspect of the quest for new forms of security, namely, the

---

[14]The case of papal doctrinal flexibility is argued by Pope John XXII, when he reacts to the 1279 papal defense of the *usus pauper* (in "Exiit qui seminat") on March 26, 1322 with the words: "... non debet reprehensibile iudicari, si canonum conditor canones a se, vel suis praedecessoribus editos, vel aliqua in eisdem contenta canonibus revocare, modificare, vel suspendere studeat, si ea obesse potius viderit, quam prodesse." L. Wadding, *Annales Minorum,* VI (Quaracchi, 1931³), 446 = *Extravag. Ioan n. XXII.*, tit. 14 c. 2; E. L. Richter and E. Friedberg, eds., *Corpus iuris canonici* (Leipzig, 1879–1881²), II, col. 1224.

Two months later (June 4, 1322), this challenge evokes the response of the Franciscan General Chapter meeting in Perugia: "... quod pro dogmate sano Sedes Apostolica comprobavit, semper teneri debet acceptum, nec ab ea licet quomodolibet resilire ..." Wadding, *ed. cit.*, VI, 448 (cf. Decr. Grat., D. 19 c. 1; Richter and Friedberg, *ed. cit.*, I, col. 58f). For the discussion of the historical aspect of Tierney's argument it is important to point to this Perugia Chapter rather than to Olivi himself as the "origin of papal infallibility." At the same time, the very fact that papal irreversibility is formulated as protest *against* a papal ruling, supports Tierney's theological critique of the infallibility decree of Vatican I.

bridging of the distance between the sacred and the profane; one could say the elimination of the ontological opposition, contrast and gap between the sacred and the profane.

In view of the present state of scholarship, we have no grounds for assuming from the beginning a common thrust pervading all late medieval movements. We are therefore well-advised to deal successively with late medieval scholasticism, the Renaissance and the Reformation. Whereas Renaissance scholarship provides us – relatively speaking – with the fewest problems, in view of the surprisingly persistent influence of Burckhardt's modernity thesis, late medieval scholasticism is still largely known, when known at all, as a chapter in the history of philosophy. Its place among the creative forces of the time is rarely mentioned. When it is dealt with, it is usually adduced to show the confusion of that epoch, the despair of reason, the divorce between faith and daily experience, and the fearful clinging to the authority of the Church. Its own self-understanding and its views on the world, on man and his society are still largely *terra incognita*. Yet late medieval scholasticism is the heyday of Franciscan thought, impregnated by ideas transmitted by the Order most deeply involved in the crisis of the times.

To refer to this movement as nominalism or *via moderna* – in themselves problematical labels – is for two reasons more appropriate than to name it Scotism in the fourteenth century, after Duns Scotus, and Ockhamism in the fifteenth century, after William of Ockham. In the first place, "Scotism" and "Ockhamism" suggest too strongly a merely academic setting, whereas the ideas of the *via moderna* are on a wide scale absorbed by non-Franciscans, infiltrating even the doctrinally well-disciplined Dominican order and shaping the piety of thousands of sermons preached all over Europe – a source still largely untapped by scholarship. In the second place, nominalism proves to be the more comprehensive category, as the movement that not only survived, but even flourished long after Ockham and Ockhamism were condemned by the University of Paris in September, 1339, and again in December, 1340.[15]

I regard it as beyond the ken of the historian to determine whether the

---

[15]Cf. Ruprecht Paqué, *Das Pariser Nominalistenstatut. Zur Entstehung des Realitätsbegriffs der neuzeitlichen Naturwissenschaft. (Occam, Buridan und Petrus Hispanus, Nikolaus von Autrecourt und Gregor von Rimini.)* (Berlin, 1970), 8ff. For the condemnation of Ockham by the Augustinian Order see Adolar Zumkeller, *Hugolin von Orvieto und seine theologische Erkenntnislehre* (Würzburg, 1941), 257f. A third reason to prefer nominalism as the more appropriate designation is that the choice of the term 'Ockhamism' is the yield of early French nationalism. The true *Inceptor* being Johannes Buridanus, the Parisian *via moderna* could well lay claim to the title Buridanism. In the condemnations, however, the foreigner Ockham is given precedence.

rapid spread of nominalist ideas reflects the spirit of the times in its search for new securities or whether it was a real (co-) agent in bringing forth these ideas. But the movement is not sufficiently charted if the following elements are not taken into consideration.

1. The insistence on God's *potentia ordinata* can easily leave the impression that we are confronted here with an 'establishment' theology. After all, the nominalist point of departure is that God could have decreed – *de potentia absoluta* – to create another world, to choose other means of salvation, and to establish another order. As a matter of fact, *de facto, de potentia ordinata*, however, God has committed himself to this world, to this Church, to this order. To remind ourselves that we are moving here in the orbit of Franciscan theology, suffices to warn us against conclusions too hastily drawn in this regard. The established reality *de potentia ordinata* is never divorced from the possibilities *de potentia absoluta*. By this, at every step, we are reminded that this, our world, is contingent, not an ontologically necessary outflow or reflection of eternal structures of being, but the result of a decree, a contract, a *pactum Dei*.

2. Contingency is perhaps the best one-word summary of the nominalist program. This contingency is understood in two directions, embracing both the vertical relation God-world-man and the horizontal relation world-man-future. We cannot pursue now this second form of contingency, which concerns the so-called question *"De futuris contingentibus."* When applied not only to the future but also to the past, it provides for a truly scholarly basis of historical studies by its tendency to eliminate supernatural factors in the interpretation of the course of events.

Contingency should not be understood to mean unreliable, threatened by the alternatives *de potentia absoluta*. The contingency of creation and salvation means simply that they are not ontologically necessary. The point is that in the vertical dimension our reality is not the lowest emanation and level in a hierarchy of being which ascends in ever more real steps to the highest reality, God.

3. Against the implication that our world is a mere reflection and shadow of higher levels of being, the nominalist insists on the full reality of our experienced world. Hunger for reality is so much the mark of nominalism that it is a perhaps humorous but certainly a misleading tradition that bequeathed upon its opponents the name "realists". What is often called Ockham's razor is the slashing away of the hierarchy of being, of ideas and concepts, which sheer speculation had invented.

4. The protest against "wild speculation" or against "vain curiosity" is not merely a sign of anti-intellectualism. Admittedly this is not alien to the Franciscan tradition, and more generally it is a trend of the times. It is particularly noticeable in the beginning stages of the *devotio moderna*, which propagated the crusade into the interior and hence presented withdrawal as answer to the challenge of insecurity.

In nominalist thought we encounter the sternest opposition to the claims of intellect and reason when not verified by the tests of experience. On this basis, nominalism provided the setting for modern science, replacing the authority-based deductive method with the empirical method. The combination of *experientia* and *experimentum* allowed for a fresh investigation, by trial and error, of such basic phenomena as movement and retardation.[16] In this way the chain of causation is reduced to observable second causes, a major advance in the transition from *the* speculative law of nature to the observable *laws* of nature.

More generally it can be said that the underlying intention of nominalism is best described in terms of the late medieval revolution against the meta-categories that obfuscate reality. Just as it rejected metaphysics to establish physics, so nominalism ventured to strip theology of her distorting meta-theological shackles, with the result that the Scriptures and the prior decrees of God were emphasized at the expense of natural theology. In this attack on meta-categories I find the most revealing parallel with aspects of Italian humanism.[17]

---

[16]Anneliese Maier is generally not partial to a more positive view of progress in nominalism. Yet – in connection with questions about *intensio* and *remissio* – she observes that the empirical evidence is new: "Noch einmal: hätten sich die Früheren diese Fragen vorgelegt, so hätten sie im wesentlichen dieselben Antworten gegeben. Aber sie haben eben diese Fragen nicht explizit gestellt. Und das ist das Neue. Es ist oft hervorgehoben worden, daß der Empirismus der Neuzeit auf den Ockhamismus zurückgeht. Hier, bei der Theorie der intensio und remissio, haben wir einen der Punkte, wo diese Entwicklung mit Händen zu greifen ist." *Studien zur Naturphilosophie der Spätscholastik*, II: *Zwei Grundprobleme der scholastischen Naturphilosophie. Das Problem der intensiven Größe. Die Impetustheorie* (Roma, 1968³), 77f. Careful not to construct a causal relation she grants that it was the achievement of the impetus theory of the 14th century "an die Stelle einer rein spekulativen Betrachtung der Bewegungsphänomene eine eigentliche, an der Erfahrung orientierte Mechanik zu setzen. Mit diesem Schritt aber war die exakte Naturwissenschaft geboren." *Ibid.*, 313. Cf. A. C. Crombie, *Augustine to Galileo: The History of Science A.D. 400–1650* (Cambridge, Mass, 1953), 273. Cf. Paqué's excellent analysis of the origins of nominalism, where he – although still too much in the tradition of the German *via antiqua* – finds the modernity of nominalism in the view of language as "nachträgliches Zeichensystem für schon fertig vorliegende und verstandene Realitäten." Paqué, *op. cit.*, 266.

[17]Valla's reduction of universals to particulars is a case in point. See Charles Trinkaus who speaks once of "counter-nominalism" (*In Our Image and Likeness. Humanity and Divinity in Italian Humanist Thought* [London, 1970], I, 152), once of "thorough going nominalism" (*op. cit.*, I, 381).

5. This sketch would be incomplete if in conclusion no mention were made of an emerging new image of God implied in the emphasis on God's *potentia ordinata*. God is a covenant God, his *pactum* or *foedus* is his self-commitment to become the contractual partner in creation and salvation. Here originates the Pelagianism of the *facere quod in se est*, which stands in the area of justification for the meager but sufficient human moral efforts which God has contracted, accepted or pledged to reward. In this emphasis on covenantal and not-necessary relationships between God and his world[18], as well as between God and his Church, man is no longer primarily a second cause moved by the prime mover and first cause. In the nominalist view man has become the appointed representative and partner of God responsible for his own life, society and world, on the basis and within the limits of the treaty or *pactum* stipulated by God.

Because of the frontal attack upon traditional ontology and meta-categories nominalism *could* make the impression upon contemporary ecclesiastical and secular authorities and *did* make the impression on later interpreters that it merely enhanced the climate of crisis and accelerated the late medieval disintegration of stability and time-honored structures. Nominalism did call traditional truths and answers into question in order to replace them with a new vision of the relationship between the sacred and the secular by presenting coordination as an alternative to subordination and partnership of persons instead of the hierarchy of being.

4. PAX AND THE THIRD AGE

Perhaps it is a revealing characteristic of times of crisis that in them the longing for peace is particularly intensive. The two most prominent themes in treatises and reform proposals throughout the later Middle Ages are *pax* and *concordia*. From Marsilius' *Defensor pacis* through the *De pace fidei* of Cusanus, from the Joachite dreams of peace and concord in the last stage of history through the imperial reform vision of the *Reformatio Sigismundi*, reform and peace are closely associated. This state of affairs provides the necessary perspective to look upon one of the least discussed of Luther's Ninety-five Theses: "' Pax, pax', et non est pax," usually bypassed by Reformation scholars, who seize more avidly upon the seemingly more central following thesis: "'Crux, crux', et non est crux."[19] It could be

[18]See William J. Courtenay, "Covenant and Causality in Pierre d'Ailly", *Speculum*, 46 (1971), 94–119.

[19]Martin Luther, Thesis 92; *W A* I, 238, 15–17; cf. already summer 1512: "... 'Pax, Pax', cum non sit pax", *W A* I, 15, 10. In 1512 Pax is still in part individually understood.

bypassed as merely a biblical reference, in this case from the prophet Jeremiah (6, 14), yet as real prophecy this verse had received a loaded meaning from St. Bernard in his widely read cycle of sermons on the *Song of Songs*: There is peace, Bernard says, and yet no peace: "Peace from the pagans, peace from the heretics, but no peace from God's own children, *sed non profecto a filiis.*"[20] For all his contemporaries the allusion to the three epochs of history was clear. In the first period, the Church withstood the Roman persecutions, and in the second, the age of the Fathers, she had been able to deal with the heretics. Now, however, the peace of the Church was much more seriously endangered, threatened as it was from within.

In this sense Pierre d'Ailly refers to the prophecy of Jeremiah, which has now come true to the point of a *generalis deformatio*; in all its scandal and horror, this had been foreseen by Joachim and Hildegard – a thoroughgoing deformation which calls for an equally thorough reformation.[21] Though we explicitly note that d'Ailly calls upon the much tainted authority of Joachim – whose words, he says, should not be held in low esteem – the conciliarist leader does not provide an answer in keeping with the spiritual tradition from Joachim through Olivi. Unlike them he does not assume the irreversibility of the final apocalyptic situation. For d'Ailly the present chaos is not the prelude to Armageddon and the last things, but a God-given opportunity for general reform of the Church and for the re-establishment of peace.[22]

The goals of conciliarism are not correctly understood when regarded as anti-papal. Such sentiments were certainly present, and the more radical aspects of Ockham's thought would later affect the decisions of the Council of Basel. In the heyday of conciliarism, however, on the long road from Pisa to Constance, the basic goal was to meet the crisis of the Church, the re-establishment of *pax* and *concordia*, or, to put it in the words of Dietrich von Niem (written in 1410): the achievement of one pope (*capitis unius*

---

[20]*Super Cantica Canticorum*, Sermo 33, 15f.: "Omnes amici, et omnes inimici ... Ministri Christi sunt et serviunt Antichristo ... Olim praedictum est, et nunc tempus impletionis advenit: 'Ecce in pace amaritudo mea amarissima.' ... Sed in qua pace? Et pax est, et non est pax. Pax a paganis, pax ab haereticis, sed non profecto a filiis." *S. Bernardi Opera* (Rome, 1957 ff.), I, 244, 6–25.

[21]"Propterea extunc quidam spirituales mala haec subtilioris intelligentiae oculo praevidentes ... et alia plura scandalosa inde sequutura praedixerunt; sicut patet in libris Abbatis Ioachim et Hildegardis, quos non esse contemnendos quorundam magnorum doctorum probat auctoritas." Petrus Alliacensis, "De Reformatione Ecclesiae", in *Tractatus de materia concilii generalis* (Paris, 1671), III, 69. Cf. Francis Oakley, *The Political Thought of Pierre d'Ailly. The Voluntarist Tradition* (New Haven, 1964), 315f.

[22]"Haec autem Deus misericordissimus, qui solus ex malis bona novit elicere, ideo permittere credendus est, ut eorum occasione Ecclesia sua in melius reformetur." *Ibid.*, 69.

declaracio), one undivided Church (*membrorum una consociacio*) and moral reform by return to the mores of the early church (*morum proborum antiquorum reformacio*).[23] Our concern in conciliar research with the *means* of implementation has lead to a deficit in attention given to the *aims* striven after. In reversing this trend we may find ourselves less mystified by the shifting development of d'Ailly and Gerson or discern more consistency in the 'papalist' defections of Cusanus and Piccolomini.

Moving our sights from the nominalist theologian d'Ailly to a humanist professor of rhetoric, we find that Lorenzo Valla's presentation of the fraudulent basis for the so-called Donation of Constantine (1440) is by no means antipapal. In a recent study, Josef Lortz and Erwin Iserloh find here a negative, subjectivistic factor, typical of the age, which undermined the authority of the Church.[24] I am inclined to see Valla's investigation as antipapalistic, but not as antipapal. It forms his contribution to the papal efforts to come to a reunion with the Eastern Church (1439). The ultimate goal of Valla's shocking argument is formulated in his very last sentence: "Tunc papa et dicetur, et erit pater sanctus, pater omnium, pater ecclesiae, nec bella inter Christianos excitabit, sed ab aliis excitata, censura apostolica, et papali maiestate sedabit."[25] When the pope functions only as successor to Christ and not also as successor to Caesar, then he will not merely be *called* but really *be* "Holy Father", Father of all men, Father of the Church; and when war is unleashed, not by him but by others, peace will return on his apostolic command and authority. – Again, as in the case of d'Ailly, Valla sees the root of all evil, the threat to peace by greed for power, *ambitio* and *avaritia*, as lying *within* the Church. On the basis of this analysis he issued his call for reform.

This omnipresent and pervading awareness of living in a New Age, in the third epoch, witnessing a threat to the sacred realm itself, reflects and sets off reflection about the interrelationship between the sacred and the secular. Before the *dignity* of man went to seed on the European cultural scene and became mere *civility* of manners, this dignity was based on the awareness that man himself stands on the demarcation line of both worlds, forming the *trait*

---

[23]Hermann Heimpel, ed., *De modis uniendi et reformandi ecclesiam in concilio universali* (Leipzig-Berlin, 1953), 13; cf. 42, 46.

[24]Joseph Lortz and Erwin Iserloh, *Kleine Reformationsgeschichte* (Freiburg i.B., 1969), 20.

[25]Laurentius Valla, *De falso credito et ementita Constantini donatione declamatio*, in *Opera Omnia* (Basel, 1540; reprint Torino, 1962 with a preface by Eugenio Garin), I. 795. These last words are introduced by the wish: "Utinam, utinam aliquando videam, nec enim mihi quicquam est longius, quam hoc videre, et praesertim meo consilio effectum, ut papa tantum vicarius Christi sit, et non etiam Caesaris . . ."

d'union, the link between the sacred and the secular. We find an application of this view in Valla's rejection and bridging of the gap between the secular faithful and those who have taken the monastic vows: Christians are all to be called *religiosi*. Just as in d'Ailly's call for reform, so with Valla we find not the Joachite quietistic approach, but rather the activistic partnership of the anthropology of nominalism; and what we see in Valla is more than an incidental expression of the humanist involvement in the spirit of the times. To use the words of Charles Trinkaus: "Valla represents the extreme of a humanist statement of position both on religion and human nature. But in his extremity much is revealed about humanism generally."[26]

The papal bull "Unam Sanctam" (1302) is usually regarded as an extreme papalist statement – and it is, in its designation of the Pope as the *homo spiritualis, the* spiritual man, who cannot be judged by anyone and who judges everything in both realms of Church and State. Yet this high papalogy is not novel, but a fine summary of the political consequences of that hierarchy of being where peace and justice in the world are derived from the sacred, from sanctification and legitimation through the sacraments and the jurisdiction of the Church. The Augustinian "Unam Sanctam" tradition holds that without the *vera iustitia* of the Church, the State has to disintegrate, can only become a *latrocinium*, a robber-state – as St. Augustine put it.

Without the sanction of the sacred, the secular cannot provide for a truly human society. If this is the case, then a relation of the sacred and the secular is assumed which itself must disintegrate under the onslaught of the crisis of the later Middle Ages. When the very sources of peace and justice themselves can no longer be regarded as sacred, sanctioned and legitimated, the guarantee for peace and justice in state and society is henceforth seen in terms of a partnership between the sacred and the secular, which provides enlightened, rational man with the basis of his covenanted responsibility.

5. "*SUMMA MISERICORDIA . . . SUPER SUMMAM MISERIAM DIRECTE CADIT*"[27]

In our final section we propose to do no more than quote three sources with some sober marginal comments. The three quotations are taken from the early writings of three later significant theologians: from the 1407 treatise on *Mystical Theology* by Jean Gerson, the 1517 *Libellus* on predestination by John von Staupitz, and Luther's *Freedom of a Christian*,

---

[26]Charles Trinkaus, *op cit.*, II, 765.

[27]Johann von Staupitz, *Libellus de executione aeternae praedestinationis* (Nürnberg, 1517), cap. X, n. 69.

written three years later in 1520. All three deal with the relation between
God and man, more particularly between Christ and the sinner in terms of
love and marriage symbolism. Each is mystical in tone, but not necessarily
mystical in the sense of describing an unusual experience of union with God.
On the contrary, what all three have in common is that this mystical
experience is no longer regarded as the privilege of a few elect aristocrats of
the Spirit; in accordance with the late medieval phenomenon of demo-
cratisation of mysticism, the bridal kiss and the intimate union of God and
man now mark the life of every true believer.

1. We pick Gerson up at the point where he has turned to the illiterate or at
least to the unschooled, for whom he emphasizes experience more than
reason. After having described the preliminary stages of the penitent on the
road to what he calls reformation,[28] Gerson goes on to say: "But when it has
finally come so far that one is sufficiently pure, that is that one has a clear
conscience so that one no longer . . . looks at God as a judge who metes out
punishment, but as the completely desirable, and lovable . . ., then fly with a
feeling of security into the arms of the bridegroom, embrace and kiss him
with the kiss of peace which surpasses all understanding [Phil. 4, 7], so that
you can say with grateful and loving devotion: "My beloved is mine and I
am his. [Cant. 2, 16]."[29]

We want to make two observations. The first serves to alert us to the
necessity, clearly stipulated here, for the soul to be fully purged and clean –
per reformationem – before it can reach the culmen perfectionis, the embrace of the
Bridegroom, where, what is his, pure divinity, becomes yours and what is
yours, pure humanity, becomes his. This is thoroughly traditional, and is
found in the same form in St. Bernard, Ficino and Cusanus. It would not

---

[28]"Scito autem nisi te prius expurgaverit timoris lima per integerrimam et non fictam
penitentiam, nisi mens insuper elimata peccati scoria claraque refulserit se per reformationem
in novitate spiritus secundum duos primos actos ierarchicos, qui sunt purgare et illuminare,
'vanum' prorsus erit tibi 'ante lucem surgere' ad hoc culmen perfectionis: 'surgite' proinde, 'qui
manducatis panem doloris', timore scilicet sine quo justificari nemo potest ante Deum." Ioannis
Carlerii de Gerson De Mystica Theologia [1407, 1422²], Tractatus secundus practicus, Cons. 12; ed.
André Combes (Lugano, 1958), 215, lines 112–120.

[29]"At vero dum eo usque pervenerit bene conscia mens et munda, ut neque gaudia neque
aliud omnino vel servile vel mercennarium recogitet, neque preterea de Deo quicquam durum,
asperum, negotiosum penset vel turbulentem, sicut de iudice retributore vel vindice, sed hoc
unicum in mentem venerit quod sit totus desiderabilis, 'suavis et mitis' [Ps. 85, 5], totus amari,
'etiam si occiderit' [Job. 13, 15], dignissimus, dum ita solum placuerit amoris negotium, tunc
vola securus in amplexus sponsi, stringe pectus illud divinum amicitie purissimis brachiis, fige
oscula castissima pacis exsuperantis 'omnem sensum' [Phil. 4, 7], ut et dicere subinde possis,
gratulabunda et amorosa devotione: 'Dilectus meus michi, et ego illi' [Cant. 2, 16], . . ." Ibid.,
216, lines 122–134.

have deserved special mention were not the other two quotations so sharply deviating. Since in the medieval exegetical tradition the individual soul and the Church are interchangeable, Gerson's view of the reformation of the Church is implied: through penance and purgation the re-establishment of the Church without spot or wrinkle. In this perspective, reformation must mean corporate purge, moral reform, withdrawal from the *negotium saeculare*.[30]

My second observation has a more general bearing on Luther scholarship. In Luther's own presentation of his development, he points to the *iustitia Dei* of Romans 1:17 as the key to his discovery of justification by faith. Before, as Luther indicates, he had feared and hated this *iustitia* as the punishing righteousness of God. Luther scholars have regarded this fear of the *iustitia Dei* as a unique experience of the unique man Luther which called for a unique psychotheological explanation. Here we should be reminded of Erik Erikson's widely hailed analysis of Luther's preoccupation with the *cloaca*, which he interpreted in the light of Luther's unfortunate childhood experiences, his particular psychological make-up. This interpretation looks considerably less convincing when we discover the existence of a well-documented medieval *cloaca* tradition. Here we find exactly this identification of feces with the diabolic sphere of influence, which proves therefore to be a transpersonal, traditional syndrome. In the same way, Gerson's description of the ascent to union with the Bridegroom de-mythologizes the uniqueness of Luther's concern with the punishing righteousness of God: Gerson describes it as a normal stage on the road to reformation through which *all* have to pass. Here again Luther can only be understood when seen as a citizen of the medieval world.

2. The second quotation stems from a precious little treatise of Staupitz which offers far more than its title indicates, "Eternal Predestination in Time and History". It is the shortest medieval *summa theologiae* known. This treatise ushers in two centuries of pre-occupation – of Calvinists, Lutherans

---

[30]The decisive point of difference between Gerson – "amor . . . naturam habet congregandi seu uniendi homogenea, et heterogenea, sic etiam separat et dividit" (*op. cit., Tractatus primus speculativus*, Cons. 41; ed. cit., 110f., lines 94–96) – and Luther – "vita haec non est habitatio iustitiae" (*W A Br* II, 372, 86), or "Christus enim non nisi in peccatoribus habitat" (*W A Br* I, 35, 29) – is lucidly presented by Steven E. Ozment, *Homo Spiritualis. A Comparative Study of the Anthropology of Johannes Tauler, Jean Gerson and Martin Luther (1509–16) in the Context of Their Theological Thought* (Leiden, 1969), 137; 184ff. Cf. Ozment, "Homo Viator: Luther and Late Medieval Theology", *Harvard Theological Review*, 62 (1969), 275–285 = *The Reformation in Medieval Perspective, op. cit.*, 142–154.

and Tridentine Catholics alike – with the doctrine of predestination as the central core of the Christian faith.

After having described what he calls the "contract" between Christ and the Christian, the point at which the soul says "Yours is mine, and mine is Yours," he goes on to explain this union: "Already you can see how appropriate it is that the tax collectors and prostitutes precede us into the kingdom of heaven ... It follows, therefore, that those have nothing in common with their Bridegroom who do not participate with Him in sin, who claim righteousness for themselves, who spurn sinners. After all, this marital love is the highest mercy, which falls immediately upon the deepest misery, concerned as it is before everything else with the extinction of sin. For this purpose 'He gave himself up for the Church that he might sanctify her, having cleansed her by the washing with water in the Word of Life that the glorious Church might be presented before Him without spot or wrinkle or any such thing, that she might be holy and without blemish' [Eph. 5:25–27]."[31] Here purgation is not the precondition for that union in which justification takes place; instead, purgation takes place in the marriage union itself. Not purgation but sin is the pre-condition for fulfillment of the contract, the exchange of possessions; Christ is only interested in real sinners. Only real sinners have something to offer Him: their sin.

Earlier, Staupitz had assigned what medieval theologians called sacramental grace, *gratia gratum faciens*, to God's eternal predestination, making Christ himself the intermediary of created grace. To put this in as short a formula as possible: justification not by ascent of the sinner but by the descent of Christ; or, justification on the level of the secular sinner, not on the level of the sacred God. To put it in Staupitz's own programmatic words: "highest mercy falls immediately – without mediators – upon deepest misery." The gap between the sacred and the secular could not have been shortened more dramatically than here in justification, the central theme of late medieval theology.

3. Without further comment we turn now to Luther's proclamation of

---

[31]"Iam vides, quam iuste in regnum coelorum praecedunt nos publicani et meretrices. Vides etiam, quare permissa sunt peccata, et quod 'omnes peccaverunt et egent gloria'. Consequens ergo est: eos nihil habere commune cum sponsa qui ei in peccatis non communicant, qui sibi iustitiam vendicant, qui peccatores spernunt. Amor enim iste sponsalis summa misericordia est et super summam miseriam directe cadit, de exstinctione peccati prae cunctis sollicitus." Johann von Staupitz, *Libellus de executione aeternae praedestinationis*, cap. X, n. 68 and n. 69. See here David C. Steinmetz, *Misericordia Dei. The Theology of Johannes von Staupitz in its Late Medieval Setting* (Leiden, 1968), 91.

freedom by faith, perhaps his single most influential writing, widely accepted also by those who would give this freedom a more political interpretation than intended by the Wittenberg Reformer.

After having interpreted faith as trust in God and identification with his Word, Luther continues: "The third incomparable benefit of faith is that it unites the soul with Christ, as a bride is united with her bridegroom. By this mystery, as the Apostle teaches, Christ and the soul become one flesh. And if they are one flesh and there is between them a true marriage – indeed the most perfect of all marriages, since human marriages are but poor examples of this one true marriage –, it follows that everything they have they hold in common, the good as well as the evil ... Christ is full of grace, life and salvation. The soul is full of sins, death and damnation. Now let faith come between them: then sins, death and damnation will be Christ's, while grace, life and salvation will be the soul's; for if Christ is a bridegroom, he must take upon himself the things which are his bride's and bestow upon her the things that are his ... Who then can fully appreciate what this royal marriage means? Who can understand the riches of the glory of this grace? Here this rich and divine bridegroom Christ marries this poor, wicked harlot, redeems her from all her evil, and adorns her with all his goodness."[32]

Luther deviates in this text, with its famous "*Fröhlicher Wechsel*" or *commercium admirabile*, just as sharply from Gerson as Staupitz had before him. At one point he intensifies the unprecedented marriage deal, *commercium*, with an explicit reference to the sinful bride as the harlot.[33] He differs with Staupitz's formulation on one significant point: for Luther the union with Christ is mediated through union with his word, through faith in his promises. This point should be stressed when the relation between the thought of Staupitz and Luther is analyzed. But in either case, we find a new proximity, even immediacy, between a twain that had not met before so pointedly, obliterating the gap between the sacred and the secular.

With this view of justification a concept of reformation is given which differs from the conciliar reform of Gerson. The profound misery of the Church, the allegorical counterpart to the misery of the soul, is not to be

---

[32]*Luther's Works* [American edition] 31, 351f.; *W A* VII, 54, 31–55, 27.

[33]The "harlot" element is unprecedented in the medieval *commercium*-tradition and a far cry from St. Augustine's one allusion to the two *commercia*, the first of Christ's compensation to the Father and the second of his gift to the sinner, offering his death for the life of man: "Mortuus est Deus, ut compensatio fieret coelestis cuiusdam mercimonii, ne mortem videret homo.... Qualia commercia! quid dedit et quid accipit? Mercantes homines veniunt ad commercia, ad res mutandas ... Tamen nemo dat vitam, ut accipiat mortem." *Sermo* 80, 1, 5 on Math. 17, 18–20; *PL* 38, 496D–497A.

purged as a precondition in order to restore the Church without spot or wrinkle. Yet the crisis of the Church is not overlooked or taken lightly; it is seen as characteristic of the Church in time and space. Henceforth reformation will not be the structural reform of Gerson or the return to the mores of the early Church, as Dietrich von Niem had put it, or the achievement of lasting peace in the words of Valla. Luther's reformation, part and child of the crises of the later Middle Ages, has a dual focal point, first in the acknowledgement of the perpetual nature of the crisis of man and his society, and secondly, the trust in the reality of the sacred embrace of the secular condition.

Looking back on the path we have travelled, we find no reason to conclude that the Reformation movement has a unique claim upon penetration into the modern era. We have not given "equal time" to the Italian Renaissance, since the Burkhardtian stress upon modernity finds ample support today and at the same time is kept under sufficient control by Kristeller's emphasis upon continuity with the Middle Ages.[34] As a matter of fact, we find not only continuity with the preceding medieval tradition but also striking congruity with contemporary Scholasticism, in some respects even more profound than the congruity of the Italian Renaissance with the learned aesthetic, apolitical piety of Erasmian Humanism, north of the Alps. The development of Italian Renaissance humanist thought in the direction of "the subordination of philosophy to rhetoric"[35] as the access route to wisdom could be and was hailed by nominalists in their revolt against meta-categories. When the debate about a "civic humanism" subsides, we shall be left in the realm of political theory with the impressive Renaissance achievement of a new diplomacy based on a balance-of-power concept, emerging out of a reality-oriented, realistic grasp of the secular condition, which is to shape the political affairs of the future.

In view of the size of the research task confronting us, we have dedicated more time and space to the ideas emerging from late medieval Scholasticism. If I seem to have sided with Troeltsch in arguing for the medieval roots and context of the Reformation movement, then it is important to formulate *expressis verbis*, what I implicitly noted in my

---

[34]Cf. Paul Oskar Kristeller, *Renaissance Thought* (New York, 1961), 92–119; Id., *Le thomisme et la pensée italienne de la Renaissance* (Montréal-Paris, 1967). Adumbrations of this view already in Kristeller's *magnum opus*, now after 35 years finally published in its original, *Die Philosophie des Marsilio Ficino* (Frankfurt am Main, 1972).

[35]Hanna Grey, "Renaissance Humanism: The Pursuit of Eloquence", *Journal of the History of Ideas*, 24 (1963), 497–514. Cf. Jerrold E. Seigel, *Rhetoric and Philosophy in Renaissance Humanism. The Union of Eloquence and Wisdom. Petrarch to Valla* (Princeton, 1968), 255; cf. 168f.

enumeration of the chief characteristics of that dominant late medieval scholastic movement which we decided to call nominalism. If the discovery of the inductive method as the basis for reliable scientific conclusions is the harbinger of modern research – and hence as important as the discovery of the New World; if the new understanding of the covenantal relationship between God and man as partners signifies the coming of a new season, the season of the dignity of man; in short, if the closing of the gap between the sacred and the secular carries the marks of the time to come, we dare to see in the crisis of the later Middle Ages the birthpangs of the Modern Era.

III

HEADWATERS OF THE REFORMATION:
INITIA LUTHERI - INITIA REFORMATIONIS

1. *DISTINCTO REALIS - DISTINCTO RATIONIS*

The "Reformation" whose origins or headwaters we seek to chart is confined here to a much abbreviated phase, focusing as it does upon Martin Luther. To be sure, the Lutheran Reformation would not have been able to profit from the protective political and military shield around its homelands without the other multiple origins in Zurich and Geneva and without their rapid developments in the middle of the sixteenth century. The additional importance of a long enduring paralysis of France – as a matter of fact until the eve of the opening of the Council of Trent – cannot be easily overestimated as a factor in the survival of Luther's heritage.

But even so, when taken in its restricted sense, reformation means more than the life and thought of Martin Luther; it carries the connotation of a movement and evokes the image of a tidal wave sweeping along not only theological but also political and social currents. It is questionable, however, whether a shift of our attention from Luther to the reception of his thought by his contemporaries can provide us with a grasp of the shape and texture of the inner structures of this movement, since at its height it swept along many elements which were to be separated out in the years to come. As symbols of such eliminated persons, groups and ideas, the names of Staupitz, Karlstadt, Sickingen, the Müntzerites, and the Erasmians can be mentioned.

Some scholars may be inclined to regard these eliminations as clarification and purification of the currents so darkened in the maelstrom of the turbulent beginnings of the Reformation movement; particularly during this last stage of the Middle Ages, academic critique, national pathos, and social unrest could not but have added interpretations and expectations alien to Luther's message. Others find instead a multiform tradition with the young Luther himself wherein the Reformation discovery was prepared, engendered, and born – in, with, and underneath nominalistic, humanistic, mystical, and Augustinian layers. In this view Luther's later opponents were early temporary allies on the common platform of genuine Lutheran elements, subsequently de-emphasized by Luther himself or even cast off like snakeskins.

To return to the original water imagery: the element of truth in the latter position seems to me to be that Luther's development can be described as a series of successive waves, one tumbling over the other. Hence the perplexing difficulty of establishing the point at which we may locate the Reformation breakthrough. Too often reduced to a single idea in Luther's mind or to an event in his study, this breakthrough has not been viewed sufficiently in relation to his public reception, which was soon to become a movement in its own right. Although we shall argue for the importance of a distinction between the *initia Lutheri* and the *initia reformationis*, the two paths for a time coincide. To express this intimate relationship between an idea and its reception, we are well-advised to think in terms of sound waves, each one reaching past an ever-widening and qualitatively different audience.

1. The first period is richly documented by the *Dictata super Psalterium* and the lectures on Romans which prove from the very beginning[1] to challenge Luther's colleagues and to appeal to the theological students. Johann Lang reports from the Augustinian monastery in Wittenberg on 10 March, 1516 to Spalatin that the students *en masse* are dropping out of the courses on scholasticism. While he does not mention Luther by name, it is obvious that he reports on the new excitement emanating from the Augustinian monk holding the chair for biblical studies. Yet he does go on to explain the rebirth (*reviviscere*) of biblical studies and the vivid interest in the *antiqui scriptores* by pointing to the learning and integrity of Reuchlin and Erasmus, "erudite and honest beyond words."[2]

A few weeks later Luther makes a crucial strategic move when he enlarges the Wittenberg sphere of influence by appointing Lang as prior of the Erfurt house of the Reformed Augustinians. Whereas Lang looks at

---

[1]See Kenneth Hagen, "An Addition to the Letters of John Lang: Introduction and Translation", *ARG*, LX (1969), 27–32. In this letter of Lang to Spalatin from the Augustinian monastery at Wittenberg dated 10 March 1516, we have now the earliest documentation of Luther's impact. This also settles the question of dating Luther's letter to Lang in Erfurt: with *W A Br*, I, 88 against the Gotha Ms., letter no. 34, it is to be dated in 1517 (8 February). Without mentioning Luther's name explicitly Lang writes: ". . . sacram bibliam antiquosque scriptores complures et anhelant et laetanter audiunt, dum scholastici doctores (quod appellant) vix aut duos aut treis [sic] habent auditores", Hagen, 30.

[2]"Quod ut fiat maximo sunt adiutorio Ioannes Reuchlinus, vir doctissimus pariter et integerrimus, et Erasmus Roterodamus ultra quem [quam ?] dicere possum et eruditus et frugis", Hagen, pp. 30–31. Lang refers to Mutian as "Rufum nostrum, non tantum amicum sed et patrem". *Ibid.*

Luther from the perspective of the Erfurt humanist circle around Mutianus Rufus,[3] Luther in informing Mutian of his decision indicates explicitly that Lang is indeed well-versed in his Greek and Latin, but what is more – "quod maius est" – he is an upright man – "syncerioris cordis."[4] It is important for us to note that in contrast to the humanist's ideal man who is equally (*pariter*) learned and upright – expressed time and again in letters and dedications – Luther indicates that for him no such balance holds: a *cor syncerum* is more important than classical learning. And that in a letter to Mutian! In Lang we meet a representative of a whole group of first adherents who, inspired as they are by humanist ideals and expectations, are bound to interpret Luther in such categories.[5] In Lang's letter to Spalatin we have the earliest reflection of Luther's emerging image; at the same time it is the earliest proof of the bewildering complexity of the question of Luther's relation to the temper and forces of his day.

2. The public disputation *Contra scholasticam theologiam* before the forum of the whole University of Wittenberg is formally a call for a reform of theological studies. Its content reveals both the deep gulf separating Luther from the tradition in which he himself was reared and the extent to which he participates in the broader Wittenberger platform *contra omnes*, against the joint medieval tradition. Hence this disputation is to be understood in conjunction with Karlstadt's earlier 151 theses of 26 April 1517, in which the later "Brother Andrew" is ahead of Luther on a number of central points.

3. Whereas the Ninety-five Theses are addressed to theologians – "docendi sunt christiani" – and are eagerly handed around by the enlightened few, the *Sermon von dem Ablass und Gnade* carries the attack on indulgences "far and wide into circles untouched by the Ninety-five Theses,"[6] establishing Luther as pastor to the nation.[7] His opting for the German language is based

---

[3]Cf. *W A Br*, I, 40–41, note 2.

[4]*W A Br*, I, 40:22; 29 May 1516, Luther to Mutian.

[5]Johannes Geiling also belongs to this group. Oswald Bayer and Martin Brecht called attention to him in connection with their important discovery: "Unbekannte Texte des frühen Luther aus dem Besitz des Wittenberger Studenten Iohannes Geiling", *Z KG*, LXXXII (1971), 229–258, 254 ff.

[6]Robert Herndon Fife, *The Revolt of Martin Luther* (New York, 1957), p. 263. Cf. note 77 referring to Knaake's list, *W A*, I, 240ff.

[7]"Es gibt in jenen ersten Jahren noch keine eigentliche lutherische Bewegung im Volk ... Luther ist hier noch nicht als Parteiführer, sondern als Seelsorger bekannt." Bernd Moeller, "Die deutschen Humanisten und die Anfänge der Reformation", *Z K G*, LXX (1959), 46–61, 51.

on the conscious decision to serve the common folk rather than the sodalities of *eruditi*. We should not too eagerly interpret this decision as an expression of "social protest." Primarily it is related to the discovery of the dimension of *experientia, Erfahrung,* which is to become thematic in Luther's tracts and sermons of the coming years, the experience of God and death which does not know social boundaries.

4. The Heidelberg Disputation on 26 April, 1518 provides Luther with the opportunity to present his theology to the Order to which he owed more, as we shall see, than to any other single influencing factor, and where he received more than a profound respect for the "Founding Father" of Hippo. In Heidelberg he pits what he self-consciously calls *mea theologia* (and a moment later *vera theologia*) against the dialectics of his Erfurt teacher, Trutvetter. It is also here that he provokes the historically loaded comment of the youngest Heidelberg Doctor Georg Niger, received at that time with hearty laughter: "If the peasants heard this, they would certainly stone you to death."[8] With foresight Niger related the swelling peasant protest to the new *theologia crucis,* particularly to the *XXI. conclusio* of Luther, where the enemies of the cross of Christ are characterized as those who "hate their cross and sufferings."[9] Whereas this warning is an effort of an opponent to ridicule him, Luther can report[10] that he has won over many among the younger generation. However, if Bucer may function as a test case, the *theologia crucis* has not come through clearly and the Wittenberger is once again seen as an Erasmian, only more courageous than the cautious scholar from Rotterdam. Among the first of the *jeunesse dorée* is Melanchthon who, a few weeks after his arrival in Wittenberg on 25 August 1518, emphasizes Luther's singularity as the "elect servant of the indestructable truth" and "expected messenger of God," even as – $\vartheta\epsilon o\pi\nu\epsilon\upsilon\delta\tau o\varsigma$ [11] – the unique mark of Holy Scripture (2 Tim. 3:16). In Luther's own "history of the reformation" of 1545, he is to single out the arrival of Melanchthon as a crucial event in the

---

[8]"Si rustici hec audirent, certe lapidibus vos obruerent & interficerent." *W A Br,* I, 173 28–29. Luther to Spalatin, Wittenberg, 18 May 1518.

[9]"Tales [sc. theologi gloriae] sunt quos Apostolus vocat Inimicos crucis Christi [Phil. 3:18]. Utique quia odiunt crucem et passiones, Amant vero opera et gloriam illorum, Ac si bonum crucis dicunt malum et malum operis dicunt bonum. At Deum non inveniri nisi in passionibus et cruce ..." *W A,* I, 362 26–29.

[10]"Ceterum adulescentulorum & totius Iuventutis animus per Bis diapason ab illis sentit. Et eximia spes mihi est, ut, sicut Christus ad gentes migravit reiectus a Iudeis, Ita & nunc quoque vera eius Theologia, quam reiiciunt opiniosi illi senes, ad Iuventutem sese transferat. Hec de me." *W A Br,* I, 174 44–47. Luther to Spalatin, Wittenberg, 18 May 1518.

[11]*W A Br,* XII, 12 5–7.

initia reformationis.[12] Even though Luther responds in kind to Melanchthon's early accolade by designating him as a God-directed *organum*, yet their profound mutual respect and *consensus* continue to be heavily tested. The severest challenge may well have been the contested interpretation of St. Augustine, so differently understood by the learned man of letters and the monk from the Order based on Augustine's Rule.[13]

5. The Leipzig Disputation in the summer of 1519 sets the defense of the *vera theologia* against the charges of heresy and deviationism before the theological world, generating reverberations among the *intelligentia*, political leaders and humanists. Here ecclesiological implications of the Ninety-five Theses are pursued, leading to the clarification that Luther's cause is not to be identified with the reemergence of late medieval conciliarism.[14] As we shall see, there is a precedent in the Augustinian Order for Luther's surprising association with the position of the abhorred heretic Jan Hus. At the council of Constance an Augustinian general had already highlighted the critical distance between the organizational Church and the elect *communio sanctorum*.

6. Finally the year 1520 with its widely read manifestos calling for joint action, inner and outer reforms, climaxes in the public burning of "Exsurge Domine" and, even more important for daily life, the burning of books of canon law, a Wittenberg happening at the Elstergate in December which could be understood also by the illiterate. For all those who could read either Latin or German, the *De libertate christiana* presents without explicit polemics

---

[12]*W A*, LIV, 182 4–8.

[13]See p. 44, n. 2.

[14]Cf. Christa Tecklenburg-Johns, *Luthers Konzilsidee in ihrer historischen Bedingtheit und ihrem reformatorischen Neuansatz* (Berlin, 1966), p. 160, n. 363, 192, 194. When Luther scholars find the concept of the general fallibility of legitimate councils in the Luther of 1518–1519, they "universalize a particular" and thus argue in the same way that Luther accused Eck of doing: "Credo autem, auditores meos forte dixisse, Concilium generale saepius errasse et errare posse, tum quod rara sunt concilia illa legitime generalia quale Nicenum fuit: hoc enim dicentes verissime dixerunt. At illi pro rusticitate sua ex particulari mox intulerunt universalem, omne videlicet concilium reprobatum assumentes." *WA*, II, 627 28–32. The same nominalistic (= scholarly!) interest appears in Luther's defense of Hus against Eck's interpretation of Constance, as distorting the various judgments "omnes in universum hereticos". *WA*, II, 288 19. The continuity with late medieval conciliarism can be seen in art. 11 in the *Defensio* of 1519: "Quod plus sit credendum simplici laico scripturam alleganti quam Papae vel concilio scripturam non alleganti." *WA*, II, 649 2–3. For Karlstadt's earlier application of this principle on the basis of Gerson, see Ulrich Bubenheimer, *Consonantia Theologiae et Iurisprudentiae: Andreas Bodenstein von Karlstadt als Theologe und Jurist auf dem Weg von der Scholastik zur Reformation 1515–1522* (Diss., Tübingen, 1971), ch. III, pp. 3–7; Tübingen, 1977, p. 166f.

44 THE DAWN OF THE REFORMATION

the platform of the new theology ranging from *iustificatio sola fide* to the priesthood of all believers and the distinction between law and gospel. The imperial Diet of Worms, *Reichsacht* and papal condemnations form no more than an epilogue to these *initia*. It is by no means obvious, however, that the designation of these early events as *initia reformationis* is appropriate. Franz Lau, for example, links the "Anbruch" and "Auslösung" of the Reformation with the decision of the Diet of Worms in May 1521.[15] As is indicated by the image of concentric sound waves, I fully agree with the emphasis upon public impact as implied in this use of the word Reformation. Yet we should be careful to integrate the *initia reformationis* with the *initia Lutheri* in the years before Worms, that is, before Luther has become both a potent political factor and a *fait accompli*.

Therefore when we try now to find a formula by which we can distinguish the *initia reformationis* from the *initia Lutheri*, with which it has too long been identified, we do so only after stressing that the two notions are intricately intertwined, particularly in the years 1516–1519. Luther is to be regarded not so much as a lonely prophet – let alone as the Hercules of the humanists – but as a leading member of the Wittenberg team which, in keeping with the motto of the university, initiated its program "in the name of St. Paul and St. Augustine."[16] In these years the difference should not be regarded as a *distinctio realis* but as a *distinctio rationis*; or to use the terminology preferred by Melanchthon and Calvin, we should distinguish only *docendi causa*.

When Luther in his joyful letter to Lang of 18 May 1517 writes: "Theologia nostra et Sanctus Augustinus prospere procedunt... Aristoteles descendit paulatim ...,"[17] he describes with his own categories the same development which Lang had regarded a year before as a victory of humanism. Yet it is not Luther's own theological program to which the "theologia *nostra*" refers, but to that of a *team* of Wittenbergers. It may well

Cf. Franz Lau, "Reformationsgeschichte bis 1532", §2.1, "Die Auslösung der Reformation durch den Reichstag zu Worms ...," and §1.9, "Reformatorische Anfänge unabhängig von Luther," *Die Kirche in ihrer Geschichte*, ed. K.D. Schmidt and E. Wolf (Göttingen, 1964), pp. 17, 13–14.

[16]Cf. my "Wittenbergs Zweifrontenkrieg gegen Prierias und Eck. Hintergrund und Entscheidungen des Jahres 1518", *ZKG*, LXXX (1969), 331–58; 334–5.

[17]"Theologia nostra et S. Augustinus prospere procedunt et regnant in nostra universitate Deo operante. Aristoteles descendit paulatim inclinatus ad ruinam prope futuram sempiternam. Mire fastidiuntur lectiones sententiariae, nec est, ut quis sibi auditores sperare possit, nisi theologiam hanc, id est bibliam aut S. Augustinum aliumve ecclesiasticae autoritatis doctorem velit profiteri." *W A Br*, I, 99 8–13. Luther to Lang, Wittenberg, 18 May 1517.

be that the "nostra" includes also Lang, addressed now as Prior of the Augustinian house at Erfurt. In that case, the statement is related to Luther's later praise of Gregory of Rimini (d. 1358) as the sole medieval representative in the battle for Scripture and Augustine against the scholastic doctors.[18]

At the same time it is necessary to distinguish *docendi causa*, since the sources compel us to acknowledge that Luther "sui ipsius interpres," when viewed in the light of the much more ample documentation at our disposal today, understood the *vera theologia* differently from his interpreters, differently not only from his opponents but also from his early followers and allies. Several factors should be taken into account.

1. Methodical research into the reception of Luther's thought by his contemporaries is still in an early stage, due partly to its preference for studying single persons and hesitancy to move on to social groups in the Hanse and *Reichsstädte*.[19] One point is nevertheless clear and striking: the converging focus of interest for all, whether positiviely or negatively, is the newly preached Christian freedom thematically formulated in Luther's *De libertate christiana*. To point first to a negative confirmation of the centrality of this theme: Staupitz addresses his critique in his farewell to Luther, concerned as he is about the spreading abuse of liberty.[20] Albrecht Dürer on the other hand, in the Nuremberg circle around Staupitz, the so-called *Sodalitas Staupitziana*, sees in Luther the prophet of liberty from the oppressive multitude of ecclesiastical laws.[21] And it is on this treatise of Luther's that the earlier prosecutor of Reuchlin, the Dominican Inquisitor van Hoogstraten (d. 1527), concentrates his perceptive and penetrating attack.[22] It is the

---

[18]*W A*, II, 303 12–15. See p. 39, n. 2.

[19]Apart from its helpful bibliography, the most recent publication in this area is paradigmatic for future investigations. Hans-Christoph Rublack, *Die Einführung der Reformation in Konstanz von den Anfängen bis zum Abschluß 1531* (Gütersloh, 1971).

[20]"... ad libertatem carnis video innumeros abuti euangelio." *W A Br* III, 264–26. Salzburg, 1 April 1524. Cf. Th. Kolde, *Die Deutsche Augustiner-Congregation und Johann von Staupitz* (Gotha, 1879), pp. 446–47.

[21]"Offensichtlich ist Dürer vor allem an der von Luther neu erschlossenen Möglichkeit rechten christlichen Lebens und der Befreiung des Gewissens von dauernder Sündenfurcht ... interessiert." Gottfried Seebass, "Dürers Stellung in der reformatorischen Bewegung", *Albrecht Dürers Umwelt: Festschrift zum 500. Geburtstag* (Nürnberg, 1971), pp. 101–31, 107.

[22]"Fratris Iacobi Hoochstrati catholicae aliquot Disputationes contra Lutheranos", *Bibliotheca reformatoria Neerlandica*, ed. F. Pijper ('s-Gravenhage 1905), III, 609–10. Interpretation and English translation of the texts concerned with Steven E. Ozment, "Homo Viator: Luther and Late Medieval Theology", *Harvard Theological Review*, LVII (1969), 275–87; 285–86.

freedom from man-made laws which motivates Karlstadt[23] and, temporarily, Melanchthon,[24] during the period of radical reform in Wittenberg before the return of Luther from the Wartburg. The same motif underlies the famous – and last – expression of appreciation on the part of the Thomas Müntzer over against the new Wittenberg theology: "Theologiam vestram toto corde amplector, nam de funibus venantium animas electorum eripuit multas."[25]

2. As it appears, all followers assent to the first proposition of *De libertate*: "A Christian is a perfectly free lord of all, subject to none." But even those who call themselves *Martiniani* differ as regards the second proposition: "A Christian is a perfectly dutiful servant of all, subject to all."[26] In the interpretation of liberty as "freedom for service" referred to by Luther as the *officium charitatis*, the above-mentioned reformers step off the common platform to give this second proposition differing interpretations in Basel and Strasbourg, in Wittenberg and Bremen, in the *Reichsritter* revolt of Sickingen,[27] and in the more widely spread but equally abortive Peasant Revolt.[28]

---

[23]"Nec scandali respectus est habendus in dispensandis humanis traditionibus, si cum iure divino observari non possint." Thesis 5 from "De scandalo et missa", Oct./Nov. 1521; Hermann Barge, *Andreas Bodenstein von Karlstadt I, Karlstadt und die Anfänge der Reformation* (Leipzig, 1905; Repr. Nieuwkoop, 1968), p. 491.

Cf. Melanchthon "De scandalo" in *Loci communes* (1521); *Melanchthons Werke*, ed. H. Engelland (Gütersloh, 1952), II, 1, 161–62, with the editions 1543 and 1559 where *ius divinum* is replaced by *mandata divina; ibid.*, II. 2, 752 ff. For Melanchthon's high regard and interpretation of *De Libertate* see ibid., VII, 1, 106–8 (April/May 1521).

The point at which Melanchthon would differ from Karlstadt is the substitution of *fides* for *ius divinum* in the evaluation of the relation *libertas-scandalum*: "Leges humanae non obstringunt conscientiam, sed sunt servandae sine scandalo. Tum rursus abolendae sunt et non servandae quando per eas periclitatur fides." *Ibid.*, VII, 1, 108 45–48. Cf. Melanchthon's letter of 5 Feb. 1522, which went via Haugold of Einsiedel to the Elector: ". . . hab auch d. Carlstatt gebetten, das er sich wolde meßigen. Ich khan aber das wasser nicht halden, were von nodten, das man zu solchen sachen, so der seelen heyl betreffen, ernstlicher thette . . . Es ist eyn reformatio vorhanden, gott gebe, das sie zu seyner ehre reyche." For this letter in its context see Nikolaus Müller, *Die Wittenberger Bewegung 1521 und 1522: Die Vorgänge in und um Wittenberg während Luthers Wartburgaufenthalt* (2nd. ed.; Leipzig, 1911), p. 181–82.

[24]In a letter to the Elector of 27 Dec. 1521, Melanchthon reports his impressions of the Zwickau prophets: "Nam esse in eis spiritus quosdam multis argumentis adparet, sed de quibus iudicare praeter Martinum nemo facile possit . . . Cavendum enim est simul, ne spiritus dei extinguantur, simul, ne occupemur a Satana." *Werke*, VII, 1, 159 20–22, 27–29.

[25]Thomas Müntzer, *Schriften und Briefe*, ed. G. Franz (Gütersloh, 1968), p. 380 3–4; letter to Melanchthon, 27 March 1522.

[26]*W A*, VII, 49 22–25; *LW*, XXXI, 344. For the designation 'Martiniani' see O. Clemen, "Georg Helts Briefwechsel", *ARG, Erg. Bd.* 2 (1907), 10–11, and Müller, 79, n. 2.

So individually determined as each one is, there is a common characteristic. Freedom is understood as freedom *from*: from the liturgical *ceremoniae*, from the theological *opiniones* and from the *humanae traditiones*. A common characteristic is that *sola scriptura* is elevated to the same level of significance as Luther's *sola fide* and *sola gratia*. This *sola scriptura* is to form the guide, lawbook, or vision according to which the freedom *for* service, for renewal of the Church, for political action and social reform is shaped.[29] For Luther, liberty and justice *coram Deo* are established and guaranteed by faith in the promises of God; i.e., in the *verbum Dei* grasped in Scripture, so that the Christian conscience is set free to act in love, determined not by set precepts of Scripture nor in order to avoid the wrath of God but by the needs of the *proximus*, the fellow man.

It is on this threshold between the first and second proposition of *De libertate* that we may find one of the characteristic lines of demarcation between the *initia Lutheri* and the *initia reformationis*.

3. A new conception of the role of Scripture arises amid the *initia reformationis* with the issue of the *tertius usus legis*. With Luther and consonant with a never-forgotten medieval tradition, Scripture is read as the only convincing basis for settling theological questions. But among those involved in the *initia reformationis*, Scripture is elevated to the same rank as *sola gratia* and *sola fide*

---

[27]See the significant advance made by Martin Brecht in showing the extent to which there is a common thrust of "Stadtreformation" as described by B. Moeller *Reichsstadt und Reformation* (Gütersloh, 1962 [Schriften des Vereins für Reformationsgeschichte 180]) and the "Reichsritterrevolte": "Wie alle gesellschaftlichen Schichten so ist auch die Ritterschaft von der Reformation stark beeinflußt worden. Daran wie dies geschah, läßt sich etwas erkennen von der weithin einheitlichen Wirkung der Reformation im sozialen Raum. Mehr als man bisher wohl erkannt hat, sind offenbar verschiedene Schichten der Gesellschaft von den gleichen Gedanken erfaßt worden, wie es das Phänomen der Ritterschaft neben den Städten beweist." "Die deutsche Ritterschaft und die Reformation", *Ebernburg-Hefte*, 3. Folge, 1969, 27–37, 32.

[28]Gordon Rupp observes quite rightly in the Peasant Revolt both the older appeal of "desperate conservatism" with "a concern not so much for abstractions – justice, liberty and the like – as for liberties ..." and a new element: "the subtle influence of Luther and the Reformation." This subtlety seems to me to exist in the reading together of liberty and justice. It is true that Luther and Melanchthon as mediators are suggested; but as Rupp observes "... there is an appeal to 'Divine Justice' (*Göttliches Recht*) which might owe something to the teaching of Ulrich Zwingli and sometimes to ancient Catholic doctrine." *Patterns of Reformation* (London, 1969), p. 232.

[29]Even when analyzing more precisely Luther's justification of armed intervention by the authorities against the peasants in revolt and also the extent to which he upholds their *gravamina*, the basic distinction is clear: the *libertas christiana* clearly warrants the "geystlich auffruhr", whereas the devil tries to compromise and suppress this threat to him by manipulating it into "ein leyplich auffruhr". *W A*, VIII, 683 30–31.

and used to determine the quest for reshaping public life, particularly in the cities. The *sola scriptura* articulated by Karlstadt before Luther (May 1518) is programmatically announced by Zwingli as the inspired reform charter for Zurich.[30]

As to the priority of Karlstadt, it should be pointed out that with all respect for the daring originalty of the Wittenberg representative of the *via antiqua*, he had literally to discover the authority of Scripture which we see presupposed in the earliest notes of Luther, the Augustinian monk. As concerns the relation between Luther and Zwingli, neither the issue of the sole authority of Scripture, nor even of hermeneutics in the technical sense of the word is at stake, but rather Zwingli's concept of Scripture as the legislative charter for the Christian magistrate.[31] For Zwingli it is a half-truth or rather a half-error due to one of Luther's paradoxes to believe that the *regnum Christi* is not also a political, visible reign, "etiam externum,"[32] as he puts it. One does not need to have been an Augustinian monk to remember with fear and trembling to what extremes curialism, with its insistence upon the political dimension of the *regnum Christi*, had led. It had been advanced in just this way by the official doctor of the Augustinian Order, Giles of Rome, and issued in Boniface VIII's "Unam Sanctam."

This pervading application and emphasis on Scripture among the Reformers, who to a large extent hail from the *via antiqua*, can also be

---

[30]Zwingli's underscored scriptural principle should not be seen in competition with the centrality of the doctrine of justification. See G. W. Locher, *Huldrych Zwingli in neuer Sicht: Zehn Beiträge zur Theologie der Zürcher Reformation* (Zürich-Stuttgart, 1969); B. Moeller, "Zwinglis Disputationen: Studien zu den Anfängen der Kirchenbildung und des Synodalwesens im Protestantismus", *Zeitschrift der Savigny-Stiftung für Rechtsgeschichte*, LXXXVII, Kanonistische Abteilung, LVI, (1970), 275–324, 294. G. W. Locher, "Zwingli und Erasmus", *Zwingliana: 450 Jahre Zürcher Reformation*, XIII, (1969), 37–61, 58: "Die Entwicklung Zwinglis ist ein prachtvolles Exempel für die Einheit von Formal- und Materialprinzip der Reformation; 'solus Christus' und 'sola scriptura' bedingen einander." The different function of the *sola scriptura* is rather to be seen in the vision of the gospel as the new law: "Wir stehen in der Freiheit vom Gesetz auf der Seite des Gesetzes. Deutlich gegen Luthers scharfe Antithetik heißt es: 'das gsatzt sye dem gotshulder (= pius) ein euangelium'. [*Huldreich Zwinglis Sämtliche Werke* (= Z), edd. Emil Egli, Georg Finsler, II, Leipzig, 1908, 232, 13 f.]". Locher, *Huldrych Zwingli in neuer Sicht*, pp. 234–35 with n. 255.

[31]*Zwinglis Briefwechsel: Die Briefe von 1527–1528* (Leipzig, 1925), ed. Walther Köhler, Z IX, 455, 26–30 (*CR*, XCVI): "... multo magis licet ei magistratui ... dum Christianus est, cum ecclesie consensu ... de externis istis, que aut servata oportet aut neglecta, statuere." Zwingli to Blarer, 4 May 1528.

[32]"... sed nos huc solum properamus, ut probemus Christi regnum etiam esse externum ... Vult ergo Christus, etiam in externis modum teneri, eumque imperat; non est igitur eius regnum non etiam externum." *Ibid.*, IX, 454 13–17. "... nobiscum videbis semierrorem istum, ex paradoxo Luteri ortum ..." *Ibid.*, IX, 454 21–22. Cf. Artur Rich, "Zwingli als sozialpolitischer Denker", *Zwingliana*, XIII (1969), 67–89, 71.

explained in terms of the large number of students of law who opted for the Reformation. At least initially, a striking number of leading men ranging from Karlstadt to Budé, Zasius, and Calvin were recruited, men who, almost without fail, stand in the tradition of the *mos gallicus* and its return *ad fontes iurisprudentiae*.[33] This is indeed one of the politically decisive points where humanism and the Reformation movement combine to perpetuate and transform the late medieval city-ideology of corporate holiness through the freedom of preaching and the firm establishment of schools replacing the monasteries.

4. Beyond or rather beneath these visible changes brought by the Reformation to an increasing number of cities, there lies a civic dream of the realization of the City of God, with explicit references, in the first stages, to Plato's *Republic*.[34] Here the relation between *temporalia* and *aeterna* or between *externa* and *interna* is seen in terms of moral progress rather than of paradox. When Luther locates his *theologia crucis* exactly at the point where these two worlds meet in the believer, it is striking that Bucer, for example, in his enthusiastic report of the Heidelberg Disputation, relegates this aspect to the background. Bucer takes Luther's repeated reference to Augustine's *De spiritu et litera*[35] as the context of interpretation of Luther's intentions. The result is that he informs Rhenanus that in Luther's view we are justified through the *lex spiritus*.[36] Rather than giving a faithful report as it is usually

---

[33]See here particularly the works of Guido Kisch: *Humanismus und Jurisprudenz: Der Kampf zwischen mos italicus und mos gallicus und der Universität Basel* (Basel, 1955); *Bartolus und Basel* (Basel, 1960); *Gestalten und Probleme aus Humanismus und Jurisprudenz. Neue Studien und Texte* (Berlin, 1969). See also Myron Gilmore, *Humanists and Jurists: Six Studies in the Renaissance* (Cambridge, Mass., 1963), pp. 85–86.

[34]See, e.g., the earliest description of Zwingli's theology by Beatus Rhenanus (d. 1547). He describes, in a letter of 6 December 1518, the content of Zwingli's preaching: "... propterea missum in terras a deo Christum..., ut doceret nos pacem et concordiam ac pulchram rerum omnium communionen (nam nihil aliud est Christianissimus), qualem olim Plato magnis annumerandus prophetis utcunque in sua republica somniasse visus est ..." *Z*, VII, 115 19–20, 115 23–116 3.

[35]*W A*, I, 355 34–35; 356 1–4: "Unde capite 8. [Rom. 8:2] appellat Legem legem mortis et legem peccati. Imo 2. Corinth. 3[: 6]. Litera occidit. Quod B. Augustinus per totum librum de spiritu et litera intelligit de qualibet etiam sanctissima lege Dei."

[36]Bucer bases his report not only on the public disputation but also on the *amica confabulatio* the next day: 'postea ab ipso fui edoctus", *W A*, IX, 162 15. "... ut summatim iam complectamur haec omnia, est lex Spiritus divina quaedam ʼἐντελέχεια humanae menti deitus illapsa, irrequieta, perenni impulsu sursum ciens omnia, qua homo et animo prono iusta percipit et summa cum voluptate operatur. Hanc vero ita dari a Deo contendit, ut nulla prorsus mortalium opera emereri queat. Eam ipsam appellari quoque subinde gratiam, nonnunquam fidem, legem vitae, legem Spiritus ac etiam novam legem." *W A*, IX, 162 44–163, 5. Cf. *Briefwechsel des Beatus Rhenanus*, ed. A. Horawitz-K. Hartfelder (Leipzig, 1886; repr. Hildesheim, 1966), p. 108

understood, Bucer at the very moment that he is won for the Reformation introduces a far-reaching variant from "justification by faith": justification through the lifegiving law of the Spirit in contrast to the killing letter of the law.[37] Lines can be drawn from here to his mediating position in the later eucharistic struggle and to the political pneumatology which would inspire his blueprint for a reformed commonwealth in England, the De regno Christi. Apparently there are limits to the extent to which Luther can be understood, even by his most dedicated adherents!

5. Significantly, these "deviations" from Luther are not a series of unrelated so-called "productive misunderstandings," nor is there reason to designate any one version as more "radical" than the others in any sense except that university reform, city reform, and reform of society may be regarded as progressive steps. They have in common, amid all other differences, a drive for political and pedagogical articulation of Christian ethics which can be regarded as one of the hallmarks of the initia reformationis, whether we look at Zwingli or Karlstadt, Müntzer or Melanchthon, Bucer or Calvin.

The theological key lies invariably in the understanding of the third Person of the Trinity. It is indeed not due to a rabies theologorum that the second generation saw the so-called extra calvinisticum as a major issue[38] which is directly related to Calvin's political testament.[39] Whereas for Luther faith is effectuated by the verbum Dei, the presence of Christ as the mode of the preached word, from Karlstadt, Zwingli, and Bucer to the most explicit statements with Calvin, faith as operatio spiritus sancti is a call to action. Faith is not, as Trent would put it, the initium iustitiae but it is the initium regni, the kingdom as the presence of Christ in the mode of the ecclesio-political community, implying the impatient reordering of creation, church and society.

It cannot be doubted that Melanchthon is respected by Luther until the very end of his life and that the Praeceptor Germaniae from his side regards himself as explicator of Luther: "Vestra collegi, et volui, quam possem

---

[37]"Haec ferme ille inter respondendum disseruit de Lege Spiritus, qua una excepta, quaecunque alia sit, nequaquam hominem possit ad iustitiam promovere sed obesse potius, libera voce pronunciabat." W A, IX, 163 21–23; Briefwechsel des Beatus Rhenanus, p. 109. In this 'libera voce' Bucer sees at this time the only difference between Erasmus and Luther: ". . . quae ille duntaxat insinuat, hic aperte docet et libere". Ibid., p. 107; W A, IX, 162 9–10.

[38]See the lucid analysis by E. David Willis, Calvin's Catholic Christology. The Function of the So-called Extra Calvinisticum in Calvin's Theology (Leiden, 1966), pp. 141–54.

[39]Heiko A. Oberman, "The 'Extra' Dimension in the Theology of Calvin", JEH, XXI (1970), 43–64; 46–47. See below Chapter Nine.

simplicissime explicare."[40] Yet even in Melanchthon's case, a true *Epitome* of Luther's theology proves to transcend his gifts of interpretation.[41] Melanchthon's *Loci*, since the 1543 version, distinguish in the characterization of the *libertas evangelica* between the work of Christ in the forensic-synthetic imputation of righteousness and the work of the Holy Spirit which evokes acts in us in keeping with (*congruentes*) the law of God.[42] There is indeed ample reason to suggest that Melanchthon implies more than the scholastic *distinctio rationis*, when he regards this distinction as made *docendi causa*.[43]

In looking from the historical to the theological distinction between the *initia Lutheri* and the *initia reformationis*, we come critically close to the suspenseful character of the Reformation movement. We sense this suspense prior to the establishment of *Landeskirchentum* and *Fürstenregime* in the constantly present tension between Luther's person-oriented rediscovery of the *solus Christus* and a community-oriented pneumatology in which, whenever *fides* is interpreted by *lex, spiritus* tends to issue in *Schwärmerei*, legalistic puritanism or both.

On the basis of our assessment we may come to the conclusion that even though a real distinction between the *initia Lutheri* and the *initia reformationis* as historical events may be dangerously artificial, we can note that the extent of the theological differences *in statu nascendi* are quite clear, notwithstanding

---

[40]*C R* III, 180 45–47.

[41]See the differentiated analysis of the "polare Einheit" by Martin Greschat, *Melanchthon neben Luther: Studien zur Gestalt der Rechtfertigungslehre zwischen 1528 und 1537* (Witten, 1965), pp. 248 ff.

[42]The conclusion can therefore be that through the *imputatio iustitae* "Abrogata est Lex, quod ad maledictionem attinet, non quod ad obedientiam attinet. Ideo et spiritus sanctus datur, ut deinde vere accendantur in cordibus nostris motus congruentes Legi Dei ..." *Melanchthons Werke*, II, 2, 771 22–26. The deviation from Luther's *De Libertate* with its *praesentia filii* expresses itself in the different evaluation of Augustine's doctrine of justification, implicitly here. *Ibid.*, II, 2, 765 32–766 7. It is explicit already in the disputation of 1536, *W A Br*, XII, 191 1–5; 193 88–94.

[43]Even more clearly than with Karlstadt and Müntzer we can see in the case of Melanchthon that he does not "distort" Luther, but rather relates to a particular phase in Luther's development, or combines – as in this case – elements from several stages of development. The conclusion of Sören Widmann is illuminating: "Bis zum Sommer 1520 liebte es Luther, das Zum-Glauben-Kommen mit der Eingiessung des Heiligen Geistes und der von ihm bewirkten Verwandlung in den Affekten zu identifizieren ... Ab Herbst 1520 glaubten wir, neue Elemente in Luthers Reflexion über das Verhältnis von Wort und Glaube entdecken zu können. Diese Veränderung äussert sich darin, daß nun die Vermittlung des Heils vor allem christologisch und erst in zweiter Linie pneumatologisch begründet wird. Christus teilt sich durchs Wort dem Glaubenden mit allen seinen Gütern selbst zu." "Die Wartburgpostille: Untersuchungen zu ihrer Entstehung und zu Luthers Umgang mit dem Text", unpublished Ph. D. diss. U. of Tübingen, 1969, mimeographed, I, 241. See *Christus in verbo veniens, W A*, X, i. 1, 17 8; *W A*, VII, 58 38–59 2; Widmann, I, 303; II, 132.

the common share in the newly found Christian liberty. Since the professional inquisitiveness of the historian drives him to the very edge of the unknowable, we cannot avoid the temptation to join in the old quest for the forces which propelled Luther in his unique direction. These forces must, however, be measured by means of the double set of coordinates of a medieval-scholastic past and the ever-widening waves of the concurrent Reformation movement.

2. CONTRA MODERNOS

I regard it as a distinct advantage to speak not of "causes" of the Reformation with the loaded connotation of a deterministic philosophy of history, but to employ instead the more poetic, or if one prefers, the literally more fluid imagery of gathering tributaries to connote the contingency and complexity of the historical connection between impetus and movement.

Even so the traditional questions as to proto-reformation or contextual movements arise, though they are now to be answered in terms of the distinction between, as well as the perichoresis of, the *initia Lutheri* and the *initia reformationis*. We choose to pursue, or in this brief context rather to comment upon, three streams we have already encountered, namely nominalism, humanism, and Augustinianism, as currents within the history of the Reformation.

When we survey contemporary interpretations of Luther's incipient theology, we discern three basic tendencies:

1. Luther creatively rethought and reshaped traditional thought to such an extent that he must be seen as *sui generis*; Luther is his own man, at once a God-made and self-made man;

2. Luther is primarily to be seen as an Augustinian reared in a nominalistic climate of thought;

3. Luther is an Augustinian carried on the waves of the rising tide of humanism in Germany.

In all three positions, concepts are used which call for clarification, but the most resistent and ungraspable concept has hitherto proved to be "nominalism." As long ago as 1931, Paul Vignaux stated in his important article on Ockham in the *Dictionnaire de Théologie Catholique* that nominalism and the influence of Ockham seem to dominate the universities in the 14th and 15th centuries, but we cannot yet give to nominalism "une notion commune, ni mesurer avec quelque rigueur l'influence d'Occam."[44] Partly due to the very phenomenon itself, we have not yet reached an established consensus in sharpening the contours of nominalism; yet the achievements particularly of Philotheus Böhner are confirmed and elaborated by others who continue to work in this field.[45]

Two points are important for our further considerations. "Nominalism" is the more encompassing designation of the movement which transcends the limits of Ockham's work and hence is not to be identified with Occamism or Occamists as the adherents to the system of the *Venerabilis Inceptor*. Secondly, it proves a distorting reduction to limit the range of nominalism to logic or epistemology, even though in these areas the most original work was done. This is borne out by the fact that the "nominalistae" do not appear in our documents until the end of the 14th century,[46] later to give place to the even more general designation "via moderna," twice removed from the *ipsissima verba magistri*. Though Ritter[47] has convincingly challenged Benary's general thesis,[48] there is nevertheless some truth in the latter's observation that the *via moderna* at the turn of the sixteenth century is, in view of its documented attraction to Thomists and Scotists, often rather the designation of a research method than of clearly defined research results. There is apparently a need for a less ambiguous designation when the term "*via* Marsiliana" emerges in Heidelberg and "*via* Gregorii" in Wittenberg.

At any rate, Luther can use "Occamistae" and "moderni" synonymously

---

[44]*Dictionnaire de Théologie Catholique* (Paris, 1931), XI, 889. See also P. Vignaux, *Nominalisme au XIVᵉ Siècle* (Montréal-Paris, 1948).

[45]See the survey and bibliography of Ph. Böhner by Helmar Junghans, *Ockham im Lichte der neueren Forschung* (Berlin, 1968), pp. 347-48. (Arbeiten zur Geschichte und Theologie des Luthertums, 21).

[46]See Damasus Trapp: "The categories of realism and nominalism characterize the theology of the 15th century very well, because very historically. When these two categories are tacked upon the theology before the Schism, the two terms are less felicitous." It seems "that the term nominalista did not have currency, did not describe the philosophical dissenter, let alone the theologian of the 14th century as such". "Clm. 27034: Unchristened Nominalism and Wycliffite Realism at Prague in 1381", *Recherches de théologie ancienne et médiévale*, XXIV (1957) 320-60, 321.

[47]"... dieser Parteistandpunkt [war] wesentlich nicht im Lehrstoff, sondern in der verschiedenen Beantwortung der Universalienfrage begründet ..." Gerhard Ritter, *Studien zur Spätscholastik: Via antiqua und via moderna auf den deutschen Universitäten des XV. Jahrhunderts* (Heidelberg, 1922), II 93; cf. pp. 15ff. (Sitzungsberichte 13).

[48]F. Benary believes: "Der Unterschied liegt in der verschiedenen Methode, ... nicht im Lehrstoff." *Zur Geschichte der Stadt und der Universität Erfurt am Ausgang des Mittelalters* III, *Via antiqua und via moderna auf den deutschen Hochschulen des Mittelalters mit besonderer Berücksichtigung der Universität Erfurt*, ed. A. Overmann (Gotha, 1919), p. 33. Cf. H.R. Abe, *Der Erfurter Humanismus und seine Zeit* (Jena, 1953), pp. 99-100.

when he argues against the condemnation by the theological faculty of Cologne (*via antiqua!*). He is not prepared to accept blind authority, even if it be that of his own school, the *secta* "Occamica seu Modernorum."[49]

Late medieval nominalism is Ockham's sphere of influence; yet it constitutes a climate of thought which does allow for an independent attitude over against central teachings of Ockham or even for bypassing him in silence. Just as Ockham is at times called the "inceptor," so we find John Buridan referred to as the "inventor" of the *via moderna*.[50] Gerhard Ritter points to a list of representatives of the *via moderna* where Ockham is just one name among many: Marsilius, Buridan, Ockham, Burleigh, Holcot, Gregory of Rimini, d'Ailly, Gerson, Biel.[51] A similar enumeration is given by Marsilius of Inghen with mention of the common characteristic that all followed "nominalium viam et modernorum doctrinam."[52] The role of Ockham is thus not denied when we insist on "nominalism" as the appropriate designation of the whole movement encompassing such varied men and minds as Holcot, Rimini and d'Ailly along with Ockham. After all, John Wesel is known as a fervent defender of the *via moderna*, yet the name of Ockham does not appear in his work.[53]

Two basic points of the *via moderna* indicated as characteristic for the Erfurt tradition, including Jodocus Trutvetter and Bartholomäus von Usingen, may also be seen as the common features of the *via moderna* as such:

1. Rejection and pruning of all concepts which are not absolutely necessary, the so-called "razor;"[54]

---

[49]"Nec hoc quaesivi, ut me ad suos autores remitterent quasi mihi incognitos, sed ut scripturae autoritate aut ratione probabili sua vera et mea falsa esse convincerent. Quae est enim ista (etiam suo Aristotele prohibita) petitio principii, mihi responderi per haec ipsa, quae impugno. Non est quaestio, quid didicerint, audierint, legerint, senserint unquam, Sed quibus firmamentis ea muniant. Alioqui, cur et meae sectae resisterem, scilicet Occanicae seu Modernorum, quam penitus imbibitam teneo, si verbis voluissem aut vi compesci?" *W A*, VI, 194 37–195 5. Cf. the two classifications in 1518 and 1520: "Thomistae, Scotistae, Albertistae, Moderni" in *W A*, I, 509 13–14, and "Aristoteles [peperit] Scotistas, Thomistas, Occanistas" in *W A*, V, 371 36–37.

[50]"Buridanus, maximus Philosophus, qui invenit viam modernorum." *Rerum Familiarumque Belgicorum Chronicon Magnum*, coll. et ed. Joh. Pistorius (Frankfurt a.M., 1654), p. 293 25; quoted by Ruprecht Paqué, *Das Pariser Nominalistenstatut: Zur Entstehung des Realitätsbegriffs der neuzeitlichen Naturwissenschaft (Occam, Buridan und Petrus Hispanus, Nikolaus von Autrecourt und Gregor von Rimini)* (Berlin, 1970), p. 22, n. 13.

[51]*Studien zur Spätscholastik: Neue Quellenstücke zur Theologie des Johann von Wesel* (Heidelberg, 1926/1927), III, 49.

[52]Quoted by Paqué, p. 22, n. 13.

[53]Ritter, III, 9, n. 2.

[54]"Secundum namque viam modernam hoc habetur tamquam principium quod nullibi habetur pluralitas sine reali distinctione." Cod. Vat. Pal. 337, fol. 94va; quoted by Erich Kleineidam, *Universitas Studii Erffordensis. Überlick über die Geschichte der Universität Erfurt im Mittelalter 1392–1521* (Leipzig, 1969), II, 22.

2. The insistence on the contextual interpretation, the so-called *proprietas sermonis*.[55] For the application of this program Ockham was twice condemned in Paris, 1339 and 1340,[56] whereas the Augustinian Order realized immediately in 1345 the theological implications of these new hermeneutics.

Contentwise we find the characteristics of nominalism in an epistemology engendered by the new logic which relates experience and experiment (the so-called *notitia intuitiva*) in such a way that the individual – be it an inanimate object, a human being or an event – is understood in its own context as potentially new, original, and unique before it is identified by classification into *species*. This epistemological stance, which one may well characterize as born out of hunger for reality, is part of a more embracing revolt against the *meta*-world of heteronomous authority and canonized speculation obfuscating, overlaying and distorting reality. It is the revolt against *a priori meta*-physics in order to provide freedom for genuine *a posteriori* physics. Indeed, there are good reasons to claim that the beginnings of modern science can be retraced to nominalism. In the same way it is the revolt against *meta*-theology to provide freedom for genuine theology. Conceived as a practical and not as a speculative "science," Ockham's razor proves to function by slicing away later crusts from more recent glosses,[57] not unlike the humanists' effort to return to the sources. Here lies as well the interest in the traditional antispeculative distinction between *potentia absoluta* and *potentia ordinata*. The description of the Church as *congregatio fidelium*, for instance, is preferred since this perception is closer to experienced reality than a "platonic" abstract universal "extra homines particulares," as Gabriel Biel put it.[58]

Where such concerns express themselves theologically, it is appropriate to speak about "theological nominalism," but it is unwarranted and confusing to designate such as "Occamism" when not expressly related to

---

[55]"... secundum proprietatem sermonis, quam intendit via moderna ..." *Ibid.*, fol. 94vb; quoted by Kleineidam, II, 23.

[56]For the text of the statute of 1340 against Occam with the explicit mention of the *proprietas sermonis* see Paqué, p. 10. The statute of 1339 is more general: Paqué, pp. 306 ff.; cf. Adolar Zumkeller, *Hugolin von Orvieto und seine theologische Erkenntnislehre* (Würzburg, 1941), p. 257, n. 4.

[57]In matters conciliar Ockham proves to be "conservative", as Brian Tierney terms it, "by preferring" to restate in detail the old arguments of Huguccio. Brian Tierney, "Ockham, the Conciliar Theory, and the Canonists", *Journal of the History of Ideas*, XV, 1 (Jan.-Mar. 1954), 40–70; Facet Books, Historical Series 19 (Philadelphia, 1971), p. 26.

[58]"... ecclesie meritum non est universale platonicum seu meritum abstractum extra homines particulares per se existens, sed est personarum et membrorum ecclesiam constituentium." Gabrielis Biel, *Canonis misse expositio* I, edd. H.A. Oberman-W.J. Courtenay (Wiesbaden, 1963), Lectio XXVI, I., p. 246.

the *Venerabilis Inceptor*.[59] When this relationship between nominalism and Occamism is inverted by making Occamism the prior category, we are forced either to confine nominalism to a movement in the school of arts,[60] or to expand the concept of Occamism so far that the umbilical cord between Ockham and the Occamists becomes stretched.[61]

These few comments about nominalism and its concerted action against all *meta*-categories make it clear that the option for nominalism meant more than the appropriation of a new system of logic. It meant the involvement in a scientific revolution. This explains the increasing concern of church and university for the continuity of doctrine, expressed in the Paris-Statutes of 1339 and 1349 and the succeeding censures by the Augustinian Order in 1345 and 1348.[62] Thus it is possible for us to grasp why Wessel Gansfort could repeatedly point to his shift in 1459 from the *via antiqua* to the *via moderna*,[63] referred to as "nominales", as the newly won basis for clearer theological arguments.[64] Furthermore it explains the tone of pride when Luther not only

[59]Erich Hochstetter, "Nominalismus?", *Franciscan Studies*, 9 (1949), 370–403; 372.

[60]In a review of E. Jane Dempsey Douglass, *Justification in Late Medieval Preaching: A study of John Geiler of Keisersberg* (Leiden, 1966) Wilfred Werbeck implies such a view when he rejects the thesis that Geiler is a nominalistic theologian: "Diese These ist in dieser Formulierung um der begrifflichen Klarheit willen nicht haltbar. Vom Nominalismus kann man nur im Zusammenhang mit bestimmten philosophischen Anschauungen sprechen, und eine nominalistische Theologie gibt es nur dort, wo solche philosophische Position theologisch unmittelbar wirksam wird ... Frau D. meint natürlich mit 'nominalistischer Theologie' letztlich stets die ockhamistische Tradition." *ThLZ*, XCIII (1968), 759–61; 760.

[61]Thus Reinhard Schwarz can comment in connection with d'Ailly's "plagiarism" from Gregory of Rimini: "Jedenfalls hat Luther bei d'Ailly – auch bei Biel – einen vielfältig gefärbten, keineswegs einen einfarbigen Ockhamismus kennengelernt!" *Fides, Spes und Caritas beim jungen Luther unter besonderer Berücksichtigung der mittelalterlichen Tradition* (Berlin, 1962), p. 20, n. 44.

[62]"Item, quod nullus dicat propositionem nullam esse concedendam, si non sit vera in ejus sensu proprio, quia hoc dicere ducit ad predictos errores, quia Biblia et auctores non semper sermonibus utuntur secundum proprios sensus eorum. Magis igitur oportet in affirmando vel negando sermones ad materiam subjectam attendere, quam ad proprietatem sermonis, disputatio namque ad proprietatem sermonis attendens nullam recipiens propositionem, preterquam in sensu proprio, non est nisi sophistica disputatio. Disputationes dyalectice et doctrinales, que ad inquisitionem veritatis intendunt, modicam habent de nominibus sollicitudinem." Paqué, p. 10. Text of the Augustinian condemnations of 1345 and 1348 in Adolar Zumkeller, *Hugolin von Orvieto*, p. 257, n. 4; p. 258, n. 3.

[63]Cf. Maarten van Rhijn, *Wessel Gansfort* ('s-Gravenhage, 1917), pp. 78–83; 236. The decisive agent was the crusading Hendrik van Zomeren. Cf. *Actuarium Chartularii Universitatis Parisiensis*, edd. A.L. Gabriel-G.C. Boyce (Paris, 1964), VI, 235–36, n. 1. See also Maarten van Rhijn, *Studien over Wessel Gansfort en zijn tijd* (Utrecht, 1933), p. 69.

[64]In his debate with Jacob Hoeck (*Actuarium* VI, 331 f. n. 11) on papal power to promulgate plenary indulgences: "Nosti, schola nostra Nominalis talem verborum dissidentiam et discohaerentiam non admittit." Wessel Gansfort, *Opera* (Groningen, 1614; Repr. Nieuwkoop, 1966), p. 890 (Monumenta Humanistica Belgica, I). In his 'conversion report' Wessel makes

claims: "Occam solus intellexit dialecticam," "Occam fuit prudentissimus et doctissimus," but also exclaims: "Occam, magister meus."[65] Finally it suggests why one must concern oneself with the relationship nominalism-reformation when dealing with the theme of Luther and the dawn of the modern era.

One cannot begin to answer this question without recalling the distinction made between the *initia reformationis* and the *initia Lutheri*. As far as the Reformation in the broader sense of the word is concerned, nominalism cannot be regarded as a factor in either a positive or a negative sense. By the beginning of the sixteenth century, nominalism had been reduced in significance by two developments: first it suffered a setback due to a rejuvenated Thomism through the work of Capreolus (d. 1444) and Cajetan (d. 1534), in Germany concentrated in Cologne. Simultaneously, the spread of religious humanism rapidly reduced the magnetism of nominalism as the possibility of academic renewal from within. Even though striking parallels can be observed between certain trends in Italian humanism and nominalism, particularly as concerns its anthropology, Paul Oskar Kristeller has done much to trace "the partial continuity"[66] of Renaissance philosophy and the Aristotelian-Thomistic tradition. Wessel Gansfort, one of the few and first Graecists of his day, uniting in one person the ideals of nominalism and humanism, could still be confident that the *via moderna* provides the means to bypass and abolish the *via antiqua* and thus to reach and read the true *antiqui*, namely the Fathers.[67] When, however, Lefèvre d'Étaples and

---

quite clear that the *via moderna* cannot be a religious authority for him: "... corrigi paratus mutavi sententiam, et Nominales adprehendi. In quibus, ingenue fateor, si quid fidei contrarium putarem, hodie paratus remearem vel ad Formales [= Scotisti], vel Reales [= Thomisti] ..." *Ibid.*, p. 877. "... quamdiu mihi videtur quod Papa, vel Schola, vel quaecunque multitudo contra Scripturae veritatem adserat, semper debeo Scripturae veritatem prima sollicitudinis parte amplecti, secundo autem, quia non probabile tantos errare, debeo diligenter veritatem utriusque partis pervestigare." *Ibid.*, p. 879. A monograph is being prepared by Sarah Reeves on the relation of Wessel to nominalism.

[65]"Occam solus intellexit dialecticam, das es lige am definire et dividere vocabula, sed non potuit eloqui." *W A Tr*, I, no. 193. "Occam fuit prudentissimus et doctissimus, sed defuit ei rhetorica." *W A Tr*, I, no. 338. "Occam, magister meus, summus fuit dialecticus, sed gratiam non habuit loquendi." *W A Tr*, II, no. 2544a.

[66]*Renaissance Philosophy and the Medieval Tradition* (Latrobe, 1966), p. 79. As to Erasmus, however, we note the conclusion of John B. Payne: "Erasmus had considerable knowledge of and appreciation for some of the scholastics, especially the late medieval nominalistic tradition. He enlists the support especially of Gerson and Durandus, but also of Biel." *Erasmus: His Theology of the Sacraments* (Richmond, Va., 1970), p. 229.

[67]"Ubicunque problematicum aliquod incideret [Buridanus] non secundum illorum [Albertum, Thomam, vel Scotum, vel universae Realium aut Formalium scholae], sed secundum Nominalium sententiam terminat. Alii sunt igitur antiqui illi, quorum sententiis, praesertim in *Moralibus* nunquam se confitetur deceptum." Wessel Gansfort, *Opera*, p. 879.

Erasmus begin to publish the first patristic editions less than half a century later, a more immediate access was provided for a return to the sources.

After the Pfefferkorn affair and the literary and, what is more, ideological success of the "Letters of Obscure Men," the German intelligentsia in large numbers turns its back on all scholastic schools to place its hopes in the study of the classics and the Fathers. In this way the renewal movement issuing from *eloquentia* and *rhetorica* stole the glitter of the *via moderna* which had raised its banner in the name of *logica* and *dialectica*. Yet whereas humanism shaped the early modern era, it is nominalism which determined the *Geist* and set the tone of the modern era, notwithstanding the protest songs of the *via antiqua* surviving in German idealism. As far as the theological world is concerned, it may not be immaterial for those who see an inner connection between nominalism and the course of the Reformation to point first to the fact that a number of nominalists belong to the earliest opponents of Luther, among them such productive authors as Eck, Schatzgeyer, and Usingen.[68]

What is more, when we go on to recall some of the leading reformers and their scholastic matrix, all evidence contradicts a more intimate relationship between nominalist training and choosing the Reformation: Karlstadt hails from the *via antiqua*, first more Thomistically, later more Scotistically oriented.[69] Zwingli's marginals to the Sentences Commentary of Scotus have not yet been published, but his having passed through the *via antiqua* cannot be contested.[70] Bucer received his theological training from the Dominicans.[71] Calvin may have been influenced by John Major but, whereas

---

[68]Cf. Otfried Müller, *Die Rechtfertigungslehre nominalistischer Reformationsgegner. Bartholomäus Arnoldi von Usingen, O.E.S.A. und Kaspar Schatzgeyer, O.F.M. über Erbsünde, erste Rechtfertigung und Taufe* (Breslau, 1940).

[69]Karlstadt describes his own road to reformation in the revealing dedication to Staupitz of his Commentary to Augustine's *De spiritu et litera*: ". . . quia sectam et capreolinam et Scotisticam manifesta interpretatione successive profitebar." Ernst Kähler, *Karlstadt und Augustin: Der Kommentar des Andreas Bodenstein von Karlstadt zu Augustins Schrift De spiritu et litera* (Halle, 1952), p. 3 19-20.

[70]Walther Köhler, *Die Geisteswelt Ulrich Zwinglis. Christentum und Antike* (Gotha, 1920), pp. 14 ff. "Bei Luther wird mit Recht im Abendmahlsstreit der Rückgriff auf die scholastischen Lehrmeister betont. Bei Zwingli steht es nicht anders, nur daß er mit dem Material einer anderen Schule arbeitet." *Ibid.*, p. 19. For the marginals to Scotus see Walter Köhler, *Huldrych Zwingli* (2nd. ed.; Leipzig, 1954), p. 22.

[71]Cf. Heinrich Bornkamm: ". . . das Studium der thomistischen Theologie, dessen Spuren man später noch bei ihm findet . . ." *Martin Bucers Bedeutung für die europäische Reformationsgeschichte* (Gütersloh, 1952), p. 8. Hastings Eells observes that Bucer "learned to detest" Aquinas, but draws on Bucer's later *Verantwortung* of 1523. *Martin Bucer* (New Haven, 1931), p. 3. He complains here that in the monastery his "Bücher, darauß man die latinisch sprach lernet", were taken away to be replaced by "sophistisch dautmären", children's tales; a quasi

we have not yet succeeded in finding unambiguous parallels, similarities with Duns Scotus are firmly established.[72]

As far as the *initia Lutheri* are concerned, our question is more complex. Increasingly refined arguments are given for Luther's dependence on the system of Ockham, whether directly or as mediated by two of Ockham's disciples well known to Luther, Petrus d'Ailly and Gabriel Biel.[73] The wholesale identification of Ockham and nominalism with Luther's theology as articulated in the tradition from Denifle to Lortz[74] is gradually disappearing. Residues of this view, however, are still operative within the concomitant Protestant apologetics. Generally it may be said that Protestant scholarship tends to reject a real connection between Luther and Ockham or nominalism. Leif Grane for example finds no "decisive influence of Occamism" in the years around the disputation against scholastic theology (1517).[75] Reinhard Schwarz argues concerning the preceding stage of the

---

knowledge drawn from "den verfuerischen unchristlichen buechern ires Thomas von Wasserburg, den sye von Aquino nennen." *Martin Bucers Deutsche Schriften, Frühschriften 1520–1524,* ed. Robert Stupperich (Gütersloh, 1960), I, 161 23–24. Whatever his later evaluation was to be, according to his report of 30 April 1518, Bucer had bought the *Scripta Thomae* with an advance from the Prior in 1516. Cf. "Bucers Bücherverzeichnis", *ibid.,* I, 281–82.

[72]Cf. François Wendel, *Calvin: Sources et évolution de sa pensée religieuse* (Paris, 1950), pp. 99 ff.

[73]Since the discovery of Hans Volz that the marginals of Luther to the 1514 Lyon edition of Biel's *Collectorium* and *Canonis misse expositio* were written partly by the young Luther – shortly before 4 September 1517 – but partly also many years later, we know that Luther continued to consult this copy. Hence we are well advised not to restrict our investigation of the influences of the *via moderna* to the years of dissociation around the "Disputatio contra Scholasticam theologiam". See Volz, "Luthers Randbemerkungen zu zwei Schriften Gabriel Biels: Kritische Anmerkungen zu Hermann Degerings Publikation", *ZKG,* LXXXI (1970), 207–19; 217. The often quoted *W A Tr,* III, 564 5–7, no. 3722 can best be understood by relating the first ("meo iudicio") and the second evaluation in the one sentence as applying to two periods in Luther's life: "Gabriel scribens librum super canonem missae, qui liber meo iudicio tum optimus fuerat; wenn ich darinnen las, da blutte mein hertz. Bibliae autoritas nulla fuit erga Gabrielem." For a critical discussion of efforts to relate Luther to representatives of late medieval nominalism from Grisar to Weijenborg, see Gordon Rupp, *The Righteousness of God: Luther Studies. A reconsideration of the character and work of Martin Luther* (London, 1953), pp. 96 ff., 175 ff.

[74]Cf. Heinrich Denifle, *Luther und Luthertum in der ersten Entwicklung* (Mainz, 1909), II, 297 ff.; Joseph Lortz, *Die Reformation in Deutschland* (4th ed.; Freiburg, 1962), II, 172 ff.

[75]"Aber soweit es in dieser Arbeit möglich war, den vorhandenen Stoff zu beleuchten, gibt es nichts, was dafür spricht, dass der Ockhamismus auf die Ausformung von Luthers Theologie dieser Jahre entscheidenden Einfluß gehabt hat. Kein zentraler Gedanke hat seinen Ursprung in der Ockhamistischen Theologie, weder positiv noch negativ. Dahingegen besteht Grund zu glauben, dass der Ockhamismus auf Luthers Formulierung der Rechtfertigungslehre befördernd und klärend gewirkt hat. Aber, wie gesagt, es handelt sich kaum um mehr als eine Folgeerscheinung." Leif Grane, *Contra Gabrielem: Luthers Auseinandersetzung mit Gabriel Biel in der Disputatio Contra Scholasticam Theologiam 1517* (Gyldendal, 1962), pp. 380–81. Cf. the clear article by Bengt Hägglund, "Voraussetzungen der Rechtfertigungslehre Luthers in der spätmittelalterlichen Theologie", *Lutherische Rundschau,* XI (1961), 28–55, in English, "The Background of Luther's Doctrine of Justification in Late Medieval Theology", *Lutheran World,* VIII (1961), 24–46.

Dictata that "the Occamistic school indeed sharpened Luther's mind," but holds that it was as an interpreter of the Scriptures and not as an Occamist that Luther came to be "the Reformer."[76]

In recent Roman Catholic Luther studies, on the other hand, we find a greater openness to the opposite thesis.[77] Among the more recent authors, Francis Clark points to Luther's use of d'Ailly in his attack on transubstantiation in *De captivitate Babylonica* and to the doctrine of the ubiquity of the Body of Christ.[78] Erwin Iserloh finds proof of the radicalization of the nominalistic separation of human and divine action in the Ninety-five Theses when Luther denies that the Church can provide forgiveness through indulgences.[79] It is again Iserloh, who discerns Luther the nominalist in the theses that images and ceremonies are neutral entities, *adiaphora*, in contrast to such realists as Karlstadt and Müntzer, who find the images so important that they call for their immediate removal.[80]

---

[76]"Luther manipulierte nicht die Traditionen, wie es im Grunde genommen die Autoren der Devotio moderna machten. Gewiss trat Luther, der seinen Verstand in der ockhamistischen Schule geschärft hatte, in die Bahnen der Devotio moderna, er griff die monastische Theologie auf, er liess sich von Bernhard anregen, vor allem suchte er die Person und Theologie Augustins zu erfassen. Dennoch wurde Luther weder als Ockhamist, noch als Anhänger der Devotio moderna, noch als monastischer Theologe, auch nicht als Vertreter einer bernhardinischen Frömmigkeit oder augustinischen Theologie zum Reformator. Zum Reformator wurde er als der Lehrer einer neuen Theologie, die in der inneren Auseinandersetzung mit den Traditionen beim Schriftstudium herangereift war. Dieser Reifeprozeß war während der 1. Psalmenvorlesung in vollem Gange." Reinhard Schwarz, *Vorgeschichte der reformatorischen Busstheologie* (Berlin, 1968), p. 297.

[77]Cf. however Jared Wicks: "His later assertions that he was of Ockham's school must refer to his philosophical training in Erfurt from 1502 to 1505 ... Luther had no interest in the dominant themes of the *via moderna*..." *Man Yearning for Grace: Luther's Early Spiritual Teaching* (Wiesbaden, 1969), p. 267.

[78]*The Eucharistic Sacrifice and the Reformation* (London, 1960), p. 320. Cf. *W A*, VI, 508 7–26. See here Leif Grane, "Luthers Kritik an Thomas von Aquin in 'De captivitate Babylonica'", *ZKG* LXXX (1969), 1–13.

[79]"Schon in der nominalistischen Theologie war göttliches und menschliches Handeln weitgehend getrennt, insofern Gott das Tun der Kirche nur zum Anlass nimmt für sein Heilshandeln, ohne darin wirklich einzugehen. Luther führt diese Trennung des Menschlich-Kirchlichen vom Göttlichen so weit, dass er der kirchlichen Strafe bzw. ihrem Erlass nicht einmal mehr interpretative Bedeutung hinsichtlich der von Gott auferlegten Sündenstrafen zumass. Hier scheint mir eine Wurzel der baldigen Leugnung des hierarchischen Priestertums als göttlicher Stiftung bei Luther zu liegen." Erwin Iserloh, *Luthers Thesenanschlag. Tatsache oder Legende?* (Wiesbaden, 1962), p. 38; repeated verbatim in *Luther zwischen Reform und Reformation: Der Thesenanschlag fand nicht statt* (Münster i.W., 1966), p. 87.

[80]"Luther nimmt als Nominalist die Frage der Bilder, Zeremonien und der äusseren Gestalt nicht wichtig. Es sind für ihn Adiaphora; sie dürfen bleiben und können wegfallen, weder dem einen noch dem anderen darf man Heilsbedeutung zumessen. Für ihn ist deshalb auch nicht die Bilderverehrung, ihre vermeintliche Anbetung, der Anstoss, sondern der falsche Heilsglaube, zu meinen, durch Stiften von Bildern, Kirchen und Altären Verdienste sammeln zu können ...

When it is said that Luther's *sola scriptura* is part of the Occamistic heritage,[81] the basis for such an assumption can be found only in a letter Luther wrote his teacher Jodocus Trutvetter on 9 May 1518. In answer to Trutvetter's obviously severe criticisms of the Ninety-five Theses, Luther says that Trutvetter was indeed the very first to teach him that "one owes faith only to the canonical books, and a serious hearing to all other (authorities)."[82] Now apart from the fact that it is a common medieval *dictum* that only the literal sense of Holy Scripture can provide for a theological *assertio*, it is precisely Ockham and the Occamists, in contradistinction to the nominalist Gregory of Rimini, who uphold Scripture *and* tradition as the basis of theology.[83] Hence Trutvetter's teaching on this point is by no means an "extra-occamisticum." Rather to the contrary! Luther reminds his teacher of a basic principle which, when carried through, means the reform – or the end – of all scholastic theology.

A few weeks earlier, Luther had already indicated what he thought about the scholastic and particularly Trutvetter's use of dialectics: "Instead of being useful to theology, (dialectic) is rather an obstacle to theological studies, because theology uses the same vocabulary in a manner quite different from that of dialectics. In what way therefore, I asked, can dialectics be of use, since once I begin to study theology I am forced to reject the dialectic meaning of a word and have to accept its [theological] meaning."[84] Hence we may conclude that the word of explicit praise,

---

Die Bilderstürmer Thomas Müntzer und Andreas Karlstadt nahmen die Sprache und die Bilder ernster. Es ist sicher nicht zufällig, dass sie ihrer theologischen Schule nach Realisten waren. Sie wollten und konnten sich nicht damit begnügen, daß die Texte der Messe erklärt wurden, sondern drängten um der 'Errettung der armen elenden, blinden Gewissen' willen zur Verdeutschung der Liturgie. Weil sie die äußere Gestalt ernst nahmen, ..." Erwin Iserloh, "Bildfeindlichkeit des Nominalismus und Bildersturm im 16. Jahrhundert", *Bild-Wort-Symbol in der Theologie*, ed. W. Heinen (Würzburg, 1969), pp. 119–38; 134–35.

[81]Cf. Friedrich Kropatschek, *Das Schriftprinzip der lutherischen Kirche. Die Vorgeschichte. Das Erbe des Mittelalters* (Leipzig, 1904), I, 309, 312.

[82]". . . sed si pateris discipuli tui et obsequentissimi famuli tui, id est meam confidentiam, ex te primo omnium didici, solis canonicis libris deberi fidem, caeteris omnibus iudicium, ut B. Augustinus, imo Paulus et Iohannes praecipiunt. Sine ergo mihi licere id idem in Scholasticos, quod tibi et omnibus licitum fuit hucusque: volo sequi, si per Scripturas aut ecclesiasticos Patres meliora fuero doctus, sine quibus volo Scholasticos audire, quoad sua firmaverint ecclesiasticis dictis, et ab hac sententia nec tua autoritate (quae apud me certe gravissima est), multo minus ullorum aliorum deterreri propositum est." *W A Br*, I, 171 71–80. Luther to Trutfetter, 9 May 1518.

[83]Cf. my *The Harvest of Medieval Theology. Gabriel Biel and Late Medieval Nominalism* (Cambridge, Mass., 1963), pp. 375 ff.

[84]"Scripsi denique ad d. Isennacensem, nostra aetate (ut videtur) principem dialecticorum, in eandem rem, potissimum allegans id, quod negari non potest, videlicet ideo non posse

"Occam solus intellexit dialecticam . . ."[85] refers to the application of logic in its own domain, not to its use as a tool for theology proper. Particularly in the field of eucharistic theology Luther employs nominalistic arguments and some of its terminology, such as d'Ailly's *transaccidentatio*, to show the arbitrariness of the Fourth Lateran (1215) in opting for the *opinio Thomae* without warrant of Scripture or reason. To this extent we can therefore agree with Leif Grane's conclusion in contrast to Clark's understanding of the *De captivitate*: Luther shows his indebtedness to Occamism in his attack against Thomism and indeed, as far as Luther's view of the *ratio*-speculation is concerned, the *via moderna* is "dem Thomismus überlegen." Grane goes on to argue that this merely applies to superiority in an area which, from the perspective of the *vera theologia*, is taboo and to which entrance is to be regarded as "impious human curiosity."[86]

This last conclusion seems to me to call for correction in one respect. Aristotle is indeed seen as the perverter of the theology of all schools, including the Occamists,[87] in paving the way to curiosity by disregarding the borderline between reason and revelation. And admittedly there is for Luther a knowledge of God which to attempt to penetrate with human reason is mere curiosity or worse.[88] Yet the triad reason-Aristotle-dangerous

---

Dialecticen prodesse Theologiae, sed magis obesse, Quod eisdem vocabulis grammaticis longe aliter utatur Theologia quam Dialectica. Quomodo ergo, inquam, prodest Dialectica, cum, postquam accessero ad Theologiam, id vocabuli, quod in Dialectica sic significabat, cogar reiicere & aliam eius significationem accipere?" *W A Br*, I, 150 21–28; Luther to Spalatin, 22 February 1518. I use the translation *L W*, XLVIII, 57.

[85]*W A Tr*, I, 85 27–28 (a. 1532), no. 193.

[86]"[Luther] ist . . . in seiner Polemik gegen Thomas abhängig von dem Verständnis des Aristoteles, das er durch den Ockhamismus gelernt hatte. Mehrere Dinge in dieser Polemik deuten auf eine direkte Benutzung des Sentenzenkommentars von Pierre d'Ailly hin. . . . Aber indem Luther sich in diese Diskussion hineinwirft, d.h. sich auf Gebieten bewegt, die seines Erachtens prinzipiell jenseits der Grenzen der christlichen Theologie und weit innerhalb der Grenzen der ungebührlichen und frechen menschlichen Neugierigkeit liegen, dann muss er sich der hier sich befindenden Waffen bedienen. Das heisst für ihn, von der ockhamistischen Aristotelesdeutung Gebrauch zu machen. Dass er also im Verhältnis zum Thomismus als Ockhamist auftritt, darf aber die Anhänger der Theorie von der Bedeutung der 'verdorbenen' Scholastik für die Reformation nicht allzu sehr freuen. Das bedeutet nämlich nur, dass er an der Überzeugung festhielt, dass die *via moderna* auf dem Gebiet der 'Vernunft' dem Thomismus überlegen war, d.h. auf dem Gebiet, wo sich seines Erachtens die *ganze* Scholastik befand. Selbst wünschte er, sich an einer ganz anderen Stelle zu befinden, und da fand er weder Thomismus noch Ockhamismus." Grane, *Luthers Kritik*, pp. 12–13.

[87]See here G. Ebeling, *Luther: Einführung in sein Denken* (Tübingen, 1964), pp. 90–91.

[88]"Legi mille et omnes doctores, nullus melius solvet hanc quaestionem. Scotus distinguit ea formaliter, moderni ratione, antiqui realiter. Ex quibus omnibus colligitur omnes eos nescire quid loquantur. Cum enim ista nemo viderit, quicquid supra fidem additur, certissimum est figmentum esse humanum. Similiter de anima." *W A*, IX, 62 19–24; quoted by Karl-Heinz zur Mühlen, "Ratio", *Archiv für Begriffsgeschichte*, XIV (1970), 192–256; 252, no. 375.

curiosity is only one side of the coin. On the other side Luther's attack is expressly addressed to Aristotle as authority in the field of theology and as interpreted *apud latinos*.[89] This does not imply that reason has no valid function of its own or that the *ratio naturalis*, when based on experience, is not a source of truth. Luther at Worms publicly acknowledges Scripture *and* reason as the two ways to convince him of his errors.[90] In *De captivitate* he rejects transubstantiation as *figmentum humanae opinionis*, because neither Scripture nor reason supports it.[91] A year earlier Luther appeals to St. Augustine for the thesis that nothing is to be believed "nisi divinis literis *aut* ratione probabili persuadeat."[92] To grasp the Gospel is beyond the reach of reason ("extra rationem")[93] and to think properly about God "non ratio, sed sola fides potest."[94] Yet it is not improper *per se* to reach beyond the domain of Scripture; to the contrary, when Scripture is silent, as in the case of purgatory, what is improper is to reach beyond the domain of reason (experience): it is *temeritas* to hold a certain opinion "in iis quae nos ratio naturalis non docet."[95] Again, it is granted that in Luther's view to argue with probable arguments is not to do theology but dialectics, "id est probabilia tantummodo tradere, non credibilia";[96] yet it cannot be minimized that Luther proclaims Ockham as the *facile princeps* in this field. It is not by chance that Luther in *De captivitate* calls upon an argument of d'Ailly; and finally it is not mere cynicism when Luther writes in the fall of 1516 to his friend Johannes Lang, who is just about to lecture in Erfurt on the second book of the Sentences:[97] "Scio quid Gabriel dicat, scilicet omnia bene, praeterquam ubi de gratia, charitate, spe, fide, virtutibus dicit."[98]

---

[89] *W A*, I, 226 28.

[90] *W A*, VII, 838 4. Cf. Bernhard Lohse, "Luthers Antwort in Worms", *Luther*, XXIX (1958), 124–34; Kurt-Victor Selge, "Capta conscientia in verbis Dei: Luthers Widerrufungsweigerung in Worms", *Der Reichstag zu Worms von 1521: Reichspolitik und Luthersache*, ed. Fritz Reuter (Worms, 1971), pp. 180–207; 200–1.

[91] *W A*, VI, 509, 20–21; see further zur Mühlen, pp. 214–17.

[92] *W A*, II, 447, 16–17.

[93] *W A*, XL 1, 371 5.

[94] *W A*, XL 1, 376 25. I regard it as an explicit rejection of – i.a. – the program of nominalistic theology when Luther in 1520 formulates the thesis: "8. Si quis terminos logice et philosophie in theologiam ducat, necesse est, ut horrendum cahos errorum condat." Conclusiones quindecim, *W A*, VI, 29 19–20. See further Bernard Lohse, *Ratio und Fides: Eine Untersuchung über die ratio in der Theologie Luthers* (Göttingen, 1958), pp. 95 ff.; Brian A. Gerrish, *Grace and Reason: A Study in the Theology of Luther* (Oxford, 1962), pp. 69 ff., 137.

[95] *W A*, I, 663 15–16.; cf. 664 25.

[96] *W A*, I, 665 2; cf. 664 36.

[97] Cf. *W A Br*, I, 73 27.

[98] *W A Br*, I, 66 32–34. Cf. Melanchthon's comment on Luther's continuing work with Biel and d'Ailly: "Nec tamen prorsus relinquit Sententiarios. Gabrielem et Cameracensem pene ad verbum memoriter recitare poterat." *CR*, VI, 159 (1 June 1546).

The *initia Lutheri* as Luther's quest for the Gospel was a path which implied a hard-fought, conscious break with theological nominalism, with the theological alliance and compound of Occam and Scotus, with the whole realm of issues where Biel "cum suo Scoto ... pelagizet."[99] Instead of the nominalistic duality of God and Church *de potentia absoluta*, we find in Luther that grace and justification as well as the word of absolution and forgiveness are glued together on the basis of God's promises.

Against Iserloh's thesis of Luther's nominalistic dissociation of God and Church it is to be pointed out that Luther called for faith in the preached and sacramental word as the word of God Himself and the *opus Dei*. Luther's insistence on the word "est" in "Hoc est corpus meum" stands contrary to the quest of late medieval mysticism and the *devotio moderna* for reform through inwardness, as is reflected in the pneumatology of the left wing of the Reformation. After his early discovery of the antitheses between faith and speculative reason (1509), the process of dissociation had reached the breaking point by 1516. After a last effort in 1515 to harmonize the *meritum de congruo* of the *doctores moderni* with the unmerited mercy of God in the *pactum misericordiae*, this remnant of nominalism can no longer be found in the content of the new theology.[100] Yet in discussing "how a nominalist doctrine

---

[99] *W A Br*, I, 66 34.

[100] "Hinc recte dicunt Doctores, quod homini facienti quod in se est, deus infallibiliter dat gratiam, et licet non de condigno sese possit ad gratiam preparare, quia est incomparabilis, tamen bene de congruo propter promissionem istam dei et pactum misericordie. Sic pro adventu futuro promisit, 'ut iuste et sobrie et pie vivamus in hoc seculo, expectantes beatam spem'. Quia quantum vis sancte hic vixerimus, vix est dispositio et preparatio ad futuram gloriam, que revelabitur in nobis, adeo ut Apostolus dicat : 'Non sunt condigne passiones huius temporis &c.' Sed bene congrue. Ideo omnia tribuit gratis et ex promissione tantum misericordie sue, licet ad hoc nos velit esse paratos quantum in nobis est." WA, IV, 262 4-13. The twice repeated *"bene de congruo"* is too explicit for me to agree with our *doctores moderni* who interpret this phrase as merely terminology without content, "Das 'facere quod in se est' der Scholastik ist zwar ... terminologisch noch zu finden, aber sachlich ist es schon jetzt überwunden." So Erich Vogelsang, *Die Anfänge von Luthers Christologie nach der ersten Psalmenvorlesung* (Leipzig, 1929), p. 70. Cf. Grane : "Hiermit ist das Bielsche Dispositionsschema trotz der Beibehaltung der Terminologie in Wirklichkeit durchbrochen worden." *Contra Gabrielem*, p. 299. A survey of the earlier literature was made by James S. Preus, *From Shadow to Promise : Old Testament Interpretation from Augustine to the Young Luther* (Cambridge, Mass., 1969). Preus does not regard this text as the rest of an old, but as the beginning of a new theology: "Like the Nominalist ideas it finds helpful, it is indeed subversive of the medieval doctrine of grace – but that is exactly what makes it new." *Ibid.*, p. 265 n. 79; cf. p. 271. New elements are here also found by Steven E. Ozment, *Homo spiritualis* (Leiden, 1969), p. 166, who points to the fact that the called for *expectio* stands "in uncompromising opposition to *meritum*". Schwarz interprets the passage à la Vogelsang, *Vorgeschichte der reformatorischen Busstheologie*, pp. 255 ff. Cf. Jared Wicks, p. 304, n. 31. An important advance is made by Oswald Bayer who after a comparison of the nominalistic (Biel) and Luther's *meritum de congruo* concludes: "Aber trotz

came to be pressed into the service of Augustinianism," Brian Gerrish puts it very well: "Luther finds himself attacking reason in characteristic Nominalist style precisely in order to destroy the other characteristic of Nominalist thought, its optimism concerning the powers of the human will."[101]

Luter's interpretation of the saints' images as *adiaphora* in *De libertate christiana* is clearly based on the freedom of Christian service as the realization of the bondage of the Christian man. If the irrelevance of the images *coram Deo* as belonging to the external man is proof of nominalism, Paul could be called a nominalist when he said, "The true Jew is not one who is such in externals . . ." (Rom. 2:18). Karlstadt for his part insists on the removal of the images not because he is a realist but because of his understanding of the Gospel as the New Law. St. Paul is for him "ein reicher prediger . . . des Evangelien und newen gesetzs, der die tiffe Moysi erreicht und tzu lichte gebracht hat."[102]

In retrospect it can be said that when applying Luther's own distinction between *credibilia* and *probabilia*, the nominalistic tradition has been consciously stamped out as far the *credibilia* are concerned. In the realm of the *probabilia*, i.e., in that of applied *logica*, Luther can respect Occam and use nominalistic tools and achievements in his own revolt against the *meta*-categories in so far as it concerns the liberation of the realm of secular experience from heteronomous authorities and the distorting *vis traditionis*.

3. *VIA GREGORII*

In his investigation of the relation of German humanism to the beginnings

---

dieser Unterschiede gehört unser Leittext auf die Seite Biels, wenn wir ihn von *De captivitate* aus betrachten." *Promissio: Geschichte der reformatischen Wende in Luthers Theologie* (Göttingen, 1971), p. 135. Two elements expressed here are of lasting significance for Luther. First is the *semper incipiens* motif, according to which there is no categorical or "vertical" progress on the *via salutis* from the preparation for grace to the preparation for glory. This theological horizon instead of being an unverifiable psychological "komplex-artige Hemmung" of Luther indicates rather the limits of the *fides incarnata*. Cf. Peter Manns, "Fides absoluta – Fides incarnata. Zur Rechtfertigungslehre Luthers im Großen Galater-Kommentar", *Reformata Reformanda: Festgabe Hubert Jedin*, ed. E. Iserloh – K. Repgen (Münster i.W., 1965), I, 265–312; 276. Secondly the "prius" category of the *iudicium Dei* before justification is to be preserved later in the relation of *persona* and *opera* (*arbor-fructus*) and of *lex* and *evangelium*, since "das Gesetz am Anfang und das Evangelium am Ziele der Bewegung steht". Wilfried Joest, *Gesetz und Freiheit: Das Problem des tertius usus legis bei Luther und die neutestamentliche Parainese* (Göttingen, 1956), p. 43. The first element which I relate to monastic passion-piety, as documented by Jordan of Sachsen, and not to Aristotle, as O. Bayer has suggested, *Promissio*, p. 139, eliminates increasingly the temporal dimension of the "prius". Cf. *Dictata, WA*, III, 292 2; *WA*, IV, 278 28.

[101]Gerrish, p. 56.

[102]Andreas Karlstadt, *Von Abtuhung der Bilder und das keyn Bedtler unther den Christen seyn sollen*, ed. H. Lietzmann (Bonn, 1911), p. 22 11–12.

of the Reformation Bernd Moeller comes to the well-argued conclusion: "Ohne Humanismus, keine Reformation."[103] At the same time the inner distance between Luther and the humanistic "Anliegen" is not be overlooked. Though Luther owes his victory to the support of humanists, especially the younger ones, he himself remains the "grosse Aussenseiter und Unzeitgemässe."[104]

When we understand humanism in terms of the attraction it exerted on German court circles and city sodalities, this movement stands for the rediscovery of poetry, rhetoric, and epistolography as marks of the man of learning. Where philosophy is concerned, it included as well a clear emphasis on ethics. Thus an educational ideal is furthered which tends to transform the school-system, also including the university curriculum. This pedagogical concern is so much one of the characteristics of what we are calling the *initia reformationis*, that humanism is not only the context in which this Reformation could flower, but, at least for a time, it was also to be its inseparable partner through the inner association of the *studia humanitatis* with the concern for religious education and sanctification.

Though Luther joined in the humanistic campaign against obscurantism, as may be seen in his engagement in university reform, there is a sense in which one can put into Luther's mouth the words of Giles of Viterbo, the General of Luther's Order, expressed at the opening ceremony of the Fifth Lateran Council: "... homines per sacra immutari fas est, non sacra per homines."[105] Early in 1517 Luther can praise Erasmus for his attack upon the "inveterata inscitia," but adds the observation: "humana praevalent in eo plus quam divina."[106]

Over against a humanism based on the optimistic anthropology implied in the *mutatio sacrorum per homines*, Luther must be regarded as an outsider. Another tradition feeding into humanism, however, apparently did reach Luther, namely the humanism developed and nurtured in his own Order. In the first half of the *Quattrocento* we find a group of influential Augustinians in close contact with Petrarch. They had strong classical interests and were concerned with literary research and hunting for old manuscripts. Dionigi da Borgo S. Sepolcro (d. 1342), Bartolomeo da Urbino (d. 1350), and Jean

---

[103]"Die Deutschen Humanisten und die Anfänge der Reformation", ZKG, LXX (1959), 46–61; 59.

[104]Moeller, p. 61.

[105]J.D. Mansi, ed., *Sacrorum conciliorum nova et amplissima collectio* (Florence-Venice, 1757–1798), XXXII, 669, Cf. John W. O'Malley, *Giles of Viterbo on Church and Reform: A Study in Renaissance Thought* (Leiden, 1968), pp. 139, n. 1; 161–2.

[106]*WA Br*, I, 90 19–20.

Coci (d. 1364) are three names among the first to participate in the new movement which later would give itself the proud name "Renaissance." Their involvement can be traced back to such early times that the Order can be said to have provided if not the cradle of Italian humanism then certainly the first allies, eagerly exploiting the new scholarly vistas for the study of St. Augustine. The work of Bartolomeo da Urbino's *Milleloquium S. Augustini* must have supported Petrarch in his intense Augustine studies, as is suggested by Petrarch's dedicatory letter: "Hinc sibi posteritas stillas studiosa salubres hauriat, hinc lectos componat in ordine flores."[107]

The increasingly employed new style of quoting within the *schola Augustiniana* is an external index to the quest for authenticity and historical concern for the sources. The anonymity of the *quidam* gives way to an exact quotation with name, title, and chapter.[108] It is in this scholarly climate, which gives birth to the *Milleloquium* and source-oriented precision quoting, that a new theology is emerging, personified by Gregory of Rimini (d. 1358), the most significant General of the Augustinian Order after Giles of Rome. Damasus Trapp has indicated the basis of this development: "What is so new in Gregory is the fact that he is the best Augustine scholar of the Middle

---

[107]Rudolph Arbesmann, *Der Augustiner-Eremitenorden und der Beginn der humanistischen Bewegung* (Würzburg, 1965), p. 54. Petrarch does not express his respect for Augustine to the exclusion of others (as for instance Jerome); but in view of the debate on the relative antiquity of the several rules it is significant that in *De otio religioso*, while discussing the great examples and representatives of the monastic tradition, he does not include "the well-known medieval founders of monastic orders and the medieval saints". Charles Trinkaus, "Humanist Treatises on the status of the Religious: Petrarch, Salutati, Valla", *Studies in the Renaissance*, XI (1965), 7–45; 17. Terrence Heath in dealing with the changing text books for *grammatica* as part of the late medieval reform of the *trivium* refers to a request of the Augustinian house in Tübingen which takes on special meaning in the context of our discussion. In 1496 the university is asked to permit the use of Perotti's *Grammatica nova* instead of the usual but clearly "meta-grammatical" *Doctrinale* of Alexander de Villa Dei. See Universitätsarchiv Tübingen XV, 17; fol. 35ʳ; quoted by J. Haller, *Die Anfänge der Universität Tübingen 1477–1537* (Stuttgart, 1929), II, 82, and interpreted by Heath as "concession to the Augustinians." Cf. T. Heath, "Logical grammar, grammatical logic, and humanism in the three German universities", *Studies in the Renaissance,* XVIII (1971), 9–64; 29. While Niccolò Perotti wrote his grammar in 1468 under the title *Rudimenta Grammatica*, it was adapted by Bernard Pirger and repeatedly published during the eighties in South-Germany as *Grammatica nova*. See Heath, pp. 16–17. The *Grammatica nova* of Jacob Locher is held to be spurious. Heath, p. 24, n. 64. Whereas the influential reform activity of the Brethren of the Common Life intended the critical pruning of the *Doctrinale* and its commentaries, Perotti's *Grammatica nova* provides an alternative textbook. In either case the chief aim is to liberate grammar from its logical and metaphysical encasement. The request of the Augustinians is granted, until in 1505 Donatus and Alexander are again required under oath and reign for another quarter of a century.

[108]Damasus Trapp, "Augustinian Theology of the 14th Century", *Augustiniana*, VI (1956), 146–274, 152 ff.

Ages ..."[109] What before Gregory had been the *schola Aegidiana* can henceforth best be called the *schola moderna Augustiniana*,[110] since in Gregory we reach a turning point away from Giles. Instead of the *cognitio universalis*, now the *cognitio particularis rei* is emphasized as the epistemological point of departure; Scripture has become the programmatic source of theology; theology is not a *scientia*, because it stands for the ability to grasp the *sensus sacrae scripturae*;[111] a much more extensive knowledge of a larger number of works of Augustine's than were used either by Thomas or Giles leads to a more intensive and exclusive reliance on the *Doctor gratiae*;[112] Gregory highlights justification *sola gratia* with Augustine rather than Giles' hierocratic-curialist interpretation of *De civitate Dei*.[113]

Gregory does not remain isolated; his authority is amazingly soon established and the high honor of the title *Doctor authenticus* assigned to him. Among his disciples we find Dionysius of Montina (*magister artium* 1374) and Hugolin of Orvieto (*sententiarius* in Paris 1348/49, d. 1374), whose Sentences commentary was available in Wittenberg.[114] All three combine nominalistic elements with a clear emphasis on the insufficiency of human works and the necessity of grace.[115] A most intriguing figure is Augustinus Favaroni (d.

---

[109]Trapp, p. 181.

[110]"Influxus nominalismi potius est externus ac formalisticus quam intrinsecus et doctrinalis, cum magis in nimia subtilitate argumentationum atque in quadam tortuositate et obscuritate sermonis quam in novitate opinionum appareat: primum est signum temporis ac defectus communis prolapsus theologiae scholasticae, a quo rarissimi scriptores illius aetatis immunes permanserunt; perseverantia in doctrina recepta, est bonum peculiare doctorum huius scholae, ut periti fatentur, quod proculdubio connexioni cum primis magistris eiusdem tribuenda est." D. Gutiérrez, "Notitia historica antiquae scholae aegidianae", *Analecta Augustiniana,* XVIII (1941–42), 39–67, 44.

[111]Gregorii Ariminensis, O.E.S.A., *Super Primum Et Secundum Sententiarum* (Venice, 1522; Repr. Louvain-Paderborn, 1955), Prol. q. 2, art. 2, fol. 8 M.

[112]John O'Malley has pointed to the fact that notwithstanding Gregory's programmatic insistence on the "ipsae sacri canonis veritates", in practice "he seems to forget all about them and, with gay abandon, throw Paul, Augustine and Euclid together..." "A note on Gregory of Rimini. Church, Scripture, Tradition", *Augustinianum,* V (1965), 365–78, 372. This "gay abandon" is explainable in terms of the arguments with which Gregory is confronted: when derived from (meta-)physics he will answer in kind "removendo dubia": Prol. q. 1, art. 2, fol. 3 K. Though Gregory's emphasis on Scripture as the sole source for theology is explicit, O'Malley can rightly point to the fact that the Church universal is for him *validissima auctoritas*. In all cases where he contrasts Augustine with the *communis opinio* Gregory does so with explicit but traditional *reverentia*.

[113]See Wilhelm Kölmel, *Regimen Christianum: Weg und Ergebnisse des Gewaltenverhältnisses und des Gewaltenverständnisses, 8. bis 14. Jahrhundert* (Berlin, 1970), pp. 304 ff.

[114]Cf. Adolar Zumkeller, "Die Augustinertheologen Simon Fidati von Cascia und Hugolin von Orvieto und Martin Luthers Kritik an Aristoteles", *ARG*, LIV (1963), 15–37.

[115]Adolar Zumkeller finds with all three in combination "mit einer nominalistischen Akzeptationstheorie... die typische Haltung des spätmittelalterlichen Augustinismus in der

1443), general of the Order, who almost a century later than Gregory[116] expresses sentiments which must have been and *de facto* were offensive to all those *Doctores*, whether curialists or conciliarists,[117] who were one with Giles of Rome in thinking of the Church as a *corpus politicum*. Alphons Victor Müller repeatedly has called attention to Favaroni as an unknown source of Luther's theology; yet Müller's biting, ironic criticism, directed especially against Denifle, Scheel, and Grisar, and his single-minded, undifferentiated identification of trends in late medieval Augustinianism and the *initia Lutheri*, provoked so much reaction that this line of research has not been pursued with sufficient energy. The scholarly form of Müller's argumentation also raised more questions than it claimed to answer. Yet notwithstanding the generally sharp and largely appropriate criticism, the existence as such of a late medieval Augustianian school cannot be contested.[118]

In Favaroni's recently discovered *Defensio contra quosdam errores hereticorum*, soon to be published,[119] this Augustinian theologian indicates that though he does not deny that the Church in one sense of the word means the *corpus mixtum*, in which the evil ones have their place *ratione sacramentorum*, the *ecclesia* as article of faith *sine macula et ruga* is the church of the elect. Of this church only Christ is the head; when the pope is *prescitus*, he is not a member of this Church, or even – as the accusation reads – of the Church militant.[120]

When we investigate the writings which led to the accusation against Favaroni, it becomes clear that his particular ecclesiology is the allegorical counterpart to the tropological *commercium admirabile* between Christ and the believer, as we find it with Johann von Staupitz and Martin Luther. On the basis of the union of Christ and his Body, "totus et solus Christus est

---

Beurteilung der Werke der Heiden und in der Forderung eines auxilium speciale." *Dionysius de Montina: Ein neuentdeckter Augustinertheologe des Spätmittelalters* (Würzburg, 1948), p. 82.

[116]Cf. G. Ciolini, *Agostino da Roma (Favaroni d. 1443) e la sua Cristologia* (Florence, 1944), pp. 13–26; Salesius Friemel, *Die theologische Prinzipienlehre des Augustinus Favaroni von Rom O.E.S.A. (d. 1443)* (Würzburg, 1950), pp. 19–26. N. Toner, "The Doctrine of original sin according to Augustine of Rome", *Augustiniana*, VII (1957), 100–17, 349–66, 515–30.

[117]At the Council of Basel an investigation is carried through, resulting in the condemnation of seven articles during the 22nd session on 15 July 1435. CF. *Mansi*, XXIX, 109 B f.

[118]Cf. the reception of Müller's interpretation with Eduard Stakemeier, *Der Kampf um Augustin auf dem Tridentinum* (Paderborn, 1937), pp. 22–60. Sharply criticized by Hubert Jedin, *Theologische Revue*, XXXVII (1938), 425–30. Cf. Steinmetz, *Misericordia Dei*, pp. 31–34.

[119]To be edited by W. Lewis from Basel Ms. A IV, 17, fol. 320ʳ – 328ᵛ; discovered by W. Pfeuffer. Cf. Adolar Zumkeller, *Manuskripte von Werken der Autoren des Augustiner-Eremitenordens in mitteleuropäischen Bibliotheken* (Würzburg, 1966), p. 83, no. 159.

[120]Art VI: "Petrus non est nec fuit caput ecclesie sancte catholice." *Defensio*, fol. 324ᵛ. Art VII: ". . . si papa est talis, si papa est malus et presertim si est prescitus, tunc ut Judas Apostolus est dyabolus, fur et filius perdicionis et non est caput sancte militantis [!] ecclesie, tamen nec sit membrum eius." *Defensio*, fol. 325ᵛ.

ecclesia," Favaroni comes to the challenging thesis: "Christus quotidie peccat."[121]

Whereas Müller argues that Favaroni anticipated Luther by some seventy years,[122] Favaroni's doctrine is clearly justification *sola caritate*[123] rather than *sola fide*. Hence a continuing line should be drawn from him to Staupitz rather than to Luther, who in his *De libertate christiana* significantly describes first a union with the word in faith[124] before he speaks about the *fröhliche Wechsel*. Furthermore, there exists no evidence pointing to a broad distribution of Favaroni's writings. Nevertheless much is gained, also for Luther research, as we reach a point where Staupitz no longer seems to arise *ex nihilo*.

It is important for us to keep in mind the words of Gordon Rupp in his splendid opening address to the Third International Congress for Luther Research: "If we are far from the end of the discussion of 'Luther and . . . Augustine,' it is because we await the elucidation of Augustine's theology in the later Middle Ages."[125] This elucidation is particularly to be expected from further work on Luther's immediate life-context after 1505, i.e., the Augustinian Order.

The aspect most difficult to establish is of course the sphere of the daily spiritual life in an Augustinian convent such as the one at Erfurt. An important beginning has been made by Martin Elze in pointing to the *De passione Domini* of the Augustinian Jordanus of Sachsen, whose *Vitas fratrum* is intensively used and quoted within the Order and taken over almost *in toto* in

---

[121]". . . Ista conclusio non ponitur ut aperiatur via sophistis, sed ut sacramentum unitatis, quod magnum est in Christo et in ecclesia, cum magna attentione notetur." *Tractatus de sacramento unitatis Christi et Ecclesiae sive de Christo integro*. Ms. Bibl. Vat. cod. B VII., 118, fol. 122[ra] – 130[va]; 125[ra]. Dr. W. Eckermann, O.S.A. kindly provided me with his transcript. In the *Defensio* Favaroni claims a thoroughgoing basis in Augustine for the contested theses in this treatise: ". . . illa dicta mea in tractatu prefato omnia fundata sunt in doctrina et dictis beati Augustini . . . nec aliquid dixi novum et inconsuetum cui non apposuerim testimonia et motiva beati Augustini." *Defensio*, fol. 320[r].

[122]Alphons Victor Müller, "Agostino Favaroni e la Teologia di Lutero", *Bilychnis*, III (1914), 1–17.

[123]"Sola caritas in homine est per essentiam suam vera iustitia per quam homo iustificatur et iuste vivit coram Deo." *Tractatus de merito Christi et condigna satisfactione pro electis*. Ms. Bibl. Vat. cod. B VII, 118, fol. 224[ra] – 241[vb]; 225[va].

[124]*W A*, VII, 53 15–23. For the ecclesiological theme of union between Bride and Bridegroom in Luther's *Dictata* see Joseph Vercruysse, *Fidelis Populus* (Wiesbaden, 1968), pp. 28–32. For its relation to the medieval tradition, particularly Augustine, see Scott H. Hendrix, *Ecclesia in via: Ecclesiological Developments in the Medieval Psalm Exegesis and the Dictata super Psalterium (1513–1515) of Martin Luther* (Tübingen, 1970), ch. I, p. 4.

[125]*Kirche, Mystik, Heiligung und das Natürliche bei Luther*: Vorträge des dritten internationalen Kongresses für Lutherforschung, Järvenpää, Finnland, 11.–16. August 1966, ed. Ivar Asheim (Göttingen, 1967), p. 14.

the *Vita Christi* of Ludolf of Sachsen, which found a wide readership.[126]

A closer textual analysis of the *Rosetum*, explicitly quoted by Luther,[127] and of the *Himmlische Fundgrube* and the *Coelifodina* of Johannes von Paltz shows the continuation of this tradition of affective meditation as it reaches Luther's immediate environment. Apart from Luther's fundamentally new theological hermeneutic and hence apart from the new connection between *affectus* and *effectus*, we find here the same warnings against speculative "high mysticism"[128] as well as the emphasis on the specific application of the

---

[126]Martin Elze, "Züge spätmittelalterlicher Frömmigkeit in Luthers Theologie", *ZThK*, LXII (1965), 381–402; *idem*, "Das Verständnis der Passion Jesu im ausgehenden Mittelalter und bei Luther", *Geist und Geschichte der Reformation: Festgabe H. Rückert* (Berlin, 1966), pp. 127–51.

[127]Elze, "Züge spätmittelalterlicher Frömmigkeit", pp. 390–9. As one example of a possible relationship between Paltz and Luther, Robert H. Fischer refers to a common quotation assigned to Albertus Magnus. "Paltz und Luther", *Luther-Jahrbuch*, XXXVII (1970), 9–36, 16. Though no dependence can be established, the juxtaposition of the two texts documents the extent of continuity in this tradition of meditation piety. "Der heilige susse lerer sant Bernhart uber das buch der lobeseng spricht, dass kein nutzer oder krefftiger ding sey tzu heylen die wunden der sunde, dan die betrachtunge der wunden Christi. Dar tzu spricht Albertus Magnus: 'Welcher mensch alle tag oben hin, als man erbes oder bonen erliseth, uberlaufft oder bedenckt das leyden Christi, der erlangeth da mit mer nutz dan das er alle freitag das gantz iar fastet. Czu dem andern ist es im nutzer, dan das er ym selber geb alle wochen ein disciplin, das das blut ernach ging durch das gantz iar. Czu dem dritten male ist es ym nutzer, dan das er alle wochen das gantze iar eynen psalter beteth.' Dartzu als man auß vil leren mag vorsteen, so ist kein nutzer ding gotes huld tzu erwerben tzu gunst der muter gotes und aller heyligen und aller engel, dan die betrachtunge des heiligen leydens Christi. Auch ist keyn nutzer ding. . ." Johann von Paltz, *Das bucheleyn wirt genannt die hymmelische funt grube* (Leipzig, 1497), sig. A. II^v–A III^r (London, British Museum, Bench mark, I.A. 1203).–Cf. Johann von Paltz, *Coelifodina* (Leipzig, 1504), sig. G II^r–G II^v (Munich, Bayr. Staatsbibliothek, call no.: P. lat. 947a [1]. 4°). – Cf. Bernhard, *Sermones in Cant. 62, 7*: "Quid enim tam efficax ad curanda conscientiae vulnera, nec non ad purgandam mentis aciem, quam vulnerum sedula meditatio?" Migne, *PL*, 183, 1079 B. See Luther, "Ein Sermon von der Betrachtung des heiligen Leidens Christi" (1519): "Zeum andernn haben ettlich angezeygte mancherley nutz und frucht, ßo auß Christus leyden betrachtung kummen. Darzu geht yrre eyn spruch, S. Albert zu geschrieben, das es besser sey, Christus leyden eyn mal oben hyn uber dacht, dan ob man eyn gantz iar festet, alle tag eyn Psalter bettet etc. Dem folgen sie blind da hyn und geratten eben widder die rechte frucht des leydens Christi, dan sie das yhre darynnen suchen. Darumb tragen sie sich mit bildelein und buechlein, brieffen und creutzen, auch ettlich ßo ferne faren, das sie sich vor wasser, eyßen, fewr und allerley ferlickeyt zu sicheren vormeynen, und alßo Christus leyden eyn unleyden yn yhn wircken sol widder seyn art und natur." *WA*, II, 136 11–20. – "Zcum zehenden. Wer alßo gottis leyden eyn tag, eyn stund, ja eyn viertel stund bedecht, von dem selben wollen wyr frey sagen, das es beßer sey, dan ob er eyn gantz iar fastet, alle tag eynn psalter bettet, ja das er hundert messen horet, dann dißes bedencken wandelt den menschen weßenlich und gar nah wie die tauffe widderumb new gepiret. Hie wircket das leyden Christi seyn rechtes naturlich edels werck, erwurget den alten Adam, vortreybt alle lust, freud und zuvorsicht, die man haben mag von creaturen, gleych wie Christus von allen, auch von got vorlaßen war." *WA*, II, 139 11–15.

[128]In this sense one can agree with Elze's conclusion, "dass alle diese Gedanken Luthers aus der Tradition jener unmystischen Frömmigkeit gespeist sind." Elze, "Züge spätmittelalterlicher Frömmigkeit", p. 399.

Passion of Christ to the individual, which suggests the context of Luther's insistence on the *pro me*.[129] The final sentence of Jordan's *Prologus* documents not only this tendency but also provides a key to Staupitz's seemingly unprecedented campaign against the scholastic *gratia gratum faciens*. Whereas Staupitz wants to reinterpret *gratia gratum faciens* not as the grace which makes us acceptable to God but vice versa as the grace which makes God acceptable to us,[130] we read with Jordan: "Omnia quae Christus passus est, ita debent homini esse accepta et grata, ac si pro ipsius solummodo salute ea sit passus."[131] Out of this tradition emerges, finally, that aspect of the first of Luther's Ninety-five Theses according to which penance is a lasting mark of the Christian life.

We encounter here the paradox that an intense preoccupation with Augustine does not always guarantee that Augustine himself comes to his own. Rather, it is the heritage of the mature Augustine marked by and protected against a long history of attack or of benign condescension to the "excessive" Augustine. Quite appropriately Eck confronts Luther right at the outset in his first proposition for the Leipzig Debate[132] with the argument that Luther cannot appeal to Augustine for his thesis of life-long penance. Since this idea is an organic development of Augustine's heritage (*humilitas*) within the order, Eck's attack came as a surprise to Luther. With some of the opponents and most of the other reformers, particularly Melanchthon and Zwingli,[133] we find an equally intensive but generally more precise use of St. Augustine. With Melanchthon, for instance, we encounter the precision of a centuries-skirting Augustine scholarship, not marked by the Augustinian's pious commitment to and reverential meditation on the works of the Founding Father. Modern scholarship cannot but agree with Melanchthon against Luther when he argues that *sola fide* does not characterize Augustine's doctrine of justification.[134] Indeed, to be immersed in and to emerge from

---

[129]Elze, "Das Verständnis der Passion Jesu", p. 134.

[130]Cf. David C. Steinmetz, *Misericordia Dei: The Theology of Johannes von Staupitz in Its Late Medieval Setting* (Leiden, 1968), pp. 84–85.

[131]Elze, "Das Verständnis der Passion Jesu", p. 134.

[132]*W A*, IX, 208 32–33. While not answering this challenge directly Luther points, not too convincingly, to a text in the *Enchiridion* on a related issue at the very end of the Disputation. *WA*, II, 377 13–17. Cf. *W A*, II, 374 4–9 (Quotation from Augustine's *Enchiridion*, Migne, *PL*, 40, 265; CChr, 46. 88, 12–13). Yet at Eck's "tangit Augustinus ut refert Gratianus", Luther cannot forego the chance to characterize this as "auctoritates consarcinare". See *W A*, II, 376 37.

[133]Cf. Arthur Rich, *Die Anfänge der Theologie Huldrych Zwinglis* (Zürich, 1949), pp. 127–30.

[134]*W A Br*, XII, 193 88–94. Luther invokes the *vox Augustini*, but quotes Bernard of Clairvaux! In the contrast between Luther and Augustine, the role of the Augustinian's tradition should be given more weight. Cf. the observation of T. van Bavel in his review of R. Schwarz, *Vorgeschichte der reformatorischen Busstheologie*: "The most striking aspect of this book, in my opinion, is the rather slight influence of Augustine on Luther." *Augustiniana*, XXI (1971), 353.

late medieval Augustianism does not *ipso facto* mean a better grasp of the historical Augustine.

The indicated thrust *ad fontes Augustini* by no means establishes an unbroken tradition in the Order. Curialistic ecclesiology like that of Giles of Rome continues at least till the times of the Council of Basel.[135] Similarly the prior of Luther's Erfurt monastery, Johann von Paltz, can by no stretch of the imagination be regarded as a partisan of either the *solus Christus* ecclesiology of Favaroni or the *sola gratia* soteriology of Gregory of Rimini. Yet the one who integrated these elements and sharpened the impact of this tradition seems to have been Staupitz, whose impact on Luther should not be underestimated. Furthermore, after Luther's Ockham-oriented *artes* training and lectorate in Erfurt,[136] he finds the nominalistic *via moderna*, referred to as the *via Gregorii*,[137] in Wittenberg.

When we take stock of the present state of scholarship, there are at least four potential agents of transmission of the indicated Augustinian tradition.

1. In the library of the Augustinians in Wittenberg, Luther had at his disposal both *De gestis Salvatoris* of Simon Fidati and the only manuscript known to us of the Sentences Commentary of Hugolin of Orvieto.[138] Either writing brings a sharper critique of Aristotle than we find with the Erfurt teachers Trutvetter and Usingen; either one carries in its own way the marks of the *via Gregorii*.

2. As is generally acknowledged, during the years of his first lectures on the Psalms, 1513–1515, Luther may well have used the main work of the Augustinian James Pérez of Valencia (d. 1490). In his doctrine of sin and

---

[135]See Adolar Zumkeller, "Die Augustinereremiten in der Auseinandersetzung mit Wyclif und Hus, ihre Beteiligung an den Konzilien von Konstanz und Basel", *Analecta Augustiniana*, XXVIII (1965), 5–56. Cf. the contemporary of Gregory, Hermann von Schildesche, (d. 1357) by whom the political predominance of the Church is argued with a "sola Ecclesia": ". . . dependet rectus usus temporalium principaliter ab Ecclesia, in quantum a gratia dependet, quae in sola Ecclesia datur." *Hermanni de Schildis OSA, Tractatus contra haereticos negantes immunitatem et iurisdictionem Sanctae Ecclesiae. . .*, ed. A. Zumkeller (Würzburg, 1970), I, cap. 13; 35, 67–68.

[136]Cf. the document dated 18 April 1508, published by Reinould Weijenborg, "Luther et les cinquante-et-un Augustins d'Erfurt d'après une lettre d'indulgences inédite du 18. avril 1508", *RHE*, LV (1960), 819–75.

[137]The new Wittenberg University statutes of 1508 establish for the arts faculty all three 'ways': the *via Thomae, via Scoti* and the *via Gregorii*. Karl Bauer draws the conclusion: "Als Vertreter der *via moderna* übernahm er in Wittenberg den auf das Augustinerkloster gestifteten Lehrstuhl für Ethik. . ." *Die Wittenberger Universitätstheologie und die Anfänge der Deutschen Reformation* (Tübingen, 1928), p. 10.

[138]Zumkeller, "Die Augustinertheologen Simon Fidati von Cascia und Hugolin von Orvieto", pp. 22–23, 26 ff.

grace Pérez proves his proximity to Gregory of Rimini and his school.[139]

3. The relation between Johann von Staupitz[140] (d. 1524) and Luther is intimate and hence complex, posing intricate problems, particularly during the period 1515–1518, when the roles of teacher and disciple may have been reversed. Yet it cannot be contested that in 1518 Luther assigns the role of *originator* and *movens* to Staupitz in his (Luther's) own discovery of *vera poenitentia*.[141] This ascription finds its partly verbatim, striking parallel in Luther's 1545 recollection of having grasped the Pauline sense of the *iustitia Dei*.[142] As with Gregory, we find with the later Staupitz after the period of the Tübingen Sermons, the *acceptatio* doctrine as interpretation of the *sola gratia*, which he has combined with the tropological application of 'Favaroni's' theme of the exchange of *iustitia* and *peccata* between Christ and the believer.[143]

4. Indebtedness to Staupitz is acknowledged by a second member of the Wittenberg coalition which was formed on the platform of the theology of Paul and Augustine in late 1516–early 1517. About this same time Andreas Bodenstein von Karlstadt dedicates his commentary on Augustine's *De spiritu et litera* to Staupitz and describes how, after Luther's first influence, Staupitz had freed Karlstadt from scholasticism by showing the "Christi dulcedinem" in the right relation of spirit and letter.[144] Karlstadt designates the brand of scholasticism he had turned away from prior to his lectures according to Scotus as the "secta Capreolina."[145] To have taught theology

---

[139]Wilfried Werbeck, *Jacobus Pérez von Valencia: Untersuchungen zu seinem Psalmenkommentar* (Tübingen, 1959); Adolar Zumkeller, "Die Augustinerschule des Mittelalters: Vertreter und philosophisch-theologische Lehre", *Analecta Augustiniana*, XXVII (1964), 167–262, 250.

[140]See Steinmetz, *Misericordia Dei; idem, Reformers in the Wings* (Philadelphia, 1971), pp. 18–29 (Lit.).

[141]*W A*, I, 525 4–14.

[142]Cf. Ernst Wolf, *Staupitz und Luther: Ein Beitrag zur Theologie des Johannes von Staupitz und deren Bedeutung für Luthers theologischen Werdegang* (Leipzig, 1927), pp. 223 ff., 253 ff. Wolf argues for formal rather than material parallels: "Gerade in ihnen ist ein wesentlicher Teil der Einwirkung Staupitzens zu suchen..." *Ibid.*, p. 248.

[143]"Nondum misericordiae domini satisfactum putes, quod nos sua iustitia iustos fecit, quod coniugium cum peccatrice non horruit. Accedit aliud, quod nostra peccata sua facit, quatinus, sicut christianus Christi iustitia iustus, Christus christiani culpa iniustus sit et peccator." *Libellus de executione aeternae praedestinationis* (Nürnberg, 1517), cap. XI, 71. Cf. the almost three weeks earlier German translation by Scheurl. Exact description by Maria Grossmann, "Bibliographie der Werke Christoph Scheurls", *Archiv für Geschichte des Buchwesens*, X (1970), 371–96, 385, no. 41 and 42. Cf. H.A. Oberman, *Forerunners of the Reformation: The Shape of Late Medieval Thought* (New York, 1966), pp. 175–203, 189–190.

[144]Kähler, *Karlstadt und Augustin*, p. 5 17–19.

[145]Cf. Kähler, p. 3 20. Already in his very first work Karlstadt employs Capreolus: "... hoc confirmat Sancti Thomae acerrimus tutor et defensor Capreolus." *De intentionibus. Opusculum compilatum ad S. emulorum Thomae eruditionem* (Leipzig, 1507), fol. 50[r].

according to the *Princeps Thomistarum* (d. 1444) implied an intensive preoccupation with Gregory, since Capreolus saw the reconciliation of Gregory and Thomas as an important task; he had transcribed Gregory page after page into his *Defensiones*.[146] This considerably strengthens the argument of Ernst Kähler that the Wittenberg discussion about the Augustinianism of Gregory has to be placed early in 1517 at the latest, i.e., more than two years before Luther praises Gregory as the only scholastic theologian to oppose the modern Pelagians.[147] In Gregory, Luther publicly and explicitly was to hail a tradition which was waiting to be used by him in his own assaults *contra modernos*.

Thus there is indeed reason to reopen the discussion about the *via Gregorii* in Wittenberg. When Luther was called in 1508 to teach philosophical ethics in the faculty of arts and later, in 1512, succeeded Staupitz in the theological faculty as Doctor of Scripture, he was supposed to represent the *via moderna*, instituted at Wittenberg by his predecessor and Erfurt teacher Trutvetter.[148] On the basis of the revised University statutes of 1508, first edited by Muther,[149] and the comprehensive critical edition by Friedensburg,[150] Scheel and Bauer concluded[151] that the *via moderna* at Wittenberg was designated in 1508 as "via Guilelmi," the way of Ockham. Muther, however, based his work on only one manuscript in which, as he noted, a later hand corrected "via Gregorii" into "via Guilelmi." Friedensburg makes use of a second manuscript which reads "Gregorii," so that in two passages in two manuscripts the three admitted "ways" are described as "via Thomae, via

---

[146]For the awareness in 1517, of the impact of Gregory of Rimini, see *Masters of the Reformation* (Cam., 1981) pp. 102ff.—In his *Distinctiones Thomistarum* (1508) Karlstadt quotes from a compendium of Capreolus' *Defensiones* by Prierias, *Opus in Ioannem Capreolum* (Cremona, 1497), in which Gregory is often mentioned and quoted. The name of Gregory is not mentioned by Karlstadt.

[147]*W A*, II, 394 29 ff.; Kähler, p. 22*, n. 5. Leif Grane argues acutely for the summer of 1519 as the time of Luther's Gregory studies: "Gregor von Rimini und Luthers Leipziger Disputation", *Studia Theologica*, XXII (1968), 29–49, 44.

[148]Cf. *Christoph Scheurls Briefbuch*, ed. F.v. Soden–J.K.F. Knaake (Potsdam, 1867) I, 142; quoted by Bauer, p. 9.

[149]"Indifferenter profiteatur Via Thomae, Scoti, Guilelmi (Gregorii Cod. Manus posterior loco Gregorii correxit Occam)." Statuta Artistarum. Caput Decimum. *Die Wittenberger Universitaets- und Facultaetsstatuten vom Jahre MDVIII*, ed. Theodor Muther (Halle, 1867), p. 45. Cf. Caput Tertium where Muther also replaces "Gregorio" with "Guilelmo"; *ibid.*, p. 41.

[150]Walter Friedensburg reads "Gregorio" both times, but comments at cap. 3: "So AB.; ob Guilelmo [von Occam] zu lesen?" at Cap. 10: "So AB.; in B. Gregorii ausgestrichen, von anderer Hand darüber: Occam." *Urkundenbuch der Universität Wittenberg* (1502–1611) (Magdeburg, 1926), I, 53, 56, 57–58. The change in one Ms. convinced Muther and influenced Friedensburg; even though we no longer possess the original copy, the total evidence speaks clearly for "Gregorii".

[151]Otto Scheel, *Martin Luther: Vom Katholizismus zur Reformation* (Tübingen, 1917), II, 395, n. 46; Bauer, p. 9, n. 4.

Scoti, via Gregorii." On the basis of this textual evidence we cannot but draw the conclusion that whatever the later practice, the statutes intended to allow for the *via Gregorii*; from Luther's course unfortunately no lecture notes are preserved. In any case Bauer is to be corrected to the extent that Luther was not obliged to lecture in ethics as a representative of the *via moderna*.[152]

Luther's second Erfurt teacher, Bartholomäus von Usingen, had already emphasized the significance of the great *Doctor autenticus*. Indeed, Ockham is for him the *Venerabilis inceptor viae modernae*; but in theology he has the highest regard, after Petrus d'Ailly, for Gregory of Rimini. Hence Luther did not come to Wittenberg unprepared.[153] The implications of teaching according to the *via Gregorii* are by no means clear, and neither is the reason why Gregory's name is replaced in one manuscript by Ockham's. When we look for a comparison we find that at Heidelberg the *via moderna* can be referred to as the "via Marsiliana"[154] after Marsilius of Inghen (d. 1396). Here again the distinction between nominalism and Occamism applies. Whereas Marsilius calls Gregory "magister noster,"[155] there is no indication in his work of exposure to Ockham's writings.[156] It is good to remind ourselves of the conclusion of Gerhard Ritter which also sets the context for understanding Gregory: the spirit of Augustine along with the philosophical elements of nominalism is the mark of theological education which later would inform the thought of Luther as a beginning teacher.[157]

---

[152]Bauer, p. 10.

[153]Luther's critique of Aristotle with its unprecedented intensity stands at the very beginning of his road to reformation. Later, in 1519, he can praise Gregory of Rimini for refuting an opposing Aristotle with the sole weapons of Augustine and Scripture: "[Gregorius Ariminensis] est enim totus aliud nihil quam Augustinus et divina scriptura, resistens quidem omnibus doctoribus scholasticis, tum maxime Aristoteli, sed nondum ab ullo confutatus est." *WA*, II, 303, 12–15. But when he tries in 1517, well over a year before his last efforts during and after the Heidelberg Disputation, to win his former Erfurt teachers for the cause of the Reformation, he chides both of them for wasting their time in meaningless work ("prorsus inutiles") in commenting on the "illusor" Aristotle. (*W A Br*, I, 88 4–89 30; 8 February 1517 to Joh. Lang.) There is no indication that he does appeal to Gregory of Rimini at a time when this would have enhanced the force of his argument. This helps us to realize that we continue to be dependent on reconstruction rather than on unambiguous evidence.

[154]G. Ritter, *Studien zur Spätscholastik: Marsilius von Inghen und die okkamistische Schule in Deutschland* (Heidelberg, 1921), I, 46 (Sitzungsberichte 12).

[155]Ritter, p. 11, n. 4, p. 38, n. 3.

[156]"Nichte genannt wird Egidius Romanus, der sonst so Beliebte; noch aufallender ist das völlige Fehlen der Originalschriften Okkams." Ritter, p. 42.

[157]"Das sola gratia ist A und O dieser Theologie. Der Geist Augustins, der sie durchdringt, in Verbindung mit den philosophischen Elementen der nominalistischen Erkenntnislehre war auch das Kennzeichen der theologischen Bildung, die dereinst das Denken Martin Luthers in den Anfängen seiner theologischen Lehrtätigkeit beherrschen sollte." Ritter, p. 183.

It is not difficult to be alert to the vast differences between Gregory and Marsilius on the one hand and Luther on the other, differences so obvious and far-reaching[158] that they cannot be explained merely in terms of a time interval. It is all the more important for us that beyond all reconstructions we now possess a newly discovered document from the hand of one of Luther's Augustinian brethren in the Erfurt monastery, to be dated around 1509. The text is well-known to Luther scholars since it was held until recently to be genuine Luther material.[159] This manifesto-like *cri de coeur* is now much more precious and crucial than before, when it was ascribed to Luther. It now serves to document the factors constitutive for the Augustinian spirituality and attitude we have been pointing to, in time and space closer to the very beginning of Luther's theology than any other text we know: first, the authority of St. Augustine *nunquam satis* praised as *apex* of the tradition; secondly, the critical stance over against scholastic philosophy with its idle questions – *nugis meris* (the philosophers can be useful for theology but they are dangerous and to be regarded as "opiniosos dubitatores"); and finally there are humanistic touches in this "Declaration of Independence" in its use of Greek mythology and its alliance with the *poetae* against the philosophers.

Taking stock of this cumulative, admittedly circumstantial evidence, we can point to the *schola Augustiniana moderna*, initiated by Gregory of Rimini, reflected by Hugolin of Orvieto, apparently spiritually alive in the Erfurt Augustinian monastery, and transformed into a pastoral reform-theology by Staupitz, as the *occasio proxima* – not *causa*! – for the inception of the *theologia vera* at Wittenberg.

As we saw in the case of the *via Gregorii* and the *via Marsiliana*, nominalism is readily incorporated into this tradition. In Luther's case we know that he continues to be proud of his Erfurt association with the *secta Occamica* as far as logic and dialectics are concerned. He uses their tools, e.g., in 1520 against a Thomistic and in 1528 against a spiritualist or "Wycliffite" doctrine of the Eucharist. Ockham, d'Ailly, and Biel could function in the field of theology for Luther in 1515–1517 in a negative sense as a magnifying glass to discover

---

[158]Cf. Gordon Rupp: "You might add a double dose of Augustine to the pre-existing mixture of Peter Lombard and Aristotle, but the result would be a Gregory of Rimini, or a Bradwardine, a recognizably mediaeval Augustinianism worlds apart from Luther's theology as it developed in these formative years." *The Righteousness of God*, p. 140.

[159]*W A*, IX, 29 4–26. In a joint effort with Hans Volz to verify Buchwald's edition of Lombard's Sentences, the Buchwald text could be confirmed on the basis of a micro-film of the Zwickau original except for minor corrections. The relatively long opening statement "auf der inneren Seite des vorderen Einbanddeckels", however, is undoubtedly not from Luther, but from another hand, contemporary, probably slightly older. *W A*, IX, 29, 1. Thus Volz.

the deviation of scholastic theology *in toto* from the *vera theologia*, particularly in its transition from a philosophical to a theological anthropology. Whereas in 1515 Luther is still able to use the nominalistic terminology of the *facere quod in se est*[160] for the role of the human will before the reception of grace and glory, though now reduced to *expectatio, gemitus* and confession of sin as the human *conditio sine qua non* in the *pactum miseridcordiae*,[161] we see that at the outset the nominalistic, experience-oriented revolt against meta-theology and the Augustinian awareness of the distance between God (*sapientia*) and man (*scientia*)[162] combine to move Luther to a decisive break with the nominalistic confidence in the *facere quod in se est* of human reason.

In the relation of Luther to humanism, I discern the peak of affinity during the period around the Leipzig Debate, when Luther in Pico-like words exclaims against Eck's claims for papal prerogatives: "Omnes homines aequales sunt in humanitate, quae est omnium summa et admiranda aequalitas, ex qua omnis dignitas hominibus . . ."[163] A *sic et non* relation seems to apply in the same real sense in which it characterizes the Reformer's relation to mysticism.[164] As a recent overall assessment of the theme "Luther and humanism" shows, an even more striking parallel with Luther's respect for nominalism "in its own domain" emerges: ". . . Luther gave enthusiastic support to humanist culture in its sphere, but sharply rebuffed its encroachments in the domain of theology where God's Word and not human letters reigns supreme."[165]

---

[160]*W A*, IX, 28, n. 1, is the most eloquent parallel text to the one discussed above, written about the same time and presented in the same context, Schol. to Rom. 3, 21: "Non enim dabitur gratia sine ista agricultura suiipsius." *W A*, LVI, 257 30–31.

[161]See *W A*, IX, 28, n. 1. In addition to the texts indicated in my article "Wir sein pettler. Hoc est verum. Bund und Gnade in der Theologie des Mittelalters und der Reformation", *ZKG*, LXXVIII (1967), 232–52, see Luther's marginal to Augustine's *De Trinitate*, I, 3 (Migne, *PL*, 42. 822; CChr, 50. 32, 5–6). "Et hoc placitum: i.e. pactum", *WA*, IX, 16 4; and "pepigit nobiscum fedus, ut daret nobis petentibus gratis ac mendicantibus", *W A*, IV, 350 13–14.

[162]"Sicut rancidae logicorum regulae somniant et puncto nulleitatis suae: infinitam deitatis latitudinem metiuntur." *W A*, IX, 47 6–7; cf. *W A*, IX, 29 20–26; 31 31–34; 65 10–22. As early as 1510 Luther argues *contra omnes*, against all schools: "Legi mille et omnes doctores, nullus melius solvet hanc questionem. Scotus distinguit ea formaliter, moderni ratione, antiqui realiter. Ex quibus omnibus colligitur omnes eos nescire quid loquantur." *W A*, IX, 62 19–22; quoted by zur Mühlen, p. 252, n. 375. In the years to come Luther frequently uses the argument that an opponent 'does not understand himself what he is saying', whenever an argument is not based on Scripture or experience: "Cum enim ista nemo viderit, quicquid supra fidem additur, certissimum est figmentum esse humanum. Similiter de anima." Continuation of above quotation, *W A*, IX, 62 22–24.

[163]*W A*, II, 631 1–2.

[164]See my "Simul gemitus et raptus: Luther und die Mystik", *Kirche, Mystik, Heiligung und das Natürliche bei Luther*. Vorträge des dritten internationalen Kongresses für Lutherforschung, Järvenpää, Finnland, 11.–16. August 1966, ed. Ivar Asheim (Göttingen, 1967), pp. 20–59, 24 ff.

[165]Lewis W. Spitz. *The Religious Renaissance of the German Humanists* (Cambridge, Mass., 1963), p. 238.

Weighing the evidence now available, it can be said that humanism, nominalism, and Augustinianism do not reach Luther as three separate and unrelated forces. Both nominalism and humanism are domesticated and put into the service of a new Augustinian theology. With their aid the authentic Augustinian emphasis on the distinction between *sapientia* and *scientia* can be preserved without being doomed to slide back into a pious conservatism, as had been the case whenever no compromise was made with the Aristotelian academic centers of learning. Yet the two movements are domesticated in different ways and put to different uses. Whereas nominalism tends to shape the prolegomena of the *schola moderna Augustiniana*[166] and thus to secure a bridge to the world of the senses, of science and of experienced reality, humanism as the quest for the *mens Augustini* by returning to the *fontes Augustini* relates to the inner core of its program. It is Luther's liaison to this "school" which suffices to explain his initial readiness to exchange Lyra for Faber and the Vulgate for Erasmus' edition of the New Testament; but it also explains his critical appraisal of the high anthropology of Erasmus from the very begining,[167] long before German Erasmians started to discover that the Wittenberger did not represent their ideals. Luther never shared the heroic vision of man, or as Charles Trinkaus has put it, the "new religious vision of *homo triumphans*," even if at times this heroicism is argued on the basis of a theology of grace.[168] Rather than Luther's contacts with individual humanists or humanistic sodalities, it is his life in the Order itself that provides us with the key to this curious mixture of respect for the historical perspective on sources and authorities, with the early preference for Augustine over Jerome,[169] and the pastoral option for the "verbositas" of the

---

[166]This aspect is to be taken into consideration when Otto H. Pesch observes in his impressive study of the relation Thomas-Luther: "Eher als mit dem Ockhamismus scheinen die Anfänge der Theologie Luthers mit einer augustinischen Reaktion gegen die *via moderna* verwoben zu sein." *Theologie der Rechtfertigung bei Martin Luther und Thomas von Aquin: Versuch eines systematisch-theologischen Dialogs* (Mainz, 1967), p. 4, n. 4.

[167]"Tempora enim sunt periculosa hodie, et video, quod non ideo quispiam sit christianus vere sapiens, quia Graecus sit et Hebraeus, quando et Beatus Hieronymus quinque linguis monoglosson Augustinum non adaequarit, licet Erasmo aliter sit longe visum. Sed aliud est iudicium eius, qui arbitrio hominis nonnihil tribuit, aliud eius, qui praeter gratiam nihil novit." *WA Br*, I, 90 21–26; letter to Joh. Lang, Wittenberg, 1 March 1517.

[168]*"In Our Image and Likeness": Humanity and Divinity in Italian Humanist Thought* (Chicago, 1970), I, xxi, 447, n. 39. The different anthropology of Luther can be shown with respect to all major humanists discussed, whether Petrarch (p. 12), Salutati (pp. 51, 76) or—especially—Valla (p. 168).

[169]The difficulty in placing the preference for Augustine over Jerome within a definite theological tradition becomes clear, however, when one observes that the young Eck takes the same position as Luther in criticizing the opposite view of Erasmus. See Eck's letter to Erasmus, 2 February 1518; *Opus Epistolarum Des. Erasmi Roterodami*, ed. P.S. Allen (Oxford, 1913), III, no. 769, 80–99. Cf. Theodor Wiedemann, *Dr. Johann Eck* (Regensburg, 1865), pp. 326–28.

German language instead of the subtlety of refined latinity.[170] The significance of the *schola Augustiniana* for Luther's development just as much as that of nominalism and humanism cannot be restricted to the *initia Lutheri*. Our understandable preoccupation with the "reformatorische Durchbruch" should not prevent us from giving more thought to another period in Luther's life, the late twenties and thirties, when the forces of the past by no means have run their full course. In his Table Talks of the early thirties, perhaps sobered by the revolutionary effect of his proclamation of Christian liberty, Luther mentions again the name of Staupitz, frequently and with great warmth, after a long period of silence.[171] In the revealing dispute with Melanchthon in 1536, Luther, unlike the *Praeceptor*, was still unwilling to admit that Augustine had at times spoken "excessively." He insists that "eum (Augustine) nobiscum sentire" as regards justification by faith alone.[172] These two examples suffice to point out that much work still is to be done on the *initia Lutheri senioris*. As far as the *initia* of the young Luther are concerned, however, the role of the *schola Augustiniana moderna* cannot be easily overestimated in our effort to assess the forces that shaped him in the years of decision. It is most certainly over-estimated, however, when a causal connection is constructed which does not take into account the contribution this same *schola* was to make to Catholic reform theology as represented by Contarini and Seripando and, at least partly, as reflected in the dogmatic decisions of the Council of Trent.

4. Epilogue

The distinction between the *initia Lutheri* and the *initia reformationis* has its limitations and accordingly its considerable dangers. It may isolate the Reformer in exactly the way in which Luther scholarship has isolated the "great and therefore lonely" man too long. It is good to remind ourselves

---

[170]"Sed nec, si quam maxime vellem, aliquid possem efficere, quod Latinis auribus tolerabile fieret, quanto minus nunc, cum dedita opera vulgi tarditati servire statuissem. Igitur te obsecro, ut e virorum eruditorum conspectu eas submoveas, quantum potes."

[171]E.g. *W A Tr*, I, 512 18–20; II 121 9–11; 227 21–25, 582 16–27.

[172]"Phil.: Augustinus, vt apparet, extra disputationes commodius sensit quam loquitur in disputationibus. Sic enim loquitur, quasi iudicare debeamus nos iustos esse fide, hoc est nouitate nostra. Quod si est verum, iusti sumus non sola fide, sed omnibus donis ac virtutibus. Idque sane vult Augustinus. Et hinc orta est scholasticorum Gratia gratum faciens... Augustinus non hoc sentit Gratis saluari hominem, sed saluari propter donatas virtutes. Quid vobis de hac Augustini sententia videtur?... Phil.: Apud Augustinum Sola fide tantum excludit opera praecedentia. Luth.: Sit hoc vel non, tamen ista vox Augustini satis ostendit eum nobiscum sentire, vbi dicit: 'Turbabor, sed non perturbabor, quia vulnerum Domini recordabor'. Hoc enim clare sentit fidem valere principio, medio, fine et perpetuo, sicut et Dauid: 'Apud te propitiatio est', 'Non intres in iudicium cum seruo'." *W A Br*, XII, 191 1–5; 23–24; 193 88–94.

that Luther could state in May 1518, that the part of his Ninety-five Theses which dealt with works and grace did not originate with him alone or with him first. He points for example to Karlstadt and to Amsdorf[173] as other members of the Wittenberg school-team. Yet in the very passages where he indicates that others have preceded him in the resistance against "modern Pelagianism" and in discovering God's initiative in the *vera poenitentia*, Luther shows his awareness that he has gone beyond this program based on an Augustinian interpretation of St. Paul. The view of the insufficiency of human works nurtured in the Order,[174] and perhaps most radically formulated by Staupitz as *opera finita* on which no hope can be built,[175] was to lead in another direction, namely to the doctrine of the *duplex iustitia* so eloquently defended at the Council of Trent by the Augustinian General Jerome Seripando.[176] Whereas the inherent "insufficient" righteousness of the *duplex iustitia* still allows for a search for the signs of election in us, a *parallelismus practicus* as described by Staupitz, this position is inverted and abandoned by Luther in his scholion on Rom. 8:28[177]. Here he says that the move from the requirement of self-analysis (*contritio*) to trust (*fiducia*) in the *iustitia Christi extra nos*[178] marks the end of medieval religious introspection

---

[173]"Deinde Positiones meae displicent, atque ita futurum suspicabar. Verum de iis, quae gratiam et opera tangunt, scias, optime vir, me neque solum neque primum esse earum assertorem. Scis ingenia eorum, qui apud nos sunt, puta Carlstadii, Amsdorfii, D. Hieronymi, D. Wolfgangi, utriusque Feldkirchen, denique D. Petri Lupini. At ii omnes constanter mecum sentiunt, imo tota Universitas, excepto uno ferme Licentiato Sebastiano, sed et Princeps et Episcopus ordinarius noster; deinde multi alii Praelati, et quotquot sunt ingeniosi cives, iam uno ore dicunt, sese prius non novisse nec audivisse Christum et Euangelium." *W A Br*, I, 170 20–29.

[174]Cf. Adolar Zumkeller, "Das Ungenügen der menschlichen Werke bei den Deutschen Predigern des Spätmittelalters", *ZKTh*, LXXXI (1959), 265–305.

[175]". . . in homine formaliter sunt et non nisi extrinseca denominatione dei sunt et finita sunt"; ". . . opera personae finitae natura finita sunt. Ergo infinitum praemium. . ." *Libellus de executione*, cap. VII, 40, 43.

[176]Seripando once appeals to Jacobus Pérez, *Concilium Tridentinum* XII, 664–65; see Zumkeller, "Augustinerschule," p. 251, n. 298 (quoted p. 78, n. 2).

[177]Compared with three kinds of love as signs of election in Staupitz's *Libellus de executione*, cap. XV, 117–120 Luther describes the third "gradus signorum electionis" as 'amara in subiectum': "Sed Amor desiderii Ille, inquam, est sicut infernus, durus et robustus, et in hoc exercet suos electos Deus in hac miris modis. Sic sponsa in Canticis: 'Amore Langueo'. Ideo Sub nomine Amoris Vel charitatis semper Crux et passiones intelligende sunt, Vt patet in textu isto. Sine quibus anima languescit, tepefit et Dei desiderium negligit neque sitit ad Deum, fontem viuum. Est quidem res dulcis, Sed non in recipiendo seu passiue, Sed actiue et in exhibendo, hoc est, Vt vulgariter dicam, dulcis in obiectum et amara in subiectum. Quia omnia bona optat aliis et exhibet, omnium vero mala suscipit in se tanquam sua. Quia 'non querit, que sua sunt, et omnia sustinet, omnia suffert'." *W A*, LVI, 388 19–28.

[178]"Phil.:. . . Vos vero, vtrum sentitis hominem iustum esse illa nouitate, vt Augustinus, an vero imputatione gratuita, quae est extra nos, et fide, id est fiducia appraehenditur ex verbo? Luth.: Sic sentio et persuasissimus sum ac certus hanc esse veram sententiam Euangelii et

and sets the Christian free for service, no longer in terms of his own salvation but in terms of the needs of his fellow-man: "Eyn Christen mensch ist eyn dienstbar knecht aller ding und yderman unterthan."

Our distinction between the *initia Lutheri* and the *initia reformationis* has allowed for the enlargement of part of the picture of the total Reformation movement in order to focus both on Luther's own theological voyage and on the extent to which it intersects with a number of contemporary crosscurrents. Our search for the headwaters has led us to the conclusion that the contributions of these three tributaries – nominalism, humanism and Augustinianism – are much more effective as categories in mapping the course of the *initia reformationis* than in locating the *initia Lutheri* before they surface in the flood of the early Reformation. In one perspective this conclusion would seem to put us on the side of those who venerate the mysterious Luther as a latter-day Melchizedek – "a man without beginnings." Efforts have been made in the past to find the key in Luther the nominalist, Luther the Augustinian or Luther the humanist – the first modern man assailing obscurantism. The opposite view that Luther's path to Reformation is determined by none of these but rather by his study of the Scriptures would seem to find ample support in the sources, in view of his explicit rejection of theological nominalism, his early critique of religious humanism, and his awareness that he had to go beyond Augustine and Gregory, Karlstadt and Staupitz when the Wittenberger coalition disintegrated. Yet the conclusion that Luther became the Reformer as "Schrifttheologe" is a confessional rather than a historical answer to our problem since it begs the question of through what spectacles he read Scripture. On the basis of the foregoing considerations we are indeed not prepared to argue that Luther made his discovery as a nominalist, as a humanist or as an Augustinian.[179] Furthermore it is clear that the headwaters

---

Apostolorum": "Phil.:. . . Vos conceditis duplicem iusticiam et quidem coram Deo necessariam esse, scilicet fidei et illius alterius, videlicet bonae conscientiae, in qua hoc, quod deest legi, supplet fides. Hoc quid aliud est quam dicere, quod homo iustificetur non sola fide. Certe enim iustificari non intelligitis Augustini more de principio regenerationis"; "Luth.: Hominem sentio fieri, esse et manere iustum seu iustam personam simpliciter sola misericordia"; "Phil.: Vtrum haec propositio sit vera: Iusticia operum est necessaria ad salutem. Luth.: Non quod operentur seu impetrent salutem, sed quod fidei impetranti praesentes seu coram sunt, sicut ego necessario adero ad salutem meam." *W A Br*, XII, 191 6–10, 18–22, 27–28; 193 95–99.

[179]We are still at the stage of *initia* in this field of research. Hence Bernhard Lohse's call for caution still fully obtains: "Es hat den Anschein, daß für den jungen Luther wichtiger als der Einfluß eines Augustinismus derjenige von Augustin selbst gewesen ist", and "der sog. Augustinismus des Spätmittelalters ist vielmehr eine höchst komplexe Größe." "Die Bedeutung Augustins für den jungen Luther", *Kerygma und Dogma*, XI (1965), 116–35; 118 with n. 6.

of the Reformation are much too widespread and interconnected to be reduced to the three indicated currents. We have not discussed the *devotio moderna*, late medieval mysticism, or the reemergence of apocalyptics, nor have we taken account of the numerous non-rational factors in a man's life, psyche and society which are so difficult to assess in the formal framework of stylized movements. We can say, however, that already in the earliest documents Luther thinks and writes as if Favaroni, Gregory of Rimini, and James Pérez combine in constituting his working library. Above all, this tradition is personified in Johann von Staupitz, to whose impetus Luther felt so deeply indebted. Luther for his part was willing to attest to Staupitz's role as forerunner of the *vera theologia*: "qui olim praecursor extiti sanctae euangelicae doctrinae et quemadmodum etiam hodie exosam habui captivitatem babylonicam."[180]

We have the optimal chance therefore to do justice to the *initia Lutheri* when we see his development and discoveries as those of the Augustinian monk finding and founding a new direction for the already established *via Gregorii*. That must suffice, for in seeking to understand the emergence of a man in relation to what he was before, we can never hope to lift the veil of mystery shrouding the birth of an original mind.

---

[180] *W A Br*, III, 264 34–36.

IV

FACIENTIBUS QUOD IN SE EST DEUS NON DENEGAT GRATIAM:

ROBERT HOLCOT O.P. AND THE
BEGINNINGS OF LUTHER'S THEOLOGY

"In manu enim illius et nos et sermones nostri, et omnis sapientia et operum scientia, et disciplina." *Liber Sapientiae* vii:16

1. *SOLA FIDE TENTUR:* HOLCOT'S SCEPTICISM

When the English nominalist and Dominican friar Robert Holcot († 1349) reaches the sixteenth verse of the seventh chapter in his *Wisdom* commentary, he seizes the opportunity to underscore the main theme which he had so passionately presented on the preceding pages as well as in his *Sentences* commentary: Wisdom is a gift of God; man's claim, therefore, that he can have a natural knowledge of God is false.

We should not be tempted to regard this statement as the solution of a Christian obscurantist who, bewildered by the challenging claims of philosophy, *scientia*, withdraws into the safe citadel of theology, *sapientia*. The riddle of Holcot's place in the medieval history of the relation of faith and reason forces itself upon the reader when, in this one lecture, both the inaccessibility of true knowledge of God and the accuracy of the natural knowledge of God on the part of the great philosophers are brought out.

It is first emphasized that the wisdom of God stands over against the wisdom of man since "we preach Christ crucified, a stumbling-block to Jews and folly to Gentiles."[1] Nevertheless at the climax of this same discussion Holcot introduces an extensive quotation from the source of all pagan philosophy, Hermes Trismegistos. He gives as his reference the eleventh book of the *De Natura Deorum*, and cites a passage which forms the last part of Asclepius in the *Corpus Hermeticum*.[2] Holcot's purpose is to show

---

[1] 1 Cor. 1:23; RSV. *Super Libros Sapientie* (Hagenau, 1494) [abbreviated as *Sap.*] Lect. 97 A. [Selections from these lectures are translated into English in H.A. Oberman, *Forerunners of the Reformation: The Shape of Late Medieval Thought* (New York, 1966), pp. 142–150.]

[2] *Sap.* Lect. 97 B= Asclepius 41; *Corpus Hermeticum*, II, Texte établi par A.D. Nock et traduit par A.J. Festugière (Paris, 1945), pp. 352–355.

that Hermes knows that God is self-sufficient. For Hermes, God has no need to receive anything from man, and so it makes no sense to burn incense for him. On the contrary, man depends on God for everything, including his wisdom; thanksgiving is therefore the best incense man can offer God.[3] Notwithstanding the fact that Hermes is a pagan, Holcot observes, he returns his thanks to God in everything.[4]

It is not the choice of Hermes Trismegistos which is the surprising element here. Holcot's contemporary Thomas Bradwardine († 1349), who has a career remarkably similar to that of Holcot, also likes to quote Hermes and regards him as "Father of the philosophers."[5] Both Bradwardine and Holcot in the thirties of the fourteenth century were part of the household of Richard de Bury, Bishop of Durham.[6] Arthur Darby Nock, in his introduction to the critical edition of Asclepius, has called attention to the familiarity with the *Corpus Hermeticum* which de Bury's important *Philobiblon* reveals.[7] In view of the fact that Holcot and Bradwardine had access to the same library, it does not surprise us that a part of Hermes' prayer at the end of Asclepius not only appears in Holcot's *Super libros Sapientiae* but also in Bradwardine's *De Causa Dei*.[8]

But here then arises the problem: it is by no means extraordinary that Thomas Bradwardine, whose first axiom is Anselm's ontological proof of God's existence, draws on the wisdom of pagan philosophers.[9] The consistent theme of the first book of *De Causa Dei* is the concordance of philosophy and theology,[10] and quotations from Hermes serve to show that

---

[3]*Sap*. Lect. 97 B. The most radically different reading in the critical edition is that of the first sentence: "Melius, melius ominare, Asclepi;" *ed. cit.*, p. 352.

[4]*Ibid.*

[5]"Pater philosophorum," *De Causa Dei contra Pelagium et de virtute causarum. Opera et studio Henrici Savilii* (London, 1618), I. 1.142 C; 1. 2.149 D. Cf. Heiko A. Oberman, *Archbishop Thomas Bradwardine; A Fourteenth Century Augustinian. A study of his theology in its historical context* (Utrecht, 1957), p. 24.

[6]*Archbishop Thomas Bradwardine*, p.43.

[7]*Ed. cit.,*p. 273. On the connection between Holcot and de Bury, see J. de Ghellinck, "Un évêque bibliophile au XIV siècle," *Revue d'histoire ecclésiastique* 18 (1922), 495. On the long debated possibility of Holcot's authorship of the *Philobiblon* see *Philobiblon: Richard de Bury,* ed. Michael Maclagan (Oxford, 1960), pp. xxxvff. Since no clear evidence is available Maclagan makes the plea "It seems simpler to suppose that Richard de Bury was in fact himself the author of the work which has so long born his name; and it is certainly more agreeable to do so," *ed. cit.*, p. lxxvi. On Holcot's life and works see Beryl Smalley, "Robert Holcot O.P.," *Archivum Fratrum Praedicatorum* 26 (1956), 7–28. Cf. her "Some Latin Commentaries on the Sapiential Books in the Late Thirteenth and Early Fourteenth Centuries," *Archives d'historie doctrinale et littéraire du moyen âge*, 18 (1950–51), 117–121.

[8]*De Causa Dei*, 1.6.182 A.

[9]*De Causa Dei*, 1. 1.2 E.

[10]1. 12.200 E. Cf. 1. 4.172 B; 1. 9.194 C.

philosophy provides a reliable natural theology.[11] Holcot, however, does not
share Bradwardine's confidence in the capacities of natural reason, and he
does not tire of showing that it is impossible to prove that God exists: "hec
propositio est mere credita"[12] or "sola fide tenetur."[13]

This denial of the possibility of a natural knowledge of God has earned
Holcot the reputation of a sceptic.[14] Gordon Leff, limiting his investigation
to the *Sentences* commentary, concluded that "Robert Holcot well illustrates
how fruitfully Ockham provided for his followers along the path to
scepticism."[15] Beryl Smalley broadens the basis of judgment when she
concludes that "Holcot admitted as an exegete to the scepticism that he
professed as a theologian."[16] The implications of this charge of scepticism
may appear from Miss Smalley's general conclusion: "Consistency was not
Holcot's outstanding virtue as a thinker, unless it may be that he was true to
his scepticism in his being inconsistent. Scepticism makes it difficult to hold a
clear-cut theory in politics as in theology, witness William of Ockham."[17]
Alois Meissner goes merely one step farther when he suggests that Holcot
stands for a stark agnosticism as regards the possibility of a natural
knowledge of God.[18] Though we cannot discuss the problem in all its
dimensions, we should at least note that the issue before us transcends the
importance of the individual case of Robert Holcot, since the scepticism of
Holcot has been seen as representative of nominalism as such and even as
characteristic of the climate of the whole fourteenth century.[19]

---

[11]. 2.154 C/D; 1. 2.155 B; 1. 2.157 B; 1. 10.195 E/196 A; 1. 12.201 C; 1. 19.226 D.

[12] *Sent.* q. 4 art. 3 M. The edition used is *Quaestiones super quatuor libros Sententiarum* (Lyon, 1497).

[13] *Sent.* q. 4 art. 3 M. cf. ib. R.

[14]C. Michalsky, "Les courants philosophiques à Oxford et à Paris pendant le xive siècle," Présenté 19 Jan. 1920, *Bulletin de l'Académie Polonaise des Sciences et des Lettres* (Cracow, 1920), p. 70; David Knowles, *The Religious Orders in England*, II (Cambridge, 1955), 80ff.

[15]*Bradwardine and the Pelagians* (Cambridge, 1957), p. 216. Leff seems to qualify his judgment when he observes (p. 218): "The human intellect can, by its own powers, believe that God is the highest good...." Leff has, however, misunderstood 1 *Sent.* q. 4 art. 3 M where Holcot categorically denies this possibility. Only when *assuming* that God exists can one show that He is to be loved above everything else.

[16]"Robert Holcot," p. 82; *English Friars and Antiquity in the Early Fourteenth Century* (Oxford, 1960), pp. 183, 185f.

[17]"Robert Holcot," p 93; *English Friars*, p. 198.

[18]"Holkot vertritt in der behandelten Frage einen schroffen Agnostizismus, Fideismus und Traditionalismus," *Gotteserkenntnis und Gotteslehre nach dem Englishen Dominikanertheologen Robert Holkot* (Limburg a.d. Lahn, 1953), p. 30.

[19]Gordon Leff, *Gregory of Rimini: Tradition and Innovation in Fourteenth Century Thought* (Manchester, 1961), p. 19. Cf. however, Damasus Trapp: "The many among the moderni [in the 14th century] never despaired of reaching eventually universal truth; at least such a general despair has never been proved." "Clm 27034. Unchristened Nominalism and Wycliffite Realism at Prague in 1381," *Recherches de théologie ancienne et médiévale* 24 (1957), 321.

If Holcot is indeed such a thoroughgoing sceptic and agnostic as hitherto has been claimed, one wonders of course why he values so highly the authority of Hermes – or for that matter the authority of Socrates, Plato, and Aristotle.[20] If there is such a radical cleavage between the realm of reason and the realm of faith, what then can philosophers, and especially pagan philosophers, offer to the field of natural theology? It is possible to answer this question by pointing out that Holcot holds the Augustinian[21] doctrine of an aboriginal revelation to Adam, his children, and the holy prophets, who handed this knowledge of God down in oral and written form. This revelation finally reached the Greek and pagan philosophers, who thus *received* but did not *produce* the knowledge of God.

Though this doctrine of "the splendid pagans" or of the philosophical cloud of witnesses is not exclusively Augustinian – we find it, e.g., also with Pelagius[22] – the fact that this revelation is a gift administered to the elect is a characteristic emphasis of Augustine.[23] In greater detail but true to Augustine's intention, Thomas Bradwardine shows that behind the natural theology of Hermes and Aristotle stands ultimately the gift of revelation given to Seth, Enoch, Noah, Abraham and Solomon.[24]

Holcot remains within this Augustinian tradition when he points out that all those who had knowledge of God without contact with Old Testament revelation were instructed by God rather than by their own rational argumentations. We are, however, forewarned that Holcot's position cannot simply be identified with that of Augustine by the fact that this gift of knowledge of God is not bestowed on the elect but on those who live according to the principles of natural law.[25] Unlike Augustine and Bradwardine, Holcot is not interested in an aboriginal revelation to explain the great insights of Hermes and Aristotle. He is more interested in the general ethical corollary that such knowledge of God is available to all who live according to the principles of natural law. It is this peculiar emphasis which throws a very different light on Holcot's understanding of the relation of faith and reason than the traditional charge of scepticism has led us to believe.

In *Lectio* 28 of his *Wisdom* commentary, Holcot explicitly asks the crucial

---

[20]111 *Sent.* q. 1 TT. Beryl Smalley quotes the parallel passage *Sap.* Lect. 156 A (in her numbering 157 A), "Robert Holcot," pp. 84f.; *English Friars*, Appendix 1, pp. 327f.

[21]Holcot refers to *De Civitate Dei* 18.28; his inclusion of Job makes it likely that instead he has in mind *De Civitate Dei* 18.47; *PL* 4.609. Cf. *Epistola* 102.2, 12; *PL* 33.374, *Epistola* 102.2, 15, and *PL* 33.376.

[22]*Epistola Pelagii ad Demetriadem* 3; *PL* 30.19.

[23]*De Civitate Dei* 18.47; *PL* 41.610.

[24]*De Causa Dei* I. 1.74 E–76 D.

[25]I *Sent.* q. 4 art. 3 Q ad.

question whether there are Christian doctrines which transcend the power of reason and yet still have to be revealed and believed since they are necessary for salvation.[26] Holcot first advances two arguments for the opposition: there are no such articles of faith which simultaneously transcend reason and are necessary for salvation since 1) nature does not fail in necessary things and, therefore, does not fail in establishing articles necessary for salvation; 2) certain doctrines such as those concerning the Incarnation and Transubstantiation are contrary to reason; since this implies a negation of the powers of reason, which is blameworthy, it is immoral to believe these articles of faith.[27]

It is not surprising that Holcot, along with the whole medieval tradition, rejects this concept of Christianity as a rational-natural religion.[28] What is important is the way in which he replies to the two arguments advanced.

In contrast to what one might expect of a radical sceptic, Holcot answers to the first point that God has so disposed nature that if man does what is in him, *facit quod in se est*, that is, uses his natural powers, he can acquire sufficient information about the articles of faith which are necessary for salvation.[29]

In his answer to the second argument Holcot points out that the supernatural articles of faith are *not contrary* to reason but go *beyond reason*. To deny reason is indeed blameworthy, but one does not deny reason if one grants that reason cannot reach beyond itself into the realm of supernatural faith which transcends the realm of the senses. The *facere quod in se est* means for Holcot that the act of faith is not merely the exercise of the theoretical reason but an exercise of the whole man: *sine discursu rationis et perceptione voluntaria veritatis, fides non habetur*.[30] The knowledge philosophers like Hermes and Aristotle possess is, therefore, not necessarily due to their acquaintance with the aboriginal revelation. They "have done what is in them" by using their natural powers and have thus reached enlightenment, though this does not exclude the possibility that they made use of the available tradition of truth.[31]

Actually it is only the latter possibility in which Holcot, the moralizing exegete, is interested. The philosophical pre-Christian tradition is not a live option any more; it has been absorbed by the Church and only there is the

---

[26]*Sap*. Lect. 28 B.
[27]*Ibid.*
[28]*Ibid.*
[29]*Ibid.*
[30] *Sap*. Lect. 28 B.
[31]*Sap*. Lect. 156 A.

true tradition to be found. One should not turn therefore to the philosophers but to Christ and his Church, since, compared with Christ, the philosophers' wisdom is stupidity.[32] Holcot does not refer here explicitly to Augustine, but the parallel with Augustine's letter to Dioscorus, *Epistula* 108, is obvious and striking: the true members of the *Plotini schola* recognized in Christ the personification of truth and went over to the Church. So it came about that only within the Church truth is to be found.[33]

Holcot proclaims, indeed, on every page of his *Wisdom* commentary the insufficiency of philosophy.[34] He holds with Augustine that only the authority of the Church can provide a solid basis for the understanding of supernatural truths.[35] Yet to embrace this authority does not mean a negation of reason or a blind jump. This indeed would substantiate the charge of scepticism. Holcot makes quite clear that the God to which the Church witnesses can to a degree be known from his creation.[36] Miracles are probable reasons which engender the act of faith.[37] The same kind of reasonable consideration, which one may call a common-sense argument or *ratio de congruo*, is admitted by Holcot when he tells the story of how a heretic who did not believe in the immortality of the soul was converted by a lay brother who argued that one cannot lose anything in believing this, but only gain eternal bliss if this proves to be true.[38]

The main reason, however, why one should be doubtful about such charges as agnosticism, fideism and scepticism is that, whereas Holcot consistently enough emphasizes that all these semi-arguments as such are insufficient without revelation on the part of God, this revelation is granted only to those who use their rational capacities to the utmost to seek and understand God. To clarify Holcot's use of the *facere quod in se est* as regards the problems of faith and understanding, we turn to his doctrine of predestination and grace which provides us with an elucidating parallel.

---

[32]*Prol. Sap.* E.

[33]*CSEL* 34.2 (Vindobonae, 1898), 697.

[34]Cf. E. Gilson: "... la doctrine d'Augustin proclame à chaque page l'insuffisance de la philosophie." *Introduction à l'étude de Saint Augustin* (Paris, 1949), 3rd ed., p. 311.

[35]*Prol. Sap.* F.

[36]*Sap. Lect.* 122 A; cf. *Sap. Lect.* 82 B.

[37] I *Sent.* q. I art. 6 J.

[38]*Sap. Lect.* 14 B; *Sap. Lect.* 18 A. Beryl Smalley concludes: "This is real scepticism. It goes with fideism." "Robert Holcot," p. 85; *English Friars*, p. 187. To the *facere quod in se est* belongs *prudentia*, and this plays a part in missionary efforts, not as demonstration but as persuasion. Christ himself is the example. *Sap. Lect.* 197 B.

2. *SOLA GRATIA SALVATUR*: HOLCOT'S PREDESTINARIANISM

In the first part we have seen that Holcot does not believe that man through his own power can acquire a saving knowledge of God: *sapientia* is a free gift of God. The transcendence and sovereignty of God is preserved and posited beyond the reach of man's *scientia*.[39] This "scepticism" is considerably mitigated, however, by the concept of the *facere quod in se est*. Man can not only acquire some knowledge of God from creation, but he can also acquire the gift of enlightenment if he makes the best possible use of his natural capacities. Since exactly the same structure of arguments reappears in Holcot's discussion of the relation of free will, grace, and predestination, we can now be more concise in our discussion.

Just as we found strong indications which seemed to support the claim that Holcot be regarded as a full-fledged sceptic, so we find explicit documentation for the claim that Holcot holds an Augustinian doctrine of unmerited grace and predestination without cause. Again God's transcendence and sovereignty are established and posited beyond the reach of man.[40]

Especially if one accepts the view that Holcot is one of the *Pelagiani moderni*, so bitterly attacked by Thomas Bradwardine, the *sola gratia* theme is striking. Though man's responsibility is not denied, all good works are clearly said to be effects of God's predestination.[41] The famous question whether God's predestination is based on fore-knowledge of future good works is answered in the negative.[42] Several times the prevenience of grace is clearly enunciated; the beginning of the process of justification is said to be due to the initiative of the Holy Spirit.[43] One can therefore very well understand that it has been argued that Holcot does not deviate from the theology of Aquinas and the Dominican order in his doctrine of grace and predestination.[44]

But again, as was the case with Holcot's "scepticism," we are confronted with a series of statements which seem to contradict this emphasis on God's

---

[39]*Sap.* Lect. 123 A.

[40]Holcot makes explicit the parallel between the problem areas of faith and reason on the one hand and will and grace on the other. *Sap.* Lect. 118 B.

[41]II *Sent.* q. I U.

[42]II *Sent.* q. I X; *Sap.* Lect. 79 D. See the more elaborate treatment by Bradwardine in *De Causa Dei* 1.35–1.46 and in *De Praedestinatione et Praescientia* published in *Nederlandsch Archief voor Kerkgeschiedenis* 43 (1961), 195–220.

[43]*Sap.* Lect. 149 A. *Ibid.* Cf. *Sap.* Lect. 148 D.

[44]"Der Grund der Prädestination liegt nur in Gott, in seinem Willen, die Prädestination ist letztlich Gnade." Alois Meissner, *Gotteserkenntnis und Gotteslehre*, p. 102. "Holkot folgt also in seiner Prädestinationslehre der allgemeinen thomistischen Ansicht," *ibid.*, p. 104.

sovereignty as expressed in the uncaused nature of predestination and in the prevenience of grace. Holcot takes I Tim. 2:4 quite seriously: "[God] desires all men to be saved and to come to the knowledge of the Truth."[45] Yet with this general will for salvation goes the condition that God only wants those to be saved who live according to the laws established by him. This, then, man can and has to decide in all freedom.[46]

Now the question arises with a new urgency how man can be held responsible to live according to the established laws and thus lay claim to the promised salvation, while the actualization of his natural capacities depends on God's granting him the gift of prevenient grace. It is again the doctrine of the *facere quod in se est* which reverses the predestinarian trend and forms the bridge between the transcendent sovereignty of God and man's responsibility for his own salvation.

Holcot solves the problem in the same way as his fellow nominalists, William of Occam[47] and Gabriel Biel.[48] God is committed to give his grace to all who do what is in them. This does not detract from His sovereignty since in eternity God was free to establish totally different laws; he was free to act with absolute power, the so-called *potentia absoluta*, subject only to the law of noncontradiction or the law of consistency. Out of sheer mercy and grace he freely decided in eternity to establish the law that he would convey grace to all who make full use of thier natural capacities. Though the law as such is freely given, and therefore an expression of God's *potentia absoluta*, God is now committed to it, in the order chosen by him, the order of His *potentia ordinata*, and therefore gives his grace "necessarily."[49]

The dialectics of the two powers of God permits Holcot, as it did Occam

---

[45]RSV; *Sap*. Lect. 144 A.

[46]II *Sent*. q. I D; II *Sent*. q. I CC.

[47]I *Sent*. d. 41 q. I G.

[48]Biel, I *Sent*. d. 41 q. I art. 3 dub 3. We note also that Biel and Occam exactly like Holcot insist that nevertheless God's predestination is to be regarded as uncaused. *Ibid*. art. 2 concl. 3; Occam, *ibid*. q. I H.

[49]"Necessitas coactionis nullo modo cadit in deo, necessitas vero infallibilitatis cadit in deo ex promisso suo et pacto sive lege statuta et hec non est necessitas absoluta sed necessitas consequentie.... Concedendo quod ex misericordia et gratia sua pro tanto quia talem legem misericorditer statuit et observat. Sed statuta lege necessario dat gratiam necessitate consequentie." *Sap*. Lect. 145 B. These two kinds of necessity reflect the distinction between the two powers. The *statuta lege* makes clear that also for Holcot God is committed to the order *de potentia ordinata*, which is therefore dependable. Cf., however, Leff, who assigns to Holcot an "extreme scepticism, which allows anything to be possible," *Bradwardine and the Pelagians*, p. 223. Though Leff has retracted some of his earlier statements he still regards the order *de potentia ordinata* as an unreliable whim of God, constantly threatened by God's *potentia absoluta*: "its [the *potentia absoluta*] purpose was not the emancipation of man from his limits *in statu isto* but of God from His obligation to abide by those limits...." *Gregory of Rimini*, p. 22.

and Biel, to hold an extreme predestinarian position which centers around the idea that God does not owe anything to any man. While this is true *sub specie aeternitatis et de potentia absoluta*, Holcot can now at the same time assert a doctrine, which one cannot but term Pelagian, according to which man can earn first grace and ultimately – in cooperation with grace – earn his salvation, *de potentia ordinata*.[50] The fact that God *accepts* this *facere quod in se est* as meritorious while this action as such has no intrinsic condignity or meritorious value, is expressed with the terminological differentiation between *meritum de congruo* and *meritum de condigno*.[51]

Holcot rejects the application of the potter and the clay simile of Rom. 9:21 – which was so important for Bradwardine in his defense of justification by grace alone[52] – on the grounds that there is no pact or commitment binding the potter over against the clay,[53] while this is exactly the mark of God's relation with his creatures.

We may conclude that the commitment by which God in eternity obligated himself conveys to man's action a dignity which it would not have in itself: if man goes halfway, God will meet him with the gift of grace. Without this gift of grace man is *helpless*; but it is just as true that, without the full use of man's own natural powers, the offer of grace is *useless*.

When we now apply our findings with regard to the relation of free will and grace to the relation of reason and revelation we are in a position to assess the validity of the charge of scepticism. There can be little doubt that Holcot denies that man unaided by grace can with his natural reason prove the existence of God, or grasp the mysteries of the Holy Trinity and of the Incarnation. In view of the foregoing we may say that Holcot holds that man cannot reach the knowledge of faith *de condigno*. Only to this extent is Holcot a sceptic. It would perhaps be more appropriate to say that for Holcot man without revelation is subject to philosophical uncertainty and that therefore man is freed from scepticism by faith.[54] This form of scepticism, however, is not without precedent in medieval theology and can even be said to be rooted in the Augustinian tradition.[55] Holcot's emphasis on the intrinsic

---

[50]*Sap*. Lect. 48 C.

[51]". . . opera nostra ex sua naturali bonitate non merentur vitam eternam de condigno sed de congruo tantum quia congruum est quod homini facienti secundum potentiam suam finitam deus retribuat secundum potentiam suam infinitam." *Sap*. Lect. 25 B. Cf. *Sap*. Lect. 116 B; IV *Sent*. q I art. 3.

[52]*De Praedestinatione et Praescientia* [69], *ed. cit.*, p. 210.

[53]*Sap*. Lect. 145 B.

[54]*Sap*. Lect. 122 B. Cf. *Sap*. Lect. 118 A.

[55]"Il n'y a pas d'augustinisme sans cette présupposition fondamentale: la vraie philosophie présuppose un acte d'adhésion à'ordre surnatùrel, qui libère la volonté de la chair par la grâce et la pensée du scepticisme par la révélation." E. Gilson, *Introduction à l'étude de Saint Augustin*, p. 311.

deficiencies of man's rational powers as compared with the confidence in natural reason on the part of Anselm, Aquinas, and Bradwardine tends to give his views an air of radicalism which places him on the left wing of the nominalistic tradition.[56]

Nevertheless, Holcot does not reject the possibility of acquiring *de congruo* the articles of faith which are necessary for salvation. Man can and therefore has to do his very best in going halfway in his search for God; thus he will receive enlightenment. Man's natural reason is *helpless* when confronted with the task of solving the mysteries of faith, but at the same time man's natural reason is the very presupposition and precondition for this enlightenment. Without man's effort to search out God with all his might, the offer of enlightenment is *useless*.

We may conclude that for Holcot the way to faith does not by-pass but presupposes the full use of natural reason. The doctrine of the *facere quod in se est* is the key to both Holcot's "scepticism" and "predestinarianism." What first seemed to be the contradictions and the inconsistencies of one who despairs of reason proves to be the reflection of the dialectic of the two powers, and the "unnecessary" but dependable commitment of God to man's serious efforts in thought and action.

3. *THEOLOGIA EST CELUM . . . HOMO AUTEM TERRA:* LUTHER'S EARLIEST POSITION (1509–1510)

One can contest the appropriateness of regarding the *De servo arbitrio* (1525) as representative of the young Luther. But his assertion there over against Erasmus' explicit approval of scepticism is the concise summary of his position from 1509 onward: "For the Holy Spirit is not a sceptic, nor are what he has written on our hearts our own doubts and opinions, but assertions far more certain and firm than life itself and all human experience."[57] One of Luther's chief objections to the prince of the humanists and his followers would always be that they moved in the realm of theology with the same scholarly attitude of uncommitted inquiry

---

[56]Cf. Occam: ". . . alique veritates naturaliter notae seu cognoscibiles sunt theologice, sicut quod deus est, deus est sapiens, bonus, etc. cum sint necessarie ad salutem." *Prol. Sent.* q. 1 F. Philotheus Boehner calls attention to a revealing observation by Peter of Candia: "Alii doctores quos videre potui, tenent quod talis propositio non est per se nota, sed est bene demonstrabilis. Et huius opinionis fuerunt beatus Thomas, Doctor Subtilis, Ockham, Adam (Wodham), Johannes de Ripa. . . ." Ms. Vat. lat. 1081, fol. 42 vb; *Collected Articles on Ockham,* ed. E.M. Buytaert (St. Bonaventure, 1958), p. 413.

[57]*W A* 18, 605; quoted by Gordon Rupp, *The Righteousness of God, Luther Studies: A reconsideration of the character and work of Martin Luther* (London, 1953), p. 272.

characteristic of and necessary in the field of philosophy, the arts, and the sciences.

This insistence on the essential difference between *scientia* and *sapientia* is not an argument especially construed to clarify a new position after the break with humanism in the mid-twenties. It can be traced back to Luther's earliest writings and perhaps best be summarized by the statement: "Smoke of the earth has never been known to lighten heaven; rather it blocks the stream of light over the earth. Theology is heaven, yes even the kingdom of heaven; man however is earth and his speculations are smoke...."[58]

For the understanding of the positive and negative relation of Luther to the nominalistic tradition, the first works, the marginal comments of 1509–1510 on one volume of Augustine's *Opuscula, De Trinitate, De Civitate Dei* and Lombard's *Sentences*, are obviously of crucial importance. As is well known Luther was educated at Erfurt by such disciples of Gabriel Biel as Jodocus Trutvetter, Bartholomaeus Arnoldi of Usingen, and John Nathin.[59] Even if Luther later developed in a radically different direction, we might expect him to show here his indebtedness to the nominalistic teachers. In view of the widespread contention that Luther denies the validity of reason and constructs an even more radical contrast between reason and revelation than Occam and Biel,[60] it is proper to compare Luther with the radical Holcot rather than with the more moderate Biel.[61] The hypothesis that Luther, as *sententiarius* in 1509, is to be regarded as a nominalist is thus investigated under the most favorable conditions.

Two recent contributions to the understanding of Luther's concept of the relation of reason and revelation are particularly important for our investigation. Bernhard Lohse has paid careful attention to the young Luther in his monograph on faith and reason in Luther's theology. The lasting contribution of his study might well be that it will no longer be possible to be satisfied with the observation that for Luther reason is the whore, *Frau Hulda*, in order to prove that Luther is antirational. Lohse has furhter shown that the distinction between the use of reason *coram mundo* or *coram hominibus* –*scientia* – in contrast with its use *coram deo* – *sapientia* – is not adequate unless one insists that it is the same reason which operates on the levels of creation

---

[58]Comment on Lombard, I *Sent.* d. 12 c 2; *W A* 9, 65.

[59]Cf. the survey by Robert H. Fife, *The Revolt of Martin Luther* (New York, 1957), pp. 32–65.

[60]See the survey of literature by Bernhard Lohse, *Ratio und Fides: Eine Untersuchung über die ratio in der Theologie Luthers* (Göttingen, 1958), pp. 7–21.

[61]Paul Vignaux misses in Holcot what he finds in Occam, d'Ailly and Biel: "un dernier écho de la *fides quaerens intellectum.*" *Luther commentateur des Sentences* (Paris, 1953), p. 100.

and redemption.[62]

As regards the study of Luther's sources, Bengt Hägglund has been the first to discuss in more detail the supposition that Luther is dependent on Occam and Occamism in the "divorce" of faith and reason. His conclusion is that for Occam and his disciples – in contrast with Luther – there exists an essential harmony between reason and revelation. This conclusion can be regarded as representative of the present state of scholarship.[63] Without mentioning him by name Hägglund points out that Vignaux's separation of Holcot from the main current of nominalism cannot be maintained. Holcot's replacement of general logic by a special logic of faith does not imply the positing of the doctrine of double truth, nor does it bring Holcot closer than his fellow nominalists to Luther's thesis that theological truths are beyond the grasp of all logical speculation.[64]

If Hägglund's conclusion could be sustained, i.e., if it could be shown that nominalism operates on the presupposition of an essential harmony between reason and revelation,[65] it is possible to suggest that Luther, at least on this basic point, had, in 1509, as *sententiarius* at Erfurt, already broken with the nominalism of his philosophy and theology professors, since the only possible theme which one can discover in the series of unconnected comments on widely varying passages is the *disharmony* between faith and reason.[66] Such a conclusion, not drawn by Hägglund himself, runs counter to the present consensus of Luther scholars.[67]

---

[62]*Ratio und Fides*, p. 135. Arnold Lunn explains the two aspects of Luther's understanding of the function of reason as "the conflict between Luther the Catholic and Luther the anarchist. . . ." *The Revolt Against Reason* (New York, 1951), p. 48. Though it is regrettable that the 19th century Roman Catholic Luther-image has apparently not yet completely disappeared, it should be pointed out that the difference between "Catholic reason" and "anarchist reason" is precisely the one intended by Luther when he distinguishes between reason *coram deo* and *coram mundo*. See also the appropriate comment by Roland Bainton in "Probleme der Lutherbiographie," *Lutherforschung Heute, Referate und Berichte des I.Internationalen Lutherforschungskongresses* (Aarhus, August 18–23, 1956), ed. Vilmos Vajta (Berlin, 1958), pp. 28f.

[63]"Hier [in Occamism] ... waltet eine ungestörte Harmonie zwischen Theologie und Philosophie, zwischen Glaubenserkenntnis und rationaler Erkenntnis," *Theologie und Philosophie bei Luther und in der Occamistischen Tradition: Luthers Stellung zur Theorie von der doppelten Wahrheit* (Lund, 1955), p. 40; cf. p. 86.

[64]*Ibid.*, pp. 93, 53.

[65]Cf. also Hägglund, "Was Luther a Nominalist," *Concordia Theological Monthly* 28 (1957), 441–452; esp. 449.

[66]. *W A* 9, 66: "Major est enim huius scripturae authoritas quam omnis humani ingenii capacitas." Cf. *W A* 9, 27; 9, 43; 9, 47; 9, 65; 9, 84.

[67]Otto Scheel's careful analysis has been most influential, *Martin Luther: Vom Kaitholizismus zur Reformation*, II (Tübingen, 1930), 430ff. Herbert Rommel, *Über Luthers Randbemerkungen von 1509/10* (Kiel, 1930), esp. p. 85. Reinhold Seeberg is an exception: ". . . so wüsste ich nichts in den Bemerkungen zu nennen, was die Ansätze zu der evangelischen Heilserkenntnis bei ihrem

In the following we want to argue that though Hägglund's thesis has to be reformulated, there is nevertheless good reason to believe that Luther at the end of 1509 has become independent of the nominalistic tradition as regards the relation of faith and reason, while retaining till 1515–1516 the doctrine of the *facere quod in se est* in its application to the relation of will and grace.

In our discussion of Holcot's position we have seen that the incompatibility of man's reason with God's revelation is not due to the fact that the articles of faith are *contrary* to reason, but to the fact that they are *beyond* the grasp of reason. Disharmony interpreted as irrationality is indeed rejected. But at the same time there is no basis for the supposition that metaphysics would provide a bridge between *scientia* and *sapientia*, as Hägglund has suggested. Metaphysics is contrasted with the authority of Holy Scripture and made responsible for the transformation of Catholics into schismatics and into unbelievers and for the change of doctors into sycophants.[68] The only bridge between the knowledge of man and the knowledge of God is the *facere quod in se est*. This is a dependable bridge insofar as it is sustained by the promises and the faithfulness of God.[69]

But this bridge should not be taken as a symbol of natural harmony between reason and faith since the range of man's rational powers falls short of the mysteries of faith. Bartholomaeus of Usingen, Luther's philosophy professor and a student of Aristotle, provides us with an illustration of how easily one is led astray on this point. He writes in his *Libellus contra Lutheranos* of 1524 that the importance of natural reason cannot be denied since it is the *rudimentum gratiae*; grace does not extinguish the light of reason but uses it as the driver uses his horse.[70] This does not imply, however, a harmonization of

---

Urheber ausschlösse," *Lehrbuch der Dogmengeschichte*, IV. I (Basel, 1953), 5th ed., 72, Bernhard Lohse finds a departure from Occamism in the epistemological parallel Luther draws between reason and will, *Ratio und Fides*, p. 27. As we noted in the discussion of the *facere quod in se est* this parallel is characteristic for nominalism. See further Biel, II *Sent*. d. 27 q. I art. 2. concl. 4 and *Sacri canonis misse expositio* (Basel, 1515) [abbreviated Lect.] Lect. 23 F.

[68]"Ita sacra scriptura omnium facultatum domina dici debet et non illa vana metaphysica quam dicta scientiarum et dominam Aristoteles vocat seu estimat. . . ." *Sap.* Prol. c. "Hoc enim catholicos in scismaticos et infideles, et doctores in adulatores convertit. . . ." Ibid. D. The reference to Aristotle is an allusion to *Metaphysicorum*, Lib. I, cap. 2; *Scriptorum Graecorum Bibliotheca Arist. Opera Omnia*, II (Paris, 1850), col. 471.

[69]Cf. Biel: Lect. 59 P. See also IV *Sent*. d. 9 q. 2 art, I nota I B; IV *Sent*. d. 16 q. 2 art. 3 dub. 4. The first explicit formulation of this doctrine is by Alexander of Hales: "Numquam deest facienti quod in se est ad esse gratuitum et spirituale. Facere quod in se est uti ratione per quam potest comprehendere deum esse et invocare adiutorium dei." *Sum.* II q. 129 me 8; II *Sent*. d. 22 q. 2 art. 3 dub. I. For the first implicit statement see *Glossa ordinaria*, super Rom. 3:22, *PL* 114.480 and Ambrosiaster, *PL* 17.79. A survey of its late medieval use is found in John Altenstaig's *Vocabularius Theologie* (Hagenau, 1517), fol. 85.

[70]"Nondum obschurati sunt seni usingo oculi fidei qui hisce videt limpide te in fide

faith and reason but it shows the possibility and necessity of the *facere quod in se est*. Again, the bridge is not man's extension of a given natural structure, but is erected by the intervening action of God.[71] The *facere quod in se est* allows the nominalist to posit at once the discontinuity of faith and reason and the moral and intellectual responsibility of the individual in search for God.[72]

In our presentation of Luther's relation to nominalistic theology as regards the *facere quod in se est*, we propose in lieu of the customary chronological sequence rather to take as our point of departure Luther's *Disputatio contra scholasticam theologiam* (1517), in which he clearly and openly attacks the medieval theological tradition. While this point is uncontested, it is not yet clear by what stages he arrived at the conclusions there formulated. From 1517 we shall search our way back towards the earliest evidence we have. This procedure makes it possible to avoid the usual "blind" approach to the marginals of 1509–1510 through the no-man's land between the last pertinent nominalistic sources and these first Lutheran documents.

There can be little discussion about the fact that Luther in 1517 in his *Disputatio contra scholasticam theologiam* has completely broken with those characteristic tenets of nominalistic theology which we have described above. He rejects here explicitly the doctrine of the *facere quod in se est*, as a liaison both between human will and grace and between human reason and revelation.[73] Applied to man's moral powers, this means that what precedes grace is not a disposition but indisposition and rebellion.[74] The proper disposition for the reception of grace is an effect of God's eternal election and predestination.[75] Applied to man's rational powers this means that

---

hallucinari. Nec obest illi lumen nature in quo olim ex aristotele profecit, quod nunc habet in rudimentum gratie que lumen nature non extinguit sed eo utitur ut sessor equi . . ." *Libellus . . . in quo respondet confutationi fratris Egidii . . . contra Lutheranos* (Erphurdiae, 1524) fol. h 3. On the use of the image of driver and horse with Augustine and Luther, see Alfred Adam, "Die Herkunft des Lutherwortes vom menschlichen Willen als Reittier Gottes," *Luther-Jb.* 29 (1962), 25–34. This should be complemented by references to its peculiar use by Scotus, Occam and Biel; see my *Harvest of Medieval Theology* (Cambridge, Mass., 1963), Chapter VI.2.

[71]Caspar Schatzgeyer, like Usingen a nominalist and one of the first opponents of Luther, is as explicit as one might wish. *Scrutinium divinae scripturae*, ed. Ulrich Schmidt, *Corpus Catholicorum* 5 (Münster i. W., 1922), 18.

[72]Holcot goes even so far as to explain the geographical boundaries of the *corpus christianum* on grounds of a lack of earnestness in the search of the unbelievers. *Sap.* Lect. 28 A/B; *Sap.* Lect. 15 B; *Sap.* Lect. 145 B.

[73]"Falsum et illud est, quod facere quod est in se sit removere obstacula gratie." *W A* I, 225.

[74]"Ex parte autem hominis nihil nisi indispositio, immo rebellio gratiae gratiam praecedit." *Ibid.*

[75]"Optima et infallibilis ad gratiam praeparatio et unica dispositio est aeterna dei electio et praedestinatio." *Ibid.*

ignorance of God is seen as a characteristic of fallen nature.[76] Aristotle does not help here; yes, one cannot become a theologian unless one breaks with Aristotle.[77] Not only syllogistic logic, but also the special logic of faith which we met with in Holcot is declared inadmissible in theology.[78] Luther sums up his conclusions with the statement: "All the works of Aristotle compare with theology as darkness with light."[79]

The 1517 disputation is not the first occasion on which Luther attacks both the moral and rational aspects of the *facere quod in se est*. When on September 25, 1516, he chairs a disputation of theses for which he himself is largely responsible,[80] one thesis is defended – the second conclusion – which states that the sinner cannot prepare himself for grace either *de congruo* or *de condigno*.[81] Inferred from this is the conclusion that the man who does what is in him – with his will or his reason – sins.[82]

This point Luther had already reached in his development while lecturing from November, 1515 till September, 1516 on the Epistle to the Romans. In his long exposition of Rom. 14:1 Luther designates the doctrine of the *facere quod in se est*, or rather the *fiducia* in this doctrine, as having overturned almost the whole Church.[83] Our point in citing this passage is not that it provides us with evidence of a remnant-ecclesiology.[84] Its import is rather that it assures us that in dealing with the problem of the *facere quod in se est*, we are not discussing a point which is alien to or even marginal for Luther's own frame of reference. He is explicitly and fully alerted to its significance.

In comparison with the quoted passages of the disputations of 1517 and 1516, there are two noteworthy aspects of the *scholion* to Rom. 14:1 of some months earlier. In the first place Luther restricts himself to a rejection of the

---

[76]". . . ignorantia dei et sui et boni operis est naturae semper invincibilis." *W A* I, 226.

[77]"Error est dicere: sine Aristotele non fit theologus; immo theologus non fit nisi id fiat sine Aristotele. . . ." *Ibid.*

[78]"Frustra fingitur logica dei. . . . Nulla forma syllogistica tenet in terminis divinis." *Ibid.* See exactly the opposite thesis with Biel, III *Sent.* d. 7 q. I art. 3 dub. I. Cf. I *Sent.* d. 5 q. I art. 2, 3.

[79]"Breviter, totus Aristoteles ad theologiam est tenebrae ad lucem." *W A* I, 225.

[80]*W A Br*, I, 65.

[81]"Homo Dei gratia exclusa praecepta eius servare nequaquam potest, neque se vel de congruo vel de condigno ad gratiam praeparare, verum necessario sub peccato manet." *W A* I, 147.

[82]"Homo quando facit quod in se est, peccat, cum nec velle aut cogitare ex seipso possit." *W A* I, 148.

[83]"Ideo absurdissima est, et Pelagiano errori vehementer patrona, sententia usitata qua dicitur 'Facienti quod in se est, infallibiliter Deus infundit gratiam,' intelligendo per 'facere, quod in se est,' aliquid facere vel posse. Inde enim tota Ecclesia pene subversa est, videlicet huius verbi fiducia." *W A* 56. 503.

[84]Thomas Bradwardine, a faithful son of the medieval Church, wrote in his preface: "Totus etenim paene mundus post Pelagium abiit in errorem." *De Causa Dei*, Praefatio, fol. 2; cf. II. 31.602 D.

moral implications of the *facere quod in se est*. It is only the "Pelagianism" of the will in relation to grace and not the "Pelagianism" of the reason in relation to revelation to which he addresses himself.[85] In the second place Luther leaves the impression that it is not so much the doctrine of the *facere quod in se est* as such which is objectionable, but rather its Pelagian interpretation, according to which man is able to prepare himself for the reception of grace.[86] This is a strange distinction since, as we have seen, this interpretation is the sole intention of this doctrine in the nominalistic tradition.

It is, of course, possible that Luther alludes here to the difference between the Thomistic and the nominalistic understanding of the sinner's preparation for grace.[87] In view of Luther's tendency to identify the various scholastic schools,[88] however, it is more appropriate in explanation to point to his exposition of Psalm 113:1, in the light of which the Romans passage affords us a glimpse of Luther in full transition. The Psalm passage dates most likely from the summer or fall of 1515. We reproduce this passage at length since here we find formulated in no uncertain terms Luther's adherence to and respect for the doctrine of the *facere quod in se est*. Again he discusses only that part of the doctrine which applies to the relation of will and grace; since he is silent in this context on the relation of intellect and revelation, we shall pursue this issue separately below. But for the rest we find all the elements of the usual nominalistic argumentation; such as that man's disposition is not meritorious *de condigno* but *de congruo*, due to God's merciful commitment.[89]

Thus in the period, probably as short as half a year, which lies between the

---

[85] *W A* 56, 502.

[86] See *W A* 56, 503, quoted above, note 83.

[87] Only in his early Sentences Commentary does Thomas teach the *facere quod in se est* as sufficient disposition for the infusion of grace. II *Sent.* d. 28 q. I art. 4. Yet even the mature Thomas does not always avoid ambiguity. The use of the Dionysian sun-image, applied to the operation of grace, neutralizes the *auxilium gratiae*. This is the case in *Summa Contra Gentiles*, III, cap. 159.

[88] "Luther zag Thomas nu eenmaal door de bril van het Occamisme. Met de theologie van Thomas was hij niet voldoende vertrouwd." Maarten van Rhijn, "Kende Luther Thomas?" *NAK* 44 (1961), 156; cf. Stephanus Pfürtner, *Luther und Thomas im Gespräch* (Heidelberg, 1961), p. 52.

[89] "Hinc recte dicunt Doctores, quod homini facienti quod in se est, deus infallibiliter dat gratiam, et licet non de condigno sese possit ad gratiam preparare, quia est incomparabilis, tamen bene de congruo propter promissionem istam dei et pactum misericordie. Sic pro adventu futuro promisit, 'ut iuste et sobrie et pie vivamus in hoc seculo, expectantes beatam spem' [Tit. 2:12f.]. Quia quantumvis sancte hic vixerimus, vix est dispositio et preparatio ad futuram gloriam, que revelabitur in nobis, adeo ut Apostolus dicat: 'Non sunt condigne passiones huius temporis etc.' [Rom. 8:18]. Sed bene congrue. Ideo omnia tribuit gratis et ex promissione tantum misericordie sue, licet ad hoc nos velit esse paratos quantum in nobis est." *WA* 4, 262.

comments on Psalm 113:1 (c. 1515) and Rom. 14:1 (c. 1516), Luther has
radically revised his position on a doctrine which in 1515 he espoused but
which in 1516 he attacks as responsible for perverting the Church. The fact
that he attempts to salvage the doctrine of the *facere quod in se est*, in the
commentary on the Letter to the Romans, by distinguishing between its
Pelagian intepretation and the doctrine itself is readily explained in the light
of his enthusiastic support of this doctrine so shortly before.[90] In the slightly
later disputations of 1516 and 1517, which we have discussed, this distinction
has also disappeared and the doctrine is without qualifications rejected.

This investigation does not lead us to claim that we have thus solved the
riddle of the dating of Luther's *Turmerlebnis*. The discussion of this question
has proved to be fruitless. The complexity of Luther's thought makes for a
plurality of levels on which his development took place.[91] We nevertheless
suggest that the search for the occurrence of the doctrine of the *facere quod in
se est* has led us to a decisive transition between two stages in Luther's
development.

When we return now to the second aspect of the nominalistic doctrine of
the *facere quod in se est*, the relation of reason and revelation, and investigate its
place in the thought of the young Luther, we find new evidence for the
plurality of levels on which Luther's development took place. While in the
disputations of 1516 and 1517 both aspects of the *facere quod in se est* are
mentioned and rejected, we were surprised to find that in his exposition of
Rom. 14:1 Luther is silent about the relation of reason and revelation.

This situation can be readily explained now that we know that this

---

[90]Less radical but connected with the reevaluation of the *facere quod in se est* is another shift in
Luther's thought in the same period. In his exposition of Rom. 4:7 Luther rejects the claim that
the sinner can obey the commandments insofar as the substance of the act is concerned. *W A* 56,
274. Contra Biel, III *Sent.* d. 27 q. I art. 3 dub. 2. His earlier exposition of Ps. 68:17, however, still
leaves room for this; here the distinction between the substance and quality of an act is still
employed, though used to expose sin. *W A* 3, 430. The humility theme in the Lectures on
Romans (e.g. *W A* 56, 259: ". . . a Deo iustus reputatur, quia respicit humiles") is characteristic
for nominalistic theology where it appears as a refined form of the *facere quod in se est*. See Biel,
Lect. 8 B; IV *Sent.* d. 17 q. 2 art. 3 dub. 7.

[91]See the survey by Wilhelm Link, *Das Ringen Luthers um die Freiheit der Theologie von der
Philosophie* (Munich, 1955), pp. 6–77. F. Edward Cranz places the reorientation of Luther's
thought on justice, law, and society toward the end of 1518. *An Essay on the Development of
Luther's Thought on Justice, Law and Society*, (Cambridge, Mass., 1959), pp. 41–71. Ernst Bizer
adduces convincing arguments for the thesis that the beginning of 1518, e.g. Luther's exposition
of Hebrews 7:12, marks a decisive change in his concept of faith: *Fides ex auditu: Eine Untersuchung
über die Entdeckung der Gerechtigkeit Gottes durch Martin Luther* (Neukirchen, 1958), pp. 74f. A. F. N.
Lekkerkerker's own presupposition of a single-level development – the concept of the
punishing righteousness of God – led him to charge Bizer with "terrible onesidedness."
"Notities over de rechtvaardigingsleer bij Luther en Trente," *Kerk en Theologie* 9 (1958), p. 161.

exposition probably harks back to and certainly is the reversal of his position taken in the exposition of Psalm 113:1; and in this latter passage the *facere quod in se est* it upheld only as applied to the relation of will and grace.

Luther's silence in 1515–1516 on the second aspect of the *facere quod in se est* should not be taken as an implicit allegiance to it. The best evidence for this assertion is perhaps Luther's comments on the *Collectorium* of Gabriel Biel since these were written, according to the editor Hermann Degering, in the crucial period of change under discussion, between the beginning of 1515 and the summer of 1516.[92] Luther here proves to be completely independent of Biel and highly critical of the main shape of Biel's theology. This criticism now is directed both against the relation of will and grace[93] *and* against the relation of reason and revelation as presented by Biel.[94] The fact that Luther in 1515 defines the *facere quod in se est* in a restricted sense is simply due to the fact that by that time he had already rejected the nominalistic application of this doctrine to the relation of reason and revelation. Actually we do not have evidence that he ever held it – though this is likely in view of his training – since in the first documents we possess, the marginals of 1509–1510, he has already rejected this point of view.

There can be no doubt that these marginals amply bear out Luther's repeated declaration that he belongs to the school of Occam.[95] Nevertheless, this observation proves to apply unambiguously only to the anthropology and epistemology of Occam and his school.[96]

There are various aspects of the fragmentary theology of the marginals which have in the past been designated as deviations from the nominalistic tradition, but it is fair to say that today they are not highly regarded as evidence for Luther's development.[97] Our investigation leads us to a different conclusion. When we restrict our purview to the relation of reason and revelation we note that on this point Luther derides his fellow

---

[92]*Luthers Randbemerkungen zu Gabriel Biels Collectorium in quattuor libros sententiarum und zu dessen Sacri canonis missae expositio* (Weimar, 1933), p. XII.

[93]Comment on Biel's statement: "... nullus peccato mortali obnoxius habet dilectionem dei." III *Sent.* d. 27 art. I nota 4 G: "Si hec vera sunt, quomodo potest ex naturalibus diligere deum? An potest ex peccato mortali per se ipsum venire? Igitur hoc vero destruuntur omnia sequentia falsa." *Ed. cit.*, p. 13.

[94]Comment on Biel's statement: "... appetitus rationalis presupponens iudicium intellectus. ..." III *Sent.* de. 27 art. I nota I B: "Sed non in fide." *Ed. cit.*, p. 12. On man before the reception of grace: "Non est intelligens, non est requirens deum. ..." *Ed. cit.*, p. 16.

[95]"Sum enim Occamicae factionis. ..." *Adversus execrabilem Antichristi bullam* (1520), *W A* 6,599; *W A* 6,195; *Tr* II, Nr. 2544: *W A* 38,160 (1533).

[96]E.g. *W A* 9,9; 9,33; 9,40; 9,54; 9,83; 9,91.

[97]See the survey by Herbert Rommel, *Über Luthers Randbemerkungen von 1509/10* (Kiel, 1930), pp. 2ff. Rommel regards all these claims as fallacious, *ibid.*, p. 85.

schoolmen for their reliance on philosophy.[98] Though Luther once mentions the distinction between merits *de congruo* and *de condigno*, he refers here to actions of the will and not of the reason of man.[99] As we have seen, he will retain this distinction until his Commentary on the Psalms.

There is no trace in the marginals, however, of the *facere quod in se est* as applied to the human reason. Perhaps the most striking evidence is that the two main points in the frontal attack against the doctrine of the *facere quod in se est* in the *Disputatio contra scholasticam theologiam* (1517), which we mentioned above, are to be found in the marginals of 1509-1510: (1) the contrast between light and darkness to express the obstacle of philosophy for theology;[100] (2) the understanding of the preparation on the part of man as an effect of God's prevenient initiative.[101] The first time, then, that we encounter Luther, we find that he so stresses God's prevenience in the act of faith that there is no place any more for the nominalistic interpretation of the *fides ex auditu* as the faith man can acquire when he does what is in him.[102] For Luther *fides ex auditu* is a gift of God.

We may conclude, therefore, that Luther's statement "theology is heaven ... but man is earth"[103] cannot be reduced to nominalistic proportions.[104] Whereas in 1515-1516 Luther finally rejects the doctrine of the *facere quod in se est* as a Pelagian reliance on the capacities of man's unaided will, we find that in 1509-1510 Luther has already discarded the other nominalistic

---

[98]Comment on Lombard's statement that God is more true than can be conceived, I *Sent.* d. 23 c 4: "Hoc verbum olim erat verum: nunc tanta est philosophorum subtilitas, ut etiam si verum esset, falsum esset: quia nihil est nostris [!] incomprehensible et ineffabile." *W A* 9,47. Cf. "... nostri [!] subtiles magis quam illustres." *W A* 9,29.

[99]On Lombard's observation "Hac voluntate concupiscitur...." II *Sent.* d. 26 c 8: "...tanquam merito de congruo, non condigno." *W A* 9,72.

[100]*W A* 1,226: "... Totus Aristoteles ad theologiam est tenebrae ad lucem." *W A* 9,65: "... nunquam est compertum fumos terrae illustrare celum, sed magis impedire lucem super terram."

[101]*W A* 1,225: "... praeparatio et unica dispositio est aeterna dei electio et praedestinatio." *W A* 9,92; "Invocatio fit de fide. Unde per contrarium est iste ordo: mittitur, praedicatur, auditur exterius...."

[102]Gabriel Biel, III *Sent.* d. 23 q. 2 art. 2 concl. I. Cf. von Usingen. *Liber Tertius* (Erphurdiae, 1524), Q I^v; quoted by Nikolaus Häring, *Die Theologie des Erfurter Augustiner-Eremiten Bartholomaeus Arnoldi von Usingen* (Limburg an der Lahn, 1939), p. 120. Cf. Holcot, I *Sent.* q. I art. 6. It is regrettable that Ernst Bizer does not start his inquiry before Luther's commentary on the Psalms; *Fides ex auditu*, pp. 15ff.

[103]*W A* 9,65.

[104]Nominalism has been claimed by Roman Catholic scholars as the cradle of Luther's theology. Its alleged un- or anticatholic nature would then explain Luther's "defection." See H. Denifle, *Luther und Luthertum*, 1 Abt. 2, pp. 522, 536, 587; Willem van de Pol, *Het Wereld Protestantisme* (Roermond, 1956), p. 36. Louis Bouyer, *Du Protestantisme à l'Eglise* (Paris, 1954), p. 176. Josef Lortz, *Die Reformation in Deutschland*, I (2 ed. Freiburg i. Breisgau, 1941), 176.

inference from this doctrine which we encountered with Holcot, but also with Occam and Biel, as the thesis that the man who does what is in him acquires all information necessary for salvation. Not merely the "young Luther," but the "youngest Luther," even *before* beginning his career as a professor, as a biblical exegete, and eventually as a Reformer, has on points which later prove to be cornerstones in the structure of his thought become independent of the nominalistic theological tradition in which he was reared.

V

"IUSTITIA CHRISTI" AND *"IUSTITIA DEI"*:
LUTHER AND THE SCHOLASTIC
DOCTRINES OF JUSTIFICATION

1. LUTHER THE BORN HERETIC

The ever-increasing respect for Luther among Roman Catholic theologians
and historians of Christian thought is not only a sign of, but also a significant
contributing factor to contemporary ecumenical openness – especially so in
Germany. Yet at the same time we should realize that this more positive
evaluation of Luther is based on the conviction that the reformer was born
under the star of heresy. While it is granted that he articulated the biblical
message of sin, grace and forgiveness in Christ within the context of the late
medieval nominalism in which he was reared, it is exactly this context
which is regarded as essentially a-catholic or even as anti-catholic to the
extent that it obstructed Luther's grasp of the full and true catholic tradition
in the Middle Ages. Therefore, from the very beginning, access to the
specifically Catholic tradition had been denied to Luther.

By way of documentation it would suffice to refer here to the works of
the Frenchman Louis Bouyer, the German Joseph Lortz, and the Dutchman
Willem van de Pol; but the most recent research also seems to support this
interpretation of Luther's relation to the medieval theological tradition. Leif
Grane in his important dissertation Contra Gabrielem relates all the theses
of Luther in the "Disputatio contra scholasticam theologiam" of September,
1517 to the nominalistic theology of Gabriel Biel, including also those theses
which Luther had explicitly designated as directed "against all scholastic
theologians," contra *omnes* Scholasticos.[1] If Grane's procedure is justified,
we have here another indication that, whereas Luther thought he opposed
the medieval tradition, he actually attacked only the nominalistic tradition,
in this case its chief representative, Gabriel Biel.

---

[1]Luthers Auseinandersetzung mit Gabriel Biel in der Disputatio contra Scholasticam
Theologiam, 1517 (Copenhagen, 1962), 46f.

Another aspect of our problem is touched upon by Werner Dettloff, who in a recent well-documented study of late medieval theology[2] undertook the task to prove as one of his main theses that "the great tradition of Franciscan theology finds in Duns Scotus its last representative." If we assume the validity of Dettloff's description, this means that exactly two hundred years before the beginning of Luther's teaching activities at the University of Wittenberg (1509) genuine Scotism had died out and was therefore in Luther's time no longer a living tradition. Indeed, according to Dettloff there is in the later Middle Ages no single true and faithful curator of the scotistic heritage.

As regards the issues pertaining to the doctrine of justification, the author notices in the works of the late medieval "disciples" of Duns Scotus three major signs of the disintegration of late medieval theology: 1, the undermining of the concept of grace (the "Entleerung der Caritasvorstellung"); 2, the distortion of the understanding of God (the "Verzerrung des Gottesbildes"); 3, the encouragement of a view of the relation of God to man in the economy of salvation which no longer grasps the interdependence between God's rule and human behavior because of the "Förderung der Auffassung von dem nahezu beziehungslosen Nebeneinander von göttlichem Walten und menschlichem Bemühen in der Heilsökonomie."[3]

Elsewhere I have tried to show that the traditional evaluation of late medieval theology as a period of disintegration in the history of Christian thought – a view supported here by Dettloff – is unable to do justice to late medieval thought as it has come down to us through the various types of sources.[4] Contrary to the supposed "Entleerung der Caritasvorstellung" we notice not only in the category of academic publications in the strict sense of the word, but also in the equally important category of sermons and pastorally oriented writings of this time, the central place of *caritas*, which is consistently presented as the main theme in the life and death of Christ and which is seen as conveyed by means of the Sacraments, always without failing, namely, "stante lege," i.e., according to God's reliable law, granted together with the "gratia gratum faciens," sanctifying grace.

---

[2]Die Entwicklung der Akzeptations–und Verdienstlehre von Duns Skotus bis Luther (Münster, Westfalen, 1963), 363.
[3]Op. cit., 364.
[4]The Harvest of Medieval Theology (Cambridge, Mass, 1963), 425ff.

The idea of the distorted doctrine of God, the "Verzerrung des Gottesbildes," is derived by Dettloff from the nominalistic thesis according to which the will of God is the rule of all justice, "sola voluntas divina est regula omnis iustitae,"[5] in which he discerns a "Willkürgott," an arbitrary God ruled only by his own whims.[6] However, it is Gabriel Biel, to whom Dettloff refers in this context, who makes completely clear that the intention of this thesis is not to ascribe to God an arbitrary and lawless code of behavior but rather to formulate that God, in all his *opera ad extra*, does not act in accordance with *our* but in accordance with *his* own justice, which transcends our preconceived ideas as to the nature of justice.[7]

When in his third criticism Dettloff points to the absence of an inner nexus between God's rule and human behaviour, we should realize that the late medieval approach to the problem of human merit and God's reward is an effort to implement a basic axiom of Duns Scotus, namely: "Nihil creatum est a deo acceptandum," there is no need for God to accept anything from a creature; in other words, the relation between human behaviour and the divine reward is established by God himself. At least in the late medieval Franciscan tradition it is clear that God's reward is due to an initiative of God and is not based on the nature of the works rewarded – in other words, there is no *necessitas dei* because there is no such *necessitas rei*.

This does not mean that a reward when it is granted by God is due to a whimsical decision on his part. On the contrary, the free God has undertaken the covenant obligation or commitment to reward man's sincere and good efforts – his *facere quod in se est* –, by stimulating man's efforts with his grace and by rewarding them with his glory. Due to these covenant decrees of God, according to which he has committed himself to reward man's best efforts with his sanctifying grace and to reward the resulting good works with the gift of life eternal, an order is established before the beginning of time which can indeed be retraced to the inaccessible will, the goodness and mercy of God but which now, "de facto" or "de potentia ordinata," forms the basis of a reliable order of justice, the order of the *iustitia dei*. The usual synonym for the expression "de potentia ordinata,"

---

[5]Biel, I Sent. d 43 q. 1 art. 4 cor.

[6]Dettloff, op. cit., 364.

[7]"... secundum ineffabilem iustitiam, non nostram sed suam ..." Canonis Misse Expositio, ed. H. A. Oberman et W. J. Courtenay, I (Wiesbaden, 1963), Lect. 23 E, 212; cf. Augustinus, De Trinitate V, PL 42.874.

namely, "stante lege," should warn us not to interpret too readily the sources in terms of an arbitrary and lawless God. In his aseity God is indeed exlex, but this means that he stands above all law and is not dependent upon any heteronomous law, extra deum, *except for* the law of his own being, the compound of his will, his goodness and mercy.

The thesis "God's will is the rule of all justice" should not be regarded as a metaphysical but rather as an epistemological axiom: God's justice transcends human calculations, and it should be interpreted in terms of the centuries-long history of the debate on the relation of revelation and natural knowledge of God.

Nevertheless, the differences between the nominalistic and scotistic traditions in the later middle ages should not be minimized. Dettloff was unable to disassociate these two because he concentrated on the doctrine of justification, which in the late medieval sources is always associated and connected with a discussion of predestination. These differences do not appear in an analysis of the *content* of statements on justification but rather in the different *context* of justification, namely, in the diverging ways of understanding the doctrine of predestination. The independence of the nominalistic theologians vis-à-vis Duns Scotus and his disciples comes through most clearly in their rejection of the scotistic doctrine of the "praedestinatio ante praevisa merita," according to which the predestination of the elect in God's eternal council precedes the foreseen good works of the elect. This doctrine is rejected by the nominalists – with the notable exception of Gregory of Rimini – and transformed into a doctrine of "praescientia," the doctrine of the foreknowledge of God of the future behavior of both the elect and the damned. Hence it is obvious that even though the nominalistic theologians can present exactly the same arguments as the scotists when justification proper is under discussion, the moral behavior of man assumes for the nominalists an importance in the process of acceptation by God which would have been impossible within the setting of the scotistic doctrine of predestination.

But again, once aware of this decisive difference between the scotistic and nominalistic theological tradition, the conclusion seems unavoidable that Luther's attack upon the pelagianism of the *whole* scholastic tradition is considerably off the target; his critique applies perhaps to the derailment of the medieval tradition within the nominalism of the later middle ages, but does not come to grips with a Duns Scotus, who is interpreted *e mente auctoris*.

When we enlarge the scope of our discussion to include a third important late medieval school of thought, namely, Thomism, the impression is only confirmed that Luther could not possibly engage the true medieval tradition; just as Scotus' soteriology had been partly misunderstood by nominalizing disciples, partly overthrown by the nominalistic revolt, just so had Thomas not been well understood. To be more precise, the authority of the Sentences Commentary of the young Thomas with its pelagianizing emphasis on the "facere quod in se est" is regarded in the later middle ages as the authoritative version of his thought. This view had not gone unopposed: Capreolus (†1444), and after him Caietanus (†1534), had pointed out that the two Summas should be regarded as the definitive expression of the teaching of Thomas Aquinas. But in the theological tradition it had already become customary to view Thomas through the glasses of his Sentences Commentary and to quote him therefore, together with such authorities, as Scotus and Biel, as a supporter of the thesis that man can in a state of sin produce good works without the aid of grace.

Without making Luther in any sense personally responsible, one would therefore be inclined to regard him as a victim of his times: his attack "contra Pelagianos" could not do more than militate against his fellow-schoolmen in the nominalistic tradition; the main currents in the medieval theological tradition did not even enter his field of vision. It is exactly these currents which, according to a consensus in contemporary research, proved to be able to acquire the status of "official Catholic doctrine" at the Council of Trent. Thus Luther seems to be the classical, or rather the medieval, example of a victim of the so-called *ignorantia invincibilis*.

2. MEDIEVAL PELAGIANISM

Before we pursue the question sketched above, whether the theological program of the Reformation is due to a clearly tragic misunderstanding on the part of Luther, we have first to clarify another point. When, after a study of the schools and school opinions in the later middle ages, one arrives at a study of Luther, for instance, of his early (1517) disputation against scholastic theology, one is struck by the fact that the reformer does not by any means identify the whole scholastic theological tradition with nominalism but rather, acutely aware of the varieties of positions, takes up each point separately in order to direct his attack especially and precisely against that theologian whom he regards as responsible for each particular thesis. From this basis, then, he directs himself several times "contra communes," against all scholastic theologians together.

An important indication of the fact that Luther has not fallen victim to a tragic lack or loss of vision – the *ignorantia invincibilis*, which, it should be noted, he himself had discarded as a valid excuse[8] – can be found in Luther's Preface to the second Disputation against the Antinomians (1538). There we find the statement: "Ita sub nomine ecclesiae et Christi ipsissimi [the 'doctores in papatu'] Pelagiani fuerunt, ut taceam, quod postea subinde peiores facti sunt. Occam enim et moderni . . ." In the name of the Church and of Christ the medieval theologians themselves became pelagians, not to mention Occam and his school who shortly afterwards became even worse (pelagians).[9] Luther clearly differentiates here between the earlier tradition, approximately from Lombard to Scotus, and the succeeding school of Occam and his disciples. It is only these last ones whom he assails on the grounds of their shameless teaching that reason without the illumination by the Holy Spirit can love God above everything else and secondly because of their teaching that Christ would have earned for the Christians only the first grace.[10] These two theses are as a matter of fact characteristic of nominalistic theology, but cannot – as modern research has clearly shown – without a considerable measure of unfairness be put on the account of Thomism and Scotism.

In the light of these findings, we have therefore to reformulate our original question in the following way: what could Luther have meant by the statement that the earlier doctors also proved to be pelagians, albeit in a more hidden and refined manner than Occam and his followers.

To answer this question we turn to another Preface of Luther, namely, the one dating from the year 1545, the Preface to the first part of the Latin edition of Luther's works which became so famous because of its description of the so-called "Turmerlebnis." In the past this Preface has been molded in so many directions and Luther scholars have deduced from its few pages so many different Luther-figures that a usage of these passages in our time has almost become *the* characteristic of unscientific Luther research. Therefore a few introductory observations:

In my opinion it has proved to be impossible to use this Preface to date with any degree of precision the so-called "Turmerlebnis." The preceding *theological* decision of the scholar involved, as to which point in the thought of

---

[8]Thesis 35: "Non est verum, quod ignorantia invincibilis a toto excusat," W A I.225 (Sept. 1517).

[9]Disputationen Dr. Martin Luthers, ed. Paul Drews (Göttingen, 1896), 340. Cf. W A 39 I. 419. 17–19 (Jan. 1538). Cf. W A I.373, 24f (1518).

[10]"Occam enim et moderni, ut vocantur, sceleste docent, quod ratio sine Spiritu Sancto possit Deum super omnia diligere, et quod tantum meruerit primam gratiam." Ibid.

Luther is to be regarded as "the centre" and what therefore is to be proclaimed as the break with the scholastic tradition, has always been the decisive factor in the *historical* fixation of the year and date of the "Turmerlebnis."

In the second place, we are not confronted with a sudden, unprepared vision. Luther himself says that before he understood Romans I, verse 17, he has "importunately beaten upon Paul at that place, most ardently desiring to know what S. Paul wanted."[11] Here Luther is describing the second of the three stages, *oratio, meditatio, tentatio,* which he had designated as the appropriate theological *ordo* in his Preface to the first part of his German writings in 1539: "Secondly [after *oratio*], you should meditate, that is, not only in your heart, but also externally, by actually repeating and comparing oral speech and literal words of the book, reading and rereading them with diligent attention and reflection, so that you may see what the Holy Spirit means by them."[12]

Some thirty-five years earlier Luther had said in his first comentary on the Psalms: "meditari est pulsare," in order to interpret Matthew 7:7, "knock and the door will be opened." Luther uses here the image of Moses, who, by his knocking (pulsare), brings forth fountains of spouting water.[13] Whereas Luther later, in 1539, is to designate the third state as *tentatio,* he

---

[11]W A 54. 186. For an early parallel to the Preface of 1545 see Heinrich Bornkamm, "Luthers Bericht über seine Entdeckung der iustitia dei," ARG 37 (1940), 123f., where one finds reference to W A 5. 144, 1–23 (1519). More explicit: idem, "Iustitia dei in der Scholastik und bei Luther," ARG 39 (1942), 27. In answer to the challenge posed by Denifle's thesis according to which Luther's intepretation of the iustitia Dei is a "discovery" of what had been always assumed in scholasticism (Die abendländischen Schriftausleger bis Luther über iustitia dei [Röm I: 17] und iustificatio. Quellenbelege zu Denifles Luther und Luthertum, 2 ed. I 2 [Mainz, 1905]), reiterated by Joseph Lortz (Luther discovers only "neu für sich"; Die Reformation in Deutschland I² [Frieburg i. Br., 1941], 183) Karl Holl as regards the exegetical tradition ("Die iustitia dei in der vorlutherischen Bibelauslegung des Abendlandes." Festschrift für Adolf von Harnack, 1921. Gesammelte Aufsätze, III [1928], 171–88) and Heinrich Bornkamm as regards the systematic tradition (art. cit., ARG 39 [1942], 1–46), called attention to the *pluriformity* and unclarity on this point within scholasticism in connection with the interrelated concepts of iustitia-misericordia. Whereas we are of the opinion that herewith the challenge of Denifle/Lortz has been answered, we believe that our introduction of the twin concepts of iustitia Dei – iustitia Christi enables us now to do justice also to the consensus and basic *uniformity* in the medieval tradition. Seen against this background, the several motives which played their part already in Luther's first Commentary on the Psalms prove to form one pattern. See section III. We should state explicitly at this point that the twin terms we employ – "iustitia Christi" and "iustitia Dei" –] are *interpretative* concepts, introduced to articulate and clarify the *duplex iustitia* operative in all medieval doctrines of justification.

[12]W A 50.659; we follow here the translation of Lewis W. Spitz, editor of vol. 34, "Career of the Reformer" IV, Luther's Works (Philadelphia, 1960), 286.

[13]"Igitur 'meditari' est pulsare cum Mose hanc petram, 'decurrere' autem 'aquas' est erumpere multos sensus et copiam intelligentie." W A 55.2. I, 15. Exod. 17: 6; Num. 20: II.

calls this in 1513 *experientia:* "Expertus novit, quod qui in lege Domini mediatatur, breviter et *subito* [!] plurima docetur ...": He who has experienced this knows that when one meditates upon the law of God, one learns many things at once and suddenly.[14] The sudden moment of insight after extended energies invested in the task of *meditari* is the characteristic of a theological break-through *as such* and should not be exclusively connected with one moment in which Luther saw the full significance of Romans 1:17.

A third fact is important for a sober interpretation of the Preface of 1545: Luther's so-called "Turmerlebnis" is by no means unique or unprecedented in the medieval tradition. In the course of history, from the autobiographical statement of St. Paul about his experience on the road to Damascus and St. Augustine's report on his conversion in the eighth book of his Confessions, we find similar "Turmerlebnisse" with Thomas Bradwardine, Richard FitzRalph, Johannes Gerson, less explicitly with Andreas Karlstadt, but again more emphatic with Gasparo Contarini and John Calvin.[15] This state of affairs allows us to conclude that there is a "Turmerlebnis" tradition which provides for a conceptual framework and an established language, in which and through which one can formulate one's own important discoveries. Luther points *expressis verbis* to Book VIII, of the Confessions of St. Augustine in his comments upon Psalm 76. Here also the experientia and meditatio are connected with each other: "If you want to have an example of this interpretation, then turn to the conversion of St. Augustine as described in the eighth book of his *Confessions* ... Therefore no words will enable one to understand this Psalm if one has not undergone this compunction and meditation."[16]

In connection with this statement of Luther, Adolf Hamel has observed

---

[14]W A 55.2.I, 16. 2f; cf. W A 55. 2. I, 55–56 and Excursus W A 55. 2. I, 39ff.

[15]Bradwardine, De Causa Dei (London, 1618), I. 35. 308 C–D; FitzRalph, cf. W. A. Pantin, The English Church in the fourteenth century (Cambridge, England, 1955), 133, Gerson, "Super magnificat VIII," Opera omnia, ed. L. E. Du Pin (Antwerpen, 1706), IV. 360 A; Karlstadt, De spiritu et litera, ed. Ernst Kähler (Halle, 1952), 5; Contarini, cf. F. Dittrich, Gasparo Contarini (Braunsberg, 1885), 488ff.

Calvin's *subita conversio,* dated by P. Sprenger in 1527–28, should also be understood in the light of this tradition. For literature see his Das Rätsel um die Bekehrung Calvins (Neukirchen, 1960).

In the augustinian epistemological tradition there is always an element of 'suddenness' (cognitio through illumination). After the aristotelian-thomistic epistemology (cognitio through sense perception) had secularized and transformed the *event* of cognitio into the *process* of cognitio, the *subito* or *statim* becomes the characteristic of a special revelation or of the supernatural gift of sapientia, often used to express the passivity of the mystic in the visio Dei. Cf. Bonaventura, Itinerarium mentis, Prol. 2; Tauler, Sermo Rom. 8:14, G. Hofmann, Johannes Tauler, Predigten (Freiburg, 1961), no. 45 [ed. Vetter, 43], 345.

[16]W A 3. 549. 26–32. See also Ernst Wolf, Staupitz und Luther (Leipzig, 1927), 145ff.

that "die durch die Bekehrung eingetretene Wandlung in Augustins theologischer Anschauung bei Luther keinen Widerhall findet, es interessiert ihn an dieser Bekehrung nur der seelische Vorgang und nicht der sachliche Gehalt."[17] In view of what we have said above, it is perhaps more accurate to state this in the following way: Luther understands the conversion of St. Augustine not historically but tropologically; in other words, contrary to the medieval examples to which we have referred, he does not understand the conversion as a unique irrepeatable event which took place in the past, once and for all, but rather as the *conditio sine qua non* of each real theological discovery, as the necessary preamble to every true insight of the interpreter of Scripture. Such a conversion is furthermore not an experience independent of Scripture but rather the "passive" reception of the Word, the true understanding of the Word. In this act, experience, and event, one's own philosophical structure of thought (ratio) is penetrated and pierced and one's own philosophical vocabulary and use of language (verbis uti) is changed in accordance with Holy Scripture;[18] this is for Luther "Sprachereignis"!

The three stages, oratio, meditatio, tentatio are well known in the preceding tradition but have not always been interpreted in the way in which we find it with Luther in his first Commentary on the Psalms. The observation in the critical apparatus of the new critical edition is appropriate: "Wo (hingegen) in der Scholastik die theologische Erkenntnis ihrerseits als praktisches Erkennen bezeichnet und gegen das spekulative Erkennen abgesetzt wird, nämlich bei den Franziskanern und Augustinern, geschieht das nicht im Hinblick auf die Anfechtung, sondern wegen der von der Erkenntnis intendierten Affektion und Tätigkeit durch die Liebe".[19] One could very well add at this point: Anfechtung, or spiritual turmoil and insecurity, is in the medieval tradition not first of all concerned with faith but rather with the works of love which – if present – provide for the assurance that one lives in a state of grace and which are thus the effective antidote against Anfechtung.

Hamel is therefore completely right when he says that in the case of St. Augustine's "conversion" Luther is interested in the spiritual experience,

---

[17]Der junge Luther und Augustin, I (Gütersloh, 1934), 160.

[18]"Sequitur tandem ex predicitis, quod Scriptura sancta aptius et melius utitur verbis, quam curiosi disputatores in suis studiis. Immo, nisi quis eorum imaginationibus renuncians velut calceos suos cum Mose exuerit, non poterit ad istum rubum flammeum appropinquare, 'terra enim sancta est.'" W A 55.2. I, 21.21–22.2. "Tercius est non docere malum (i.e., maxime docere bona). Quos tres gradus in Augustino ..." W A 55. 2. I, 24. 12f.

[19]Ed. cit., 56. 8–13.

but – and this is an important qualification – only insofar as this experience, in close conjunction with oratio, gives access to and opens one up for the word of Scripture. In the tentatio one does not therefore transcend the state of faith by way of the evidence for the presence and sincerity of one's faith found in the actual works of love, but it is through tentatio that one appropriates this faith. The true theological sequence: oratio, meditatio, tentatio, is therefore intimately related to the insight into the relation of Word and Spirit, of spiritus and litera.[20]

The gulf between Luther and Gabriel Biel is striking; with Biel the sequence is turned exactly the other way around: lectio, meditatio, oratio. According to Biel, the lectio or reading of Holy Scripture enables one through the natural virtue of prudentia to discover what one should ask from God in one's prayer, in the last stage of this sequence. Meditation about the basic principles established by the reading of Scripture, namely God's power and goodness and one's own sinfulness, produces fear and love, timor and amor. Thus the will is propelled and guided towards the bonorum petitio, the prayer for God's good gifts.[21]

In 1539 Luther has explicitly rejected the divorce of letter and spirit which is implicit in the view which regards the relation of lectio (the letter) and meditato (the spirit or intention) as two *successive* stages; meditation is lectio and relectio, reading and rereading "with diligent attention and reflection, so that you may see what the Holy Spirit means. And take care that you do not grow weary or think that you have done enough when you have read, heard, and spoken them once or twice and that you then have complete understanding . . ." But it was already in his first commentary on the Psalms that he based meditation directly upon the word of Scripture, upon the literal sense of Scripture, which is for him the sensus propheticus.

The difference between Luther and Biel comes through even more clearly when we realize that it is exactly the central place of prudentia, the virtue of natural wisdom, which enables Biel to enlist the sequence, reading, meditation, prayer, into the service of the "facere quod in se est," as part therefore of man's best efforts to which God has committed himself. In

---

[20]Emphasized by Gerhard Ebeling as the main theme in the first Commentary on the Psalms: "Die Anfänge von Luthers Hermeneutik," ZThK 48 (1951), 172–230; 187. Cf. his Luther, Einführung in sein Denken (Tübingen, 1964), 100ff.

[21]"Primum ergo est per prudentiam cognoscere petenda, que confert lectio. Secundum vigilans et studiosa cognitorum masticatio, que est meditatio excitans fervorem et affectum. Demum sequitur desideratorum bonorum petitio." Sermones Dominicales (Hagenau, 1510), 47 C. Cf. Gerson, "De mystica theologia speculativa," cons. 8 G; Opera III. 4IIf. Cf. Thomas ST II II. q 82. art. 3.

answer to the question how God could possibly in the new law have required such a spontaneous and spiritual virtue as love, Biel answers that love is indeed not a human task insofar as it is *God* alone who can infuse it in us; but *we* are responsible for the preparation and the later preservation. The preparation for the infusion of love takes place exactly in this reading, meditation, prayer.[22]

By emphasizing the difference between Luther and Biel on the basis of the Reformer's first biblical commentary from the years 1513–1516, it might seem that Luther due to his biblical studies outgrew his nominalistic teachers. As a matter of fact, it is clear from the earliest literary evidence, the marginals of 1509 to Peter Lombard's Sentences, that the "facere quod in se est" of the human reason is rejected.[23] This means that what was the function of the human prudentia in Biel's thought is here assigned to the insight or illumination granted by God.[24] The prudentia cannot discern in the biblical passage anything else than the litera occidens; it is the spirit which shows the true literal sense.

But it is in the first commentary on the Psalms that we see that with the theme "spiritus et litera" a second theme is interwoven: the relation of the lex vetus and the lex nova, the relation of Law and Gospel. We believe that it is exactly in the conjunction of these two themes that we can show that Luther has radically re-interpreted the "facere quod in se est," both as regards the preparation for the reception of the gift of love and as regards the preservation of this gift. With this new stance Luther assumes a position which is not only independent of the nominalistic position but independent of the whole medieval scholastic tradition. Luther looked beyond the central issue in nominalistic theology, namely the *preparation* for grace, to the problem of the *conservation*, or preservation, of grace. In pursuing the traditional battle contra Pelagianos in this larger framework, he had to confront the whole scholastic tradition.

3. AGAINST A COMMON FRONT

We can now return to Luther's Preface of 1545 and read there: "Though I

---

[22]"Sed quomodo ad hanc dilectionem perveniemus? Responsio: . . . lectio, meditatio, oratio, quam sequitur contemplatio . . ." Sermones Dominicales, 85 C/D.

[23]Cf. my "'Facientibus quod in se est Deus non denegat gratiam.' Robert Holcot O.P. and the beginnings of Luther's Theology," HTR 55 (1962), 317–42.

[24]"Sed confitemur tibi, quia indigemus ostensore bonorum, et ex nobis non videmus ista bona. Sed lumen vultus tui (i.e. fides . . .) signatum est (. . .) super nos (i.e. desursum . . .)." W A 55. 2. 1, 80, 28–81, 2; cf. 83, 5: "et revelata parvulis (sine dubio super quos 'signatum est hoc lumen')."

lived as a monk without reproach, I felt that I was a sinner before God with an extremely disturbed conscience. I could not believe that he was placated by my satisfaction (satisfactione).[25] I did not love, yes, I hated the righteous God who punishes sinners; and secretly, if not blasphemously, certainly murmuring greatly, I was angry with God and said: 'As if, indeed, it is not enough, that miserable sinners, eternally lost through original sin, are crushed by every kind of calamity by the law of the Decalogue, without having God add pain to pain by the Gospel and also by the Gospel threatening us with his righteousness and wrath!' At last by the mercy of God, meditating day and night, I gave heed to the context of the words. There I began to understand that the righteousness of God is that by which the righteous lives by a gift of God, namely by faith."[26]

Two hundred years earlier Thomas Bradwardine had posed a seemingly identical but essentially different question; he discovered, when illumined by God, that grace is always prevenient. That is the traditional point of departure in the centuries-long battle against the Pelagians. Bradwardine was concerned to establish from Scripture and the Fathers "justification by grace alone" and thus to show that the sinner cannot acquire grace with his own powers. Luther also wrestled with this problem, as we can already clearly see in his first marginal annotations to Lombard's Sentences. But here, in this Preface, Luther is not dealing with the works of *sinners* but rather with those of the *just*; as he says, the issue is satisfaction required of the penitent following absolution. Put in the terminology of scholasticism, the first concern is not the reception of grace, the praeparatio, but the continuation of its presence, the conservatio. His question is: what does it mean when Paul says that the *justified* lives by faith?

It should be granted at this point that from the perspective of Luther's radical answer, according to which justification is always and in each case opus Dei extra nos, this distinction seems to evaporate and has all the appearance of being artificial. But when we want to compare Luther with the preceding tradition, we have for a moment to abstract from his later insights and place ourselves at the moment at which he lived as "a monk without reproach." This expression "without reproach" does not only indicate a certain degree of perfection, but first of all that Luther, as

---

[25]Cf. "Ergo oportet nos [pro actualibus peccatis] satisfacere. Illa est doctrina papatus et inventa ab illis sua opinione, inventae sunt multae viae reconciliandi Deum. Hoc argumentum videmus esse fontem et originem omnium monasteriorum, missarum, peregrinationum, invocationis sanctorum et similium, quibus omnes conantur satisfacere pro peccatis." Disputatio de Iustificatione, 1536, Drews, op. cit., 59. Cf. W A 39 I. 111.

[26]W A 54. 185; cf. Luther's Works, op. cit., 336f.

"confessus et absolutus," tried after the reception of the sacrament of absolution to live in the right way in the *state of grace*.[27] Luther's problem was the elevation in the New Testament of the standard of justice presented by the Old Testament, especially the Decalogue. If the New Testament is new insofar as it requires a higher degree of righteousness, how can it then possibly be the good tidings of the redemption in Jesus Christ?

One recognizes here without difficulty the old problem which had agitated medieval theologians in their effort to understand St. Augustine, according to whom the New Testament goes beyond the Old Testament in that it claims not only "man's hand" but also "man's heart," his interior motivation, his will. We are faced then not with a mere personal question of Luther, necessitated by this or that psychological structure of his personality or determined by his adherence to this or that theological school. It is *the* question of scholasticism par excellence in connection with the clarification of the relation of the lex vetus and the lex nova.[28]

It is impossible within the context of this article to describe with the necessary detail all the different solutions which the middle ages have produced. The striking lack of monographs in this area is an indication that quite a lot of preliminary research is still to be performed. Some chief moments in the medieval history of the discussion of this question deserve our attention. In the meantime we keep in mind the thesis of Luther, quoted above, according to which all the "doctores in Papatu" are to be regarded as pelagians, though Occam and his disciples, as worse specimens, are "peiores."

In a time not too distant from Luther, we find with *Gabriel Biel* a florilegium, a multiform collection of quotations from Bonaventure,

---

[27]This emphasis on conservatio rather than on praeparatio also underlies Luther's second most important autobiographical statement, contained in his letter to Staupitz of May 30, 1518. W A I.525–527; Luther's Works, Vol. 48, ed. Gottfried G. Krodel (Phil. 1963), 65–70. Here the key word is not 'satisfactio' but its related 1517 parallel 'poenitentia': ". . . poenitentia is genuine only if it begins with love for iustitia and for God"; "The commandments of God become sweet when they are read not only in books, but also in the wounds of the sweetest Savior." Ibid., 65f. This understanding of poenitentia is expressed in the first of the 95 theses: "Dominus et magister noster Jesus christus dicendo: Penitentiam agite etc., omnem vitam fidelium penitentiam esse voluit," W A 1.233; cf. Luther's Works, Vol. 31 , ed. Harold J. Grimm (Phil., 1957), 25. Luther's point is therefore lost if one translates 'penitentiam agite' with 'repent.' As the characteristic of the life of the faithful in a state of grace it should be rendered by 'do penance'. This first thesis assails the indulgences exactly because this 'do penance' applies to omnis vita, not merely to justification (iustificatio impii) in the sacrament of penance.

[28]Cf. Lombardus, III Sent. d. 40, q 1, n. 1; Bonaventura, III Sent. d. 40, art. I q. 3 resp. 5 ad 5; Thomas, ST I II q. 107, art, I, ad 2; Scotus, Ox. III d. 40, q. I, n. 8; Biel, III Sent. d. 40, q. I, art. 3, dub. I.

Thomas, Scotus, and of course from Augustine. He does not seem to be particularly interested in carving out a special position for himself. Yet it is remarkable that, compared with his sources, he places a comparatively greater emphasis on the lex nova as *lex*: "the righteousness of the Christian has to be greater than that of the scribes and the Pharisees . . ."; "if we want to be saved, our righteousness has to be more abundant"; "this righteousness is not just determined by our external deeds but also by our internal deeds."[29] Biel understands the fulfillment of the law by Christ as a "making complete" and he uses as evidence the opinion of St. Augustine that in the new covenant not only the hand but also the will is subject to the law.[30] Together with the whole medieval scholastic tradition he is of the opinion that the Old Testament as ceremonial and civil law is now cancelled, precisely because in those two kinds of law only the hand and therefore only the external actions were dealt with.[31] The law of Christ is the fulfillment of the Mosaic law in a few words because of the interiorization of the righteousness intended by it. From this point of departure it is understandable that Biel can regard the merits of Christ as the chief and principal merits, but never as the "sola et totalis causa meritoria,"[32] by which we are saved. Thus he can say in one sermon, "if our merits would not complete those of Christ, the merits of Christ would be insufficient, yes, nihil."[33] It is therefore *necessary* that Christ is not only Redeemer but also Legislator, since, without the complement of obedience to His Law, His redemption would fall short of assuring man of his eternal salvation.

We find with *Duns Scotus* – though in another context – the same ideas about Christ as Legislator and about the extension of the old law of the hand to the new spiritual law of the New Testament which claims the obedience of the whole man, hand and will. As we saw above, the doctrine of predestination functions here as the protective wall round the doctrine of justification. Nevertheless, the will has to produce the good works, since these good works are presupposed by the acceptatio dei. Scotus too understands the fulfillment of the law by Christ as "making full," "making more complete." Christ the Legislator has after all stipulated love as a requirement, a duty; the yoke of the new law, however, is less heavy than that of the Old Testament because of the cancellation of the ceremonial and

---

[29]Sermones Dominicales, 60 B.C.

[30]Loc. cit., 60 F; III Sent. d. 40, q. i, art. 3, dub. i.

[31]III Sent. d. 40, q. i, art. 2 concl.

[32]III Sent. d. 19, q. i, art. 2 concl. 5.

[33]"Cui, nisi nostrum meritum iungatur, insufficiens, immo nullum erit." Sermones de Festivitatibus Christi, 11 G.

civil laws.[34]

Thomas Aquinas has especially emphasized the continuity between Moses and Christ while yet, at the same time, showing quite clearly the newness of the Gospel.[35] It seems clear that the quotation from St. Augustine's De spiritu et litera is most central: "What are the laws of God which God has written in our hearts, other than a presence of the Holy Spirit, the finger of God, through whose presence in our heart that love is poured in, which is the fulfillment of the Law and the end of all constraint."[36] Yet Thomas too can refer to Christ as the Legislator:[37] though the new law is primarily the Holy Spirit written in our hearts, yet, at the same time, the new law comes through also in the moral and sacramental precepts; the law therefore exists also outside of man as his "Gegenüber." These precepts concern the "dispositiva ad gratiam Spiritus Sancti et ad usum huius gratiae pertinentia."[38] The natural works are being elevated ontologically by grace to a higher level, so that – without the scotistic link of the acceptation by God – the works of the righteous, in whom the Holy Spirit is sacramentally operating, can now count as fully meritorious, de condigno, in a divine "quid pro quo" secundum debitum iustitiae.

---

[34]The yoke of the new law is lighter: "In lege nova, moralia sunt eadem quae tunc [i.e., in lege vetero], sed magis explicita; caeremonialia sunt multo pauciora et leviora, quae imposita sunt per Christum; iudicialia nulla sunt posita per Christum, sed magis est lex mititatis et humilitatis, in qua non oportet habere iudicialia." Oxon. I, III, qu. 40 (Vives, tom 15, n. 3, 1085a). Fear and love represent the contrast between the Old and the New Law: "Illa dicitur esse lex timoris, haec autem amoris." (Ibid. n. 8, 1097). The ceremonial laws were heavier and more in number: "Quantum ad caeremonialia dico, quod illa fuit multo gravior et quantum ad multitudinem et quantum ad difficultatem observandi." (Ibid. n. 4, 1085). The new law is lighter in as much as it is accompanied by more and more effective help and aid to accomplish this law: "Simpliciter ergo plura adiutoria et efficaciora sunt in lege christiana quam veteri, et ideo ex ea parte lex nova est levior." (Ibid. n. 7, 1093) By far the greatest help is an incitement which the Old Testament did not provide; when we fulfill the New Testament law, there is the promise of life eternal: "Est autem unum adiutorium valde notabile, quia nobis pro observatione legis christianae promittitur explicite vita aeterna; illis autem vel raro vel numquam nisi bona temporalia promittebantur; numquam autem tantum alliciunt animam ad servandum legem bona temporalia sicut bona aeterna." (Ibid. 1094)

[35]Cf. Yves M.-J. Congar, O.P., "Le sens de 'l'Économie' salutaire dans la 'théologie' de S. Thomas d'Aquin (Somme Théologique)," in Festschrift Joseph Lortz, ed. Erwin Iserloh and Peter Manns, II (1958), 73ff. As far as I can see, it has not yet been noticed that though there is no parallel in scholastic theology for Luther's expression "iustitia Dei passiva," Thomas knows a "iustificatio passive accepta": "iustificatio passive accepta importat motum ad iustitiam sicut et calefactio motum ad calorem," ST I II q. 113, art. I. This word "passive" is however understood here from the point of view of man who is drawn into this process of justification; "passive" thus interpreted stands for what we have designated as the iustitia inhaerens or iustitia Christi.

[36]PL 44. 222. Cf. the concise summary by Anselm Forster, Gesetz und Evangelium bei Girolamo Seripando (Paderborn, 1963), 69f.

[37]ST I II q. 108, art. I c.a.

[38]ST I II q. 106, art. I ad I.

In the *Acta of the Council of Trent* we find that Ambrosius Catharinus, who definitely understood Luther better than the first opponents, noted among the errors of the Lutherans: "Christus non est legislator."[39] The General of the Augustinians, Seripando, still tried at Trent to remove from the records the formula "Christus etiam legislator" exactly because the Christian is, according to him, "per Christum liberatus a lege Dei."[40] In an impressive intervention Seripando reminds the fathers of the fact that St. Augustine applies Psalm 9, verse 21 – "appoint him, oh Lord, to be Legislator over them" – not to Christ but exactly to the Antichrist.[41] Seripando's opposition was too much associated with his doctrine of double justification to have his stance influence the final conciliar decrees. Christ remained for all the representatives of all the schools the Legislator: those who are Christ's have to earn their salvation with fear and trembling.[42] Thus the "conditio observationis mandatorum" is retained as the Roman Catholic conciliar doctrine.[43] The condition remains that the laws are to be fulfilled. As before in the Middle Ages, those who are in a state of grace have indeed sacramentally received the "iustitia Christi," but their works have in one way or another to meet the requirements of the "iustitia Dei," whether by ontological elevation or by acceptation.[44]

Luther's discovery of the iustitia Dei passiva was not that grace is always prevenient. That would have been nothing new, since after all that was exactly the main theme of the traditional medieval anti-pelagian campaign. With such a discovery Luther would have indeed only attacked the disciples of Occam. Neither was the novelty of his discovery located in the fact that he would have taught that the sinner is justified through sanctifying grace, the gratia gratum faciens, and thus receives into himself the iustitia Christi. This the Thomists and Scotists had also known. If this had been the case, then Heinrich Denifle would have been right when he described Luther as a "Halbwisser." Luther has, however, attacked the whole medieval tradition as it was later confirmed at the Council of Trent. According to this tradition the "iustitia Christi" is granted in the justification to the sinner as gratia or caritas. But the iustitia Dei is not granted together with the iustitia Christi. According to this tradition the "iustitia Christi" is granted in the process of

[39]CT V. 472. Cf. Forster, op. cit., 76f.
[40]CT V. 472.
[41]Enarr. in Ps. 9; PL 36. 125. CT V. 666. Applied by Luther to Christ!! W A 55. 1 1, 76.4.
[42]Denz. 806. In the new edition Denzinger-Schönmetzer, Enchiridion Symbolorum (Freiburg, 1963³²), 1541.
[43]Denz. 830; ed. cit., 1570.
[44]Compare the verb "debere" in the Tridentine Decree on justification (Denz. 836–1576) with Luther's "pro quibus debemus nos satisfacere"; Drews, op. cit., 59.

justification, but the iustitia Dei is not granted together with or attached to the iustitia Christi. The iustitia Dei remains the finis, the goal, or the "Gegenüber" of the viator who is propelled on his way to the eternal Jerusalem by the iustitia Christi. The iustitia Dei is the standard according to which the degree of appropriation and the effects of the iustitia Christi are measured and will be measured in the Last Judgment. The iustitia Dei is the eternal immutable Law of God.

One can summarize, therefore, Luther's discovery in the following sentence: *the heart of the Gospel is that the iustitia Christi and the iustitia Dei coincide and are granted simultaneously*. It is on the basis of this view that the disciples of Occam are not presented or unmasked as Pelagians as such, but rather as "worse Pelagians," as those who "postea subinde peiores facti sunt!" It is not the task of those who are justified to implement the iustitia Christi by relating themselves in an optimal fashion to the iustitia Dei. The Pauline message is the Gospel exactly because the iustitia Dei – revealed at the Cross as the iustitia Christi – is given to the faithful per fidem. The "fides Christo formata"[45] replaces the medieval "fides charitate formata"; in other words, "faith living in Christ" has come in the stead of "faith active in love" as it had been formulated and defined in a unanimous medieval tradition and as it can be found with Thomas Aquinas, Duns Scotus, Gabriel Biel, et al., including the Council of Trent.

4. THE LAST JUDGMENT: NOW!

Herewith our original question has been answered, at least in broad outline. Yet the last phrase we used, "fides Christo formata," calls for some further clarification to protect it against an otherwise too easy criticism. Therefore, two closing observations about the expressions "extra nos" and "pro nobis."

1. From the earliest times onward there has been a strong tendency in the history of Luther research to be highly suspicious of such terms as habitus and forma, c.q. forma inhaerens, usually regarded as typically scholastic and

---

[45]"Sicut vos dicitis charitatem ipsam imbuere fidem, sic dicimus nos Christum esse formam istius fidei." W A 40 I. 229, 8f. Cf. ". . . sic dicimus nos Christum esse formam istius fidei et sic apprehensus est iustitia Christiana; propter hanc reputat nos iustos et donat vitam." (Ibid.) Karin Bornkamm points to Luther's statement ". . . quod Christus sit mea forma, sicut paries informatur albedine. Sic tam proprie et inhesive, ut albedo in pariete, sic Christus manet in me et ista vita vivit in me; et vita, qua vivo, est Christus." W A 40 I. 283, 7ff. Luthers Auslegungen des Galaterbriefs von 1519 und 1531. Ein Vergleich (Berlin, 1963), 97. Very important is the section entitled "Christus als forma fidei," 93ff.

therefore as un-Lutheran. Indeed, it would not be difficult to introduce ample evidence that Luther rejected the Aristotelian anthropology, at least insofar as this anthropology was employed in medieval scholasticism. It is only insofar as such terms as habitus and forma represent this particular anthropology that it would be inappropriate to use them in a characterization of Luther's thought such as we suggested with the expression "fides Christo formata."

It is much more precise and relevant, however, to investigate the basis of Luther's criticism and the reason this tradition of suspicion against these terms originated: Luther criticized the philosophers because they claimed to be able to say *how* man is without learning from theology *whence* and *whither* man is, where he comes from and what his goal is.[46] Of the two usually employed medieval anthropological frameworks, the historical-dynamic image of "driver and horse" is therefore more attractive than the ontological-static image of "form and matter."

The first image is much more suitable for a genuine theological anthropology which regards man as a "viator," as a being *en route*. The "extra nos" is for Luther the connection between the doctrine of justification and a theological anthropology. This expression should, however, not be misunderstood in the forensic sense of the word. The central concept "extra nos" does not stand on the side of an imputatio-justification over against a unio-justification. It does not prove that we are justified "outside ourselves" before the chair of God the judge (*in foro Dei*), in such a way that grace would not be imparted but "only" imputed. The intention of the "extra nos" is to show that justification is not based on a claim of man, on a debitum iustitiae.

The righteousness granted is not one's property but one's possession. It is not *proprietas* but rather *possessio*. We cannot pursue here the subtle implications of the connotations of these two words in the history of Roman law, nor describe the extent to which the contrast between the two terms plays its part especially in marriage law, and hence in that whole mystical tradition in which marriage provides the symbol for the exchange of goods between Christ and the faithful, a tradition with which Luther via Staupitz was well acquainted.

We point here so emphatically to the difference between proprietas and possessio because we believe that an understanding of the meaning of both

---

[46]Römerbriefvorlesung 1515–16; Rom. 12: 2: "Et sic est [Christianus] in peccato, quoad terminum a quo, et in iustitia quoad terminum ad quem." W A 56. 442. "Nam philosophia efficientem [causam] certe non novit, similiter nec finalem." Disputatio de homine, 1526; Drews, op. cit. 90–92. Thesis 13. Cf. W A 39 I. 176.

implies a terminological advance after centuries of debate in the history of Luther intepretation between those who have argued in favor of a justification by imputation against those who claimed that impartation was definitely the best one-word summary. The meaning of the words "extra nos" comes through in connection with the term possessio: "Extra nos esse est ex nostris viribus non esse, et quidem iustitia possessio nostra, quia nobis donata est ex misericordia, tamen est aliena a nobis, quia non meruimus eam."[47] The "extra nos" is therefore directed against the separation of iustitia Christi in us from the iustitia Dei over against us and thus directed against the fides caritate formata.

2. In the history of Luther research it is customary to emphasize the expression "pro nobis" as one of *the* characteristic points in Luther's theology which marks him off from the preceding tradition. However, with Alexander of Hales, Bonaventure, and Thomas we find that quotations from the Vulgate which contain such words as *vos* or *vobis* are freely and without a trace of hesitancy changed into *nos* or *nobis* – apparently to facilitate an existential application of such a biblical quotation.

In the theology of the later Middle Ages we encounter the expression "pro nobis" again and again, especially in connection with the work of salvation by Christ. To employ here the Augustinian distinction, so popular in the Middle Ages, between sacrament and example one could say: the work of Christ is not only "pro nobis" as sacrament over against the Father, but more especially "pro nobis" as example over against the Christians. As sacrament the work of Christ has fulfilled the justice of God, the iustitia Dei, and "pro nobis" opened the gates of heaven. As example the work of Christ incites the faithful to travel towards these gates and encourages them to endure all the hardships "on the road"; in this way the work of Christ is "pro nobis" the law of the New Testament.

The Council of Trent designates Christ both as Redemptor *and* Legislator. It is exactly this idea which Gabriel Biel expresses when he speaks about "the two works of Christ" – an idea built upon the distinction between the

---

[47]Disputatio de Iustificatione, Luther presiding, 1536; Drews, op. cit., 58. arg. 17. Cf. W A 39. I, 109. Luther's Works, Vol. 34, ed. L. Spitz (Phil., 1960), 178.

To summarize the Roman law tradition in one sentence: *aliquid proprium* [proprietatem] *habere est iure possidere*. Possessio stands with ususfructus over against proprietas or dominium. Cf. Max Kaser, Eigentum und Besitz im älteren römischen Recht (Weimar, 1943), 310ff. Ernest Levy, West Roman Vulgar Law: the law of property (Phil. 1951), 19ff. Hugonis Grotii, De iure belli ac pacis, libri tres, ed. P.C. Molhuysen (Lugduni Batavorum, 1919), II. II.3, 143, note I.

opus spei (misericordiae) and the opus iustitiae.[48] The expression "pro nobis" functions with Biel – as it does in the decree on justification of Trent – in the gap between the iustitia Christi and the iustitia Dei where the two works of Christ keep man on the right path towards the heavenly Jerusalem, balanced between fear and hope. Strengthened by the iustitia Christi provided by the opus misericordiae, the viator sets out in hope – and trembling – to fulfill the requirements of the iustitia Dei.

It is therefore not the existential roots or the frequency of the use of the expression but rather the function of the term "pro nobis" which is characteristic of Luther's theology. Already in 1509 Luther had noticed while reading Augustine that the "founding father" of his order relates both sacramentum and exemplum to man, the external and internal man.[49] Though he will retain this Augustinian theme for quite some time and though there is a neo-platonic flavor to his anthropological statements until the late teens, we find already in his first Commentary on the Psalms: Christ is the sacramentum not only as the fulfillment of the Old Testament, understood as signum; Christ is also the root sacrament, the mother sacrament, which stands behind the seven ecclesiastical sacraments, through which in the Spirit, that is to say by faith, everything *signified* in the Old Testament by way of *signs* is now granted.[50]

It is already at this early stage that we find interwoven in one pattern all the themes that we have touched upon hitherto: litera and spiritus, lex vetus and lex nova, signum and sacramentum. Here we find the point of departure from which the contrast and difference between the iustitia Dei and the iustitia Christi is to be abrogated, a contrast which had been assumed, articulated, and defended by all medieval schools of thought. This point of departure is the "fides Christo formata," which – if well interpreted –

---

[48]"... quecunque in Scriptura continentur et in praedicationibus sonant, vel misericordiam dei vel iustitia dei ... commendant." Sermones Domincales, 101 G. "Et attendite, quam pulchre opus iustitiae sequitur opus spei, ne fiat vana praesumptio, si non conversi, nec penitentes, vitam speramus." Sermones de Festivitatibus Christi, 12 E.

[49]"... duplae morti nostrae salvator impendit simplam suam; et ad faciendum utramque resuscitationem nostram in sacramento et exemplo praeposuit et proposuit unam suam ... Cum in ea fieret interioris hominis sacramentum, exterioris exemplum ..." De Trinitate IV.3; PL 42. 891; W A 9. 18. Cf. Gerhard Ebeling, Evangelische Evangelienauslegung. Eine Untersuchung zu Luthers Hermeneutik (Darmstadt, 1962²), 238, note.

[50]"... omnia in uno christo implentur et inveniuntur, quia quicquid in lege tam multis verbis et factis agitur, totum unus christus habet in veritate ... Sicut modo in spiritu unica ceremonia, scilicet sacramento, omnia tribuit, que olim multis carnalibus et imperfecte, i.e. signo dedit." W A 3. 262. 16–29 (±1515). Cf. W A 39 I. 462. 20ff. (in 1538).

stands for: fides Christo *pro nobis* formata *extra nos*.[51]

The characteristic of Luther's doctrine of justification can therefore be designated as the reunification of the righteousness of Christ and the justice of God by which the sinner is justified "coram deo," which forms the stable *basis* and not the uncertain *goal* of the life of sanctification, of the true Christian life. Doubtlessly driven by the interest to emphasize the difference between the Protestant and Roman Catholic doctrines of justification, Luther scholars have been tempted to interpret the "extra nos" as evidence and proof for a forensic doctrine of justification. Ever since the ensuing reaction, especially of the school of Karl Holl, which wanted to account for

---

[51]The first time that Luther clarifies the expression "iustitia dei passiva" is in De servo arbitrio, 1525: "... sic iustitia Dei latine dicitur, quam Deus habet, sed Ebraeis intelligitur, quae ex deo et coram Deo habetur." W A 18. 769, 1. The identification of iustitia Dei and iustitia Christi as expressed here in "ex [!] deo et coram deo" is especially striking when one puts it side by side with a pasage out of an All Saints sermon of Bernard of Clairvaux. In connection with Psalm 142 (143): 2 –, "non enim iustificabitur in conspectu tuo omnis vivens" – Bernard points out that this "omnis vivens" embraces both men and angels so that even angels, though they live so much closer to God, can be presented as justified "ex eo" but not as justified "coram eo"; the expression "in conspectu tuo" is understood to mean: "munere eius, non in eius comparatione." Dominica I Novembris, Sermo V, 9. Sermones de Tempore, ed. J. M. Mandernach (Coloniae, 1863), 494. Cf. Luther in the Dictata super Psalterium, the gloss on the same verse: "quia non iustificabitur: i.e. non erit iustus nisi per tuam iustitiam in conspectu tuo, coram te, omnis vivens, quantumvis in sua iustitia iustificetur." W A 3. 443. 13–14.

The natural sequel to this article is a discussion of the iustitia Dei which in a new de-eschatologized form – as iudicium in via – underlies Luther's earliest 'simul' doctrine, later formulated as *simul iustus et peccator*: "In inferno enim solum erit iudicium, in coelo autem sola misericordia: hic autem simul utrumque ..."; "... per misericordiam et iudicium [in via], de iudicio sine misericordia [in inferno], ad misericordiam sine iudicio [in coelo] pervenias. Amen ..." "Iustorum autem est unum tantum flagellum, non multa ... scilicet in carne tantum, quia misericordia circumdat eum." W A 4.133, 13f.; 19f.; 29ff. (Dictata, Ps. 100 [101]).

In view of the fact that humilitas is the lasting context of the iustitia Dei, interpreted as iudicium, we remain unconvinced by Ernst Bizer's argument that the "Turmerlebnis" is to be dated in 1518, since till then "der Begriff der Iustitia ist noch der alte, der humiliatio entsprechende." Fides ex auditu (Neukirchen, 1958), 96. For the most detailed and convincing answer to Bizer see Heinrich Bornkamm, "Zur Frage der Iustitia Dei beim jungen Luther" I, ARG 52 (1961), 16–29; II, ARG 53 (1962), 1–60. I deviate from Bornkamm *formally* in that I am more inclined to regard Luther's autobiographical statement of 1545 (with its parallels) as an important source, to be taken seriously with the indicated provisos; *materially* in that Luther's interpretation of the crucial Ps. 70 [71] – W A 3. 462, 36f: per Iudicium ... fit Iustitia, and W A 3. 465, 32: Iudicium is tropologice humiliatio by which we forestall the final judgment – does indeed already identify iustitia Dei with Christ litteraliter, and with fides Christi tropologice (moraliter), but through humiliation. Though this humiliation is itself a work of God in man [W A 3.462, 36], it is the *precondition* for the gift of iustitia: huic dat deus gratiam (W A 3.462, 37f.). Later, when Luther develops his marriage theme, Christ accepts our possessions, i.e., our sins, and thus, *He* carries the iudicium, whereas we acquire his possessions and thus receive his iustitia. In the interpretation of this Psalm Luther is still involved in what he, on April 8, 1516, calls an error. See next note.

the many Luther texts which could not be forensically intepreted, scholars have tried to come to terms with the seemingly irreconcilable alternatives of imputation and impartation.

For a proper interpretation of what we call the "fides Christo formata," but at the same time for the preservation of the elements of truth in both of these positions, it is of essential importance that we no longer ignore the crucial distinction between righteousness as *possessio*[52] and as *proprietas*. Derived from the tradition of Roman law, this distinction is of eminent importance for the proper description of Luther's doctrine of grace and justification, because by these means it is possible to express that justification, received in Word and Sacraments, is at once God's Deed *and* God's Word, *really* granted and really *granted*.

---

[52]Whereas one root of the understanding of the new righteousness as possessio rather than as proprietas is to be found in Roman civil law, the other root can be discerned more specifically in the application of marrige imagery – contractus, sponsalia, consummatio – with the exchange of possession between the partners. See Luther's sermon on the two kinds of righteousness (Palm Sunday 1518 or 1519), W A 2.145–52; transl. L. J. Satre in Luther's Works, Vol. 31, Career of the Reformer, I (Philadelphia, 1957), 297–306. This marriage theme should be interpreted in the light of John of Staupitz' De Executione aeternae praedestinationis (Nüremberg, 1517), translated and discussed in my Forerunners of the Reformation, 138f., 175–203.

Staupitz may on this point have been influenced by Luther. See the application of the marriage vow in Luther's letter to George Spenlein, April 8, 1516, a monk in one of the major augustinian monasteries, Memmingen. W A Br. I. 35f.: "tu, domine Iesu, es iustitia mea, ego autem sum peccatum tuum; tu assumsisti meum et dedisti mihi tuum; assumsisti, quod non eras, et dedisti mihi, quod non eram". Before this description of justification, Luther allows us a revealing glance into his life by pointing to the basic ailment of his time which he has not yet been able to suppress completely in himself: "Fervet enim nostra aetate tentatio praesumptionis in multis, et iis praecipue, qui iusti et boni esse omnibus viris student: ignorantes iustitiam Dei, quae in Christo est nobis effusissime et gratis donata, quaerunt in se ipsis tam diu operari bene, donec habeant fiduciam standi coram Deo, veluti virtutibus et meritis ornati, quod est impossibile fieri. Fuisti tu apud nos in hac opinione, imo errore, fui et ego: sed et nunc quoque pugno contra istum errorem, sed nondum expugnavi." For a (questionable) translation of this letter see Luther's Works, Vol. 48, 12f.

As for Staupitz, so for Luther, theology is not scientia nor attributio per analogiam. The theological enterprise is for both an act of thanksgiving, the imputation of the highest praise to God, confessio laudis. Imputare Deo and laudem dare are synonymous with the key verb cantare. The confessional rather than ontological nature of the unity in justification by marriage with Christ comes through in the verb cantare in the preceding words: ". . . disce ei cantare et de teipso desperans dicere ei. . ." This cantare is explained in the Dictata super Psalterium Ps. 100 [101], W A 4.127, 2ff. and 132, 11–25. Note esp. the parallel example of adoption, ibid. 130, 36–131, 8.

The locus classicus for the contractus between Christ and the believer is Luther's 1520 "Reformation writing," The Freedom of a Christian, written on the instigation of Staupitz to Pope Leo X. W A 7. 25ff. Cf. Luther's Works, Vol. 31, 351–54. See further, on Rom. 2:15, W A 56.204, 22.

VI

SIMUL GEMITUS ET RAPTUS: LUTHER AND MYSTICISM

"We will deal with that material than which none is more sublime, none more divine, and none more difficult to attain ..." Jean Gerson[1]

"That [mystical] rapture is not the passageway [to God]." Martin Luther[2]

1. INTRODUCTION

It cannot be our task to determine whether Luther is to be regarded as a mystic. For an empathic biographer it is interesting that Luther himself testifies to the highest degree of mystical experience when he writes: "once I was carried away (*raptus fui*) to the third heaven."[3] Yet, in complete accordance with a widespread concern and hesitancy almost monotonously expressed in late medieval pastoral literature, he also states in 1516 that this "negotium absconditum" is a rare event.[4] Furthermore there are grave dangers in the pursuit of the *suavitas* which "is rather the fruit and reward of love than love itself."[5] Luther never based his authority on special revelations or high mystical experiences, nor does he write for the "aristocrats of the Spirit" who are granted a special foretaste of the glory to come. Rather it is our task to investigate the relation between Luther and medieval mystical theology and its possible significance for the formation and understanding of Luther's theology.

---

[1]*De mystica theologia, Tractatus primus speculativus. Prologus*, ed. André Combes (Lucani, 1958), cons. 2, pp. 27–29.

[2]*W A* 56,300 7f.; Cl. (= *Luthers Werke in Auswahl, I–VIII*, hrsg. von Otto Clemen). 5.248.16f (to Rom. 5:2; 1516).

[3]*W A* 11.117. 35f. (1523): cf. 2 Cor. 12:2. Thomas Aquinas relates the "third heaven" to the *contemplatio intellectus*, and he understands the rapture of Paul as a higher level "quod pertinet ad affectum." (S. Th. II/II, q. 175, a. 2, c.a.).

[4]*W A* 9.98.19 (Marginal Notes on Tauler's Sermons, 1516). See Johannes Ficker, "Zu den Bemerkungen Luthers in Taulers Sermones (Augsburg, 1508)." *Theol. St. u. Kritiken* 107 (1936), 46–64

[5]*W A* 9,100. 38f.; Cl. 5,308.11f. (1516).

The fact that *mysticism* is a form or degree of religious experience, and hence to some extent individually determined, makes this topic highly elusive. We have to turn, therefore, to mystical theology, which is the effort of those who may or may not have had these experiences themselves to report, order, or teach the methods and goals of "the mystical way." Even so we shall find that there is a considerable variety of views both as to the method and goal germane to Christian mysticism. Furthermore, in the particular case of Luther, I believe that a consensus can be reached among scholars in the field that it is highly precarious to separate the mystical tissue from the living organism of Luther's spirituality. The tissue of mysticism cannot be treated as one aspect of Luther's theology, such as his relation to certain historical events, men, or movements (e.g. the Black Death, Karlstadt, or the Hussites) but it is part and parcel of his overall understanding of the Gospel itself and therefore pervades his understanding of faith, justification, hermeneutics, ecclesiology, and pneumatology.

2. METHODOLOGICAL CONSIDERATIONS

In view of the complexity of the question before us it is not my intention to offer any final solutions, but rather to indicate a series of desiderata for research and suggest the direction in which the problem might be fruitfully pursued in the years ahead.

Centuries of controversy are reflected in the varying views presented on Luther's relation to mysticism: the tension between Philippism and Pietism; the differing views on the relation of the young Luther to the mature or – more descriptively – the old Luther; the evaluation of the thesis of "the Reformers before the Reformation"; the Holl-Ritschl debate on justification as impartation (*sanatio*) versus imputation; the intimate interplay of politico-nationalistic and theological factors in the clash of *Deutsche Christen* and the *Bekennende Kirche* reflected in the confrontation of Luther as the spokesman of an endemic "Deutsche" or "Germanische Mystik" (Eckhart-Luther-Nietzsche!) versus an appeal to Luther as the witness to the God who is *totaliter aliter*, without a natural point of contact (*Seelengrund*, etc.) in man; the unclarity regarding the relation of the *Via moderna* to the *Devotio moderna* – and more generally of nominalism to mysticism. It will prove to be impossible to bypass these battlefields, but we will have to approach them with appropriate caution.

Yet the greatest obstacle methodologically is doubtless the fact that the terms "mysticism" and "mystical theology" themselves shift in meaning from author to author. The preliminary question is therefore: what is mysticism and with what structure of thought do we compare Luther?

1. On first sight the most obvious procedure for answering this question, which has indeed recently been suggested, is: "What is common to mystics, and where do we find these common elements in Luther?"[6] On two scores we cannot accept this solution. In the first place there is no guarantee that the common denominator gathers in much more than a general structure such as *purgatio, illuminatio, unio,* or the contrast between scholastic theology and mystical theology as *sapientia doctrinalis* versus *sapientia experimentalis.* Perhaps more important, the search for the common mystical denominator presupposes that one knows what authors are to be regarded as mystics and therefore the proper subject of investigation.

2. The alternative approach is a dogmatic answer. Protestant theologians are not too helpful for our purposes because they have by and large chosen the *via negativa* in their evaluation of mysticism, inclined to regard the *Christus pro nobis* and *extra nos* as alternatives to the *Christus in nobis.*

A clearer answer can be garnered from Roman Catholic manuals and encyclopedias. In Thomistically oriented works one frequently encounters the name of Philipp of the Holy Trinity, well known as interpreter of St. Thomas and famous for his *Summa Theologiae Mysticae,* first published in Lyon in 1656. His influential definition is: "mystical and heavenly theology is a kind of knowledge of God drawn forth or produced by divinely infused light through the union of the will with God."[7] We are fortunate in that there is a recent and learned example of the application of this standard to a topic similar to ours: Augustine's relation to mysticism.[8]

Without explicitly mentioning the definition quoted above, the author relies on Philipp for the corresponding description of the stages leading to mysticism in the strict sense of the word. In a few words we report his outline to clarify both his final conclusion and the technical terms we shall use later on. The first stage is ascetics or mysticism in the general sense of the word. It starts with oral prayer and meditation characterized by "discursive, decisional thinking."[9] Not study as such but love is the goal, and

---

[6]Artur Rühl, *Der Einfluss der Mystik auf Denken und Entwicklung des jungen Luther* (Theol. Diss. Marburg, 1960), p. 6.

[7]"Theologia mystica coelestis est quaedam Dei notitia per unionem voluntatis Dei adhaerentis elicita vel lumine coelitus immisso producta." So reported by Thomas de Vallgornera O.P., *Mystica theologia divi Thomae* (Barcelona, 1662). Philipp and Thomas were both dependent upon the commentary of John of St. Thomas (†1644) on Thomas of Aquinas, *S. Th.* I/II, q. 67–70, Cf. *Les dons du Saint Esprit,* trans. R. Maritain (Juvisy, 1950²).

[8]Ephraem Hendrikx O.E.S.A., *Augustins Verhältnis zur Mystik* (Theol. Diss. Würzburg, 1936); in abbreviated form in *Zum Augustin-Gespräch der Gegenwart,* ed. Carl Andresen (Darmstadt, 1962), pp. 271–364.

[9]*Ibid.,* p. 272.

the more love is elicited the more an irrational element characteristic of love is introduced so that finally in persistent meditation the intuitive mode replaces the discursive mode of thought. From the resulting affective prayer, "the state of meditation, in which purification and inner unification is achieved, transforms itself, with the aid of God's grace, into an acquired state of contemplation."[10] The ensuing peace of soul and enjoyment of divine truth should not be confused with mysticism proper. What is important is that "the acquired state of contemplation is a habit and a fully controllable act which is accessible to every individual soul, given the assistance of ordinary grace."[11]

It is only from here onward that one embarks upon the *via mystica* proper – to which I shall refer as "high mysticism" – when the soul suffers in sheer receptivity and passivity the divinely infused contemplation, is transformed in spiritual marriage, and finally absorbed into God, gazing upon God Himself or upon the Holy Trinity. Applying this definition to the thought of St. Augustine, Hendrikx argues that Augustine teaches merely the achievement of *sapientia* with the aid of ordinary grace, typical of acquired and not of infused contemplation; therefore "in the closed system of Augustinian convictions there is no place for mystical knowledge of God in the genuine sense of the word."[12]

Since the two stages of acquired and infused contemplation are alien to Luther's thought, acceptance of Hendrikx' definition of mysticism would mark the end of this essay. Furthermore, this scholastic understanding of mysticism – which is anachronistic with regard to Augustine – excludes with St. Augustine a large group of eastern and western theologians from

---

[10]*Ibid.*, p. 274. L. G. Mack points out: "Above all the humanity of Christ should be meditated upon, for man is more deeply impressed by visible objects. ... As to the acquired contemplation, Domenichi seems to admit a contemplation, inferior to the infused, it is true, yet genuine contemplation, which can be reached by human efforts." *The Liber de contemplatione Dei by Dominicus de Domincis, 1416–1478* (Rome, 1959), pp. 14, 16f. In the Thomistic mystical tradition it is unthinkable that the higher levels of mysticism should be subject to the efforts of man. Marie Louise von Franz suggests that this Commentary could be a transcript of the last words which Thomas Aquinas spoke in his ecstasy on his deathbed. *Aurora consurgens: A document Attributed to Thomas Aquinas on the Problem of Opposites in Alchemy* (New York, 1966), pp. 430f. On the other hand, the identity of the soul with God, which in one place even looks to such union from the side of man (*ibid.*, p. 363), suggests the opposite conclusion.

[11]Hendrikx (note 8), p. 275.

[12]*Ibid.*, p. 346. It may be noted that a generally respected authority on mystical theology, writing in the same year as Hendrikx and working with a different definition of mysticism, came to the opposite conclusion about Augustine. Joseph Maréchal, *Etudes sur la psychologie des mystiques* II (Brussels, 1937), 180ff.; cf. 250, 255. A more balanced judgment is made by Ernst Dassmann in regard to Ambrosius: "Ein wie auch immer akzentuierter *moderner* Begriff von Mystik kann nun aber wiederum nicht als Maszstab an die Aussagen des Ambrosius gelegt werden." *Die Frömmigkeit des Kirchenvaters Ambrosius von Mailand* (Münster, 1965), 181.

the realm of mystical theology "in the genuine sense of the word," since it presupposes the thirteenth century secularization of Neoplatonic and Augustinian epistemology.

3. In addition to the phenomenological and dogmatic solutions, there is still a third option, namely, the historical-genetic approach. Again in the year 1936 Erich Vogelsang made a significant contribution by no longer operating with the general and usually vague concept of mysticism. After first enumerating the mystical authors said to be known to Luther – Dionysius Areopagita, Hugh and Richard of St. Victor, Bernard, Bonaventure, Gerson, Brigit of Sweden, Tauler, and "the Frankfurter" – Vogelsang distinguished between "Dionysian mysticism" (*areopagistische Mystik*), "Latin mysticism" (*romanische Mystik*), and "German mysticism" (*Deutsche Mystik*). With this more differentiated view of mysticism, Vogelsang could give a more refined answer to our question: (1) From 1516 onward Luther renders the clear verdict of "No" to "Dionysian mysticism" as a speculative bypassing of the incarnate and crucified Christ;[13] (2) *re* "Latin mysticism" both a "Yes" to its emphasis on the earthly Christ and on mysticism as experience rather than doctrine, and a "No" to its bypassing spiritual *Anfechtung*, to its erotic marriage mysticism, and to its ultimate goal of ecstatic union with the uncreated word;[14] (3) an enthusiastic "Yes" characterizes Luther's evaluation of the third type of mysticism, "German mysticism," in which Luther found what he hailed in "Latin mysticism," but beyond that a spiritual understanding of purgatory as self-despair characteristic of the Christian life, and the idea of the *resignatio ad infernum*,[15] both presented in his German mother tongue and representative of a nearly forgotten, submerged, genuinely German theological tradition.

---

[13]"Luther und die Mystik," *Luther-Jb*, 19 (1937), 32–54, esp. 35. Vogelsang was not the first to go beyond an often unrewarding general definition of mysticism. He acknowledges the merits of Hermann Hering, *Die Mystik Luthers* (Leipzig, 1879). Cf. also W. Köhler, *Luther und die Kirchengeschichte I* (Erlangen, 1900), 368, where an "areopagitische und germanisch-bernhardinische Mystik" are described.

[14]Vogelsang (note 13), pp. 40f. In his later essay, "Die unio mystica bei Luther," *ARG* 35 (1938), 63–80, Vogelsang focuses his earlier exposition as he now expressly applies the "yes" and "no" to bridal and union mysticism; see especially the reference (p. 70, n. 4) to Luther's emphasis on faith as "copula." Cf. further Friedrich Th. Ruhland, *Luther und die Brautmystik nach Luthers Schrifttum bis 1521* (Giessen, 1938), pp. 54ff., 142f. Vogelsang could still write in 1937 that Luther preferred Tauler to Bernard because, among other things, the bridal mysticism "bei Tauler ganz zurücktrat" (42). Cf. however Ruhland, pp. 59ff., and Vogelsang, *ARG* 35 (1938), 78ff.

[15]On the spiritual nature of temptation (*Anfechtung*) and the *resignatio ad infernum* in Jean Gerson. cf. Walter Dress, *Die Theologie Gersons. Eine Untersuchung zur Verbindung von Nominalismus und Mystik im Spätmittelalter* (Gütersloh, 1931), pp. 167, 180ff.

3. TOWARD A NEW CLASSIFICATION: *"SIC ET NON"*

1. Insofar as Erich Vogelsang works here with concepts and categories which have been operative and influential in Luther research until this present day, it is appropriate to raise some fundamental questions which lead us, I believe, *in medias res.*

The medieval use of authorities is seldom characterized by a total endorsement of an earlier theologian as such; rather it is an effort to establish support on a particular point under discussion, while leaving ample room for overt criticism in another context. The relation of Thomas Aquinas to Augustine, of Jean Gerson to Bernard of Clairvaux, and of John Eck to Gregory of Rimini may serve here as three well-known examples drawn from the traditions of the *theologia speculativa* and the *theologia affectiva.* The same "sic et non" procedure can be amply documented with regard to Luther's attitude toward many preceding theologians, including Augustine, Bernard, Thomas, and Scotus.[16]

Hence it is inappropriate to chart on the basis of one or two references, whether positive or negative, reliable lines of relationship and dependence. When Luther refers to or praises a medieval doctor whose thoughts on other accounts prove to be completely alien to his own theology, it is often suggested that Luther "misunderstood" him, or – as it is sometimes put more nicely – that Luther is led into a "productive misunderstanding." If one collects these kinds of statements from a wide range of Luther studies, one cannot but conclude that Luther is uniquely naïve and ignorant!

In the case of Pseudo-Dionysius we have the very positive statement by Luther in 1514 that the *via negativa* is the most perfect. "Hence we find with Dionysius often the word 'hyper,' because one should transcend all thought and enter darkness."[17] Luther seizes here upon an aspect of the theology of Dionysius[18] which in the *Disputation Against Scholastic Theology* in 1517 will be

---

[16]For Augustine see *W A Tr.* 1,140.5; Cl. 8,45.36 (Nr. 347); cf. *W A* 54,186.16. For Bernard esp. *W A Tr.* 3,295.6 (Nr. 3370b). For Thomas: *W A Tr.* 1,135.12 (Nr. 329). For Scotus: *W A Tr.* 3,564.3; Cl. 8,150.4 (Nr. 3722).

[17]*Schol.* to Ps. 64 (65):2 (*W A* 3,372.13–27; early 1514). Martin Elze has warned that one cannot interpret this passage as a positive reference to Dionysius; see his important article, "Züge spätmittelalterlicher Frömmigkeit in Luthers Theologie." *ZThK* 62 (1965), 381–402, 395, n. 51. If one examines this text as a whole, one finds that in the "attamen"-sentence Luther indeed says that the text of Dionysius should not be undertood in an anagogical sense. In the sentence which begins "Nam ut dixi . . ." however, it is necessary to understand the words "unde nimis temerarii sunt nostri theologi" as a reference to the "hyper" of Dionysius. Cf. also the *Schol.* to Ps. 17 (18):12 (*W A* 3,124.29–39; Cl. 5,94.14–25).

[18]Soon thereafter, perhaps in the summer of 1514, Luther emphasizes in the *scholion* to Ps. 79 (80):3 the "supra rationem" of faith. This passage shows that by "contemplativi" Luther can

formulated as "the whole of Aristotle relates to theology as shadow to light."[19] I am inclined to classify this theme with the earliest statement on this matter in 1510: "Theology is heaven, yes even the kingdom of heaven; man however is earth and his speculations are smoke. . . ."[20] It is the "hyper" element which Luther approves and by no means the anagogical *facere quod in se est* of man which would bypass God's revelation in Christ.[20a]

In 1514 it is already clear that "darkness," – *tenebrae, umbra,* or *caligo* – shares in the double meaning of *abscondere* and *absconditus:* not only apart from faith is God obscured in our speculations, but even in faith the faithful live "in umbraculo," in God's protective custody,[21] as friends of God on earth. If one turns for comparison to a passage from the hand of such a true disciple of Pseudo-Dionysius as Dionysius the Carthusian (†1471), where he discusses the *unio mystica* in terms of the most intimate sons of God (*secretissimi filii Dei*), elevated halfway between the blessed and the average believers and through

---

mean not the spiritually privileged among the faithful, but the faithful as such: "Christi fides non potest esse nisi in iis, qui supra rationem contemplativi sint. Apparet enim, quando in eum creditur. Sed credere nequent, nisi filii Rachel, elevate mentis." *W A* 3,607.22–24. On the significance of "in eum credere" in place of "eum credere" or "eo credere" cf. my book *The Harvest of Medieval Theology* (Cambridge, Mass., 1963), pp. 229, 119. I fully agree with the important observation of Bernhard Lohse that "positiv . . . die contemplatio letztlich mit dem Glauben identisch gesetzt (wird)" and that Luther "zumindest der Sache nach die contemplatio mit dem Glauben gleichsetzt oder doch auf die entscheidende Bedeutung des Glaubens hinweist." *Mönchtum und Reformation. Luthers Auseinandersetzung mit dem Mönchsideal des Mittelalters* (Göttingen, 1963), pp. 230f. To be sure, to the extent to which *contemplatio* = *elevatio mentis* = *excessus mentis*, Luther's interpretation is not completely without precedent; cf. infra, n. 93. But in the *Dictata* for the most part "contemplativi" refer to a particular group in the Church and is often connected with the "doctores." For further documentation of this point see Joseph Vercruysse, *Fidelis Populus. Een onderzoek van de ecclesiologie in Martin Luthers Dictata super Psalterium (1513–15)* (Diss. Gregoriana, Rome, 1966), typed ms., pp. 176–182.

[19] *W A* 1,226,26; Cl. 5,324.8.

[20] *W A* 9,65.14–16; Cl. 5,9.29–31 (Marginal Notes to Lombard, *Sent.* I, d. 12, c.2). In regard to Luther's rejection of the "facere quod in se est" between reason and revelation, cf. my essay "Robert Holcot O.P. and the Beginnings of Luther's Theology," *HThR* 55 (1962), 317–342, esp. 330ff. [See Chapter IV above]. On sinful blindness as "caligo" in the later years, cf. the commentary on Gen. 42. *W A* 44.472.38; 473.42 (1535–45).

[20a] See Luther's later statement in the *Operationes in Psalmos*, Ps. 5:12 (*W A* 5,176.29–33).

[21] *Schol.* to Ps. 90 (91):1 (perhaps early 1515; *W A* 4.64.24–65.6; cf. 65.28–31). In Ps. 121 (122):3, another aspect of this theme is touched upon. Here Luther warns: be careful with the idea of participating in Christ! In this life, he writes, not even the most perfect of the saints have the whole Christ (". . . nunquam habet aliquis sanctorum totum Christum, sed quilibet partem eius, etiam perfectissimi"). *W A* 4.401.25–30. The significance of this passage has been noted by L. Pinomaa, "Die Heiligen in Luthers Frühtheologie," *St Theol.* 13 (1959), 1–47, 6f., and by B. Lohse (note 18), p. 230. n. 15, who quotes the second half of the citation. It is precisely the first half of the citation, however, that shows that Luther consciously sets forth this theme as a major and not a minor motif. Luther's conclusion, the Bernardian "stare est regredi," harkens back to the "in hac vita": in this life the *activi* and the *contemplativi* remain *viatores*.

love and rapture absorbed in the ocean of God's infinity,[22] one sees
immediately that it would be misleading to overlook the "sic et non"
character of this and other asides Luther makes to Dionysius in the early
years.[23] When from 1519–1520 onward Luther attacks "Dionysian
speculations" there is no reason to base on this finding a theory of
development, let alone of reversal. Rather, he now associates the name of
Dionysius with a theological position which had never been his own, a
phenomenon perhaps not unrelated to the fact that his earliest opponents had
started immediately to make use of Pseudo-Dionysius to defend the validity
of the papal hierarchy.[24]

2. Turning now to the second category of "Latin mysticism," we begin by
stating that it makes exceedingly good sense to establish a separate category
for medieval authors from Bernard to Gerson who, in contrast to the
tradition characterized by the *Doctor Ecstaticus*, Dionysius, do not
allow for the absorption of the believer into the abyss of the Godhead. As
Etienne Gilson has shown clearly for Bernard, the Christian has to lose his
proprium in the process of union with God through love, but this *proprium* is

---

[22]Dionysius the Carthusian, *Enarratio in canticum canticorum Salomonis* in *D. Dionysii Cartusiani Enarrationes piae ac eruditae in quinque libros sapientiales* (Coloniae, 1533), *Opera omnia* VII (Monstrolii, 1898), 386 B-387 B.

[23]Although I do not believe that John Eck was in any way decisively indebted to the Aeropagite, Eck still makes reference in a completely understandable way to the *via negativa* of Dionysius as representative of the tradition of the Church. *Chrysopassus, Centuria* IV, 44 (Augsburg, 1514), Cf. *W A Tr.* I, Nr. 257.

[24]See in regard to Eck, *W A* 2,55.34–56.1 (1519). Ambrosius Catharinus Politus (†1552) writes: "As the great theologian Dionysius says, the ecclesiastical hierarchy is as much like the heavenly hierarchy as possible." *Apologia pro veritate ... adversus impia ac valde pestifera Martini Lutheri Dogmata* (1520), ed. Josef Schweizer, *Corpus Catholicorum* 27 (1956), 2.7.18f. One finds this concept of the Church also with Sylvester Prierias. *De potestate papae dialogus* (1518) in Valentin Ernst Loescher, *Vollständige Reformations-Acta und Documenta*, II (Leipzig, 1723), 14. For the insistence upon the authenticity of the works of Dionysius as a disciple of Paul by Johannes Cochläus, see Martin Spahn, *Johannes Cochläus. Ein Lebensbild aus der Zeit der Kirchenspaltung* (Berlin, 1898; 2nd ed. Nieuwkoop, 1964), p. 234. For the high rating of Dionysius among northern humanists in the beginning of the sixteenth century we note, besides the well-known analysis by Nicolas Cusanus and the editorial work of Faber Stapulensis (cf. Eugene F. Rice, *Renaissance Studies* XI [1962], 126–160; 142), a letter by Konrad Peutinger (Augsburg, June 13, 1513), where Dionysius heads the list of the Greek and Latin Church fathers. *Briefwechsel des Beatus Rhenanus*, ed. Adalbert Horawitz and Karl Hartfelder (Leipzig, 1886; Hildesheim 1966²), pp. 57f. In a letter of Dec. 1, 1508. Beatus Rhenanus ranks him even with Paul and John as an instrument of revelation (*ibid.*, p. 18). Shortly before (Oct. 10, 1508), Rhenanus had already indicated as the most important reading "altissimam Dionysianae theologiae lectionem," "sublimem Cusani de Sacris philosophiam," "Bonaventurae commentarios" – "the other theologians are not worth your time" – and the *Quincuplex Psalterium* of Faber. *Ibid.*, pp. 576f. In the later letters Dionysius is no longer mentioned!

not the individuality of the *viator*, but rather the distortion of his image by the impact of sin.[25]

In Bernard's influential *De diligendo Deo* there is an acute awareness of the limits and limitations of man's bond with God on this earth. After distinguishing four degrees of love – of oneself for one's own sake (*se propter se*), of God for one's own sake (*Deum propter se*), of God for God's sake (*Deum propter Deum*), of oneself for God's sake (*se propter Deum*) – of which the first three are familiar to us from late medieval scholastic debates as *amor sui, amor concupiscentiae,* and *amor amicitiae,* Bernard confesses that he is not certain that anyone can attain to the fourth degree in this life: "I for one confess that it seems impossible to me. But without doubt this will come about when the good and faithful servant will have entered into the joy of his master, exhilarated by the abundance of God's house."[26]

3. It is not without good reason that in so many fifteenth century meditations and sermons Bernard and Gerson constitute the two major authorities, often mentioned in one breath and interchangeably. Without denying Gerson's independent synthesis in his *Theologia mystica speculativa,* it is, e.g., at such a climax in his work as the description of the several interpretations of transformation and union with God that Gerson falls back on *De diligendo Deo*. In a fascinating sermon preached on the Feast of St. Bernard, dated August 20, 1402, he appropriates Bernard's heritage, and extols the *Doctor Mellifluus* by having Bernard speak autobiographically.[27] Here three stages of contrition, meditation, and contemplation are described as the way to peace and union with Christ with the usual reference to Gal. 2:20: "it is no longer I who live, but Christ who lives in me."[28] Gerson selects two points which the young Luther would also associate with Bernard: (1) not to progress is to regress (*non progredi, regredi est*),[29] and (2) the hermeneutical principle that for a proper interpretation one has to clothe oneself in the affective state of the writer (*affectus induere scribentis*).[30] In my opinion the most revealing index of the intimate relation between Gerson

---

[25]*La théologie mystique de Saint Bernard* (Paris, 1947), pp. 21, 138, 155. The destruction of the false *proprium* means "reformation"; "transformamur cum conformamur." *Cant. Cant.* 62.5. as cited by Friedrich Ohly, *Hohelied-Studien. Grundzüge einer Geschichte der Hoheliedauslegung des Abendlandes bis um 1200* (Wiesbaden, 1958), p. 152.

[26]*De dilig. Deo* 15.39 (*PL* 182, 998 D).

[27]*Jean Gerson, Oeuvres complètes*, V: *L'Ouevre oratoire*, ed. P. Glorieux (Paris, 1963), 326.

[28]*Ibid.*, p. 329

[29]*Ibid.*, p. 335. Cf. Luther, *W A* 9,69.36f.; 107.23. See also the *scholion* to Ps. 4:2 in the Vatican Fragment: *Unbekannte Fragmente aus Luthers zweiter Psalmenvorlesung 1518*, ed. Erich Vogelsang (Berlin, 1940), p. 41. On Bernard, *Ep.* 91. 3 (*PL* 182, 224).

[30]Gerson (note 27), p. 334. Cf. *W A* 3,549.27–37.

and Bernard is the fact that on the one point at which Gerson warns his listeners against Bernard, he refers to a Pseudo-Bernardian work. Not yet five months before the exuberant encomium and completely in accord with the "sic et non" tradition, Gerson expresses his disapproval of a too intimate and proleptic description of the union of love in Bernard's *Epistola ad fratres de Monte Dei*, which actually is from the hand of William of St. Thierry.[31]

I am not convinced that Bonaventure should be mentioned in the same breath with Bernard and Gerson. Though one can interpret Gerson's theological program as an effort to reestablish in the Parisian theological faculty the balance of mind and heart which had characterized Bonaventure's *opus* a century and a half before, and though Gerson regrets that the Franciscan *moderni* abandoned the great tradition of Bonaventure,[32] it is questionable whether Bonaventure would have reciprocated this admiration and whether he would have sided with the Parisian Chancellor in his critique of Ruysbroeck's transformation (eucharistic) mysticism, or would have appreciated Gerson's insistence on the "conformitas voluntatis" as the axis of mystical theology.[33]

Furthermore, when Bonaventure develops his own typology[34] in accordance with the threefold spiritual sense of Scripture, and hence distinguishes between *doctores (fides)*, *praedicatores (mores)*, and *contemplativi (finis utriusque)*, Bernard of Clairvaux is classified as a preacher rather than with Dionysius and Richard of St. Victor as one concerned with the *studium contemplativorum*. Whereas Hugh of St. Victor[35] forms the apex of Bonaventure's typology, embracing the offices of doctor, preacher, and contemplative, we find in a parallel typology with Luther's later opponent, Kaspar Schatzgeyer, that Bonaventure has replaced Hugh of St. Victor. In his *De perfecta et contemplativa vita*, a hitherto hardly noticed work dating from 1501,[36] Schatzgeyer distinguishes – according to a psychological instead of an

---

[31]Sermon "A Deo exivit" (Mar. 23, 1402), 14. Cf. *PL* 184, 337.

[32]*Opera omnia*, ed. L. Du Pin. I (Antwerp, 1706), 91 D.

[33]Cf. my book, *The Harvest of Medieval Theology*, pp. 338f.

[34]*De reductione artium ad theologiam*, cap. 5, ed. Julian Kaup (Munich, 1961), 246.

[35]On the relation between Hugo of St. Victor and the Pseudo-Dionysius, see Roger Baron, *Etudes sur Hugues de Saint-Victor* (Angers, 1963). Baron, who edits Hugo's commentaries, regards them as late works, ca. 1130–40 (*Ibid.*, p. 88).

[36]Otfried Müller cites from this work without calling attention to its early date. *Die Rechtfertigungslehre nominalistischer Reformationsgegner: Bartholomäus Arnoldi von Usingen O.E.S.A. und Kaspar Schatzgeyer O.F.M.* (Breslau, 1939). The same is true for another work on Schatzgeyer by Heinrich Klomps, *Freiheit und Gesetz bei dem Franziskanertheologen Kaspar Schatzgeyer* (Münster, 1959). Together with the equally neglected yet quite significant *Apologia status fratrum ordinis minorum de observantia* (1516). *De Perfecta et contemplatita vita* forms the main source of our knowledge of Schatzgeyer before 1517, and hence it permits us by way of comparison with the

exegetical scheme – between doctors who have special gifts "in vi rationali" (Augustine, Ambrose), "in vi irascibili" (Jerome), and "in vi concupiscibili" (Gregory the Great, Bernard). While Jerome does not seem to have any intellectual progeny, Thomas, Alexander, Scotus, and the later commentators on Lombard stand in the succession of Augustine and Ambrose. Bonaventure, however, stands out as the appropriate guide for all those in orders, since he combines the characteristic gifts of both Augustine and Bernard.[37]

This classification finds its echo in Luther's evaluation. He can place Bernard before Augustine as the *preacher* of Christ[38] but refers to Bonaventure as "the highest among the scholastic *doctores*."[39] It is exactly where Bonaventure straddles the two schools and combines the *theologia speculativa* with the *theologia affectiva* that Luther deviates from him and testifies: "he almost drove me out of my mind, because I wanted to feel the union of God with my soul, as a union of both the intellect and the will."[40]

4. From the point of view of Luther, it is not so obvious that Gerson should be classified under the rubric of "Latin mysticism" rather than with Tauler and the Frankfurter as "German mysticism." Conceding that Luther hails in Tauler a concept of spiritual temptation,[41] we note that it is exactly this aspect of Gerson's writing which leads Luther to say: "Gerson is the first who came to grips with the issue which concerns theology; he too experienced many temptations."[42] And: "Gerson is the only one who wrote about spiritual temptation."[43]

In 1516 Luther notes explicitly the anthropological parallel between

---

Scrutinium and other later works to measure the influence of the *causa Lutheri* on the development of Schatzgeyer's thinking. The pre-Reformation writings of Counter-Reformation authors deserve our special attention. Cf. the conclusion of Ernst Walter Zeeden: "Der Protestantismus hatte Augen, Herzen und Sinne auch der Katholiken geöffnet für das Wirken der Gnade." "Aspekte der Katholischen Frömmigkeit in Deutschland in 16. Jahrhundert," in *Reformata Reformanda. Festgabe für Hubert Jedin*, ed. Erwin Iserloh and Konrad Repgen. II (Münster i. W. 1965), 1–18; 12.

[37]Kasper Schatzgeyer, *De perfecta atque contemplativa vita* (Conventus Monarchiensis, 1501) in *Opera omnia* (Ingolstadt, 1534²), fol. 318r–333v; directio 20, fol. 325.

[38]*W A Tr.* 1,435.32f (Nr. 872); *W A Tr.* 3,295. 6–8 (Nr. 3370b); *W A* 40/3.354.17.

[39]*W A Tr.* 1,330 I (Nr. 683).

[40]*W A Tr.* 1,302.30–34; Cl. 8.80.17–22 (Nr. 644). Cf. *W A* 40/3,199.32–35 (Ps. 126:6–1532-33, pub. 1540).

[41]In the *Dictata* Luther breaks consciously with medieval tradition in the *scholion* to Ps. 90 (91):6 (*W A* 4.69.6–22 – probably early 1515), in that he interprets the text not in the sense of "tentationes corporales," but as "tentationes fidei."

[42]*W A Tr.* 2,114.1–3 (Nr. 1492); cf. *W A Tr.* 5.213.16 (Nr. 5523).

[43]*W A Tr.* 1,496.7 (Nr. 979). Vogelsang notes "Gersons Sonderstellung" and refers to his earlier book, *Der angefochtene Christus bei Luther* (Berlin, 1932), p. 15, n. 56. Nevertheless, he finds with Gerson the same bypassing of the incarnate Christ as with Bernard and Bonaventure, "wenn auch auf dem methodisch gestuften Umweg über den Menschgewordenen, Gekreuzigten." *Luther-Jb.* (1937), p. 41 and n. I.

Gerson and Tauler[44] – characteristically replacing their *apex mentis* and *syntheresis*, regarded as the highest part of the soul, by faith.[45] In view of the dramatic importance sometimes attached to the influence of Tauler upon Luther, it may be noted that this position of Luther can be traced back to a reference to Gerson in the earliest layer of the *Dictata*, more than two years before the discovery of Tauler.[46]

If the different classification of Gerson and Tauler is argued on the basis of Gerson's adherence – with Bernard and Bonaventure – to the mystical ascent by way of *(per christum)* rather than *to* the incarnate Christ *(in christum)*, we may recall that Luther noted in 1516 that Tauler preached one sermon on the basis of *theologia mystica*, which for Luther is characterized by its concern with the spiritual birth of the *uncreated* word, in contrast with theology in the normal sense *(theologia propria)*, which is concerned with the spiritual birth of the *incarnate* word.[47] Luther insists on the right relation between the two – "Leah [*theologia propria*] ought to precede (*prius ... ducere oportet*) Rachel [*theologia mystica*]"[48] – but does not now or later deny the possibility or

---

[44] *W A* 9,44.38–39; Cl. 5,307.22 (Marginal Notes to Tauler's Sermons).

[45] *W A* 9,103.41; Cl. 5.310.27. I do not pursue this further pending the study by S.E. Ozment of the influence of Gerson and Tauler on the anthropology of the young Luther (a Harvard Ph.D. dissertation). [Now in print: *Homo Spiritualis: A Comparative Study of the Anthropology of Johannes Tauler, Jean Gerson and Martin Luther (1509–16)* (Leiden, 1969).] On the solidarity of Thomas and Tauler vis à vis Luther who "misunderstood" Tauler, cf. Heinrich Denifle, *Luther und Luthertum* I/I (Mainz, 1904²), pp. 150ff. Cf. also A.M. Walz, "Denifles Verdienst um die Taulerforschung," in *Johannes Tauler. Ein deutscher Mystiker; Gedenkschrift zum 600. Todestag*, ed. E. Filthaut O.P. (1961), pp. 8–18. For Protestant assessments of the independent nature of Luther's appropriation of mysticism see Reinhold Seeberg, *Die religiösen Grundgedanken des jungen Luther und ihr Verhältnis zu dem Ockhamismus und der deutschen Mystik* (Berlin, 1931), p. 30; Willhelm Thimme, "Die 'Deutsche Theologie' und Luthers 'Freiheit eines Christenmenschen,'" *ZThK* NF 13 (1932), 193–222, esp. 222; and Hering (note 13), p. 27.

[46] *W A* 3,151.5–13 (*schol.* to Ps. 26 [27]:9 – ca. Autumn, 1513). Cf. Gerson, *De mystica theologia* (note 1) 28.42–29.47; 34.24–35.31; 97.35f.

[47] *W A* 9,98.20–25; Cl. 5,306.28–307.3.

[48] *W A* 9,98.34: Cl. 5,307.13. For a parallel to this in a sermon from Aug. 15, 1517 (according to Vogelsang it is from 1520 – see *Z K G* 50 [1931], 132, 143), see *W A* 4,650.5–15; Cl. 5,434.19–30. To my knowledge the earliest treatment of this matter is in Luther's use of "deinde" with reference to the transition from the *vita activa* to the *vita contemplativa* in the *scholion* on Ps. 52 (53):7 (*W A* 3,298.31). Cf. the almost hymnic development in the *scholion* on Ps. 113 (114):9 (*W A* 4,94.40–95.11), where an attack on the "*prius*" is already considered dangerous. Cf. the striking parallel to this "*prius*" in John Geiler of Kaysersberg in L. Dacheux, *Die ältesten Schriften Geilers von Kayserberg* (Freiburg I. Br., 1882), pp. 215f. Cf. also the letter written a century earlier by Geert Groote, "Ad curatim Zwollensem" (1382), which warns of the importance of the "*prius*" by calling on the authority of the Pseudo-Dionysius, *Geraldi Magni Epistolae*, ed. W. Mulder, S.J. (Antwerp, 1933). p. 135. On Groote cf. K. L. C. M. de Beer, *Studie over de Spiritualiteit van Geert Groote* (Brussels, 1938), pp. 84–187. Groote warns of the serious danger of a mystical contemplation which is not preceded by ascetic purification (*ibid.*, pp. 186f.). While he has praise for Heinrich Seuse, Groote is very critical of Meister Eckhart and speaks in a qualified way about Jan van Ruysbroeck. It is noteworthy that Luther warns us not "festinari ad opera ... antequam credimus." (*W A* 57,143.5f. – Hebr. 3.7, 1517).

validity of "high mysticism" in the sense indicated above, however qualified it is as *difficile* and *rarum*. When the "old Luther" refers to Gerson in a most revealing comment on Genesis 19, probably sometime in 1538, he notes first that Caspar Schwenckfeld *cum suis* speculates about God as the monks used to when they bypassed Christ. Against this dangerous *commercium* with the *Deus nudus* Luther pits the true specultive life which concerns God's *potentia ordinata*, the incarnate and crucified Son.[49] It is quite clear, however, that Luther does not here condemn Gerson as the spiritual father or ally of Schwenckfeld.

Whereas it is often argued that the young Luther was a mystic until he saw the dangers of mysticism in the encounter with the left wing of the Reformation,[50] we note that Luther's reference to Gerson in 1538 reveals basically the same attitude as in his marginals to Tauler's sermons of 1516. High mysticism is not said to be out of the question or impossible, but "often extremely dangerous and a sheer trick of the Devil. . . . If one wants to be safe, one had best flee these speculations altogether. . . ."[51] Not even in this last stage of his development does Luther put Gerson on the Index. To the contrary, he exhorts his audience to study Gerson (and other authors of his genre), though with a restriction similar to that we noted with Gerson vis à vis Bernard: he should be read "cum iudicio."[52]

One could, of course, argue that beyond the earlier qualifications of the mystical union as "difficult" and "rare", the old Luther adds the warning "dangerous." However, we find this implicitly[53] stated in Luther's comment

---

[49]Cf. *W A* 43,72.9–14, 22–28 (to Gen. 19:14).

[50]More cautious is Johannes von Walter, *Mystik und Rechtfertigung beim jungen Luther* (Gütersloh, 1937), p. 21. Horst Quiring presents a representative view when he argues that Luther's (negative) relation to mysticism after 1520 is determined by his "Antithese zum Schwärmertum." "Luther und die Mystik," *ZSTh* 13 (1936), 150–174, 179–240, 234. Over against this view cf. Karin Bornkamm's instructive juxtaposition of Luther's exposition of Gal. 2:20 ("Vivo autem non iam ego, sed vivit in me Christus") in 1519 and in 1531. *Luthers Auslegungen des Galaterbriefs von 1519 und 1531. Ein Vergleich* (Berlin, 1963), p. 98. In 1531 the intimacy of the union between Christ and the believer is described in stronger terms ". . . multo arctiore vinculo quam masculus et femina" (*W A* 40/1.286.1). Despite our emphasis on continuity, we do not deny a certain fluctuation and noteworthy parallels in the lectures on Romans and especially in the lectures on Hebrews. Cf. J. P. Boendermaker's study which comes to the conclusion that Luther's lectures on Hebrews are concerned "die neuen Erkenntnisse in alten, grösstenteils von der deutschen Mystik geprägten Begriffen auszudrücken." *Luthers commentaar op de brief aan de Hebreeën 1517–18* (Assen, 1965), p. 119; cf. p. 101. As we are trying to demonstrate, such was Luther's effort to depict the "*vera* vita contemplativa" from the very beginning.

[51]*W A* 43,73.11–13, 21–23.

[52]*W A* 43,72.31–73.9.

[53]More explicit is the comment on Tauler at *W A* 9,100.28–30. Cf. Luther's Aug. 1517 (?) sermon. *W A* 4,647.19–25, 35–40; 648.13–16.

on Romans 5:2, dating from approximately the same time as his marginals on Tauler. Again, as in the example of Leah and Rachel, Luther insists on the priority of *accessus to raptus*, of justification by faith through the incarnate and crucified word to the *raptus* by the uncreated word. "But," Luther concludes this passage, "who would consider himself so clean, that he would dare to pursue this, unless he is called and, like the Apostle Paul, lifted up by God (II Cor. 12:2). . . . In short, this 'raptus' cannot be called 'accessus.' "[54]

There is here a transition from "rare" to "dare", from *rarum* to *periculose*; yet this transition is not so unexpected and is understandable in the light of the fact that in the prologue of the most important nominalistic *Sentences* commentaries, the Apostle Paul is introduced on the basis of II Cor. 12 as an exception to the rule *de potentia ordinata* according to which the status of the *viator* is contrasted with that of the *beatus* in that he is not yet a *comprehensor*, not yet face to face with God, and hence without immediate knowledge of God.[55] Though Luther employs the concept of the *potentia ordinata* of God, so characteristic for nominalistic theology; in his commentary on Genesis, he gives it a Christological point instead of its primary epistemological meaning: the *potentia ordinata* is here not primarily the order established by the inscrutable free God who could as well have established another order, but it is clearly the order of redemption in Jesus Christ, established out of God's mercy to provide sinful man with a refuge from danger. If we remind ourselves of the striking parallel with the *Dictata* passage (early 1515), which insists, against those who want to be more immediately related to God, on the protection (the *umbraculum*) which is necessary in this life because we are not yet face to face with God,[56] we are forced to conclude that there is a basic continuity throughout this large span of years (1515–1538), notwithstanding Luther's encounter with Tauler and the *Schwärmer*.

The fact remains that Tauler seems exempted from the "sic et non" rule which generally applies to all Luther's authorities. This cannot be due—as in the case of Wessel Gansfort[57] and Pupper of Goch[58] or the author of "Beatus

---

[54] *W A* 56,299.17–300.8. Cf. *W A* 57,168.18–22; 167.17f.; *W A* 56,298.1f. On the basis of Luther's contrast between *raptus* and *accessus* Otto Scheel concludes: "So verliert die mystische Theologie ihre Bedeutung für die Praxis des religiösen Lebens . . ." "Taulers Mystik und Luthers reformatorische Entdeckung." in *Festgabe für Julius Kaftan* (Tübingen, 1920), pp. 298–318, esp. 318.

[55] Cf. my *Harvest of Medieval Theology*, p. 41. On the debate between Ockham, d'Ailly, and Biel, cf. Altenstaig, under article "Viator," fol. 263rb – 264va.

[56] *W A* 4, 64.24–65.6.

[57] Cf. the preface to Gansfort's *Epistolae*, *W A* 10/2,316f. (1522); 317.3.

[58] Cf. *W A* 10/2 329f. (1522). R. R. Post, the *connoisseur* of the *Devotio moderna*, has recently established that Pupper is a typical late medieval theologian. "Johann Pupper van Goch," *Nederlandsch Archief voor Kerkgeschiedenis* 47 (1965–66), 71–97, esp. 93.

Vir"[59]—to temporary enthusiasm and later disappearance from the sources. Bernd Moeller was able to compose a list of twenty-six references to Tauler over the years 1515–1544 which remain positive to the very end.[60] We believe that Tauler and the *Theologia Deutsch*[61] are and remain of vital importance for Luther, among other things because they showed the growing Reformer how the mystical *affectus* could be retained while breaking with both the synergistic elements in the *contemplatio acquisita* and the speculative elements in the *contemplatio infusa*. Indeed, it is a question whether it was not precisely this mystical *affectus*, with its proximity to *sola* categories, which made it possible for Luther to carry out this double break, or at least to formulate it theologically.

It is important that we do not assume that all the so-called "mystical authors" listed by Vogelsang have been read by Luther as *mystical* authors. In the first place and more generally one can point to the democratization of mysticism[62] in late medieval devotional literature: what is retained of such an author as Bernard of Clairvaux or Hugh of St. Victor is often his piety, not his mysticism.[63] There is still a margin left for the "aristocrats of the Spirit," but the traditional mystical terminology is appropriated for the description of the Christian life of the average believer.[64] The *Via moderna* and the *Devotio moderna* share a common concern for the *theologia affectiva* rather than for the *theologia speculativa*, for ascetics rather than for mysticism, for the *contemplatio acquisita* rather than for the *contemplatio infusa*.[65]

---

[59]Luther declares that he has nowhere found a better (i.e. nonphilosophical) treatment of original sin than in the "Beatus vir" (i.e. "De Spiritualibus ascensionibus") of Gerhard Groote (i.e. Gerhard Zerbolt von Zütphen). *W A* 56,313.13–16; Cl. 5.252.23–26. Cf. the Cologne ed. (1539), chap. 3. J. van Rooij considers Luther's praise a misunderstanding, since Zerbolt did not represent a "Protestant" doctrine of the total corruption of man. *Gerhard Zerbolt van Zutphen* (Nijmegen, 1936), p. 254.

[60]"Tauler und Luther" in *La mystique Rhénane* (Paris, 1963), pp. 157–168, esp. 158, n. 3.

[61]See the preface to the first, incomplete edition of the *Theologia Deutsch* (1516). *W A* 1,153: "... ist die matery fasst nach der art des erleuchten doctors Tauleri, prediger ordens." Henri Strohl points out that Tauler by comparison is more Thomistic (Dominican), whereas the *Theologia Deutsch* is more Scotist. *Luther* (Paris, 1962), p. 191.

[62]Cf. *Harvest of Medieval Theology*, pp. 341ff.

[63]Cf. Elze (note 17), esp. pp. 391ff. Cf. Jean Chatillon, "La devotio dans la langue chrétienne," in *Dic. de Spiritualité, ascétique et mystique*, III (Paris, 1957), 705–716, esp. 714.

[64]François Vandenbroucke characterizes this era as marked by "le divorce entre théologie et mystique," *La Spiritualité du Moyen Age* (Paris, 1961), p. 533. Indeed, a general upsurge of affective theology can be noted, usually critical of the debates "in scholis." If theology is understood in this latter academic sense, Vandenbroucke's conclusion can be amply validated. Late medieval affective theology, however, with its elaborate use of mystical terminology, can perhaps better be assessed as a protection against such a divorce. This upsurge of affective theology and what I have called the democratization of mysticism are two sides of the same coin.

[65]I shall deal elsewhere more extensively with the relation between the Observant movement and the *Devotio moderna*.

In the second place, and more specifically with regard to Tauler: the very fact that Luther comes to the conclusion that Tauler develops one particular sermon on the basis of mystical theology[66] alerts us to the fact that Luther apparently does not assume this always to be the case. It is a daring step to build around Tauler—and the *Theologia Deutsch*[67] mentioned by Luther in the same breath—a whole category of so-called "German mysticism," especially if this is to include, as it usually does, an author such as Meister Eckhart to whom Luther has not related himself in any sense. Granted the generally acknowledged proximity of Eckhardt and Tauler, there are noticeable differences which, when seen from the vantage point of Luther, are too formidable to overlook.[68] At any rate, the main conclusion drawn by Luther from the *Theologia Deutsch* is certainly not mystical: ". . . man should not confide in anything else but in Jesus Christ alone, not in his prayers, not in his merits or his works. Since it is not due to our efforts that we are to be saved but due to the mercy of God."[69] As appears from the final words of the 1518 preface to "Eyn deutsch Theologia" Luther regards it as a representative of the category "German Theology" rather than that of "German Mysticism": "hence we will find that the German theologians are without doubt the best theologians. Amen!"[70]

---

[66]*W A* 9,98.20; Cl. 5,306.28.

[67]On Luther's description of the *Theologia Deutsch*, see the title page of the second (and first complete) edition (1518), *W A* 1,376.A. Cf. the exposition of Ps. 51:3 in 1517. *W A* 1,186.25–29. Finally, cf. *Eine Deutsche Theologie*, cap. 42, modernized by Joseph Bernhart (Munich, 1946), p. 229.

[68]On the distinction between Eckhart and Tauler see Käte Grunewald, *Studien zu Johannes Taulers Frömmigkeit* (Berlin, 1930), p. 41: "Statt einer Schaumystik also eine in diesem neuen Sinne wirklich voluntaristische Mystik." We do not, of course, deny that there are parallels between Eckhart and Luther; it is a more complex matter than mere "Verbindunglinien," as Rühl argues (note 6), p. 91. If Rühl is justified in describing as *the* point of distinction between scholasticism and mysticism the "Denkform" of the latter which "von einem Begriff ausgeht, andere anschliesst und wieder zum Ausgangsbegriff zurükkehrt" (38), and hence "die essentielle Einheit von diametral entgegengesetzten Konzeptionen enthüllt" (45), then the question must be raised: is not a minimal interpretation of just this "Denkform" encountered in every affective theology and hence no further typical for "high mysticism" in the described sense of the word? To the extent that one seeks an interpretation which would embrace "high mysticism," the "Denkform" rests then upon a "Denkinhalt" which presupposes a thorough-going monism in which opposites are present only in appearance. Further, Rühl's effort to distinguish Luther and mysticism generally on the basis of anthropology is unclear and does not take account of the fact that the anthropologies of Eckhart and Tauler are different. Cf. Grunewald, p. 8. Finally, there is a decisive difference between Luther's and Eckhart's understanding of creation. While for Eckhart creation is alienation (cf. *Harvest of Medieval Theology*, p. 326), it is for Luther "gnad und wohltat." *Tagebuch über Dr. Martin Luther*, ed. H. Wrampelmayer (Halle, 1885), p. 1559.

[69]*W A Br.* 1,160.10–20; Cl. 6,10.15–18.

[70]*W A* 1,379.11f.

4. CHRIST'S EMBRACE: DEATH AND HELL[71]

1. Although we seemed to remain within the realm of methodological issues when we discussed the problems involved in extracting from Luther a "Yes" or "No" with respect to schools of mystical theology which did not present themselves as such to him, we have already moved beyond the state of formal considerations. The only viable method open to us is to study and define mysticism on the basis of Luther's description and evaluation, hence, at least initially, bypassing the issue of the appropriate definition of mysticism as such and of the classification of its several schools.

On the basis of the foregoing discussion we can come to the following preliminary conclusions:

a) There is as yet no reason to assume that Luther rejected mystical theology as such.[72] Rather he opposes the dangers of what we called "high mysticism."

b) The first characteristic of this form of mysticism is for Luther the union of soul and body ("unio animae et corporis"). So far as I know, this is not a standard expression. Altenstaig brings in his *Vocabularius theologie* a definition of "beatitude" which includes both soul and body.[73] It may be that Luther hints at this form of final beatitude to expose the proleptic nature of this high mysticism as a presumptuous *theologia gloriae*. More specifically, however, the context of his remarks indicates that he has in mind a psychosomatic experience through which the human senses experience the object of speculation,[74] i.e. the union of the soul with Christ.[75]

Luther's stance is not due to the fact that he rejects the idea of union as such or that he holds that spiritual realities cannot be experienced. On the contrary, while they cannot always be formulated, they can be experienced,

[71]*W A* 5,165.23. See note 82.

[72]Cf. the discussion of Luther's use of the concept of bridal mysticism in my article, "Iustitia Dei' and 'Iustitia Christi': Luther and the Scholastic Doctrines of Justification," *HThR* 59 (1966), 1–26, esp. 25f. On the use of the expression, "du bist min, ich bin din," among German mystical authors, see the register assembled by Grete Lüers. *Die Sprache der deutschen Mystik des Mittelalters im Werke der Mechthild von Magdeburg* (Munich, 1926), pp. 309f. On the use of the expression, "minnende Seele," cf. Romuald Banz, *Christus und die minnende Seele. Zwei spätmittelhochdeutsche mystische Gedichte* (Breslau, 1908), p. 119.

[73]"Illa autem unio animae et corporis..." (*W A* 43,73.11). Altenstaig writes in the article on "beatitudo," fol. 25ra: "Beatitudo est duplex (ut scriptis reliquit Richardus di. XLIX ar. V, q. 2, li. IV), sc. anime et corporis." Under the article on "unio" (fol. 269[va]) he writes: "unio quedam est corporalis, quedam spiritualis," although it is only in regard to the latter that mystical experience is discussed.

[74]Bonaventure writes of such an experience: *Itinerarium mentis in Deum*, ed. Julian Kaup (Munich, 1961), IV,3. 112–114.

[75]Cf. *W A* 40/3,199.5–10.

and on the basis of experience they can be learned. The point is, however, that true negative theology is "theology of the cross" and, as we shall see, its corresponding experience is the crying and groaning of the soul, the "gemitus inenarrabiles" (Rom. 8:26).[76]

c) The second characteristic of the kind of mysticism rejected by Luther is the bypassing of Christ in order to rest *in Deo nudo*. In his comment on Romans 5:2 Luther had insisted on the double requirement "per fidem" and "per Christum."[77] The single requirement "per Christum" could still be— and indeed was generally—understood as the necessary preparation for union and contemplation since it axiomatically presupposed the earlier and now transcended stage of faith. Especially the meditation upon the passion of Christ as the basis of all merits is advocated as the most useful means to generate intense devotion.[78]

A treatise by Schatzgeyer, in time (1501) close to Luther and filled with that monastic spirituality which was to evoke Luther's wrath, has by no means slighted Christ. The "pro nobis"—in this warm treatise put as "pro te"—establishes the intimate bond between Christ and the believer.[79] Furthermore the treatise insists that "there is but one way to heaven, through the cross of Christ." This proves, however, to evoke love and lead to the sweet embrace of Christ.[80] The true Christian turns away from the bitterness of this valley of tears to the beauty and splendor of Christ. Over against this *per Christum (et charitatem)* Luther places *per Christum* in the abiding context of faith *(per fidem)*.[81] For Luther the embrace with Christ is not sweet but death and hell:[82] "God wants us to be trained (by the cross), not absorbed."[83] The Christian does not turn away from the bitterness of this

---

[76]*Enarratio* Ps. 90:7 (1534–35. pub. 1541), *W A* 40/3,542.27–31; 543.8–13. A similar point is made in *W A Tr.* 1,108.1–11 (Nr. 257; 1532), where Luther writes against Eck as a disciple of Plato.

[77]See note 54.

[78]See Schatzgeyer (note 37), fol. 329[b], Dir. 32. Cf. John Geiler of Kaysersberg in Dacheux (note 48), p. 247, and Jane Dempsey Douglass. *Justification in Late Medieval Preaching* (Leiden, 1966), pp. 180ff. In this connection we refer the reader to Gerson's "Ars bene vivendi," which appeared in Wittenberg in 1513 "apud Augustinianos" with Luther's publisher Johannes Grunenberg. It is inconceivable that Luther should not have known this edition, and it increases the number of Gerson's works which Luther probably had read.

[79]Schatzgeyer (note 37), fol. 325[b], Dir. 21.

[80]*Ibid.*, fol. 329. Dir, 29.

[81]Compare by way of contrast Dionysius the Carthusian, *Opera* VII, 301 D–302 A.

[82]*Operationes in psalmos*, Ps. 5:2 (1519–20), *W A* 5,165.21ff.: "Sicut et filii patrem carnis dulcius amant post virgam, qua verberati sunt, Ita carni contraria voluptate sponsus sponsam suam afficit Christus, Nempe post amplexus. Amplexus vero ipsi mors et infernus sunt."

[83]Cf. note 75. For both parallel and contrast cf. the emphasis on *exercitium* in Gerhard Zerbolt, note 59.

world but is in that very valley of tears identified with the cross of Christ.[84]

d) At this point one may wonder whether the question as to Luther's relation to mysticism has not already been answered. If, indeed, the *contemplatio acquisita* is ruled out because it presupposes man's strenuous cooperation with grace,[85] and if *contemplatio infusa* is ruled out as presumptuous *theologia gloriae*,[86] it seems that no latitude is left. Yet the contrast of *accessus* and *raptus* is not the last word. If Luther, on the one hand, rejects the *raptus*, he indicates, on the other hand, that the *accessus* takes on a number of traits which are usually characteristic of the *raptus* itself. Although the embrace and union cannot be experienced through the senses and the *gemitus* continues to characterize the human crying need for the full manifestation of God (Rom. 8:26),[87] still the embrace and union are not ruled out but grasped by faith. As appears from the third Galatians commentary, the confrontation with the left wing of the Reformation does not force Luther to break with his alleged mystical past. The amazing thing is that he does not criticize the *Schwärmer* for being too radical, but for not being radical enough. They separate faith in the heart and Christ in heaven, whereas, for Luther, these are inseparably interwined. As regards this identification of Christ and the Christian Luther says concisely: "Es geht nicht speculative sed realiter zu" – it is not an imagined but a real matter.[88] It is important for us that this "realiter" is interpreted – undoubtedly expressing Luther's intention precisely – as the Christ in us who works "realiter," clarified by the eloquent adverbs "most present" (*praesentissime*) and "most efficaciously" (*efficassime*).

In the concluding section we want to probe Luther's use of typical mystical terminology in a series of thesis-like short paragraphs. To collect Luther's explicit statements *re* mystical theologians and their theology would prove to be an illegitimate short-cut. We have to take here the same

---

[84]See the *scholion* to Hebr. 2:14 (1517), *W A* 57³,129.20–25.

[85]*W A Br.* 1.160.

[86]Cf. the exposition of Hebr. 9:5, *W A* 57³,201.15–202.6. Cf. the earliest exposition of Ps. 17:11 ("Ascendit et volavit super pennas ventorum") in *W A* 3,114.15; 124.16ff. On the two theologies which Luther contrasts in his exposition of Hebr. 9:5 – "sapientia Christi gloriosi" and "sapientia Christi crucifixi" – cf. *W A* 39¹,389.10ff.

[87]As we hope to show, this "gemitus" is closely related to the "syntheresis." On Luther's assessment and use of the concept "syntheresis," see Emanuel Hirsch, *Lutherstudien I* (Gütersloh, 1954), pp. 109–128. Without connecting "gemitus" and "syntheresis" with one another, M. A. H. Stomps collects a series of citations under the viewpoint "expectatio" – a term which is central for Luther's *theological* anthropology. *Die Anthropologie Martin Luthers. Eine philosophische Untersuchung* (Frankfurt a. M., 1935), esp. pp. 14ff.

[88]Commentary on Galatians 3:28 (1531). *W A* 40¹,546.3–8, and the printed text of 1535. *W A* 40¹.546.25–28.

seemingly unexciting or at least unspectacular way as in the study of other aspects of Luther's theology: patient comparison with the preceding tradition, with a special emphasis on the devotional tradition immediately before him.

5. THE MYSTICAL CONTEXT: FUNDAMENTAL CONCEPTS

1. *Exegetical mysticism.* When one consults such a source as Altenstaig's *Vocabularius theologie* – published in the same year that Luther published his 95 theses – for the contemporary understanding of such technical mystical terms as "excessus," "extasis," and "raptus," one notices that the article on "extasis" is drawn up on the basis of two authorities. The first witness is the late medieval Church father, Gerson;[89] but in second place we find the Augustinian bishop and biblical exegete Jacobus Perez de Valencia.[90]

In the Prologue to the Psalms Commentary (1484) of Perez, we read that the *excessus* is the gift of vision to all prophets, a supernatural illumination which transcends the capacity of human knowledge. *Extasis* is a higher stage in which one is alienated from one's inner senses, as if he were outside himself (*quasi extra seipsum*). The third and final *elevatio* is called *raptus*, which is granted to but a few.[91] Perez, just like Luther half a century later, could and probably did find this description dispersed throughout the works of Augustine.[92]

---

[89]Luther speaks of "Gerson et ceteri patres" (*W A Tr.* 2.27.6f. [Nr. 1288] –1531). On the pulpit of the Amanduskirche in Urach, which was constructed in the last third of the 15th century, Gerson is depicted together with the four fathers of the Church. Cf. Georg Dehio, *Handbuch der Deutschen Kunstdenkmäler*, III (Berlin, 1925³), 548.

[90]See Altenstaig, *Vocabularius theologie* under article on "extasis" (fol. 83va); cf. the article on "raptus" (fol. 213va-b). Cf. also the earlier *Vocabularius* (Tübingen, 1508; 2nd ed. Basel, 1514) under article on "ecstasis" (fol. 25³⁻⁴). As the epigram of Heinrich Bebel put it, this Latin schoolbook was considered an "antidote" to such little-valued books as the "Catholicon." The "Catholicon," a comprehensive book completed in March, 1286, and often published (there is a Cologne, 1497, edition), was a lexicon compiled by Joannes Balbus de Janua (Giovanni Balbi), and it was still used as an authority by Luther in 1509–10. Cf. *W A* 9,68.14. In 1524 Luther considered it (along with the *Florista, Grecista, Labyrinthus,* and *Dormi secure*) typical of the "tollen, unnützen, schedlichen, Müniche bücher," which glutted the libraries. *An die Ratherren aller Städte deutsches Lands, W A* 15.50.9f.; Cl. 2,461.10f. Humanists north of the Alps probably followed the variegated judgment of the work by Erasmus; *Opus Epistolarum* I, 115.89 (1489); 133.85 (1494); 172.32 (1497). At the time he wrote his first lectures on the Psalms (1513–15), Luther still considered the "Catholicon" authoritative.

[91]*Prologus in Psalterium, tract.* II, a.2 (Venetiis, 1581), 16 F–17 B. For the larger context cf. Wilfrid Werbeck, *Jacobus Perez von Valencia. Untersuchungen zu seinem Psalmenkommentar* (Tübingen, 1959), pp. 81f. Cf. Luther *W A* 3,185.26f.: "in spiritu raptus intellexit in eo facto quid mystice significaret."

[92]Cf. the by no means dated work of A. W. Hunzinger, *Lutherstudien,* I, *Luthers Neuplatonismus in der Psalmenvorlesung von 1513*-1516 (Leipzig, 1906), pp. 105ff., esp. p. 106, n. I, Cf. p. 74, where

In the exegetical application, however, Perez does not retain the indicated distinctions. In commenting upon Psalm 115:11, Vulgate: "I said in my *excessus*: every man is a liar" – "excessus" is identified with "extasis" and interpreted by the verb "rapi" to describe the transition of David from "fides sola" to "contemplatio." Thus David is able to foresee the mysteries of the New Testament as prefigured in the law of Moses.[93] More important for the hermeneutical implications, exactly the same applies to the Apostles. First they have an implicit faith in Christ; but after Pentecost their minds are brought into ecstasy so that they grasp the mysteries of faith.[94] One may use here the term "exegetical mysticism" since it is the elevated state of mind, *excessus* or *extasis*, which allows the Apostles to understand Scripture.[95] The humiliation of which the preceding verse 10 speaks ("I am completely humiliated") is understood by Perez as the "sacrificium intellectus," the preparatory pre-Pentecostal state of mind. Thus, in a second stage, the "excessus" takes place in which David, the interpreter, comes to understand that only the divine law is reliable in the sense revealed by the Spirit.[96]

When we turn now to Luther's exposition of this text, we find that in his first comment on the *Psalterium* of Faber Stapulensis, the "excessus" is related to self-knowledge: elevated above himself man sees himself as he is, full of clouds and darkness.[97] Luther refers back to his exposition of Ps. 30 (:21) where he had said even more explicitly that *humiliation* is the result of the "excessus" or "extasis."[98] In contrast to Perez, humiliation is not the preparation for but the result of the "extasis."

In the interlinear gloss on the words "in my excessus," Luther notes the two meanings of "excessus" as either "raptus" or fear,[99] as he charts the four possible meanings of *extasis*.[100] Apart from this second connotation of fear,

---

Hunzinger argues that Luther's Neoplatonism is not that of the Pseudo-Dionysius. For a necessary clarification of the basic differences, cf. the characterization by J. Koch, "Augustinischer und dionysischer Neuplatonismus und das Mittelalter," *KantSt.* 58 (1956–57), 117–133. I owe this reference to F. Edward Cranz, "The Transmutation of Platonism in the Development of Nicolaus Cusanus and of Martin Luther," which appears as part of the reports of the Cusa Congress of 1964.

[93]Perez (note 91), fol. 837 F–838 A.

[94]*Ibid.*, fol. 838 B.

[95]*Ibid.*, fol. 838 D/E.

[96]*Ibid.*, fol. 838 E/F.

[97]*W A* 4,519.26–29. Cf. Augustine, *Enarr.* in Ps. 115, n. 3; Gl. ord., *PL* 113, 1038A; Peter Lombard, *PL* 191, 1030B.

[98]*W A* 3,171.19–24.

[99]*W A* 4,265.22 (Spring, 1515). Cf. Altenstaig, *Vocabularius* (1508), fol. 253–254.

[100]*W A* 4,265.30–36. With Cassiodorus the connection between *excessus* and martyrdom is given prominence. See his exposition of Ps. 115:10f., *Corpus Christianorum* 98, col. 1042, lines 9–16.

Luther interprets the term "excessus" ("extasis") in its mystical sense first as related to the "raptus" and the clear knowledge of faith; second, it stands for the understanding of faith (*sensus fidei*) which exceeds the literal understanding (*sensus litere*). This first understanding is the *true* literal sense;[101] the "sensus litere" is the interpretation on which the unbelievers stubbornly insist. The understanding of faith is the understanding of Scripture, the Gospel itself, the "face" of God, elsewhere distinguished from the eschatological vision of God's face in heaven.[102]

In his comments Luther makes three successive attempts to interpret this text. He is especially concerned to bring together the "excessus" as (1) the transition of the sinful man (*homo mendax*) to the man who is spiritual through faith (*homo spiritualis per fidem*), and (2) as the state of man stricken by fear particularly the fear due to persecution,[103] in which the believer experiences his complete dependence upon God.[104] "In my excessus" proves to become a synonym for both "in faith" and "in struggle"; it designates man's place "coram Deo" where the demarcation between "verax" and "mendax" is revealed.[105] This "excessus" does not imply the transcendence of this valley of tears and a rest in the peace of God, but the "demasquer" of the enemies of truth (i.e. the flesh and the world) and marks the beginning rather than the end of the battle.[106] There is definitely an elevation involved in the "excessus," an elevation which gives the believer a true perspective on the "futura bona" and produces the humiliating acknowledgment that he has no claim to these.[107]

Though the exegetical tradition concerning Ps. 115:11 will have to be explored in more detail, we suggest that four conclusions can be drawn from the preceding exposition.

a) The mystical term *excessus* is related by Luther to the idea of battle or

---

[101]Cf. *W A* 4,492.5–8 (Ps. 40, Faber). Luther's comments here are an exact mirroring of Faber's prologue to his Psalter. This important text is discussed in my book, *Forerunners of the Reformation* (New York, 1966), pp. 281–296.

[102]*W A* 4,482.25–483.4. On this usage of "face" (*vultus/facies*), cf. John Staupitz, *Tübinger Predigten*, ed. G. Buchwald and E. Wolf (1927), pp. 239.13–15. Cf. also the study by David C. Steinmetz, *Misericordia Dei: The Theology of Johannes von Staupitz in its Late Medieval Setting* (Leiden, 1968).

[103]*W A* 4,267.16–33; Cl. 5,196.16–197.2. Compare Augustine's interpretation. *Enarr. in Ps.* 115, n. 3; *Corpus Christianorum* 40, col. 1654, lines 1–27.

[104]*W A* 4,268.29–35.

[105]*W A* 4,269.3–15.

[106]*W A* 4,269.15–20.

[107]*W A* 4,273.14–22.

struggle typical for the life of the *viator*, the soldier of Christ.[108] As such this is by no means unusual; ever since Augustine it had been noted that *excessus* refers to an extraordinary state of mind either due to fear and suffering or to revelation. It would remain for Luther characteristic that the *excessus* through which the *homo mendax* becomes the *homo spiritualis* continues to be seen in the context of *pugna, tribulatio, Anfechtung*. What must have fascinated Luther most in Tauler is the idea that man *suffers* the birth of God.[109] This is what Luther means when he contrasts "realiter" with "speculative."

b) There is another aspect to this very same contrast. The "realiter" also means that one does not leave Scripture behind as a mere starting motor for the *affectus*.[110] Against the usual monastic order of *lectio (oratio), meditatio, contemplatio*, Luther prescribes a *lectio* initiated by *oratio* and leading toward *relectio*. When compared with the preceding tradition, it is striking that Luther no longer regards *lectio* (letter) and *meditatio* (spirit) as two *successive* stages. In 1539, dealing explicitly with the proper order, it is stated that true *meditatio* is *lectio* and *relectio*.[111] The axis of this Scripture-oriented meditation is not speculation (*prudentia–intellectus*) but the affective state (*affectus*) which prepares man's intellectual powers for the sudden insights and break-throughs which we should not limit to a once and for all *Turmerlebnis*.[112] The scope of the *affectus* is exactly the reality *coram Deo* which, as we saw, is revealed *in excessu mentis*,[113] when the knowledge of *futura bona* and the self-knowledge that *omnis homo mendax* coincide.[114] Luther can refer here to the believers exactly because it is to them, as the *spirituales* or the *mystici*,[115] that the mysteries of redemption and Incarnation are revealed.

c) Just as Luther rejects a false Christological mysticism – which, as we saw, speculates on the uncreated word and is not satisfied with the "homo

---

[108]Cf. Olavi Tarvainen, "Der Gedanke der Conformitas Christi in Luthers Theologie," *ZSTh* 22 (1953), 26–43, esp. 40. See also the *Operationes in Psalmos*. Ps. 5:12 (*W A* 5, 167.36–168.7). Cf. *W A* 5, 188.30–32.

[109]*Schol.* to Ps. 4:2 (Autumn, 1516), *W A* 55², 57.3–58.11. On Tauler's view of passivity as spiritual self-elevation, cf. Bengt Hägglund, "The Background of Luther's Doctrine of Justification in Late Medieval Theology," *Lutheran World* 8 (1961), 24–36, esp. 30f.

[110]*W A* 4,467.24–26.

[111]*W A* 50,659.22–24; cf. the discussion in " 'Iustitia Christi' and 'Iustitia Dei' " (cited in note 72), p. 12. See above Chapter V.

[112]For a more exact analysis of the term "affectus" in the young Luther, cf. Günther Metzger, *Gelebter Glaube. Die Formierung reformatorischen Denkens in Luthers erster Psalmenvorlesung* (Göttingen, 1964). Metzger's definition of "extasis" in the excursus on "excessus" (*ibid.*, pp. 111f) requires further work.

[113]Cf. Reinhard Schwarz, *Fides, Spes und Caritas beim jungen Luther* (Berlin, 1962), p. 148, n. 213.

[114]Cf. *W A* 1,342.37–343.8 (*Sermo de Passione*, 1518).

[115]Comments on Rom. 8:6 as an explanation of Ps. 31(32):9; *W A* 3,176.14–24; Cl. 4,107.25–108.1.

abscondens divinitatem" – so also he rejects a false exegetical mysticism which forces access to the Father "through the mysteries of Scripture." Either way makes for pride or desperation, *superbi* or *desperati*, a traditional allusion to the two erring groups on the left and the right of the *via media* of the Church militant.[116]

d) The dual aspects of the *excessus mentis* as faith and tribulation may help us to explain why, in the first lectures on the Psalms (1513–1515), Luther repeatedly slights the fourth sense of Scripture, the anagogical interpretation.[117] It is certainly not completely absent; but when it occurs it stands increasingly for the horizontal perseverance of the faithful and not for the vertical ascent of the aristocrats of the Spirit. Accordingly, in one central passage the anagogical work of God is not mystical elevation but the goal of God's work in history, either in heaven or in hell.[118] The deviation from the principles of Bonaventure[119] and from the practice of men like Dionysius the Carthusian and Kaspar Schatzgeyer cannot escape our attention. I am inclined to find here support for the conclusion of Gerhard Ebeling, accepted by the editors of *W A* 55, that the reduction of the fourfold sense is to be related to another hermeneutical schema: head-body-members.[120] Just as its head, Jesus Christ, so does the body, the *ecclesia militans*, march toward history's goal through the same valley of tears as its suffering Lord:[121] "Therefore if you look for a sign of the grace of God or wonder whether Christ himself is in you: no other sign is given to you but the sign of Jona. Therefore if you were to be in hell for three days, *that* is the sign that Christ is with you and you in Christ."[122]

2. *Raptus.* Not only *excessus* but also *raptus* and *rapi* function in Luther's theological vocabulary. The well-known sharp contrast between the *temporalia* and the *aeterna*, etc., referring to the difference between existence

---

[116]*W A* 4,647.24f. (Sermon, Aug., 1517 [?]).

[117]Cf. the discussion of this important discovery by Gerhard Ebeling, "Die Anfänge von Luthers Hermeneutik," *ZThK* 48 (1951), 172–230, esp. 226, and "Luthers Psalterdruck von Jahre 1513," *ZThK* 50 (1953), 43–99, esp. 92ff. Cf. also the suggestion by Werbeck (note 91), p. 104, that in the medieval tradition the anagogical sense "weniger häufig . . . zum Zuge kam." Cf. Henri de Lubac, *Exégèse médiévale. Les quatre sens de l'Ecriture*, I (Paris, 1959), 139.

[118]*Schol.* to Ps. 76(77):13, *W A* 3,532.7f.; Cl. 5,160.28f.

[119]Cf. above, pp. 226–229.

[120]Ebeling (note 117), pp. 95ff.; cf. *W A* 55/1,9.28ff.

[121]Although the early ecclesiology of Luther is not a topic for detailed discussion here, I believe that the usual criticism by Roman Catholic scholars, which spies in the first lectures on the psalms documentation for an individualistic interpretation of the "congregatio fidelium," must be corrected by Luther's conception of anagogy as the *common* history of the people of God, without foregoing individual exceptions. On the literature, cf. Gerhard Müller, "Ekklesiologie und Kirchenkritik beim jungen Luther," *Neue ZSTh* 7 (1965), 100–128.

[122]*Schol.* to Ps. 68 (69):17, *W A* 3,433.2-4; Cl. 5,147.7–10.

coram hominibus and *coram Deo*, can be summarized by Luther on the inside of the title-page of his Psalter with the words: "In Holy Scripture the most important thing is to distinguish the Spirit from the letter; this is what truly makes one a theologian."[123] In a significant parallel in early 1514, Luther had noted that a true theologian is born "in rapture and ecstasy; this is what makes a true theologian" (*in raptu et extasi, et hec facit verum theologum*).[124] After we have seen that *excessus* or *extasis* is at once *fides* and *pugna*, we are no longer tempted to oppose without far-reaching qualifications the mystical Luther of 1514 to the mature one of 1520 who states in the *Operationes in Psalmos*: "By living, indeed by dying and being damned, one becomes a theologian, not by thinking and reading and speculating" (*Vivendo, immo moriendo et damnando fit theologus, non intelligendo, legendo aut speculando*).[125]

Raptus is the reliance on the righteousness of Christ outside ourselves (*extra nos*) and can be described as a complete transformation into Christ (*in Christum plane transformari*).[126] Again, as we noted with *excessus*, *raptus* does not mean an ontological transformation but a transformation of *affectus* and *fiducia*, of our love and trust. Hence we do not argue that Luther is a mystical theologian because of his use of these terms. Rather we stress that their new function cannot be understood without a thorough grasp of their original mystical context. If future research confirms my suggestion that Luther's concept "extra nos" is related to *raptus*, one of the major arguments for a forensic interpretation of Luther's doctrine of justification has been preempted.[127] Though we have no claim to the *iustitia Christi* which is not our "property" (*proprietas*), it is granted to us as a present possession (*possessio*).[128] *Extra nos* and *raptus* indicate that the *iustitia Christi* – and not our own powers – is the source and resource for *our* righteousness.[129] Epithets such as

---

[123]*W A* 55/1,4.25f.

[124]*Schol.* to Ps. 64(65):2, *W A* 3,372.23–25; Cl. 5,130.11f. Cf. *W A* 1,336.10–12 (*Sermo de passione Christi*, 1518).

[125]*W A* 5,163.28f.

[126]*W A* 8,111.29–5 (1521).

[127]Cf. Thomas M. McDonough O.P., *The Law and the Gospel in Luther: A Study of Martin Luther's Confessional Writings* (Oxford, 1963), p. 53: "Indisputably, Luther understands imputative righteousness as an extrinsic or forensic relation...."

[128]*W A* 39¹,109.1–3 (*Disputatio de iustificatione*, 1536). In the Roman legal tradition "possessio" and "ususfructus" from the contrast to "proprietas" or "dominium." Cf. Max Kaser, *Eigentum und Besitz im älteren römischen Recht* (Weimar, 1943), pp. 310ff. and Ernst Levy, *West Roman Vulgar Law: The Law of Property*, (Philadelphia, 1951), pp. 19ff.

[129]One should concede that in one of its very earliest statements the "extra se (nos)" designates simply the contrast between God's aseity and the dependence of man on divine providence. *W A* 4,481.20f. (to Faber, *Quincuplex Psalterium*, Ps. 15(16):2). The "extra-dimension" is, therefore, not only applicable to fallen man and his justification, but also to man as a created being.

"external" and "forensic" righteousness cannot do justice to Luther's doctrine of justification.

Luther can use the *raptus* not only because of its connotation of "extra nos" but also because of its implication of absolute passivity. According to what we called "high mysticism," sheer passivity is typical of the last stage of true mysticism experienced by the elect few. Luther takes this term and applies it to the life of faith as such and hence to *all* true believers. Parallel to his deletion of the wall of separation between the *praecepta* and the *consilia evangelica* – the shaking of the foundations of monasticism – Luther's particular kind of democratization of mysticism robs high mysticism of one of its main characteristics. At the same time, its original context alerts us to the fact that when Luther uses *rapi* in one breath with *duci* and *pati*,[130] the sinner is not a dead instrument of the omnipotent God, and justification by faith is not quietism.

3. *Gemitus*. Both *excessus* and *raptus* imply that faith and justification are not the harmonious realization of man's capacities and desires. In his Romans commentary Luther uses a term which he could have read in Gerson's *De mystica theologia*, the "juxtaposition of opposites" (*antiperistasis*), synonymous with "sub contrario," in the transcript rendered as "in abscondito."[131] Here we are in the immediate proximity of Luther's own use of the word mystical: all wisdom and love are hidden in the suffering and dying Christ – "hidden because visible to mystical and spiritual eyes (*mysticis et spiritualibus oculis visibiles*)."[132]

At this point we should at least mention the term *gemitus*, though its absence in the relevant literature and the limits of this paper do not allow for more than some introductory observations. In the light of the preceding tradition with regard to *gemitus*, two points are particularly noteworthy in Luther's earlier works. In the first place the parallel between *fides* and *gemitus*. Justification, and more precisely the nonimputation of sin, takes place "on account of faith and groaning" (*propter fidem et gemitum*), and culpable sin is not found "in those who believe and cry out [to God]" (*in credentibus et gementibus*).[133] *Gemitus* is not another word for *facere quod in se est* or *humilitas* as some kind of condition for justification; rather it characterizes

[130] *W A* 5,144.34–36 (1519–21); *ibid.*, 176.12. *W A* 40¹,41.3–5. Cf. Karl Holl, *Ges. Aufs. zur KG*, 1, 131. Cf. *W A* 56,386.24f., where it is clear that "rapi" need not necessarily mean an "excessus mentis" to God.

[131] Gerson (note 1), pp. 190, 129f. Luther, *W A* 56,387.2–4; Cl. 5,270.14–16. Cf. the transcript. *W A* 57,199.6ff.

[132] *W A* 1,340.35–341.3 (*Sermo de passione*, 1518).

[133] *Schol.* to Rom. 4:7; *W A* 56,289.18–21; Cl. 5,245.11–15. *Ibid.*, 276.7ff; 289.29–31.

the life of the *sancti*, whose righteousness is hidden.[134] It describes the state of complete identification with Christ.[135] Whereas in the connection between *gemitus* and true penitence there is a basis for comparison with Abelard,[136] Bernard and Gerson refer to *gemitus* as part of the preparatory stage in the triad "purgation-illumination-contemplation"[137] or as initiation of the birth of God in the soul.[138]

The real significance of the fact that Luther can combine *gemitus* and *fides* appears, however, when we realize that the use made of *gemitus* by both Bernard and Gerson as a stage on the mystical way is by no means a coincidence. According to an influential gloss by Jerome *gemitus* refers to *synderesis*, which means that the gloss attributes to the human spirit what Romans 8:26 describes as the operation of the Holy Spirit: "the Spirit petitions for us with unutterable groanings."[139] This combination of *gemitus* and *synderesis* functions in scholasticism in such a way that we are not allowed to study the one concept without the other. For Bonaventure the *synderesis* is the affective power in man which intercedes with God with "unutterable groanings,"[140] since it makes man desire the good. Since this *synderesis* is an inalienable part of man, Geiler can exhort his readers to self-purgation by going "diligently into the inner ground [of the soul]."[141] It is this same virginal part of man which, according to Dionysius the Carthusian, is kindled by love until the soul is completely absorbed in God.[142] And it is in a call for the full exploitation of these divine resources in man that Schatzgeyer's 1501 treatise on the spiritual life culminates in the Epilogue.[143]

As is well known, there is a marked interest with the young Luther in the *synderesis*, [144] which I am inclined to relate to his early defense of the *facere quod*

---

[134]*W A* 56,290.18–22; Cl. 5,245.30–34.

[135]*W A* 1,558.4f (1518).

[136]Peter Abelard, *Ethica* c. 19 (*MPL* 178, 664, D).

[137]Bernard, *Tractatus de gradibus humilitatis et superbiae*, c. 6, n. 19 (*MPL* 182, 952).

[138]Gerson, *In festo S. Bernardi* (Aug. 20, 1402), Glorieux, v, 336.

[139]Commentary on Ezekiel 1:10 (*MPL* 25, 22); cf. Commentary on Malachi (*MPL* 25, 1563).

[140]II *Sent.*, d. 39, a. 2, q. I, ad 4; *ibid.*, ad I. Cf. *ibid.*, a, 2, q, 3, ad 5. Cf. also Alexander of Hales, *Summa* I/II (*Ad Claras Aquas* II, Nr, 418); Scotus, *Ox.* II, d. 39, q. I (Vives, XIII, 409ff); *Rep., ibid.* (Vives, XXIII, 203). For our purposes it is not important to discuss further the relation of *synderesis* and conscience or to distinguish *synderesis, apex mentis*, and *scintilla animae*. In this regard cf. Hirsch (note 87). pp. 11ff. An interesting variation of this concept appears in Wessel Gansfort. *De Providentia* in *Opera omnia* (Groningen, 1614), p. 722.

[141]Geiler of Kaysersberg, fol. 6^b (note 48), p. 222.

[142]*Opera*, VII, 313 a/b.

[143]Schatzgeyer (note 37), *Epilogus et conclusio*, 330^b.

[144]*W A* 1,32.1–16 (Sermon, Dec. 26, 1514).

in se est and the *merita de congruo.*[145] Yet in the most explicit statement in this period it is quite clear that the *synderesis* points man to the proper *goal* but does not show him the *way* to that goal.[146] Even here the *gemitus* is not the emotional expression of the *synderesis* but the mark of its impotence and hence of man's absolute dependence on God. The *synderesis* characterizes man's *esse*, not his *bene esse.*[147] Schatzgeyer had – in accordance with the tradition – based his high expectations of man's innate *synderesis* on Ps. 4:7: "the light of your face is manifest to us, O God." In the *Dictata* (1516) and again emphatically in the *Operationes in Psalmos* Luther says explicitly that this interpretation is false: "The first principle of all good works is faith."[148] *Gemitus* (just as much as *oratio*) presupposes faith and does not refer to a stage of preparation or to a virginal sinproof part in man, but to the life of faith itself: "Prayer is his desire for Christ; the cry is for Christ to transfigure his wretchedness."[149]

Reviewing our conclusions it can be said that Luther has gathered in terms characteristic of the extremes of the *via mystica* to clarify its center and axis. On the one hand *excessus* and *raptus*, on the other *gemitus* have been put to the service of clarifying the Christian life. It is exactly in the balance of these ideas that I discern the genius of Luther's theology of the Christian life. The *gemitus* aspect neutralizes the dangers of the *theologia gloriae* of the mystical *raptus*. The *excessus* and *raptus* aspect neutralizes the synergistic elements in the traditional scholastic combination of *synderesis* and *gemitus*. The test for this conclusion can be carried out in a separate discussion of Luther's use of bridal imagery and his view of the *unio fidei*, which we cannot execute here. Searching our way among the many pitfalls inherent in the theme "Luther and Mysticism," we hope to have shown that this crucial area cannot be regarded as a side issue in the rich world of thought of the Reformer.

One can designate the theology of Luther with the generally recognized summarizing formula, "simul iustus et peccator" – simultaneously righteous and sinful. The very same reality which is summarized by this formula can be expressed in the language of mystical spirituality, and that means for

[145]Cf. my "Facientibus quod in se est Deus non denegat gratiam," *HThR* 55 (1962), 317–342, esp. 333ff. See above Chapter IV.

[146]*W A* 1,32.33–40 (Sermon, Dec. 26, 1514), *ibid.*, 33.36f.; 34, 4–7.

[147]*Ibid.*, 36.37–37.1 See the connection between *gemitus* and *homo vetus, Operationes in Psalmos,* Ps. 5:12; *W A* 5.164.22–31. For a more detailed analysis of the texts which deal with the *synderesis* and *fides*, see S.E. Ozment (note 45).

[148]*W A* 5,119.12–18 (1519–21); cf. *W A* 55²,80.29–81.2 (1516) and the detailed annotations in *W A* 55¹ 22.34–25.9. Cf. the thesis of Arnold of Heisterbach in Gerhard Ritter, *Via antiqua und Via Moderna* (Heidelberg, 1922; Darmstadt, 1963), 155.16ff.; cf. 63f.

[149]*W A* 1,196.25f. (*Die sieben Busspsalmen,* 1517).

Luther in the language of the personal experience of faith, by the formula, "simul gemitus et raptus."[150] For both formulas it is characteristic that they do not indicate a *via media*, but a *simul* which reveals a *coincidentia oppositorum*.

---

[150]*Operationes in Psalmos.* Ps. 5:12; *W A* 5,176.11–22.

VII

THE GOSPEL OF SOCIAL UNREST:
450 YEARS AFTER THE SO-CALLED
"GERMAN PEASANTS' WAR" OF 1525

1. THE GERMAN PEASANTS' WAR

In spite of intensive research, it has proven difficult to set aside terms and concepts that have been current since the time of the Reformation. Thus, we continue to speak without further reflection of the *"German* Peasants' War" although this limitation has long since proven untenable. For a period of almost two centuries, the so-called *tumultus rusticorum*, best translated as social unrest or countryside agitation, was a phenomenon extending across all of Europe, from Italy to the Low Countries and from Southern France to Bohemia.

We also continue to speak of the *Peasants'* War even when our sources suggest that the term *"rustici"* must be used in a more differentiated way and be best translated as "country folk" or – when viewed from the humanist perspective – be translated as "uneducated" or "simple folk." Furthermore, throughout the later Middle Ages and in the first twenty years of the sixteenth century, part of the urban population pursued the same political and social goals as the peasants. These townspeople not only offered the "peasants" "solidarity," as it is often put, but they decisively participated in and supported the consequent revolutionary movement. Hence we find in the so-called *Artikelbriefen*, or peasant manifestos, the common political platform of town and country. We read in one *Artikelbrief*: the poor must suffer under "great hardships (burdens) which are contrary to God and all justice. These burdens are placed upon the poor by secular and sacred authorities in 'city *and* country.'"[1]

---

[1]*Flugschriften des Bauernkrieges*, ed. Klaus Kaczerowsky (Hamburg: 1970) 15. The careful collection of texts offered by Gerald Strauss (*Manifestations of Discontent in Germany on the Eve of the Reformation* [Bloomington: 1971]) provides a good survey of several modes of protest on the eve of the Reformation. In contemporary research, too often the distinction between "town" and "country" is emphasized. As far as the Peasants' War is concerned, it must be borne in mind that the town market served as an effective liaison. See David Sabean, "Markets, Uprisings and Leadership in Peasant Societies: Western Europe 1381–1789," *Peasant Studies*, Newsletter 2 (Pittsburgh: 1973) 17–19. Note especially point three in n. 45 below. Volker Press in a

The *Mühlhausen Articles* of September 1524 demand the reform of the city council at the urging of "the weavers [of St. Jacob] and other craftsmen in various city districts."[2] The *Erfurt Articles* of May 9, 1525 are the result of a meeting of "all craftsmen belonging to the various districts of the city of Erfurt to discuss the need for social reform."[3]

Particularly in this sensitive area of research, ideological spectacles tend to obscure our grasp of historical reality. Historians from East Germany emphasize the Peasants' War as a *German* event because they want to be able to compete for historical glory with the French and Russian Revolutions. In regard to the *Peasants'* War as an affair of town and country, however, Marxist research with *its* ideological presuppositions has indeed the edge. It is not Marxism but National Socialism that has most distorted the proper perspectives. In the Nazi effort to play the "völkische" peasants against the "klassenkämpferische" workers, Hitler is presented as the fulfillment of the Peasants' Revolt.[4]

Finally, the expression "Peasants' *War*" covers only that military phase which first developed *after* May 1524 (Forchheim, May 16) with its dual climax in Mühlhausen on May 25, 1525, and the flight of Gaismair a year later on July 2, 1526.[5] But the *roots* of this movement had long been present in European history as a non-violent impulse for reform, as what might be called the "Gospel of Social Unrest." Indeed, it is true that the early twenties saw a radicalization across the board. The fundamental Reformation concepts of *freedom (Freiheit)* and the *priesthood of all believers*

programmatic article calls for the further investigation of the "village" and of the phenomena in the proximity of the "*Ackerbürger der Kleinstädte*" and the "*grosstädtische Unterschichten*" to the peasants ("Der Bauernkrieg als Problem der deutschen Geschichte," *Nassauische Annalen* 86 [1975] 158–77, especially 168, 173). "Für die Artikulation der bäuerlichen Forderungen spielte die Mithilfe städtischer Gruppen eine wichtige Rolle – aus den städtischen Unterschichten fanden die bäuerlichen Erhebungen überdies Zulauf aus einer traditionell unruhigen und im Gegensatz zu ihnen selbst leicht mobilisierbaren und organisierbaren Gruppe. Agrarische und städtische Konflikte gingen so ineinander über" (ibid., 176f., point 6).

[2]*Akten zur Geschichte des Bauernkriegs in Mitteldeutschland*, II, ed. Walther Peter Fuchs in collaboration with Günther Franz (Jena: 1942; Aalen: 1964) 47, no. 1128.

[3]*W A* 18, 534, 1–3.

[4]Cf. Günther Franz, *Der deutsche Bauernkrieg* (Munich and Berlin: 1933) 481.

[5]"Bei diesem Überblick über die Ursachen, welche die Bauernunruhen auslösen, wird aber auch deutlich, dass alle diese Auseinandersetzungen einschliesslich der ersten des Jahres 1525 noch gewaltlosen Charakter haben. Lösungen werden zunächst friedlich-schiedlich gefunden und meistens vertraglich festgelegt. Beschwerden über einzelne Punkte bringt man schriftlich nur dort vor, wo man mit Entgegenkommen rechnet, nicht aber dort, wo man im Begriff ist, loszuschlagen, sondern wo zunächst von Verhandlungen etwas zu erhoffen ist. Besonders in Zeiten, in denen man nicht gern viel schreibt, fasste man solche Beschwerdebriefe wohl doch nur ab, wenn man sich etwas davon versprechen konnte" (Adolf Waas, *Die Bauern im Kampf um Gerechtigkeit 1300–1525* [Munich: 1964] 38).

(Priestertum aller Gläubigen) became slogans that electrified and mobilized the peasants everywhere. But Luther and the Reformation are merely accelerators. Far from freeing the soul by means of a sublimation of worldly *gravamina*, as Marx, Engels and Marcuse have put it, the Wittenberg and Zürich Reformations brought a clearly traceable tone of impatience into the political petitions and polemical pamphlets of the time.

The pre-Reformation rebellious "hordes" *(Haufen)* and "mobs" *(Rotten)* had appealed to the old "common" law and rights. They congregated around preachers of repentance who summoned the people to prepare for the coming Kingdom of Peace. They banked on a non-violent reform from above. Hence *conversio cordis* and *patientia mentis* were extolled as the most prominent virtues, i.e., a personal disposition of penance and a patient awaiting of the coming Kingdom of peace and justice.[6]

The new ferment of reformation proved to imply political radicalization by a biblical-spiritual opposition to the secular power of the Church, with its tax privileges in both city and country and its Rome-oriented economic policies.[7] Yet, during the time of the so-called Peasants' *War*, peasant leaders

---

[6]The interpretation of the *Reformatio Sigismundi* as a revolutionary manifesto has been convincingly refuted by Lothar Graf zu Dohna: "Es war ein arges Missverstehen, dass man die Erneuerung der Ordnung, die Reform, als neue Ordnung ansehen wollte. Man hatte die Aktualisierung der vorfindlichen, wenn auch weitgehend verdeckten Ordo wegen seiner Zukünftigkeit für etwas grundlegend anderes gehalten als die vorhandene Ordnung. Es gibt aber im Denken des Verfassers nur eine Ordnung. Sie ist ihrem Ursprung und Wesen nach göttlich und zugleich in die Geschichte eingetaucht. Sie kann auch als 'rechte' oder als 'heilige, selige Ordnung' bezeichnet werden. Ihr Wesen könnte man vielleicht, besser als in einer Definition, durch einen gehorsamheischenden Anspruch der Schrift zum Ausdruck bringen, in dem beide Aspekte der Ordnung enthalten sind, einmaliger Vollzug und ewige Geltung: 'man soll halten, was Christus mit Leib und Leben geordnet hat'" (*Reformatio Sigismundi: Beiträge zum Verständnis einer Reformschrift des fünfzehnten Jahrhunderts*, Veröffentlichungen des Max-Planck-Instituts für Geschichte, no. 4 [Göttingen: 1960] 115, cf. 182). For the significance of the *Reformatio Sigismundi* in the following period, especially for Luther's "An den christlichen Adel," see *Reformation Kaiser Siegmunds*, in Monumenta Germaniae Historica (Stuttgart: 1964) 6.27.

[7]Die Reformation scheint eine erhebliche Intensivierung dieser Unruhen gebracht zu haben, die sich dann in dem grossen Aufstand von 1524/25 entluden" (Horst Gerlach, *Der englische Bauernaufstand von 1381 und der deutsche Bauernkrieg: Ein Vergleich* [Meisenheim am Glan: 1969] 66). Although Luther viewed reform "from above" as the only answer and rejected violence "from below" on principle as legalistic, his evaluation of the situation – economically and psychologically – at the beginning of 1522 conforms exactly to what will be articulated three years later in the Peasants' Articles: "Es ist von gottis gnaden yn dissen iaren das selige licht der Christlichen warheyt, durch Babst und die seynen tzuvor vordruckt, widder auffgangen, da durch yhre manchfeldige schedliche und schendliche vorfurunge allerley misztadt und tyranney offentlich an tag bracht und tzuschanden worden ist. Das es sich ansehen lest, es werde gelangen tzu auffruhr und Pfaffen, Munich, Bisschoff mit gantzem geystlichen standt erschlagenn und voriagt mochten werden, wu sie nit ein ernstliche merkliche besserung selbs fur wendenn, denn der gemeyne man, yn bewegung und vordriesz seyner beschedigung am gut, leyb und seel erlitten, tzu hoch vorsucht und ubir alle masz vonn yhn auffs aller untreulichst

repeatedly and explicitly distanced themselves from any use of violence; while, on the other hand, long *before* Luther's call to reformation, armed clashes were frequent.[8] To be sure, the problem of the use or non-use of violence did not become thematic until after the rebellions of 1512–13 in rural and urban areas – from Deventor to Regensburg and from Swabia to Saxony – when the call for divine justice had fully taken the place of the old common laws and rights.[9] The term "War" is an overdramatization that distorts our historical perspective and tends to isolate the events of 1525.

Therefore, in all its three parts the term "German Peasants' War" is to be used with caution and according to its differing contexts.

2. THE NEW HORIZON OF EXPECTATION

When we make the difficult – but for our modern understanding necessary – attempt to distinguish within the maze of programs and tendencies of this epoch between reform attempts and revolutionary movements, we have to point to the changed horizon of expectation. On the eve of the Reformation, an important change took place. Earlier, the appeal to old "common" law and custom over against the irresistible spreading of centrally administered territories, the precursors of our modern states, was a cry of distress and a plea for help from those "below" to those "above." This plea was grounded in a trust in the authorities which, given the circumstances, has remained for a long time surprisingly shock-resistant.

However, where the appeal to the new divine law penetrates, the injustice experienced because of unbearable tax burdens, encroachment on the common pasture land, and further disenfranchisement of free men starts to spark off intensified reflection and action. At this point we have left the plane of longing for *restitutio* and for a return to the multiple forms of an earlier, regional autonomy. We now hit upon a new awareness of all men being equal under the just will of God, which is seen as equally binding,

---

beschweret, hynfurt solchs nymmer leydenn muge noch wolle, und datzu redliche Ursach habe mit pflegeln und kolben dreyn tzu schlagen, wie der Karst hans drawet" (*Eyn trew vormanung Martini Luther tzu allen Christen, sich izu vorhuten fur auffruhr unnd emporung, WA* 8.676, 6–18).

[8]There were other rebellions in 1478 (Salzburg), 1489/90 and 1513/15 (Eidgenossenschaft), 1499 and 1502 (Vorlande), 1514 (Württemberg, "Armer Konrad"), 1520 (Tirol) planned. Cf. also Wilhelm Stolze, *Bauernkrieg und Reformation*, Schriften des Vereins für Reformationsgeschichte 44 (Leipzig: 1926) 39f.

[9]This "pre-history" is yet to be taken into consideration in the field of Anabaptist research. See James M. Stayer, *Anabaptists and the Sword* (Lawrence: 1972). Cf. the relevant reviews by John H. Yoder in *Church History* 43 (1974) 272f.; and Steven E. Ozment in *Renaissance Quarterly* 27 (1974) 213ff.

embracing, and obligatory for the entire society, city *and* country, peasants *and* cityfolk, ecclesiastical *and* civil authorities. What had been active in the self-understanding of both imperial city and city-state for two hundred years, namely, the joint and equal responsibility of all citizens and residents in respect to the will of God, caused tangible reverberations in circles of the rural population in the last decades before the Reformation.

One can concur with earlier research which held that the city riots of the years 1513–15 are to be traced back to peasant disturbances. It is to be borne in mind, however, that the basic structure of the peasants' program did not arise *ex nihilo* in the country. Instead, their program is rooted in the idea of the God-willed balance between rights and duties which had long been tested in the cities.[10]

It has been argued that the peasants were too unrealistic in their dreams about a new society with justice for all. The one point of critique in Marxist studies on Müntzer is that he was utopian in his aspirations. But we would be missing the point if we regarded the appeal to divine law and the vision of an ideal rural state as political utopianism. The designation "utopian" is a mere *vaticinium ex eventu*, a prophecy from hindsight. This is as ludicrous as

---

[10]Cf. Bernd Moeller, *Reichsstadt und Reformation*, Schriften des Vereins für Reformationsgeschichte 180 (Gütersloh: 1962). The transition from "Pflegschaftspflicht" to "Pflegschaftsrecht" with the accompanying theories of a sacral civic community is a *pre*-Reformation phenomenon. Here we encounter the rise of the "bürgerlichen Kirchengemeinde als genossenschaftliches Gegenstück zur herrschaftlichen Auffassung der Kirche" (Rolf Kiessling, *Bürgerliche Gesellschaft und Kirche in Augsburg im Spätmittelalter: Ein Beitrag zur Strukturanalyse der oberdeutschen Reichsstadt* [Augsburg: 1971] 126; cf. 312, 360). The deepening of urban consciousness as a result of the Reformation remains for the time being a working hypothesis. More appropriate would be such designations as "appropriation," "application" or "use" of the *genossenschaftliche* traditions – inside and outside the city walls! – by the spokesmen for the Reformation, including Martin Luther. According to Moeller (*Reichsstadt*, 33), the Reformation in the imperial cities had "jedenfalls zunächst eine Neubesinnung auf deren genossenschaftlichen Grundlagen, neue lebhafte Anteilnahme der Bürger an den kommunalen Angelegenheiten erweckt ..." The careful qualification of this in the accompanying note (63) has unfortunately not been included in the otherwise excellent American translation by H. C. Eric Midelfort and Mark U. Edwards, *Imperial Cities and the Reformation: Three Essays* (Philadelphia: 1972) 69, n. 65. Heide Stratenwerth (*Die Reformation in der Stadt Osnabrück* [Wiesbaden: 1971] 123, n. 81) has pointed out that the holdings of the Osnabrück archives offer no proof that the citizens understood their commune as a religious community. Hans-Christoph Rublack (*Die Einführung der Reformation in Konstanz von den Anfängen bis zum Abschluss 1531* [Gütersloh: 1971] 2f., 16, 50ff.) and Helmut Maurer ("Die Ratskapelle: Beobachtungen am Beispiel von St. Lorenz in Konstanz," *Festschrift für Hermann Heimpel* 2, Veröffentlichungen des Max-Planck-Instituts für Geschichte 36/II [Göttingen: 1972] 225–36; 234f.) offer examples of the pre-Reformation intertwining of town and church in the town council. Only through comparison with the rapidly increasing research dealing with the Italian urban communities will it be possible to differentiate the various types of transalpine urban communities. Cf. Marvin B. Becker, "Some Common Features of Italian Urban Experience (c. 1200–1500)," *Medievalia et Humanistica* NS 1 (1970) 175–201.

dismissing the ideals of the late-medieval city-state with its religious covenant-theology as a utopian dream merely because in the 1530's the city-state could no longer extricate itself from the clutches of the princes' absolutism.[11] Just as much, it would be unfounded to deny the rural people of the territories the realistic demand to align their living conditions – in the realm of existing political and economic possibilities – with the tested judicial structures of the city. In the *Bundschuh* movement, e.g., the freedoms of the cities – with their own election of pastors, their tax and market privileges – provided a realistic basis for incorporating its concept of freedom in the sense of a covenant community interpreted according to the Old Testament. This occurred years before Luther's fundamental Reformation writing, *The Freedom of a Christian*, had been printed and rapidly and widely circulated.

Here we touch upon another assertion that even today haunts the literature concerning the Peasants' War: It is felt that Luther gave birth to the idea of freedom but that this idea was then misunderstood by the peasants. This interpretation[12] is based on the earliest Counter-Reformation propaganda, which even predates Cochläus. It argues that the revolutionary Luther with his pseudo-prophetic sense of calling and his impatient attitude toward Church and Pope could not but evoke *tumultus*, social unrest and subversive action. In the humanist circles influenced by Erasmus, it was just this charge which prepared for the break of many humanists with Luther – years before Erasmus publicly attacked Luther in his 1524 treatise on "The Freedom of the Will."[13] This kind of propaganda did not come

---

[11]Thomas A. Brady has already shown for the year 1530 "the essential weakness of the cities in the political world of Reformation Germany" ("Jacob Sturm of Strasbourg and the Lutherans at the Diet of Augsburg, 1530," *Church History* 42 [1973] 1–20, esp. 20).

[12]Not how such a misunderstanding of Luther's *libertas christiana* actually has, but how it could have (!) resulted, has been reconstructed by Hans J. Hillerbrand, "The German Reformation and the Peasants' War," *The Social History of the Reformation*, ed. Lawrence P. Buck and Jonathon W. Zophy (Columbus: 1972) 106–36, esp. 118ff.

[13]Since 1521, *tumultus* – not only as "*Uffrur*" but more generally as "agitation" – to an increasing extent is reason for concern on the part of the city fathers. This agitation is an important factor in the introduction and advancement of the Reformation. Cf. Eberhard Naujoks (*Obrigkeitsgedanke, Zunftverfassung und Reformation: Studien zur Verfassungsgeschichte von Ulm, Esslingen und Schwäb. Gmünd* [Stuttgart: 1958] 56): "Indem die religiöse Reformbewegung die obrigkeitliche Position an der empfindlichsten Stelle, dem kaum beruhigten Verhältnis zwischen Rathaus und Zünften, angriff, löste sie bei den Stadtvätern die nie ganz eingeschlafene Furcht vor unberechenbaren Strassenaufläufen aus." An advance in the recognition of the relative weight of the religious factor is made by Heinz Schilling in his rich analysis of "the second wave" of town revolts and agitation from 1570–1620; cf. his article "Bürgerkämpfe in Aachen zu Beginn der 17. Jahrhunderts: Konflikte im Rahmen der alteuropäischen Stadtgesellschaft oder im Umkreis der frühbürgerlichen Revolution," *Zeitschrift für Historische Forschung* 1 (1974) 175, 231.

unexpectedly. As early as 1521, when the first rumors about armed mobs reached Wittenberg, Luther forecasts that he and his interpretation of the Gospel will be held responsible for the revolutionary freedom movements.

Due to our modern resources which grant us a better insight into the social status and education level of the peasant leaders and "*Rottenpastoren*,"[14] it has become highly improbable that the peasants either warped Luther's ideas or deluded themselves about them. This is especially clear when one bears in mind that for over a century the *libertas christiana* had been a current issue and a central question in pub and marketplace. With the peasants, Luther's concept of freedom did not fall into a vacuum to be distorted by their fanatical enthusiasm. For those who no longer expected reform from the feudal establishment, the higher obedience toward the *iustitia Dei* had already started to imply freedom from the Old Law obligations in dealing with temporal authorities [see Appendix]. There the ground had long been prepared by "the Gospel of Social Unrest."

That does not mean, however, that Luther functioned as nothing more than a catalyst. Whereas Reformation research likes to present Luther as a Biblical scholar who influenced people through his publications, Luther, at that time, functions primarily as a symbol, a beacon, a sign of the times, a means to read the timetable of God. Admittedly, a shift *did* take place: the appeal to divine justice is transformed into an explicit appeal to the Gospel which – as it is put – is now at last proclaimed clearly and without additions.[15] Further, Luther's proclamation of the priesthood of all believers highlighted the contrast between the justice of God and the existing inequality between the priests and the laity and provided a rationale for abolishing this inequality.[16]

---

[14]Usually leadership did not emerge from the peasant class, but from the pastors, nobles, artisans, and innkeepers. See Gerlach, *Der englische Bauernaufstand*, 144–75; further, Rudolf Endres, "Der Bauernkrieg in Franken," *Festschrift für Gerd Wunder*, Württembergisch Franken, Jahrbuch 58 (Schwäbisch Hall: 1974) 153–67, esp. 162f.

[15]In his essay "Die deutsche Ritterschaft und die Reformation" *Ebernburg-Hefte*, 3. Folge (1969) 27–37, Martin Brecht has convincingly pointed to the significance of *urban* communities and brotherhoods for the non-urban "Ritterschaftsbewegung." The Thirty Articles attached to Martin Bucer's *Neuw Karsthans* (an addition by the printer H. Schott, Strasbourg: 1521) contain the several *gravamina* as they came to be represented in the Wittenberg disturbances (*Karsthans*, Art. 23–25) *and* in the Peasants' Articles; see Arnold E. Berger, *Die Sturmtruppen der Reformation* (Leipzig: 1931), 202–04.

[16]Cf. *Flugschriften des Bauernkrieges*, ed. Kaczerowsky, 10 ("Die 12 Artikel der Bauernschaft"). The seventh thesis, defended by Christoph Schappeler in the Memmingen Disputation on January 2, 1525, reads: "Ein einiges geistliches Priesterthum mit gleichem Opfer und Amt, nicht zweierlei, sei allen Christgläubigen gemein." Friedrich Dobel, *Memmingen im Reformationszeitalter nach handschriftlichen und gleichzeitigen Quellen*, I: *Christoph Schappeler, der erste Reformator von Memmingen, 1513–1525* (Memmingen: 1877) 59.

To give an example from the demands of the so-called "peasants": the right to free election of pastors.[17] This is not a new call; however, its basis is now clearly founded on Reformation principles. According to the "Twelve Articles," a pastor has to be elected who will proclaim the Gospel on the basis of Scripture alone.[18] And that means here: a Gospel not molded in the cast of canon law. In a parallel context, from the side of the cities, the "Hallenser Articles" of May 6, 1525, state that every congregation should be allowed to call a minister, since Christ has freely proclaimed the Gospel and has us *"zu wissen frei gemacht. . . . "*[19] This freedom intended by God for all men, the right to elect a pastor and to hear the Gospel, joins with a third demand: the civic incorporation of clerics, i.e., the end of their extra-legal status, which later is put into practice in the cities won for the Reformation.[20]

Friedrich Engels, the historical engineer of Marxism, has advanced the thesis that the resistance by the cities against feudalism was a merely conservative opposition, the conservative heresy, as he called it.[21] The real

---

[17]In addition, see Dietrich Kurze, *Pfarrerwahlen im Mittelalter*, Forschungen zur kirchlichen Rechtsgeschichte und zum Kirchenrecht 6 (Köln and Graz: 1966) esp. 465f., 471f. For the late-medieval thrust towards the full incorporation of the priests not from an ideal of faith but from economic motives, see Kiessling, *Bürgerliche Gesellschaft*, 97f.

[18]*Flugschriften des Bauernkrieges*, ed. Kaczerowsky, 10: "Der selbig erwölt Pfarrer soll vns das hailig Evangeli lauter unnd klar predigen one allen menschlichen zusatz, leer und gebot, dann uns den waren glauben stetz verkündigen, geyt uns ain ursach got umb sein gnad zu bitten, unns den selbygen waren glawben einbylden und in uns bestetten, Dann wann seyn genad in unss nicht eingepyldet wirdt, so bleyben wir stetz fleysch unnd blut, das dann nichts nutz ist, wie klärlich in der geschrifft stat das wir allain durch den waren glauben zu got kommen kinden, und allain durch seyn barmhertzigeit sälig müssen werden, Darumb ist uns ain söllicher vorgeer unnd Pfarrer von nötten unnd in dieser gestalt in der geschrifft gegrindt."

[19]*A G B M*, II 216f., no. 1345[4]: "Nachdem der ewige, unser gutiger gott und vater aus besundern seinen gottlichen gnaden sein heiliges teures, ja unuberwintlichs wort wunderbarlich, ja wie zur zeit der aposteln Christi, unsers einigen behalters, in die weite welt seinen gleubigen zum heil mitteilt, ausgebreit und zu wissen *frei* gemacht hat, wil der gemeine zu besundern lob und ehren desselbigen unsers einigen gotts geburen, das ein ider in sonderheit und semptlich, ja auch wes standes der sei, zu fordern und so zu geleben vorpflicht sein, dem also auch raum und stadt zu geben und gelart zu werden, sal es und muss sein, das eine ide gemeine einen frommen, aufrichtigen, vorstendigen desselbigen worts des hern zu wehlen, zu entsetzen macht haben sal, dorumb die gemin hir in Halle u.g.h. undertenig bittende, so zu gescheen, pfarner und prediger zu wehelen, gnediglich nachhengen wolle."

[20]Cf. Bernd Moeller, "Kleriker als Bürger," *Festschrift für Hermann Heimpel* 2 (Göttingen: 1972) 195–224; *Pfarrer als Bürger*, Göttingen Universitätsreden 56 (Göttingen: 1972). In the first article mentioned (p. 211, n. 102), Moeller refers to the demands for equal taxation in Erfurt, 1521, and to a similar council decision of Strasbourg in March, 1523. About a year later than in Strasbourg, but a year earlier than in Nuremberg, the council in Memmingen attempted to place the religious under secular jurisdiction. Cf. the council protocol from July 22 and November 28, 1524. See Dobel, *Memmingen im Reformationszeitalter*, 54, n. 110f.

[21]Friedrich Engels, *Der deutsche Bauernkrieg* (Lepzig: 1870; 9th ed. Berlin: 1970 [1946]) 48f.

opposition was the radical heresy of the peasants. He argues that the bourgeois heresy deviates from the plebeian heresy because of the different economic conditions and hence (!) motivations. It seems to me crucial, however, to see that for both town *and* country, it is divine justice and not merely economic betterment that provides the key for the basic propulsion and highest motivation. Both see divine justice as the guiding line; yes, more strictly, as the law for Church *and* society. As a matter of fact, one of its major characteristics over against later conceptions of justice is the inner connection between *iustitia coram Deo* and *iustitia coram hominibus*, between the vertical and horizontal dimensions of justice. This city ideology provides the breeding ground for the early Reformed tradition by virtue of its emphasis on the idea of covenant and an ethic of common rights and duties.[22]

Yet, it is by no means a Reformation "first" to have exported this urban theology beyond the city walls to the villages and countryside.[23] The desire of the peasants for social change is based on ideas which were indigenous and vital to the late-medieval city long before it had been influenced by the Reformation.

Admittedly, the effort to put these models which were determined by the "justice of God" into practice in the countryside was to be frustrated by the prevailing political, economic, and cultural conditions there. As a reaction, these attempts often led to a return to the city, as in the cases of Tabor, Münster and Geneva. Conversely, since the beginning of the seventeenth century, we can note time and again "a trek into the wilderness";[24] in the case of the poor German country folk, it became "a trek into the Americas."

Animosity against the cities is often said to be a major thrust in the peasants' program. One can indeed point to some peasant writings of that time, particularly to Gaismair's appeal to remove the walls of the cities and

---

[22]Cf. Rudolf Endres ("Bauernkrieg in Franken," 160): "Allgemein in Franken ist die Forderung nach Aufhebung der wirtschaftlichen und juristischen Sonderstellung der Geistlichen, nach ihrer völligen Gleichstellung mit Bauern und Bürgern und ihrer Teilhabe an den kommunalen Pflichten."

[23]In contrast to the construction of an opposition between city and country, the village community must be taken into consideration: "Gerade in den Klein- und Zwergstädten, deren Rechtscharakter als Stadt unbestreitbar ist, ergeben sich zahlreiche Berührungspunkte und Verwandtschaften zwischen Stadt und Dorf" (Karl S. Bader, *Studien zur Rechtsgeschichte des mittelalterlichen Dorfes*, I: *Das mittelalterliche Dorf als Friedens-und Rechtsbereich* [Weimar: 1957] 231). Cf. "Einen burger und einen gebür scheit nicht me wen ein czuhen und ein mür" (ibid., 234). For the *coniuratio* in town and village, see Bader, II: *Dorfgenossenschaft und Dorfgemeinde* (Köln and Graz: 1962) 271–74.

[24]Cf. George H. Williams, *Wilderness and Paradise in Christian Thought* (New York: 1962).

make them into villages.[25] This evidence, however, does not contradict the fact that the peasants claimed the *urban* freedoms and privileges for themselves. When Gaismair calls for the destruction of the city walls, this is the necessary response to the challenge of a city unwilling to extend its human rights to the countryside, thus hoarding the treasures meant for all. To use Engels' terminology, the conservative heresy is to be found just as much with the peasants in so far as they were motivated by anti-urban tendencies. To sum up: the programs of the peasants which aimed purely at reestablishing the past were not realized and were, in hindsight, reactionary. The later history of social emancipation – e.g., in the battle for freedom in the Netherlands – shows that a movement based on the idea of divine justice can become political reality only when it joins forces with the emancipatory tradition of urban rights.

3. Three Contemporary Testimonies as Judgments of the Peasants' War

The collections of documents on which our picture of the so-called Peasants' War is based refer chiefly to the events of 1525. And understandably so! This is the final phase of the Peasants' War with its spectacular climax of the princes' expedition to level punishment on the peasants. But because of this limitation in the selection of sources, essential impulses from the beginning stages remain unconsidered.

Perhaps the earliest attempt to understand the Peasants' War historically by placing it in the history of the Reformation came from the pen of Desiderius Erasmus. For him, the history of the Reformation until 1525 is a drama in three acts. The first is the campaign of humanism; the second is the battle around Luther; and the third and final act is the armed clash between the princes and the peasants: *"prodierunt in scenam nobiles et agricolae."* For the humanist from Rotterdam, however, this is not merely a chronological succession of three acts, but rather a spiritual descent in the direction of catastrophe. After the main event of the century, the rebirth of the *studia humanitatis*, there follows the rough, uncouth battle over religious doctrine. According to Erasmus, the intemperate Luther had kindled this fight which

---

[25]". . . alle rinckhmauren an den stetten . . . [sollen] niderprochen werden und hinfur nimer stött, sonnder dorffer sein . . ." Gaismair's "Landesordnung," April, 1526, *Flugschriften des Bauernkrieges*, ed. Kaczerowsky, 79. See also Heinz Angermeier, "Die Vorstellung des gemeinen Mannes von Staat und Reich im deutschen Bauernkrieg," *Vierteljahrschrift für Sozial- und Wirtschaftsgeschichte* 53 (1966) 329–43, esp. 341.

consequently, and due to him, grew into a fiery and bloody confrontation.[26]

As if he were sitting at a central news desk, Erasmus in his European correspondence is able to survey and assess the entire complicated situation. Thus, his judgment regarding the motives present in this drama is of particular significance. Although taking part only as a "spectator,"[27] he displays understanding for the unbearable economic position under which the peasants suffer. He views the Peasants' War not as a rebellion against the princes and secular authority, but as resistance provoked by monastic exploitation: "*Multis in locis dure tractati sunt monachi; verum plerique cum sint intolerabiles, alia tamen ratione corrigi non poterant. Tot privilegiis, tot exemptionibus, tot phalangibus armati sunt.... Quanquam immane videtur quod rustici monasteria quaedam diripuerunt, tamen huc istorum improbitas provocauit, qui nullis legibus corrigi possunt*":[28] it is a reaction against the evil doings of the monks who swim in their privileges and seem to be beyond the control of law.

In succinct phrases Erasmus sketches "the state of the nation" as follows: The Franciscans and Dominicans have been expelled from 's- Hertogenbosch, the capital of Brabant; in Antwerp, in spite of prohibitions by king, regent, and rural magistrate, "Hagepreken" are being held outside of the city walls; the majority of the people in Holland, Seeland, and Flanders are driven by hate of the monks, *"odio plusquam capitali fertur in monachos."*[29] Spurred on by Luther's writings, the rebels have brought about a situation which is now completely out of control. Urban culture is mortally threatened.

In "Germany" (!) a similar fury against the monks has broken out. The cloisters of nuns and monks have been destroyed. The magistracy here and there intervenes to moderate things by introducing a stricter control of the

---

[26]"*Prima turba erat de bonis literis. Hic suas partes egit Reuchlinus, nonnihil etiam Erasmus. Mox ad fidei negocium deuoluta est actio. Hic primas egit Lutherus, non incruentae fabulae princeps. Saltarunt et reges suam portionem ... Nuper prodierunt in scenam nobiles et agricolae. Actio fuit mire sanguinaria. Ea nunc recrudescit; quae sit futura catastrophe nescio*" (*Opus Epistolarum Des. Erasmi Roterodami*, ed. P.S. Allen and H.M. Allen, VI: *1525–1527* [Oxford: 1926] 153.1–10 [Letter to Guillaume Budé, August 25, 1525]).

[27]Valentin Lötscher (*Der deutsche Bauernkrieg in der Darstellung und im Urteil der zeitgenössischen Schweizer*, Basler Beiträge zur Geschichtswissenschaft II [Basel: 1943] 234–36) regards Erasmus too much as a mere spectator.

[28]*Opus Epistolarum*, ed. P.S. Allen and H.M. Allen, 156.53–55; 157.90–92 [Letter of August 28, 1525, to Willibald Pirckheimer].

[29]"*Est civitas Brabantiae satis ampla frequensque, Syluam ducis appellant; hic populus eiecit Minoritas et Dominicanos omnes ... Antwerpiae quidam ausi sunt extra civitatem concionari; nec veritus est illo populus confluere, contemptis omnibus Caesaris, Margarethae et magistratuum edictis. Itaque tota civitas illa feruet periculoso tumultu ... Maxima populi pars apud Hollandos, Zelandos et Flandros scit doctrinam Lutheri, et odio plusquam capitali fertur in monachos: qui cum plerique sint mali, tamen pro his nunc belligerabimur. Qui si vicerint, actum erit de bonis omnibus. Incipiunt nunc ferocire.*" (*Opus Epistolarum*, 155.15–31).

cloisters, but they too are of the opinion that the monks are a pest no longer to be endured: *"has coniuratas phalangas et tot privilegiis armatas diutius ferri non posse."*[30] On September 5, 1525, the tumult of war has come so close to Erasmus' study in Basel that he can hear the cries of the wounded. The bloody end is near: *"Agricolae ruunt in mortem."* The peasants are drowning in their own blood. Then he comments cautiously, but with a scarcely veiled critique: "The princes react with the usual measures – I fear that they only increase the misery."[31]

In contact with humanist, and that means with urban circles, Erasmus has seen the Peasants' War from the perspective of a city man. Averse to everything which threatens his academic peace, especially when it develops into tumult, he sees his cause, that of the *bonae literae*, endangered. The basis and responsibility for this, however, do not lie with the "folk" (*infima plebs*), but rather with the monks and their intolerable claims. For Erasmus, the Peasants' War is a "Pfaffenkrieg," that is, a war against the priests and cloisters.[32] For Erasmus this war is an understandable, in its motivation justified, rebellion by city and country. In responding to it, the city magistrates have reacted more reasonably (*moderatius!*) than the princes, who do not appear as a party until the last phase of the war.

Erasmus' perspective from the city distorts the picture: In the country not only cloisters but also castles and manor houses were stormed as symbols of subjugation. Nevertheless, his perspective offers a correction over against our contemporary tendency to view the Peasants' War mainly as a war against princes and nobles. Thus, Erasmus' interpretation is not to be ignored. For the initial phase of the Peasants' War, in spite of all the local peculiarities varying throughout the Low Countries and Germany, Erasmus' judgment is relevant and noteworthy. In contrast to his friend Bonifatius Amerbach, who sees in the peasants only murderers who use the Gospel merely as a pretext,[33] Erasmus does not hesitate to emphasize that the

---

[30]Ibid., 150.22f. [Letter of August 25, 1525, to John Selva in Paris].

[31]*"Principes tantum agunt vulgaribus remediis. Metuo ne magis exasperent malum, sed Christus insignis artifex solus potest hanc fatalem tempestatem vertere in laetos exitus"* (*Opus Epistolarum*, 160.25–28 [Letter of September 5, 1525, to Polydore Vergil]); see also Lötscher, *Der deutsche Bauernkrieg*, 236.

[32]The "Klosterkrieg" as the first phase of the *tumultus* is one of the most important parallels between the Peasants' War and the Hussite Revolution. See Frederick G. Heymann, "The Hussite Revolution and the German Peasants' War: An Historical Comparison," *Medievalia et Humanistica* NS 1 (1970) 141–59, esp. 145f.

[33]*"Videres passim suboriri tumultus et ubique per totam Germaniam multa sese coniungere rusticorum millia, monasteria devastantia ac cuncta diripientia, nec dubitandum, quod exhaustis cenobiis ac direptis idem contingat vrbibus. Et tamen interim tam insignibus latrociniis ac rapinis Evangelicam pretexunt libertatem. Evangelicum illis nunc est cuncta diripere, operas patrono detrectare, census debitos non amplius solvere, omne obedientiae*

complaints (*gravamina*) of the peasants are legitimate. But, ultimately, for him the cause of the *bonae literae* has precedence; this cause stands or falls with the *pax Christi*, with peace and order, which has now been threatened in a diabolical fashion. He could have taken over without change the concluding sentence of Amerbach's report: *"Faxit deus, ut tumultus sedari possit; quod nisi fiat, periimus omnes"*:[34] If God does not squash this revolt, we will all perish.

Another contemporary document grants us a close-up of the military situation and is one of the first reactions to the "Twelve Articles of the Peasants" – that Upper-Swabian manifesto which became a prototype for the articles of the peasants in all of Germany.[35]

Our source here is a letter of April 1525 to Rutger Rescius by the ambassador from Margrave Philipp of Baden, who had the commission of reporting to the regent of the Netherlands, Margaret of Parma, about the situation in Southern Germany. The ambassador emphasizes how numerous the Swabian peasants are – 120,000 with daily additions –, how disciplined – 600 officers –, how pious – with daily sermons by many chaplains –, and how self-confident. He writes further that it is assumed that they have made

---

iugum excutere et, si ita pergant, nullum non flagitii genus sub Evangelica scilicet tuebuntur libertate. Ius non ex bono et aequo sed ex viribus metiuntur, nempe vi, qui minus fortis sit, potentiori cedere cogatur." (*Die Amerbachkorrespondenz*, ed. Alfred Hartmann, III: *Die Briefe aus den Jahren 1525–1530* [Basel: 1947] 18. 44–54 [Letter of April 28, 1525 to Alciato in Basel]); Lötscher, *Der Deutsche Bauernkrieg*, 220.

[34]Ibid. 19, 63f. The moderate course, followed to avoid a catastrophe, recommended by Erasmus, was carried out by Basel's neighbor, Constance. After the defeat of the peasants, this neutrality was sharply criticized. See Rublack, *Reformation in Konstanz*, Excursus III: "Konstanz im Bauernkrieg," 142–44.

[35]Since the following presentation is based on a letter which, to my knowledge, has until now not received any attention, I cite here the entire report from Memmingen: *"In loca vicina Vlme, oppido Suevie, convenit exercitus conscriptus ex rusticis factionis illius qui nomine Evangelicorum sese iactitant. Numerus eorum, ut perscriptus est ad Dominum Marchionem Badensem, fertur esse centum et viginti millium. Castrametati sunt in septem locis, ut commodius eis commeatus suppeditetur; in singulis castris sunt quindecim millia, quibus brevi decem millia adiuncta sunt, indiesque fit major numerus eorum. Dux Wittembergensis* [sic] *petiuit cum eis inire federa; responderunt ei, nullum se velle cum ipso habere commercium, quum constet illum querere mundana et sua; se autem agere negocium Evangelii et libertatis Christiane. Habent in exercitu suo sexcentos consiliarios, quorum nutu omnia aguntur. Habent concionatores multos; quos singulis diebus audiunt. Miserunt legatos suos ad Vicarium Imperatoris cum quibusdam articulis, super quibus cupiunt sibi et Christianis reliquis administrari iustitiam. Articuli autem maxime attingunt Episcopos et prelatos Ecclesie; quidam etiam principes. Nolui interrogare ex legato qui cum illis ad Dominam Margaretam a Vicario Imperatoris mittebatur. Audivimus tamen antea multos ex articulis esse de tollendis gravaminibus Germanie: nolunt amplius solvere decimas; cupiunt liberari a teloneis et nescio quibus aliis oneribus. Episcopi et Principes Germanie conati sunt conscribere exercitum ad resistendum eis, sed ne unum quidem invenire potuerunt qui nomen dare vellet. Respondent se nolle pugnare contra suos; posse enim incidere ut vel parentes vel fratres occiderent. Multi etiam suspicantur multas Civitates cum illis esse foederatas . . ."* (*Literae ad Franciscum Craneveldium 1522–1528*, ed. Henry de Vocht, Humanistica Lovaniensia 1 [Louvain: 1928] 417.55–416.86 [Letter from Rutger Rescius – born in Maeseyck, died in 1545, first recipient of the chair in Greek at the Collegium Trilingue – cited in a letter from Joh. de Fevyn to Francisco Cranevelt, Bruges, April 9, 1525]).

solemn alliances with many cities. They could even afford to refuse an offer of alliance from Duke Ulrich of Württemberg. They wish to have nothing to do with the Duke since he has only his own worldly interests in mind while they themselves represent the "concerns of the Gospel and Christian freedom": "*negocium Evangelii et libertatis Christianae.*"

In this report with its assessment of the "Twelve Articles," three points are of prime importance for our consideration. *First*, the Articles demand justice not only for the peasants, but explicitly also "for other Christians"; *second*, the Articles are aimed against the Church – the bishops and prelates – with only a few directed against the princes; *third*, the attempts by the bishops and princes to raise an army have failed because no one was ready to run the risk of having to kill family members, their own flesh and blood: "*posse enim incidere ut vel parentes vel fratres occiderent.*"

This diplomatic report certainly allows us to get closer to the real situation than the perspective of Erasmus' armchair assessment permits. Indeed, the judgments of both agree that the goals of the program for change went beyond the concerns of the peasants themselves and that, above all, these goals signify a religious revolt against the ecclesiastical establishment. Furthermore, the diplomat does not see the Peasants' War as a regional rural rebellion but as a revolt by both city *and* country which is well-organized and, by means of a successful policy of alliance, is gathering momentum and cannot be stopped. In his view, it seems, it cannot be stopped, because it is not simply a "*Pfaffenkrieg*" directed against the monks, but a civil war which sets citizen against citizen and brother against brother.

Our correspondent obviously wants to present and report his data free of value judgments. He is impressed by the seriousness of the peasants in practicing the *negotium Evangelii*. At one point, he reveals his own standpoint when he writes that the peasants boast (*sese iactitant*) that they are evangelical. But his view is characteristic in that he does not regard the peasants as a blind lot of rabble led by the Devil, but much more as sober and secular; he sees before him a revolutionary project with a considerable chance for success. This document warns us not to view the Peasants' Revolt as a utopian movement which, from the beginning, was destined to fail. In many areas and cities it has been touch-and-go. If the Emperor's troops had not been available after the victory at Pavia, the balance of power would have looked different; and if the trend toward centralism which was favorable for the princes had been politically weakened, German parochialism would not just have been a stumbling block in the path of the peasants.

Finally, we turn to a third document, written by one of the peasants' leaders. It is an evaluation of the final phase of the Peasants' War. Written by Christoph Schappeler in Memmingen on May 2, 1525, and directed to Zwingli, it brings us even closer to the event itself. Schappeler, co-author of the "Twelve Articles,"[36] shows himself to be well-informed concerning the abuses in the country. Far better than anyone else known to us from that time, he penetrates the psyche of the underprivileged class and describes with a gripping rhetoric what it means for the peasant to have to groan under crushing tax burdens.[37] When he tends to be more critical of the movement, it is on the basis of his own observations and because of his involvement in the revolt from its earliest beginnings; Schappeler's new attitude over against the consequences of the "Twelve Articles" cannot yet have been occasioned by Luther's *Ermahnung zum Frieden auf die Zwölf Artikel.*" What he describes is the radicalization of an – in principle – fully justified resistance.[38]

From close quarters he reports how the poor people were torn by conflicting claims of obedience to God, to the civil and ecclesiastical authorities, and to their feudal lords, who were hostile to the Gospel.[39] They decided, however, to obey God more than men. But when the resistance developed into a blind destructiveness, no trace of the Gospel was to be found any more. After they initiated blood baths and destruction, their reference to "justice" became a pretext (*praetextus*) and an attempt at self-justification.

In the apocalyptic end of the revolt Schappeler sees a just punishment for all, because – as he says – we leaders of the revolt have sinned against Jesus Christ in that we have "embraced the Gospel and doctrine of salvation impatiently and clumsily"; we have used the Gospel "*sinistre et impatienter*" for our own needs.[40]

---

[36]It is illuminating for Schappeler's reputation that Konrad Peutinger in a letter of May 11, 1524, to the mayor and city council of Memmingen warns in regard to Schappeler: "Wa und wan ainer, der sich berömbt, nichtz anders dann das war und clar gotswort gepredigt zu haben ... demnach gar leichtlich widerwill und aufrur daraus entsteen möchten, das doch meniglich zu verbieten und zufurkomen schuldig" (*Konrad Peutingers Briefwechsel*, ed. Erich König [Munich: 1923] 395; cf. 382–89.

[37]"*Audientes enim atque scientes, immo et in ceteris sentientes seipsos, proavos, denique posteros gentili ritu ac iudaica hypocrisi preter modum in dispendium et animae et rerum omnium delusos, extenuatos, onere ac iugo iniquo oppressos et quasi in ventum misere datos, animo in ea servitute vivere omnino nolunt, onera Christiano indigna ferre renuunt, servire diis, ut est in proverbio, alienis respuunt, voce una omnes clamant, reclamant, sua potius querentes*" (*Huldreich Zwinglis sämtliche Werke*, CR 95 = ZW VIII: *Zwinglis Briefwechsel*, II: *Die Briefe von 1523–1526*, ed. Walther Köhler [Leipzig: 1914] 325, 12–19).

[38]For a different emphasis, see Lötscher, *Der deutsche Bauernkrieg*, 230f.

[39]"...*ipsorum ducibus, hominibus scilicet Christum eiusque evangelium et manibus et pedibus impugnantibus...*" (*ZW* VIII 325.22–24).

[40]"... *Christi Iesu evangelium atque doctrinam sanam, sinistre impatientesque amplectantes*" (*ZW* VIII, 326.6f.). Cf. also Lötscher, *Der deutsche Bauernkrieg*, 230 and esp. n. 61.

As a man of the moderate center and a man of the first hour, Schappeler is outflanked by the "left" because, as he sees it, the peasants have ignored the conditions stipulated in the final clause of the "Twelve Articles": "*Wol man vns mit dem Wort Gots für vnzimlich anzaigen, wolt wyr daruon abston . . .*"[41] We do not want to use force but are prepared to cede to anyone who can prove us wrong on the basis of Scripture. When the Articles are no longer a basis for negotiation, but rather a program which must be pushed through immediately and with violence, one proceeds *sinistre* and *impatienter*.[42]

According to Schappeler's interpretation, the Peasants' Revolt is programmatically a justified movement for liberation, grounded in Christian doctrine. In its concluding phase, however, it degenerated into an economic battle and a war of interests. The fault for this lies not with the monks or princes, but with the peasants' impatience which threatens to transform Southern Germany into a Sodom and Gomorrah, into a place of destruction as a sign of God's wrath in the last days: "*Indulgentiam queramus ne simul in unum cum Zodoma et Gomorra increduli pereamus omnes.*"[43] We pray for forgiveness and ask that we who started because of faith will not perish without it.

4. "*IUSTITIAE PRAETEXTU*": JUSTICE AS PRETEXT OR MOTIVE

Now we turn to our final question. Do the "Twelve Articles," as has been argued from Friedrich Engels to Hans Hillerbrand, present a social program in religious dress which we can strip off so that we are left with a hard core of economic interests? I believe not. Rather, what initially was not a pretext but a genuine and original motive rooted in a knowledge of the justice of God could not be realized. The original vision of justice for all collapsed under the weight of ungovernable fanaticism. Schappeler's prayer is at once an assessment: "God forbid that the one-time righteous should perish as unbelievers."

No other contemporary document, and no modern presentation, confronts the reader so directly with the awesome turn from initial hope to final, terrible shock. Apparently, neither fact-filled diplomatic dispatches nor the armchair wisdom of a scholar can replace daily, direct contact with the combatants themselves.

---

[41] *Flugschriften des Bauernkrieges*, ed. Kaczerowsky, 14.

[42] Bernhard Fleischlin comes to the conclusion that Schappeler himself "das Evangelium der Revolution gepredigt hatte" (*Schweizerische Reformationsgeschichte* I [Stans: 1907] 551).

[43] *ZW* VIII 326.9f. This belief in the approaching end of the world permeates all parties and factions in this period.

According to its own sources, the Peasants' War is a religious revolt of people in town and country who, on the basis of divine justice, pressed for improved social conditions. And they did so not only for the benefit of one social group, but for the benefit of "all Christians."

The accusation of a merely simulated thirst for divine justice – *iustitiae praetextu* – was raised in one form or another during that time by each party against the other: against the old believers, the Lutherans, the Anabaptists, and finally against the peasants themselves.[44] Modern research has made significant progress due to its recognition of the genuine motives of the parties concerned – but this is a task that is yet to be undertaken as far as the Peasants' War is concerned.[45] The main thrust of present research is oriented towards economic and social history, hence providing an insight into a large number of elements that go into the making of history. Yet, this should not tempt us to permit Biblical ideas, Christian-apocalyptic ferment, and the horizon of religious expectation on the part of the rebels to be relegated to the background, since it is only through these means that the birth and spread of the Peasants' War are to be understood.

In its differing expressions, varying from Luther and Karlstadt to

---

[44]Beatus Rhenanus is definitely not thinking only of the peasants when he writes on September 1, 1525, of those *"qui sub evangelici nominis praetextu impostores agunt"* (*Briefwechsel des Beatus Rhenanus*, ed. Adalbert Horawitz and Karl Hartfelder [Leipzig: 1886], 334).

[45]We are quite aware that our emphasis on Schappeler's letter and on the diplomatic dispatch – more than Erasmus' report of the situation – can give rise to the suspicion that one is trying to interpret the *entire* Peasants' War from a limited, regional viewpoint. As a justified correction in *this* regard, we can accept Hans Hillerbrand's thesis ("The German Reformation," 125) that "there can be little doubt that the famous Twelve Articles convey an utterly erroneous picture of the relationship between the Reformation and the peasant uprising. The bulk of the peasant documents does not echo the sentiment of that document. The majority of the grievances are concretely economic or social." The statistic results he uses to show that less than five per cent of the *gravamina* "have to do with religion or exhibit religious terminology" (ibid.) can all too easily favor the *'iustitiae praetextu'* critique of the earliest period. In order to grasp the importance of the religious factor, one must consider all letters and documents, along with the Articles analyzed by Hillerbrand, including the last piece of evidence, a protocol of the interrogation of March 12, 1527, which reports that in the abortive attack on Mühlhausen "die losunge were gewest: das wort gots" (*Akten* II 873, no. 2081 [20]). The instructions (dated February 25, 1522) of William IV and Ludwig X, Dukes of Bavaria, for negotiations with the Archbishop of Salzburg, Matthäus Lang, are most illuminating in three respects: 1. They give us proof of the highly explosive revolutionary climate in early 1522: "... they want to slaughter all the 'Pfaffen'" (*Acta Reformationis Catholicae*, I: *1520 bis 1532*, ed. Georg Pfeilschifter [Regensburg: 1959] 7.14f., 13.15; cf. 58.6f., 76.11f., 92.25). 2. Their religious motivation: they argue "that the modern priests behave in such a way ... that to tolerate that any longer would be contrary to the Christian faith" (ibid., 16f.). 3. This revolutionary ferment is generally found "under den layen in stetten, markten und sonderlich auf dem lant in den dörffern ..." (ibid., 9.9f). The contrast is seen more between the laity and the priests than between the peasantry and their "Obrigkeit."

Müntzer and Hut, the Reformation movement attempted to influence, to strengthen or to regulate the religious factor operative in the long history of social agitation in town and countryside, to redirect the "Gospel of Social Unrest."[46] The term "religious factor" is open to the charge that it is used in a modern and thereby anachronistic way when it is not clearly seen that at that time the religious factor reaches far into the other domains of life, so that social conditions and factors are also included. We have noticed the cohesion between horizontal and vertical justice. The two most prominent religious traditions, apocalypticism and mysticism, go even further in making it a programmatic point to fuse the outer and the inner orders, the world of the soul and the world of the senses. The so-called "religious factor" then embraced a much larger range of experience than applies for most of us today. Yet, it cannot be denied that there is a second sphere not covered by the religious factor. Not only Luther, but also Schappeler and Müntzer speak of a development in the program and action of the peasants which is no longer in tune with the Christian faith. The religious factor itself, however, is for all three so much an uncontested category and a common criterion that the *purely* social demands of the peasants are characterized with a surprising unanimity as "*que sua sunt querunt*," the self-serving quest for gain; by all three, this is regarded as the selling-out of God's cause.

The characterization of the Peasants' War, implicit in the condensed formula *iustitiae praetextu,* under the cloak of righteousness, is therefore not only an out-group judgment, conditioned by ignorance or class distance. It is also an in-group self-analysis and self-critique which stems from a mixture of disappointment and solidarity.

In its initial thrust and program, the so-called Peasants' War for both its moderate critics and its radical leaders is basically a religious movement. It seems to me that we have no right to question this any more than in the case of the movements originating in Wittenberg, Geneva, and Trent. This conclusion itself is not unimportant vis-à-vis Marxist interpretations in Eastern Europe and a recent sociological trend in Reformation history in the United States. But beyond this, there are two more points to which I want to call attention in thesis form by way of conclusion. I have found it a sound rule for my own work to illustrate a historical movement on the basis of its extremes but to interpret it from its mean. In our case this rule helps us to see that Thomas Müntzer serves as an excellent illustration of the

---

[46]Cf. Heiko A. Oberman, "Thomas Müntzer: van verontrusting tot verzet," *Kerk en Theologie* 24 (1973) 205–14.

apocalypticism on the edges of the "Gospel of Social Unrest." Except for the very last stages of the uprising, he remains a marginal figure who would never have played such a prominent role in our modern presentations if he had not been singled out for attack by Luther's verbal bombardment. If any single figure should be named, it is not Müntzer but Hus who fathered the movement both in its moderate and more radical manifestations. For the bloody climax not only the monks, the princes, and to an extent Martin Luther, but also Müntzer has to carry part of the responsibility. In his hands and due to his apocalyptic impatience and misreading of the eschatological timetable, the "Gospel of Social Unrest" became transformed into the assembly call for the elect, for the children of righteousness to take up arms in the final battle against the children of darkness and wrath.

The enormous religious potential in an extensive lower-middle class layer of society in central Europe was squandered. This potential proved to be badly missing when half a century later it was most needed, at a time when the religious impetus of the Reformation and Counter Reformation movements issued in a new scholasticism. That seems to me the real drama in what we misleadingly call the German Peasants' War.

5. APPENDIX: PEASANT PLOT AND PROGRAM
A CONTEMPORARY REPORT ON THE EVENTS OF 1502[1]

Anno domini 1502 magna ubique per totam Germaniam pestilentia grassabatur, et multa milia hominum consumpsit, praesignata, quemadmodum multorum opinio fuit, per cruces quas in lineis hominum vestibus etiam abditis et cistis inclusis, ante biennium apparuisse narravimus, quarum casus sive lapsus in annum tertium, non simul et semel omnibus in locis duravit. Videbantur etiam nonnulli cruces habuisse suis corporibus nudis impressas qui ut plurimum eodem anno peste sunt consumpti.

Eodem anno rustici quidam diocesis Spirensis in agro Bruchsellano iuramentorum suorum et fidelitatis praestitae temerarii transgressores contra dominos suos, episcopum et canonicos in malum conspiraverunt,

---

[1]*Memorabilium omnis aetatis et omnium gentium chronici commentarii a Ioanne Nauclero I.V. Doctore Tubing. Praeposito, et Universitatis Cancellario, digesti in annum Salutis M.D. Adiecta Germanorum rebus Historia de Svevorum ortu, institutis ac Imperio. Complevit opus F. Nicolaus Basellius Hirsaugiensis annis XIIII, ad M.D. additis. Ex Tubinga sueviae urbe. Cautum Maxaem. Aug. decreto privilegio, ne quis intra decennium excudat* (1516) fol. 305f.

iuramento se mutuo colligantes, ac paulatim occulte numero crescentes multiplicati sunt. Et nisi tempestive conspiratio illorum denudata fuisset, in brevi multitudine insuperabiles evasissent.

Sumpsit ortum liga rusticorum quam ipsi "Buntschuch" vulgariter nominabant, in villa quadam Spirensis diocesis, Undergrunbach dicta, primo per duos rusticos qui per callidas suas persuasiones paulatim in eandem coniurationem plurimos traxerunt, nedum in praedicta villa, sed in plerisque aliis circumcirca. Et ut duo eorum in tormentis confessi sunt, media pars virorum oppidi Bruchsal in eandam coniurationem consensum dederat. Submittebant autem secretius quosdam ex liga sua callidos sollicitatores, qui per vicos et oppida circumeuntes, quos potuissent, in sui consortium contra clerum, contra principes et omnem maioritatem traherent. Delegerat iam sibi haec malignantium congregatio duos capitaneos, qui omni colligationi et ligae praeessent atque ad quorum imperium omnia fierent et agerentur, et quibus reliqui sine contradictione oboedirent.

Ititur ex insidiis hinc inde latenter prorumpentes parato vexillo bicolorato in unum convenire satagentes, diem statuunt et locum; ubi convenientes, divina disponente providentia, consilium eorum infatuatum et denudatum fuit, plurimis eorum captis et trucidatis. Siquidem capti huius coniurationis primi auctores quaestionibus expositi arcanum impietatis suae ac initae coniurationis denudant, atque in tredecim aut xiiii articulos, quae conceperant mala, dinumerant, quos breviter et succinctim hic complectemur:

Primus, ut aucti numero iugum omne servitutis abiicerent, et omnimodam sibi libertatem more Helvetiorum armis vindicarent.

Secundus, ut quisquis in hanc sotulariam ligam assumptus fuisset, singulis diebus quinquies dominicam orationem cum angelica salutatione in memoriam quinque vulnerum Christi principalium flexis genibus oraret pro obtinenda victoria.

Tertius, symbolum sibi constituerunt deiparam virginem Mariam et divum Ioannem Evangelistam. Signum vero mutuae[2] inter se cognitionis erat, dum aliquis ex coniuratione interrogatus fuisset, alteri interroganti respondere potuisset in hunc modum: *Was ist nun für ain Wesen;* respondit interrogatus, si fuit de coniuratis: *Wir mogen vor den Pfaffen nit genesen.* O iniquitas diu fermentata ut clericis laici oppido infesti praedicentur.

Quartus, conabantur omnem principatum et dominium extinguere, atque

---

[2]Rosenkranz reads *mutae.* Cf. Albert Rosenkranz, *Der Bundschuh – die Erhebungen des südwestdeutschen Bauernstandes in den Jahren 1493–1517,* II: *Quellen* (Heidelberg: Carl Winters, 1927) 93.

contra omnes turmatim cum vexillo in bellum procedere, omnesque sibi resistentes miserabili clade trucidare.

Quintus, confessi sunt primum Bruchsal oppidum se invasuros, atque id quidem facile, quod dimidiam virorum in eodem oppido partem sibi coniuratam habere gloriabantur, quo facile, ut praesumebant, obtento ulterius contra Marchionatum Badensem armati procederent.

Sextus, constituerunt inter se bona monasteriorum, ecclesiarum et clericorum in circuitu direpta dividere, atque ministros ecclesiae humiliare, ac quantum possent eorundem numerum imminuere.

Septimus, ut ad sufficientem numerum congregati amplius xxiiii. horis in uno loco haud quaquam moras traherent, sed ad ulteriora semper procederent, donec omnia suae coniurationi subiicerent.

Octavus, tantum sibi praestabant, ut, dum semel conglobatim ad bellum procederent apertum, omnes sibi adhaerere cives et rusticos libertatis amore, etiam non compulsos.[3]

Nonus, intendebant extinctis monasteriis et ecclesiis atque in nihilum ecclesiastica libertate redacta neque decimas neque census dare velle, neque monachis neque clericis neque principibus neque nobilibus.

Decimus, coniurarunt ad diem S. Georgii eiusdem anni convenire et armata manu, ut diximus, oppidum Bruchsal mane diluculo invadere.

Undecimus, libertatem sibi armis vindicare[4] invicem coniurarunt omnimodam, nec deinceps alicuius pati dominium velle, nec census dare nec decimas, non precarias principibus, non vectigal, aut quippiam tale, sed ab omni tributorum genere se liberos esse et penitus exemptos.

Duodecimus, proposuerunt venationes, piscationes, pascua, nemora et omnia, quae principum consueverunt exceptione usibus deservire privatis, in communitatem revocare, ut cuique liceret venari atque piscari quando, ubi et quomodo vellet, sine cuiuscunque prohibitione et impedimento.

Tertiusdecimus, decreverunt manu valida suorum procedere, primo contra Marchionem Badensem, deinde contra episcopum Spirensem, et demum contra monachos et clericos; et quicunque contradixisset, sine misericordia interficeretur tanquam iustitiae dei contrarius, inoboediens et rebellis.

Haec autem in perniciem reipublicae contra episcopos, principes, religiosos et clerum omnem excogitaverat rusticorum temeritas in Undergrunbach, Iolingen et in oppido Bruchsal, aliisque villis et locis in

---

[3]Trithemius' addition provides a smoother reading: *in eorum venissent consortium. Annales Hirsaugiensis* 2.590. Rosenkranz adds: *aestimarent; Quellen*, 94.

[4]Rosenkranz reads *vendicare: Quellen*, 94.

circuitu, quorum tamen praesumpta temeritas a deo fuit denudata, receperuntque iustam suorum male gestorum poenam publicis expositi cruciatibus, ut supra patuit, quam quidem Maximilianus Germanorum rex suis in litteris propterea emanatis inflixit.

The Fight for Freedom and the Justice of God:
The First Phase of the German Peasants' War[5]
A Tübingen History from 1516[6]

In 1502 the Plague raged throughout Germany and found thousands of victims. Many were convinced that two years previously there had been warning signs of its approach: crosses had been found in the clothes of people who were now ill or dying. Those who were thought to have had crosses impressed upon their naked bodies usually died within the year.

In that same year some peasants from the Diocese of Speyer, in the area of Bruchsal, criminally disregarded their oaths of loyalty and started a conspiracy against their lords, the bishop [Ludwig], and the canons of the Chapter. Through the secret swearing in of more and more people, their number grew into a movement. Just in time there plot was discovered; otherwise they would have become too strong to be squelched.

The "Bundschuh," as this league of peasants was called, originated in Untergrombach. It was here that two men began to draw other peasants from the surrounding area into their plot and eventually to find support with half the population of Bruchsal. Secretly they sent propagandists to organize resistance against the clergy, the princes, and all authority. Two of their number were chosen as leaders and were given absolute obedience and loyalty.

They decided on the meeting place, the day to initiate the uprising, and

---

[5]In view of my introductory section concerning the need to broaden the concept "Peasants' War" it should not be surprising that I relate the revolt of Untergrombach to the great uprisings of 1525 and consider the events in 1502 to be a phase in the same "Bauernkrieg." That I regard "1502" as the *first* phase, notwithstanding earlier revolts – particularly one nine years earlier in nearby Elsass (1493) – is based on the fact that our document brings the first full-fledged peasant program.

[6]My digest is based on the Chronicle of Nicolas Basellius, published Tübingen, 1516. For the period 1501–1514 he brought up to date the medieval history by Johannes Vergenhans (1510, Nauclerus), chancellor of the University of Tübingen. Basellius made extensive use of the historical account, written in his own monastery, the *Annales Hirsaugienses* (1514). Its author, Johannes Trithemius, had relied in turn on Vergenhans for the period preceding 1501. Cf. Paul Joachimsen, *Geschichtsauffassung und Geschichtsschreibung in Deutschland unter dem Einfluss des Humanismus* (Leipzig and Berlin: B.G. Teubner, 1910), 1.247; Klaus Arnold, *Johannes Trithemius (1462–1516)* (Würzburg: Ferdinand Schöningh, 1971) 154.

the moment at which to unfold their two-colored flag.[7] When they finally came together, their plans proved to have been unveiled, and many of their number were caught and dismembered. When the masterminds were questioned, they owned up to a program of thirteen articles:

1. As soon as their number would permit, they were to seek freedom by force – like the Swiss had done – and throw off the yoke of slavery.

2. Upon initiation, as a supplication for victory, every participant was pledged to kneel and say the Lord's Prayer with an Ave Maria five times every day, in memory of the five wounds of Christ.

3. As their common symbol they chose the Virgin Mary and St. John the Evangelist. For their password they decided upon: "What the hell is wrong?" to be answered by the initiated with the words: "The priests are squeezing on and on!"

4. They planned to extinguish every trace of rule and ownership and by every form of force to remove opposition.

5. They admitted that their military plan was first to attack Bruchsal – expected to be ready for a takeover in view of the popular support within the town – and from there to invade Baden.

6. They further planned to divide the spoils of the monasteries, churches, and clergy in the occupied territories, to remove the ministers from their high pedestals, and as far as possible to reduce their number.

7. They committed themselves never to stay longer than 24 hours in one place and then to move on to other targets until the whole country would be under their control.

8. They were cocksure enough to assume that once they had taken up arms, once they were in the open and on the march, townsmen and peasants alike would take their side because of their common longing for freedom.

9. After destroying the monasteries and churches, they intended to abolish the privileges implied in the so-called "freedom of the Church" by no longer paying tithes and taxes to monks, clerics, princes, or nobility.

10. The day chosen for the armed march upon Bruchsal was that of St. George, the 23rd of April, 1502, at the crack of dawn.[8]

11. They swore to gain their freedom by force, no longer to suffer submission or to stand for taxation in any form.

---

[7]Trithemius adds that on one side of the blue-white flag were inscribed the words: "Nothing less than the justice of God." *Annales* 2.589–92, esp. 590.

[8] One fact overlooked until now points to a striking continuity between the events of 1502 and 1525. It is too much for coincidence that Bruchsal was taken by the insurrectionists on this same St. George's Day, the 23rd of April 1525. This time, however, not only in the name of the justice of God, but also in the name of the Gospel and on the basis of the 12 Articles. Cf. Günther Franz, *Der deutsche Bauernkrieg*, 230f.

12. They proposed to return to the whole community the rights usurped by the princes, thus reestablishing free hunting and fishing together with access to and usage of pasture and woods by all men at all times.

13. Once they had gained full strength, they planned to direct their first offensive against the Margrave of Baden, the next against the Bishop of Speyer, and finally to proceed against all monks and clerics. Every form of resistance would be treated as opposition to the justice of God.

This criminal offense with its grave danger to the state, directed as it was against bishops, princes, monks, and all clergy, was plotted in Untergrombach, Jöhlingen, and the town of Bruchsal, as well as in other villages and manors in the area. But this evil plan was revealed by God; those responsible received their deserved punishment by pubic hanging, authorized by the German Emperor Maximilian.[9]

---

[9]Cf. Wilhelm Zimmermann, *Der grosse deutsche Bauernkrieg* (Volksausgabe; Berlin, DDR: 1952 [Stuttgart: J. H. W. Dietz, 1841–43; 3 vols.]) 46.

VIII

REFORMATION AND REVOLUTION: COPERNICUS' DISCOVERY IN AN ERA OF CHANGE

This address is not to be just an interesting commemoration of the historical past. Copernicus has become more than a private scholar who made a scientific discovery. Copernicus has become a symbol if not a syndrome; and it is not easy to define exactly what this symbol stands for, so varied are the reactions to his name and the associations it evokes. The nerves of Western man are hit, titillated, or hurt, and sometimes all of these at once. By no means without precedent, but certainly most intensively, the community of scholars and, with a remarkable intuition for essentials, society at large is probing the ultimate questions of man and matter, of time and space.

The inability to present the Copernican Revolution in a more or less objectively descriptive fashion, myth-proof as it were, is already obvious from the first series of articles and television programs so far presented to the public – and many more are to follow in this commemoration year! But the serious scholarly tradition on which these popularizations had to rely gave ample occasion, reason, and cause for the spread of myth. With ill-hidden ideological passion the name of Copernicus has been used to propagate the values of the French or Russian revolutions as his legitimate heirs. Replacing the Aristotelian hierarchy of multiple spheres, Copernicus then would mark the end of feudalism and emerge as the herald of our modern society. His name also suffices to connect the Christian faith with the dark Middle Ages. Pre-Copernican man is seen as caught in the blinding spiritual captivity of the "Ptolemaic Church," from which this astronomical giant liberated us to lead us into the promised land of modern times.

What is at stake in this complex issue – indeed a central issue underlying our Western Copernicus complex – is the question of what the access-route to knowledge is and, concomitantly, what the universities on the tightrope – tottering between impatient relevance and vain curiosity[1] – can do and

---

[1]The association of astral (meta) physics and irrelevance has a classical root. This association is reflected in Christian antiquity when St. Augustine applied to it the term *curiositas*. Since that

should do. It concerns the question of theory and practice, of reason and test, speculation and experience. It is the classical clash between Plato and Aristotle, today intermittently illuminated by tensions between the German and the Anglo-American tradition of scholarship and research underlying in parallel but different ways the student revolution of our times.

Finally, the Copernican Revolution touches upon, and is rooted in, man's new relation to nature, suggested by the development from prehistoric animistic veneration to the classical adoration of nature, and via Christian admiration to the post-Christian administration of nature – therefore implying man's own changing role.

This year's celebrations may appear as a feast for fools: after all, Copernicus' heliocentric cosmology places man off center and unmasks him as cosmically eccentric. Yet we have to reconcile this with another phenomenon, on the level of anthropology, where we see a geocentricity reemerging in a sublimated form as anthropocentricity: Man in a succession of stages developed from the microcosm and image of God into the *Homo faber*[2] and partner of God, to end up, finally, as the *Homo manipulator*, God in his own realm. At that very point, what used to be the mysterious dwelling place of man and dewed path for the feet of God becomes the secular "environment" – the mechanical context of Man's survival; that is, the contemporary sore point where cosmological, behavioral, and environmental studies converge.

This short "tour d'horizon" suggests the range of concerns and apperceptions with which I have approached the given theme. If done well, this lecture will be a festive historical commemoration but at the same time something of an acupuncture of nerve centers, without the Chinese promise that it will not hurt.

---

time the growth – and stagnation – of intellectual European man is reflected in his attitude to "the heavens," "*quae supra nos*" (See Note 16). For the classical root cf. the wise Thales falling in a pit while watching the heavens; Werner Jaeger, *Paideia. Die Formung des griechischen Menschen*, second edition (Berlin, 1954), vol. 1, p. 211.

[2]"During the first Christian millennium, in both East and West, God at the moment of creation is represented in passive majesty, actualizing the cosmos by pure power of thought, Platonically. Then, shortly after the year 1000, a Gospel book was produced at Winchester which made a great innovation: inspired by Wisdom of Solomon 11:20, '*Omnia in mensura et numero et pondere disposuisti*,' the monastic illuminator showed the hand of God – now the master craftsman – holding scales, a carpenter's square, and a pair of compasses. This new representation spread and, probably under the influence of Proverbs 8:27, '*certe lege et gyro vallabat abyssos*,' the scales and square were eliminated leaving only the compasses – the normal medieval and renaissance symbol of the engineer – held in God's hand." Lynn White, Jr. "Cultural Climates and Technological Advance in the Middle Ages," *Viator*, vol. 2 (1971), pp. 171–201, esp. p. 189.

We begin by looking into the first encounter between the two 16th-century reform movements –in theology and in cosmology – for a time suspended in a precious but precarious balance between partnership and rivalry. In a second part we gain historical perspective and distance by dealing with the preceding late medieval phase in which both the modern sciences and the modern consciences prove to evolve simultaneously, in terms awaiting translation to reveal their effect on modern man.

1. THE ENCOUNTER BETWEEN COSMOLOGY AND THEOLOGY

In his play *Galileo*, Bertolt Brecht has the old cardinal say to Galileo:[3]

> So you have degraded the earth despite the fact that you live by her and receive everything from her. I won't have it! I won't have it! I won't be a nobody on an inconsequential star briefly twirling hither and thither. I tread the earth, and the earth is firm beneath my feet, and there is no motion to the earth, and the earth is the center of all things, and I am the center of the earth, and the eye of the Creator is upon me. Above me revolve, affixed to their crystal shells, the lesser lights of the stars and the great light of the sun, created to give light upon me that God might see me – Man, God's greatest effort, the center of creation. "In the image of God created He him."[4]

The scene here presented by Bertolt Brecht is as moving as it is misleading. Granted, there is some truth in seeing in Galileo's plight the clash of science and faith; therefore, we cannot avoid asking whether the same applies in the case of Copernicus – whether, just as the Roman Catholic Church forced Galileo to recant, so, some twenty years after Luther's appeal to his conscience at Worms, the Reformation did not unmast itself as an intolerant, repressive, and anticonscientious movement, which tried to suppress, and for a time succeeded in subverting the Copernican Revolution.

It is to be said with all possible clarity, however, that pre-Copernican cosmology did not posit the earth at the static center as a place of glory but as a place of inertia, the farthest removed from divine movement so perfectly reflected in the circular movement of the stars. Man, not his earth, held the cosmic place of honor, reaching in the summit of his soul (*apex mentis*) the greatest proximity to God. As far as I can see, we owe it to the mystical tradition that "center" and "summit" could become interchangeable and

---

[3]Bertolt Brecht, *Galileo*, English version by Charles Laughton, first publication, 1952. Scene 5.

[4]For the original presentation of this paper, the Laughton translation authorized by Brecht was not available to me in a European library, so Mr. Philip J. Rosato made an elegant translation. Generally, I am most indebted for his critical perusal of my English efforts. In the following notes, Prof. Owen Gingerich, Harvard University, has provided various English translations.

equivalent in dignity[5] – as can still be noticed in the parallel mixture of spacial and anthropological components in the words "depth" or "profundity."

The resistance against Copernicus may have had other causes than the normal healthy resistance in intellectual man to novelty; it might have been furthered by a mystical sense of the cohesion of man and his cosmic environment. This resistance, however, cannot be explained in terms of hurt pride as the defence mechanism of Ptolemaic-Medieval man. To the contrary, Copernicus gave the earth a cosmic dignity in keeping with the ontological rank of man, its divine inhabitant. It is thus all the more important to analyze the first reactions to Copernicus from close quarters. In order to test the traditional story of Copernicus'-lone-battle-against-the-mighty-Church we have to listen to Luther's oft-quoted *Tischrede (Tabletalk)* and weigh more extensively the arguments in the famous case of Osiander's "fraud." If this story can be substantiated, Copernicus would have a valid claim on the gratitude of all those who see in the emancipation from Christian faith the basis for the cultural progress of Western man; more gratitude, at least, than is owed to Galileo, whose similar claim is convincingly rejected by Friedrich von Weizsäcker[6] and, for very different

---

[5]Cf., Maximilianus Sandaeus, editor, *Theologiae mysticae clavis*, (Cologne, 1640), f. 12. The problem of Cusanus as "forerunner" of Copernicus is best presented by A. Koyré, in a fashion that deserves a full quotation: "No doubt it could be objected that a century before Copernicus, in 1440, Nicholas of Cusa in *De docta ignorantia* (II, 17) had already proclaimed 'the Earth is a noble star' (*terra est stella nobilis*), and had removed it from the centre of the Universe, declaring, moreover, that this centre has no existence, seeing that the Universe is 'an infinite sphere having its centre everywhere and its circumference nowhere'; and it could be maintained that the work in question was probably known to Copernicus, whose mind could have been influenced by it (R. Klibansky, 'Copernic et Nicolas de Cues' in *Léonard de Vinci et l'expérience scientifique du XVIᵉ siècle*, Paris, 1953). I do not dispute it. Yet, it is nonetheless true that the metaphysically very bold concept of Nicholas of Cusa, namely that of an undefined, if not infinite, Universe, was not accepted by Copernicus, nor by anyone else before Giordano Bruno; that his cosmology, scientifically speaking, is non-existent; and if he attributed any motion to the Earth, he does not endow it with any motion around the Sun. On the whole, his astronomical notions are so vague, and often so erroneous (for example, he endows both the Moon and the Earth each with its own proper light) that Nicholas of Cusa cannot by any means be ranked among the forerunners of Copernicus (except in dynamics); nor can he claim a place in the history of astronomy." A. Koyré, *The Astronomical Revolution, Copernicus – Kepler – Borelli*, translated by R. E. W. Maddison (Paris-London-Ithaca, 1973), p. 72.

[6]"We can thus even maintain that the Inquisition desired nothing more from Galileo than that he should not say any more than he was able to prove. In this argument he was the fanatic." Weizsäcker's radicalization, and romantization of inquisitional objectives, is decisively mitigated when he introduces his views on the parallels between faith and science: "In this it was appropriate that he was the fanatic. The great advancements of science do not happen while one sticks anxiously to proof. They happen through bold propositions which themselves open the path to their own confirmation or refutation. All that I have said about the fall of

reasons, by Bertolt Brecht himself.[7] Subjectively the case is clear: Copernicus felt intimidated by the anticipation of the charge of innovation; the very fact and the carefully worded content of his letter of dedication to Pope Paul III make this abundantly clear (see Appendix). This is the element of truth in Arthur Koestler's *Sleepwalkers*[8] where he casts Copernicus as a fearful and submissive weakling. Objectively seen, however, Copernicus' expectation of curt, if uninformed, rejection had already been proven to be well founded. Luther spontaneously exclaims on hearing the advance rumor:

---

bodies and about the principle of inertia is illustrated by this sentence, and we cannot doubt that Galileo himself was fully aware of this methodological situation. Science, as well as religion, needs faith, and both kinds of faith submit themselves, provided that they understand themselves, to their adequate tests: the religious faith in men's lives, the scientific in continuous research." Translated from "Kopernikus, Kepler, Galilei: Zur Entstehung der neuzeitlichen Naturwissenschaft," in Klaus Oehler and Richard Schaeffler, editors, *Einsichten, Gerhard Krüger zum 60. Geburtstag* (Frankfurt am Main, 1962), pp. 376–394, esp. p. 392. Galileo as the "glorious fanatic" is also reflected in the words of Albert Einstein. See his Foreword to a translation of Galileo's *Dialogue*: "A man who possessed the passionate will, the intelligence, and the courage to stand up as the representative of rational thinking against the host of those who, relying on the ignorance of the people and the indolence of teachers in priestly and scholarly garb, maintained and defended their positions of authority. His unusual literary gift enabled him to address the educated man of his age in such clear and convincing language as to overcome the anthropocentric and myth-ridden thinking of his contemporaries." Quoted by Stillman Drake, *Galileo Studies: Personality, Tradition, and Revolution* (Ann Arbor, 1970), p. 65. The puzzling complexity of the assessment of the significance and "human dimension" of Galileo's achievement may be seen in the fact that exactly the anthropocentrism of Copernicus, as basis for his faith in the cosmic order, marked the path toward his discovery. See his Dedication to Pope Paul III [Appendix to this article].

[7]"In reality Galileo enriched astronomy and physics while robbing these sciences of a great part of their social meaning. With their discrediting of the Bible and the Church, they stood for a time on the front lines of all progress. It is true that a change nevertheless took place in the following centuries and they were involved in it, but it was a mere reform instead of a revolution, and the scandal – so to speak – degenerated into a dispute among experts. The Church, and with her the whole reactionary wing, could execute an orderly retreat and more or less preserve its power. As for these sciences themselves, they never again reached the high place in society held then, and no longer touched the common man.

"Galileo's crime can be considered as the 'original sin' of modern science. Out of the new astronomy, which deeply interested a new class, the bourgeoise, since it promoted the social revolutionary currents of the times, he made a severely restricted special science, which because of its 'purity,' i.e., its indifference to the means of production could develop relatively undisturbed.

"The atomic bomb, both as a technical and social phenomenon is the classical end product of scientific accomplishment and its social failure." Translated from Bertolt Brecht, *Gesammelte Werke* (Frankfurt am Main, 1967), vol. 17, p. 1108ff.

[8]Koestler ponders a number of explanations of why Copernicus did not object to or have Osiander's Preface removed, and concludes that it is more likely he submitted to Osiander's proposal since he had already submitted his whole life long. "... More likely he procrastinated, as he had done all his life." Arthur Koestler, *The Sleepwalkers* (London, 1959), p. 171; second edition, 1964, p. 175.

Nowadays people try to show their genius by producing new deviating ideas; this man subverts the whole field of astronomy. Even when that whole field stands topsy turvy I believe Holy Scripture. After all Joshua (10:13) commanded the sun to stand still and not the earth.[9]

Calvin – who without documentation and basis in fact is held by some recent scholarship to have been a critic of Copernicus[10] – seems to present an alternative to Luther by introducing another relation between revelation (in Scripture) and (experienced) reality. After all, in his commentary on Genesis Calvin points out[11] that the story of creation does not compete with the "great art of astronomy," but accommodates to and speaks in terms of the unlettered idiota, the common man.[12] Exactly the same argument we find a

---

[9]See Martin Luthers Werke, Kritische Gesamtausgabe Tischreden (Weimar, 1916), vol. 4, art. 4638, pp. 412–413; cf. ibid. (Weimar, 1912), vol. 1, art. 855, pp. 418–421. Basic literature: Werner Elert, Morphologie des Luthertums, I: Theologie und Weltanschauung des Luthertums hauptsächlich im 16. und 17. Jahrhundert, second edition (Munich, 1958), pp. 363–393. Heinrich Bornkamm, "Kopernikus im Urteil der Reformatoren," Archiv für Reformationsgeschichte, vol. 40 (1943), pp. 171–183; reprint in Das Jahrhundert der Reformation: Gestalten und Kräfte, second edition (Göttingen, 1966), pp. 177–185. John Dillenberger, Protestant Thought and Natural Science: A Historical Interpretation of the Issues behind the 500-year-old Debate (New York, 1960), pp. 28–49. Klaus Scholder, in a broad cultural and historical setting: Ursprünge und Probleme der Bibelkritik im 17. Jahrhundert. Ein Beitrag zur Entstehung der historisch-kritischen Theologie (Munich, 1966), pp. 57–65.

[10]See Thomas S. Kuhn, The Copernican Revolution: Planetary Astronomy in the Development of Western Thought (Cambridge, Mass., 1957), p. 196: "Protestant leaders like Luther, Calvin, and Melanchthon led in citing Scripture against Copernicus and in urging the repression of Copernicans. Since the Protestants never possessed the police apparatus available to the Catholic Church, their repressive measures were seldom so effective as those taken later by the Catholics, and they were more readily abandoned when the evidence for Copernicanism became overwhelming. But Protestants nevertheless provided the first effective institutionalized opposition."
Since the Protestant "attack" is interpreted as being due to its "sola scriptura," the Catholic reaction to Galileo has to be explained in different terms, and much to the historian's surprise, it is presented as anti-Protestant reaction and part of Catholic reform.
R. Hooykaas has eloquently opposed the myth that Calvin mentioned and rejected Copernicus in his works " 'There is no lie so good as the precise and well-detailed one' and this one has been repeated again and again, quotation marks included, by writers on the history of science, who evidently did not make the effort to verify the statement. For fifteen years, I have pointed out in several periodicals concerned with the history of science that the 'quotation' from Calvin is imaginary and that Calvin never mentioned Copernicus; but the legend dies hard." Religion and the Rise of Modern Science (Edinburgh-London, 1972), p. 121.
Furthermore, Hooykaas dealt with the theological thrust of Calvin's Genesis commentary by pointing to another aspect: "Thus Calvin's exegetical method was based on the Reformation doctrine which held that the religious message of the Bible is accessible to everybody. The Spirit of God, as he put it, has opened a common school for all, and has therefore chosen subjects intelligible to all. Moses was ordained a teacher of the unlearned as well as of the learned; had he spoken of things generally unknown, the uneducated might have pleaded in excuse that such subjects were beyond their capacity; therefore, Moses 'rather adapted his writing to common usage'." Ibid., p. 118.

[11]See Corpus Reformatorum, vol. 51 (Calvini Opera, vol. 23), col. 20–22.

[12]Calvin, loc. cit.

hundred years later with Kepler, when this admirer of Copernicus reconciles Joshua with his new cosmology.[13]

Since we touch here, in this difference between Luther and Calvin, upon one of the main phenomena of change in the Copernican era, we want to take a closer look. For those who know this period, Luther's reaction is predictable: he does not give his considered opinion of the Copernican thesis; he sees him merely as an instance of the sickness of the times, "*vana curiositas.*" Luther stands in a late medieval tradition "*contra curiositatem,*" which is pre- and supra-confessional, as can be seen from the identical views of Gerson and Erasmus. More generally a characteristic of the *via moderna* and *devotio moderna*, this acute aversion to *curiositas* is the awareness of the danger of one-sided intellectualism. At its worst this "modern" attitude is pietistic and anti-intellectualistic, reeling back from secular scholarship as a threat to the sacrality of the inner life. At its best – and closer to its historical origins and main thrust – it calls for a reform of the universities to discard intellectual games, far removed from experienced reality. As we shall see, this very thrust of seeming obscurantism proves to be the great wedge that is to provide Copernicus with the metaphysical antidote and the intellectual antecedents presupposed in his discovery.

The appropriate slogan for this campaign "*contra curiositatem*" we find in the *Adagia* of Erasmus: "*Quae supra nos nihil ad nos*"[14] ["The things above us do not concern us"]. Erasmus found it as a *dictum socraticum* (a Socratic saying) in the Church-father Lactantius (†320) and he knows that its main thrust is directed against cosmic speculation as "the curious investigation of things celestial and the secrets of nature."[15] After Lactantius, Augustine had dedicated an excursus in his *Confessiones* to the dangers of curiosity,[16] but left the deepest impression in a more direct parallel to Lactantius in his *Enchiridion,*[17] confronting the Greek metaphysical-cosmological speculation by arguing that to know the cosmic forces, the *causas motionum*, does not bring happiness; what we should know are the causes of good and evil.

---

[13]See K. Scholder, op. cit. [note 9], p. 68 ff. and Heinrich Karpp, "Der Beitrag Keplers und Galileis zum neuzeitlichen Schriftverständnis," *Zeitschrift für Theologie und Kirche*, vol. 67 (1970), pp. 40–55, esp. p. 46 ff.

[14]*Adagiorum chiliades*, vol. 1, p. 6, 69, in *Ausgewählte Werke*, vol. 7, edited by Theresia Payr (Darmstadt, 1972), p. 414 ff.

[15]Erasmus von Rotterdam, *Ausgewählte Werke*, vol. 7, ed. cit., pp. 414, 416. In a learned and stimulating article Eberhard Jüngel pursues the function of the "Socratic saying" in Luther's theology: "*Quae supra nos, nihil ad nos.* Eine Kurzformel der Lehre vom verborgenen Gott – im Anschluss an Luther interpretiert," *Evangelische Theologie*, vol. 32 (1972), pp. 197–240.

[16]Augustine, *Confessiones*, book 5, 3, 3.

[17]Augustine, *De fide, spe et caritate sive Enchiridion*, in J. P. Migne, editor, *Patrologiae completus cursus*, vol. 40, p. 235 (= *Corpus Christianorum*, vol. 46, p. 52 ff.).

Hence not metaphysics, but ethics fully deserve our dedication and pursuit. This Augustinian legacy of the contrast and even mutual exclusiveness of metaphysics and ethics, of cosmology and theology had been submerged[18] and was lying dormant throughout the era of the successful Aristotelian band wagon, till in the 14th century human experience in physics and theology started to pull at the dogmatic Aristotelian chains. It is this pulling that is expressed in the campaign "*contra vanam curiositatem.*"

It would be a fatal mistake to see in this campaign the high tide of medieval obscurantism thwarting the emergence of modern science. On the contrary, "*contra vanam curiositatem*" is best translated as "against distorting intellectualism" and marks the revolt that not only paved the way, but also provided method and models, for the coming era of science.

Before reform and revolt grew into religious reformation and scientific revolution as two distinguishable movements, we see how a man like Gerson can hold in one hand the threads of renewal in both fields. The common impetus is the call for experience as the best antidote against curiosity. On the one hand the reform of religion, Church, and theology urged a return to mystical piety (Bonaventure!) and thus stressed experience as the hallmark of the true Christian. On the other hand, the renewal of the sciences called for a revolt against metaphysics and thus based the new physics on experiment and experience. Less than a century and a half later, the common impetus was severely tested when the experience of faith and the experience of science were in the process of turning against each other as alternative bridges to the future. It is here that the voice of John Calvin carries particular weight. Calvin applies the slogan "*Quae supra nos nihil ad nos*" not to the reader of Scripture, but to the intention of Moses as the author of Scripture ("*nihil attinet supra coelos volare*"; "It accomplishes nothing to fly above the heavens"). The discrepancy between the story of creation and the secured data of astronomy is not to be solved by condemning astronomy as the obscurantists (*phrenetici*) do, who arrogantly reject everything unknown to them. Nor should the data of astronomy be taken as proof that Moses erred. Moses was not a teacher of astronomy, but a theologian, hence concerned with the glory of God, which, contrary to vain curiosity, is most useful to man. In his field, the astronomer does exactly the same: his field is not only exciting, but also most useful, providing access to the breathtaking wisdom of God: "*nam astrologia non modo iucunda est cognitu,*

---

[18]We find a restrictive interpretation of the Augustinian position with Hugo of St. Victor in his *Expositio in Hierarchiam coelestem S. Dionysii Areopagitae, Patrologiae completus cursus*, vol. 175, p. 925 A.

sed apprime quoque utilis: negari non potest quin admirabilem Dei sapientiam explicet ars illa"[19] ["for astronomy is not only nice to know, but also very useful: it cannot be denied that this study reveals the marvelous wisdom of God."]

In words almost identical with Kepler's in his *Astronomia nova*,[20] Calvin sees theology no longer in competition with astronomy or as penetration of the heavens to be rejected with the charge of vain curiosity and audacious preoccupation with the things "*supra nos.*" The sky above us is no longer the realm beyond us, beyond our ken, *supra nos.* Calvin's solution is not the obscurantist rejection of astronomy, nor does he go along with the adherents of the doctrine of "double truth" – what is true in theology is not true in philosophy. Rather one has to respect the limits. To stay within one's personal limits – the medieval definition of humility and the alternative to proud curiosity[21] – means now to stay within the limits of one's field of competence. The medieval differentiation between the university faculties, programmatically transcended in the preceding stages of the Renaissance, is here recaptured by Calvin to defend and respect the different methods of illuminating the common object, the glory of God.

It is here that I find the historical basis for the early latitude in Calvinism to favor or reject the Copernican vision. This stance helps as well to explain why, against all expectations, the relationship between Puritanism and science is to be a most intensive and fruitful union.[22] After all, before the restoration, the Puritans "were the main support of the new science."[23]

The so-called fraud of Osiander, who in his introduction to *De revolutionibus* tried to pass off Copernicus' heliocentricity thesis as "hypotheses,"[24] was intended to raise the toleration level in the scholarly

[19]*Calvini Opera*, vol. 23, ed. cit. [note 11], col. 22.

[20]Johannes Kepler, *Astronomia nova*, in Max Caspar, editor, *Johannes Keplers Gesammelte Werke*, vol. 3 (Munich, 1937), pp. 28–34, "Introductio."

[21]Cf. Thomas de Aquino, *Contra Gentiles*, vol. 3, book 4, "De unione hypostatica," chap. 55: ". . . *virtus humilitatis in hoc consistit ut aliquis infra suos terminos se contineat, ad ea quae supra se sunt non se extendens, sed superiori se subiiciat.*" (". . . the virtue of humility consists in this, that someone contains himself within his limits, not extending himself to those things that are above him, but subjugating himself to the higher things.")

[22]Cf. John Dillenberger, op. cit. [note 9], p. 130: "Statistical evidence points to a predominant Puritan membership in the Royal Society."

[23]See R. Hooykaas, op. cit. [note 10], p. 148; cf. p. 94ff.; pp. 135–138.

[24]*Nikolaus Kopernikus Gesamtausgabe*, II: *De revolutionibus orbium caelestium* (Munich, 1949), pp. 403–404. ". . . *astronomus eam* [*hypothesim*] *potissimum arripiet, quae comprehensu sit quam facillima. Philosophus fortasse veri similitudinem magis requiret; neuter tamen quicquam certi comprehendet, aut tradet, nisi divinitus illi revelatum fuerit. Sinamus igitur et has novas hypotheses inter veteres nihilo verisimiliores innotescere, praesertim cum admirabiles simul et faciles sint, ingentemque thesaurum doctissimarum observationem* [*sic; lege: observationum*] *secum advehant. Neque quisquam, quod ad hypotheses attinet, quicquam certi ab astronomia expectet, cum ipsa nihil tale praestare queat, ne si in alium usum conficta pro veris*

world. It may explain Melanchthon's shift from early condemnation to cautious support;[25] it could, of course, not provide a more lasting basis for welding together the new science and religion. Such a basis could only be found in the conviction formulated by Calvin that Scripture is not a supernaturally revealed book of nature, so that religious experience and scientific experience can go hand in hand.

Only after Darwinism as the scientific "arm" of Cartesianism programmatically separated these two hands, was the threat of Descartes to Christian faith met with obscurantist fanaticism.[26] One of these means was to hold the book of *Genesis* against the book of Darwin and to match God's Adam with Darwin's ape, hence falling back into a pre-Calvin stage of unenlightened obscurantism, all the more offensive since science had made such remarkable progress in the meantime. It is a serious mistake, however – and very often made – to read the reactions against Copernicus in the light of the anti-Darwin crusade. Even the 17th-century stir over Galileo is a misleading paradigm. Apart from the overcautious suspicion of vain curiosity, which all that emerged from academic circles had to face in late medieval society, the opposition to Copernicanism was due rather to weaknesses and obscurities immanent in the Copernican system itself, as well as to his assumptions (i.e., hypotheses!), which were not to be substantiated until the time of Kepler, Galileo, and Newton.

"It is safe to say that even had there been no religious scruples whatever against the Copernican astronomy, sensible men all over Europe, especially the most empirically minded, would have pronounced it a wild appeal to accept the premature fruits of an uncontrolled imagination, in preference to the solid inductions, built up gradually through the ages, of man's confirmed sense experience.... Contemporary empiricists, had they lived in the sixteenth century, would have been [the] first to scoff out of court the new philosophy of the universe.[27]"

---

arripiat, stultior ab hac disciplina discedat quam accesserit. Vale." Ad lectorem de hypothesibus huius operis. [For an English translation, see pp. 301–304 of Gingerich.] Note: The title page of the 1543 Nuremberg edition is enlarged by a publisher's blurb: "Habes in hoc opere . . . motus stellarum . . . novis insuper ac admirabilibus hypothesibus ornatis." ("You have in this work . . . the motion of the stars . . . newly arranged with fine and admirable hypotheses.") For the bibliographical data see Gottfried Seebass, *Bibliographia Osiandrica* (Nieuwkoop, 1971), p. 130 ff.

[25]H. Bornkamm, op. cit. [note 9], p. 182 ff.; K. Scholder, op. cit. [note 9], p. 63.

[26]On the Cartesian dichotomy between the two experiences see J. Bots, *Tussen Descartes en Darwin: Geloof en natuur wetenschap in de 18ᵉ eeuw in Nederland, Speculum Historiale* (Assen, 1972), vol. 8., pp. 136–139 (for a German summary of this section, see p. 186ff.).

[27]E. A. Burtt, *The Metaphysical Foundations of Modern Physical Science*, second edition (New York, 1951); p. 25 ff. cited by Dillenberger, op. cit. [note 9], p. 26 ff. Franz Wolf, though more restrained, presents the same argument in his 1943 commemoration address: "Furthermore, in its details the superiority of the Copernican system over Ptolemy's was not yet clearly

2. OSIANDER'S UNAUTHORIZED PREFACE

The unauthorized introduction or preface to *De revolutionibus* by the astronomer and first Lutheran minister in Nuremberg, Andreas Osiander, has been characterized by Bishop Tideman Giese as a "fraud"[28] and has, ever since, drawn a major portion of research energy away from the real subject, Copernicus. Some of the charges against Osiander can be easily disposed of. There is no sly effort on his part to suggest that his preface is actually written by Copernicus. Content and style – he speaks about the author in the third person – clearly pointed to a third person, often a friend of the author who introduced the book to the reader, as was often the case in this *genre* during the 16th century.[29]

One more aspect of Osiander's subjective honesty: The basic structure of his preface can be found in a letter sent two years earlier to Copernicus and to the first Copernican and original editor, Georg Joachim Rheticus. Here we already find the proposal to placate and then win the Aristotelians and theologians by emphasizing that the Copernican theory is based on a series of assumptions (hypotheses) and hence cannot claim ultimate truth. Since several hypotheses can be offered to explain one and the same phenomenon, it should be regarded as belonging to scholarly freedom (*"Freiheit in Forschung und Lehre"*) that more convincing hypotheses can be always advanced: "In that way the potential opponents will be lured away from massive criticism to more intensive research; and, through newly gained respect and a lack of counter arguments, be moved to fairness and ultimately to acceptance."[30]

---

perceived.... From the world of Copernicus to the distances of the spiral nebulae is but a moment in the development of scientific knowledge of the heavens." Translated from *Karlsruher Akademische Reden*, vol. 22, pp. 5–23, esp. p. 11, 1943. Cf. Norbert Schiffers, "Die Schwäche des Kopernikus," *Fragen der Physik an die Theologie: Die Säkularisierung der Wissenschaft und das Heilsverlangen nach Freiheit* (Düsseldorf, 1968), p. 13 ff.

[28]Karl Heinz Burmeister, *Georg Joachim Rhetikus 1514–1574, III: Briefwechsel* (Wiesbaden, 1968), p. 55. It seems clear that Giese refers to Osiander as responsible for putting pressure on Petreius. Giese's interpretation of Osiander's motives is, understandably, more malicious than convincing: "... *dolens descendendum sibi esse a pristina professione, si hic liber famam sit consecutus.*" ("... unfortunately stooping to have the opening declaration in case this book would later become famous.") In letters to Copernicus and his co-editor Rheticus, Osiander had, as early as 20 April 1541, developed his battle plan for winning over the two expected opposition parties. See Burmeister, op. cit. [note 28], vol. 3, p. 25: "... *Paripathetici et theologi facile placabuntur* [instead of: *placabunter*], *si audierint, eiusdem apparentis motus varias esse posse hypotheses...*" ("... Aristotelians and theologians will be easily placated if they hear that the same motion as perceived can be explained by means of different hypotheses ..."). Cf. note 30.

[29]In early copies the name of Osiander is identified; as a matter of fact, this is the way in which Kepler could name Osiander as the author of the Preface. Yet even as late as Laplace, the Preface was read as being written by Copernicus. See Koyré, op. cit. [note 5], p. 99, n. 14.

[30]See Burmeister, op. cit. [note 28], vol. 3, p. 25. For the parallel, partly identical, letter of Osiander to Copernicus dated on the same day, 20 April 1541, see *Apologia Tychonis contra Ursum, Kepleri opera omnia*, ed. Ch. Frisch (Frankfurt, 1858), vol. 1, p. 246.

The word "hypotheses" should not be as offensive to us as it was to Kepler and many a Copernican scholar since.[31] In one of the most concise, but also most accurate, treatments of the Copernican discovery, Edward Rosen[32] has established Copernicus' own use of the term in his main works. And the first believer, Rheticus, describes the achievement of his beloved master as "*renovare hypotheses.*"[33] In his own dedicatory letter to Pope Paul III, Copernicus describes the genesis of his break-through and provides us with a number of significant parallels with Osiander's preface. But more importantly, the letter lays the basis for our effort to place the Copernican Revolution in an era of change.

For Copernicus the point of departure was that the hypotheses of preceding astronomy – the theoretical explanations of the postulated mathematical astral movements – did not jibe with observed reality; i.e., the actual forecasts of future movements of sun and moon on the basis of the assumption of concentric circles did not prove true. Above all – and now comes the explicit goal that Copernicus had set for himself – earlier assumed explanations did not lead to the discovery of the true shape of the universe (*forma mundi*), or to the symmetry of its structure (*partium eius certam symmetriam*). What had been lacking was a blueprint explaining the inner workings of the universe (*ratio motuum machinae mundi*), the world machine which, after all, the greatest and the most orderly machinist has produced for us (*propter nos*), because of us:

"Encouraged by the witness of classical authors I too started to think in terms of a moving earth. And even though this seemed an absurd view [*opinio*],[34] I felt that I had the same freedom to advance hypotheses to explain astral phenomena as others before me; and hence that it would be permissible to find out whether on the assumption of global motion [*ut experirer an positio terrae aliquo motu*] a more reliable explanation could not be advanced for the revolution of the celestial spheres."

Up to this point there is a striking double parallel with Osiander: First, the appeal to the freedom of scholarly investigation in a time of emancipation from the homogenizing weight of tradition. This is the very juncture at which the ideal of self-directed research frees itself from the pious shackles

---

[31]*Johannes Keplers Gesammelte Werke*, ed. cit. [note 20], p. 6.

[32]Edward Rosen, *Three Copernican Treatises*, second edition (New York, 1959), pp. 28–33. The appendix of annotated bibliography (pp. 201–269) proved to be invaluable.

[33]Ibid., p. 31. Cf. Rheticus' dedicatory letter to the *Narratio Prima*, quoted by Leopold Prowe, *Nicolaus Copernicus* (Berlin, 1884), vol. 2, p. 321, 27.

[34]In contrast to *assertio*, which means "conviction," *opinio* means "view" in the sense of "assumption."

of metaphysical orthodoxy. This is an implicit plea against "vain curiosity" and for respecting the limits of each discipline. For Copernicus the piety of the Church Father Lactantius leads to obscurantism – quite audaciously put in a letter to the Pope! After all, Lactantius, who handed down to posterity the slogan "*Quae supra nos, nihil ad nos*" came to ridicule those who discovered the rotundity of the earth. Secondly, there is the common description of the Copernican research-process in terms of "hypotheses." This is as far as the parallel goes. What Copernicus now discovers remains for Osiander on the level of *opinio*, that is, "assumption," or "hypothesis," without an ultimate claim to a true explanation of cosmological causality, of what makes the universe tick. For Osiander that was the sole domain of God and of those with whom He cares to share His wisdom.[35]

Copernicus, on the other hand, left the level of assumption behind at the moment when he made his breakthrough: at that moment – namely, when his hypothesis of the movement of the earth was hardened, as he claimed, by experience and confirmed by observations (*multa et longa observatione tandem repperi*), sense-data suddenly fell into place, and above all, showed a universal-pattern,[36] a true cosmos, where blueprint and global machine fit perfectly together.

We are now in a better position to assess the charge of fraud against Osiander. Osiander is a misleading guide to the world of Copernicus. Without questioning the former's good intentions, the worlds of Osiander and of Copernicus are as a matter of fact light-years apart. But we would miss the true nature of science's advance, if we cede traditional scholarship the point that these two worlds are to be designated as "medieval" and "modern." With great erudition, as well as with dizzying rhetorical magnetism, Hans Blumenberg has advanced the thesis that Osiander embodies a basic nominalist position. As Blumenberg sees it, the nominalist stands in an alien, unreachable universe, which is metaphysically systematized as "astronomical resignation."[37] Out of this heteronomous

---

[35]". . . *neuter tamen quicquid certi comprehendet aut tradet nisi divinitus illi revelatum fuerit.*" (". . . neither of them will learn or teach anything certain, unless it has been divinely revealed to him.") For an accessible and emendated Latin text of Osiander's Preface, see Emanuel Hirsch, *Die Theologie des Andreas Osiander und ihre geschichtlichen Voraussetzungen* (Göttingen, 1919), App. 1, p. 290.

[36]This universal vision as the essential advance beyond Ptolemy is highlighted by Matthias Schramm in his commemoration address in Tübingen, 1 February 1973, entitled "Die Leistungen des Copernicus." The author kindly supplied me with his manuscript.

[37]"Man is not, as the Stoics would have it, disposed to examine the arrangement of the heavens, but on the contrary, his theoretical inquisitiveness puts before him the appearance of a heterogeneous and unattainable cosmology [*Weltregion*] for whose perception Nature provides him no basis. The epistemology of astronomical resignation is therewith metaphysically

world, the great humanist Copernicus, as it is claimed, freed us to relate man to his *Umwelt* within which he is to gain his conscious autonomy.[38]

In a last section, I shall attempt to show that where the Copernican Revolution is a cause of celebration for modern man, it presupposes and is based on a nominalist platform – and that when we let ourselves be waylaid and lured away from his platform, we are bound to regress into something worse, to confuse again astrology and cosmology, *Weltbild* and *Weltanschauung*. Neither Protestantism nor Roman Catholicism, much less Blumenberg's philosophical humanism, gave birth to modern science. For that we have to look at a preceding stage, a true fertile crescent.

3. THE NOMINALIST BACKGROUND TO THE COPERNICAN REVOLUTION

"Nous avons du ciel trop peu d'expérience."[39] That is an exclamation, a *cri de coeur* of the leading nominalist philosopher in the generation between Ockham and Gerson (†1429), Nicole Oresme (†1382), 150 years before Copernicus, younger contemporary of Thomas Bradwardine (†1348) and disciple of Jean Buridan (†1348). We do not quote Oresme here because we believe that he influenced Copernicus directly, though Copernicus had in his library, besides some Bradwardine, at least one nominalist source, the *Quaestiones* of Pierre d'Ailly (†1420).[40] Copernicus, however, probably did not know French; and it is in beautiful, indeed creative French, that Oresme made available the works of Aristotle – in translation, commentary and critique. In France we find Oresme quoted by d'Ailly and Gerson, and his name was soon respected both in Germany and in Italy. Moreover nominalism is such a powerful and all pervasive movement that we cannot ignore Oresme, one of its pacesetting spokesmen, if we want to catch at least a glimpse of its

---

systematized." Translated from Hans Blumenberg, *Die kopernikanische Wende* (Frankfurt am Main, 1965), p. 64. Cf. *Die Legitimität der Neuzeit* (Frankfurt am Main, 1966), p. 346 ff.

[38]"Copernicus had not only used the humanistic rules, but with his astronomical reform he had exactly hit the genuine mentality of the humanistic movement of the fading Middle Ages and had more essentially realized it than many of those who had explicitly formulated the program of this movement." Translated from H. Blumenberg, op. cit. [note 37], p. 77.

[39]Nicole Oresme, *Le Livre du ciel et du monde*, edited by A. D. Menut and A.J. Denomy, translated by A.D. Menut (Madison, 1968), p. 356ff (= book 2, chap. 8, f. 89d).

[40]See Ernst Zinner, *Entstehung und Ausbreitung der Copernicanischen Lehre: Sitzungsberichte der Phy.-Med. Sozietät Erlangen* (Erlangen, 1943), vol. 74, p. 406. These *Quaestiones* are part of a genre of composite volumes described by Pierre Duhem, *Les Origines de la statique* (Paris, 1906), vol. 2, p. 59, n. 1; p. 337 ff. n. 1.

originality and constructive revolt.[41]

It is by no means a novelty to introduce Oresme's name in our attempt to understand the significance of Copernicus. Since Pierre Duhem, modern scholarship has been very aware of this point; among others, Lynn Thorndike,[42] Anneliese Maier, and Marshall Clagett have furthered our knowledge of Oresme significantly. Yet the high claims of Duhem for Oresme's role as precursor and even as preemptor of later discoveries has now generally led to an overcautious reaction. With their usual nod to Anneliese Maier's impressive phalanx of manuscript-based evidence,[43] scholars invariably tend to come to the conclusion that Oresme may have had some theoretical insights but remained "Aristotelian" and offered mere speculative possibilities without relation to fact and reality.[44] It is, however, misleading to speak here of "mere speculation" for we then miss, I believe, the decisive access-route to the phenomenon of modernity. Hence we should be prepared to listen more patiently to the sources.

The systematic application of the theological distinction *potentia absoluta* (absolute power) – "what God could have done without contradiction" – and *potentia ordinata* (God's commitment) – "what God *de facto* did," or, as Oresme puts its "*selon verite,*" actually "revealed, decided to do or ordained" – functioned, in line with the condemnations of Averroism in 1277, to place God beyond the fangs of necessity in thought or action. In other words, the transcendence of God is what really concerned the nominalist here. The distinction – and this we have not seen before – works itself out in two different ways: in theology and physics, which includes, of course, astronomy. In theology, the distinction shows the irrelevance and irreverence of speculative theology and man's absolute dependence on

---

[41]In another context – with respect to the significance of neostoicism as "setting" for Descartes, Spinoza, and Calvin – the French philosopher Eric Weil observes that such "authors are credited with an originality they themselves would not have admitted, simply because we do not study what every cultured man in their times had always present in mind." See his article "Supporting the Humanities," *Daedalus*, vol. 102 (1973), pp. 27–38, esp. p. 33.

[42]On a broad (often manuscript) basis Lynn Thorndike presents Oresme's view on astrology, magic, and miracles, *A History of Magic and Experimental Science* (New York, 1934), vol. 3, pp. 398–471.

[43]Anneliese Maier, herself, has often been more ready to grant Oresme his subjective sense of exploring reality; see *An der Grenze von Scholastik und Naturwissenschaft* [*Studien zur Naturphilosophie der Spätscholastik*, vol. 3], second edition (Rome, 1952), p. 354 ff. In a characteristic formulation Anneliese Maier now ascribes to Oresme a view (earlier assigned by her to Albert of Sachsen) "in whom one can see the first hint of the equivalence principle of modern set theory," *Die Vorläufer Galileis im 14. Jahrhundert* [*Studien zur Naturphilosophie der Spätscholastik*, vol. 1], second edition (Rome, 1966), p. 309.

[44]See A.D. Menut's bibliography in N. Oresme, ed. cit. [note 39], pp. 753–762.

God's own revelation. Speculation makes us leave reality behind and orbit in the infinite realm of the *potentia absoluta*, disoriented and lost amongst the infinite number of possibilities God *could* have decided to realize. To penetrate this realm of the *Deus absconditus*, is *vana curiositas*, to fathom the thoughts of God is vain curiosity, whereas it is the task of religion and faith to base itself on God's own revelation, the *potentia ordinata*. Together with the humanist quest for authentic sources (*fontes*), the insistence on nothing but God's commitment, the *sola potentia ordinata*, may evolve into a *sola scriptura*, the Reformation principle "Scripture alone." As history can document, however, nominalism has left its profound impact not only on Luther, but also on Erasmus and the decrees of the Council of Trent.

In both theology and physics the distinction between possibility and reality helped to free man from the smothering embrace of metaphysics. Yet in physics the same distinction works itself out in a different way. Here the main shift from preceding tradition is that the investigation of final causality is recast in terms of efficient causality.[45] This means that the *Weltbild*, the experienced world, is set free from the fangs of a *Weltanschauung*, the postulated world. Simultaneously the unmoved Mover thus cedes his place to the inscrutable Lawgiver. Here the *potentia ordinata* stands for the realm of nature, the "present order," or as Oresme puts it, "*le cours de nature.*"[46] Whereas in theology the established order (e.g., of the Church) is at the same time the revealed order (through Holy Scripture, and/or Tradition), in the realm of physics the established order is the order of the established laws of nature,[47] still to be investigated and freed from the Babylonian captivity of metaphysical a priori.

In this climate there emerge before our eyes the beginnings of the new science. I see the first contours of this science in a double thrust:

1. The conscious and intellectually ascetic reduction and concentration on *experientia* both as collective experience entered in the historical record of mankind; *and* as sense or "test tube" experience (*cognitio intuitiva*) that allows

---

[45]Anneliese Maier assigns to Jean Buridan the central role: "Buridan deserves the credit for having drawn the metaphysical and methodological consequences from all this knowledge; he is the first who thought he saw that these principles suffice to explain the events of nature and that on this basis one can refrain from adopting final causes and final tendencies. And hereby he has in fact anticipated the idea that would dominate the science of the following century." Translated from *Metaphysische Hintergründe der spätscholastischen Naturphilosophie* [*Studien zur Naturphilosophie der Spätscholastik*, vol. 4] (Rome, 1955), p. 334 ff.

[46]Oresme, op. cit. [note 39], book 1, chap. 2, f. 7a; ed. cit., p. 58. See also the synonyms used by d'Ailly, as quoted by Francis Oakley, "Christian Theology and the Newtonian Science: The Rise of the Concept of the Laws of Nature," *Church History*, vol. 30 (1961), pp. 433–457, esp. p. 454 ff. n. 74.

[47]Oresme, op. cit. [note 39], book 2, chap. 2, f. 71a; ed cit., p. 288.

for general conclusions and the discovery of laws; and such only by induction.[48]

2. The discovery of the scientific role of imagination[49] allows for mental experiments. Where facts are not in the reach of experience, we grope for the facts with our imagination, the realm of the *potentia absoluta*, the *terra incognita*, the unknown realm of logical possibilities. In the field of theology this would be "vain curiosity"; in the field of natural philosophy this is research, *investigation*. This is the breeding ground of the so-called hypotheses that are completely misunderstood as "mere speculation": hypotheses are at once the feast of free research unhampered by *a priori*, unassailable assumptions and the forecast of possibilities based on experiments, the formulations of scientific expectations. The nominalist scientific revolution cannot be sufficiently measured when one merely looks at the research results, even though these are most impressive; but nominalism brings about a revolution in research methodology, which is strictly oriented to experiment and experience.

In the field of astronomy the nominalist hunger for reality is all the more acute, since the heavens are so far removed from collective (the incomplete lists of observations!) and individual experience. Hence the *cri de coeur* of Oresme: "... *nous avons du ciel trop peu d'expérience.*" While this very hunger will lead to the development of such instruments as the telescope (the needed extensions of the human senses), in the meantime imagination has to fill the gap left by actual experiments, in a conscious suspension of final judgment. All in all mental hypotheses reach out to reality and expect to be verified by it.

When the distinction is allowed between *microcosm* (for man), *macrocosm*

---

[48]See, however, G.W. Coopland: "Of Oresme's use of experience in the everyday sense little need be said; it is illustrated at every turn and furnishes the most attractive part of his work. It is evidently the result of wide interests and knowledge of his world, although in this connection, again, we discern that strange stopping short of closer and more searching enquiry demanded by modern standards. Of organized and controlled observation in the form of experiment we can find no trace." *Nicole Oresme and the Astrologers: A Study of his "Livre de divinacions"* (Cambridge, Mass., 1952), p. 35.

[49]For the double function of *"imaginatio"* as "not-fact" and as point of departure for inquiry, see Jean Buridan, as quoted by Pierre Duhem, *Le Système du monde* (Paris, 1916), vol. 4, p. 317 ff.; *"imaginatio"* as *"modus inveniendi loca planetarum"*, and therefore merely as *calculatio* à la Osiander, see ibid., p. 146 ff. Even the editors of Oresme's *Livre du ciel et du monde* have not always differentiated between matter and method: "Under these conditions, we may suppose that a ship could float on the surface of the sphere of air just as naturally as it would on the Seine River or on the surface of the sea (199d). This final 'ymagination' in Oresme's long critique of Aristotle's *De caelo* exhibits impressively the distance that separates the science of today from that of the 14th century," ed. cit. [note 39], p. 30.

(for the universe) and *metacosm* (for the realm of God)[50] we may say that (1) nominalism has discovered "space" by transforming the metacosm from the habitat of God into the infinite extension of the macrocosm,[51] while the omnipresence of God binds Him no longer to circumscribed space, hence placing His presence squarely in the macrocosm – an aspect pursued in Luther's theology and particularly in his doctrine of the Eucharist.[52] (2) In concentrating on the macrocosm as *machina mundi* or the reliable "horloge" set by God,[53] under the exclusion of the metacosm, the demarcation line between God and nature is clearly marked and hence space is demythologized and dedivinized.[54] The thrust of this development is better expressed in the designation "naturalization of the universe" than in the more depreciating two-dimensional "mechanization of the universe." (3) The demarcation line drawn by God himself between his own being and his creation terminates the centuries-long argument that the very existence of

---

[50]Jean Gerson uses for our "metacosm," *mundus archetypus*, in *Opera omnia*, vol. 3, edited by L.E. du Pin, "Definitiones terminorum ad theologiam moralem pertinentium" (Antwerp, 1706), col. 107B.

[51]See Anneliese Maier's Addenda to the second edition of her *Die Vorläufer Galileis im 14. Jahrhundert* [*Studien zur Naturphilosophie der Spätscholastik*, vol. 1] (Rome, 1966), p. 315, and the comparison with Bradwardine's view of the *immensitas Dei*, in note 1 on the same page. Cf. John E. Murdoch: "It is of note that in the Middle Ages such speculation on the infinite centered on the older problem, in itself less scientific, of the eternity of the world. Analyses of the infinite were initially designed to resolve this more traditional problem. On the other hand, in the 14th century in many instances the problem of the possibility of an eternal world had simply become an occasion to discuss the mysteries of the infinite." Translated by John Murdoch from his "'Rationes Mathematice,' Un aspect du rapport des mathématiques et de la philosophie au Moyen Age" in *Conférence donnée au Palais de la Découverte le 4 Novembre 1961. Histoire des Sciences* (Paris, 1962), p. 22.

[52]The significance of this "breakthrough of God" for Luther's theology is described well by W. Elert, op. cit. [note 9], vol. 1, p. 386 ff.

[53]For Oresme's fascination with the image of the clock, see also Lynn Thorndike, op. cit. [note 42], vol. 3, p. 411, n. 1. For Jean Buridan, Oresme's teacher also in this respect, see *Quaestiones super libris quattuor de caelo et mundo*, edited by Ernest A. Moody (Cambridge, Mass., 1942), book 2, qu. 22, pp. 226–233.

[54]The wide spread of popular astrology is one of the many indications that the Arabian "myth screen" had not been sufficiently effective. See here Manfred Ullmann: "The interpretive possibilities of planetary positions depended on setting the planets equivalent with the gods, a procedure already established in the 6th century B.C., next by the Pythagoreans, and then generally in colloquial speech. All the attributes, capabilities, and actions of the gods that had been found deposited in their myths were now associated with the planet in question, and thus it became possible also to interpret the constellations. For the Arabs and Moslems the names of the planets lost in translation their character as gods' names. But the Arabs undertook the complicated articulation of the interpretive possibilities, which without the ancient mythological background necessarily remained a purely mechanical, inexplicable system." Translated from *Die Natur- und Geheimwissenschaften im Islam* (Leiden, 1972), p. 348.

God requires celestial movement including the orbiting of the sun.[55]

The example from the book of Joshua (10:13) that was going to be used as a biblical argument against Copernicus to prove that the sun moves – "Sun stand still" – is adduced by Oresme to show that creation is not a necessary function of the Highest Being, but the result of a voluntary decision of the Highest Person.[56] It is important to note that for Oresme Scripture admits the possibility that the earth moves – "*qui commovet terram de loco suo*" (Job 9:6) – so that henceforth the investigator is forced to offer a physical instead of a theological solution.[57] Therefore for Oresme, as well as for those who stand in his tradition, the issue of the heavenly movements – of the orbits of the sun, the moon, the moving stars and the earth – is no longer to be solved in terms of a deductive speculative cosmo*logy*, but in terms of an experiential inductive cosmo*nomy*, with the aid of imagination but without claim on scientific accuracy until the mental experiments are confirmed by experience.

It is impressive to see how far Oresme has come in opening up the realm of imagination and of theoretical astrophysics – the impetus theory, the three-point requirement in perspectives, the diurnal rotation of the earth – thus finding significant pieces in the puzzle that would reveal to Copernicus the vision of heliocentricity. But again, outlasting by far the significance in material progress, we emphasize the advance in scientific attitude, an

---

[55]Conversely developments in the field of physics show effects on theology. After the Thomistic ontological relation between grace and movement, the new impetus-doctrine transforms "motion" and personalizes the concept of grace. We have pursued the history of theology and the history of the medieval sciences so long in separate departments that we stand only at the very beginning of seeing the interactions between shifts in these fields.

[56]"Thus, it is clear from what we have said that it does not follow that, if God is, the heavens are; consequently, it does not follow that the heavens move. For, in truth, all these things depend freely upon the will of God without any necessity that He cause or produce such things or that He should cause or produce them eternally, as we explained more fully at the end of Chapter Thirty-four of Book I [see f. 58b]. Moreover, it does not follow that, if the heavens exist, they must move; for, as stated, God moves them or makes them move quite voluntarily. He demonstrated this action at the time of Joshua when the sun stood still for the duration of an entire day, as the Scripture states: Was not . . . one day made as two? It is probable that the daily motion of the whole heavens and that of the planets stopped, and not only the sun. In relating this event, the Prophet said: The sun and the moon stood still in their habitation, etc." N. Oresme, op. cit. [note 39], book 2, ch. 8, f. 92b; ed. cit., p. 365.

[57]"Therefore, assuming that the earth moves with or contrariwise to the heavens, it does not follow from this / (92d) that celestial motion would stop, and so, in and of itself, this circular motion of the heavens does not demand that the earth remain motionless at the center. It is, indeed, not impossible that the whole earth moves with a different motion or in another way. In Job 9, we read: Who shaketh the earth out of her place . . ." N. Oresme, op. cit. [note 39], book 2, ch. 8, f. 92d; ed. cit., p. 367.

attitude that is not tacked on but integrally related to the new religious and theological attitude: *vain* curiosity is the effort to penetrate the unknown realm of God omnipotent (*qui supra nos; potentia absoluta*); *true* and *valid* curiosity is concerned with the whole *machina mundi*, which includes earth *and* heaven (*quae supra nos; l'ordre selon nature*). Programmatically God and the heavens are separated: the wise Greek Thales, once the laughing stock and object of jokes about the ivory tower of speculative Platonism, may still stumble into his pitfall, but now because of his proud penetration of divine mystery, no longer because of his astronomical curiosity. In our modern parlance, the mysteries of the heavens have been "declassified."

4. THE COPERNICAN MANIFESTO

I have presented a sketch of Oresme because I sense here a remarkable proximity to the birth of the modern theory of research in the natural sciences. With much truth, yet with little humility and hence in a strikingly post-medieval way, Oresme concludes[58] his *Livre du ciel et du monde* with the words: "I dare say and insist that there is no human being who has seen a better book on natural philosophy than this one."[59]

I have not dealt with Oresme, the Parisian master, to reopen the issue of the forerunners of Copernicus, though it may have become clear that I do not support the theory of "spontaneous generation."[60] The point is rather

---

[58]Hardly more cautious is the explicit of a physics commentary, *Quaestiones*, assigned to Buridan: "*Tu melius scribe, qui dixeris hoc fore vile/Si melius fuerit, plus tibi laudis erit*" ("Write it better, in case you say this is worthless; if you do better, it will be more praise to you."). Quoted by Pierre Duhem, op. cit. [note 49], p. 132. The same desideratum from the inverse perspective is formulated by John Murdoch in his "Philosophy and the Enterprise of Science in the Later Middle Ages," *History of the Interaction between Science and Philosophy: Proceedings of the International Symposium on Science and Philosophy held at the Van Leer Jerusalem Foundation, Jerusalem, Israel, January 15-January 19, 1971, Honoring Professor S. Sambursky*, p. 28 (MS).

[59]With all respect for my fellow countryman, E.J. Dijksterhuis, who belongs to the pioneers in the history of science, I cannot share his view of Parisian nominalism: "The decadence into which Scholasticism has fallen is typified by the fact that in their works there is no question of any further development of the fruitful, but as yet totally unexplored, ideas contained in his theory; nevertheless, one can at least appreciate in the Parisian philosophers of this time, that they were at least able to keep the good aspects when in the same period the Italians were falling back in the field of mechanics to the Aristotelian-Averroistic errors that had in Paris long since been conquered." Translated by Arthur Loeb from *Val en worp. Een Bijdrage tot de Geschiedenis der Mechanica van Aristoteles tot Newton*, Chapter II: "Val en Worp in de Scholastiek" (Groningen, 1924), pp. 117–121, esp. p. 118.

[60]See, however, Koyré: "... but no-one except Copernicus produced a heliocentric astronomy. Why? It is an idle question: because no-one before Copernicus had his genius, or his courage. Perhaps, it was because no-one between Ptolemy and Copernicus had been both an inspired astronomer and a convinced Pythagorean," op. cit. [note 5], p. 42.

that we gain a revealing perspective on Copernicus, and this evaluation necessarily includes his two unfortunate editors. To begin with, there is Georg Joachim Rheticus, who had cause to feel slighted by his beloved master Copernicus when the latter decided not to mention this Protestant disciple in his dedicatory letter to Pope Paul III. In a letter to Peter Ramus, dated Cracow 1568, Rheticus describes his future program as the task of liberating astronomy from hypotheses; henceforth astronomy was to be, as he insists, solely based on observation (*solis observationibus*);[61] in the field of physics, modern research should be freed from the shackles of tradition and be allowed a direct approach, based only on the analysis of the phenomena of nature (*ex sola naturae contemplatione*). We find here, some two centuries after Oresme, a reformulation of the nominalistic antimetaphysical program that envisioned the replacement of metaphysical *a priori* assumptions by experiment and experience. In discarding classical sources as a hindrance to progress, Rheticus proves that he has outgrown the scientifically unproductive phase of the Renaissance which, with its sun-symbolism and *magi*, blinded many a scholar until our own day.[62]

As far as Osiander is concerned we are, I think, now in a position to do justice to his vision of reality and to see the element of truth in his Preface – better, I believe, than either those who are understandably irritated by his face-saving (but not faith-saving!) devices or those who have opted for the *via antiqua* and reject the nominalist stance on principle. However harsh it may sound, astronomy cannot reveal the "true causes" of astral phenomena

---

[61]See Burmeister, op. cit. [note 28], vol. 3, p. 188; cf. "Near the end of his life Rheticus sought to build out of his rich experience as astronomer, physician and alchemist, a new philosophical system whose foundation should be only nature, *ex sola naturae contemplatione*. Only in this way, he wrote in 1568 to Ramus, would his natural philosophy be grounded. As we know, Rheticus placed this demand equally on medicine, astronomy, and astrology." Translated from Burmeister, *Georg Joachim Rhetikus 1514–1574, I: Humanist und Wegbereiter der modernen Naturwissenschaften* (Wiesbaden, 1967), p. 173.

[62]See the in-other-respects excellent study by Francis A. Yates, *Giordano Bruno and the Hermetic Tradition*, second edition (London, 1971), pp. 241–243. See also Peter J. French, *John Dee: The World of an Elizabethan Magus* (London, 1972), p. 103; "Renaissance Hermeticism prepared the way emotionally for the acceptance of Copernicus' revolutionized universal structure. In this case, then, scientific advance was spurred by the renewed interest in the magical Hermetic religion of the world." The Sun-analogies and Hermetic traditions – alluded to by Copernicus in his Preface – are certainly important characteristics of a movement we can trace from protohumanism (Richard de Bury's library, used by Bradwardine and Holcot) to Pico and Reuchlin. See further Eugenio Garin, *Portraits from the Quattrocentro*, second edition (New York, 1972), pp. 145–149, and Wayne Shumaker, *The Occult Sciences in the Renaissance: A Study in Intellectual Patterns* (Berkeley, 1972), pp. 201 ff., on the "centrality" of the sun, ibid., p. 221. For a perspective on Copernicus' discovery, this tradition does not help us a step further. Here Koyré's evaluation of the parallel case of Cusanus applies; see note 5.

insofar as final causality lies beyond its purview. It can deal with efficient causality – what is called in German "systemimmanente Faktoren." In our terms, however, it can deal with cosmonomy in contrast with cosmology. But even here astronomy and science in general provide "hypotheses" whose validity cannot be established without experiment and experience, which, most literally, were not yet "in sight" in Osiander's day. Whatever we may think of his claims for the Christian faith, I for one am prepared to grant that the goal of the natural sciences is validity in the sense of *accuracy*, whereas that of the humanities, particularly of philosophy and theology, is validity in the sense of *truth*. Where this distinction is lost, a mechanized and not a naturalized world view has emerged out of the process of nominalist demythologization.

And now finally the case of Copernicus himself. In the first place, heliocentricity is a significant advance and breakthrough in the accurate charting of the universe. Before Copernicus, the theological, philosophical, and physical possibility of the daily and yearly (dual) movement of the earth had been probed and approved – but indeed only as possible. Hindrances in all three fields had been cleared to make Copernicus' theory conceivable, a "Denkmöglichkeit."[63] But it was Copernicus who formulated heliocentricity with clarity and audacity, particularly when the limited bases of facts established by experience are taken into consideration. Yet, on that very point Copernicus, though materially in advance, is formally a step backwards in comparison to nominalistic research standards.[64] Copernicus

---

[63]Thomas S. Kuhn, *The Structure of Scientific Revolutions,* second edition, (Chicago-London, 1969), p. 62: "... characteristic of all discoveries from which new sorts of phenomena emerge. Those characteristics include: the previous awareness of anomaly, the gradual and simultaneous emergence of both observational and conceptual recognition, and the consequent change of paradigm categories and procedures often accompanied by resistence."

[64]And as Randall has shown, the Paduan Aristotelians a century later dominated the climate of thought with which Copernicus must have become familiar during his Italian study years. Cf. John Herman Randall, *The School of Padua and the Emergence of Modern Science* (Padua, 1961), p. 24 ff.; p. 71 ff.

Note also R. Hooykaas op. cit. [note 10], pp. 35–36: "Thus Kepler and Galileo, in contrast to Plato, put forward a mathematical empiricism. This was quite evident in one of the most decisive moments in the history of science. It had been a dogma of the 'church scientific', up to the time of Kepler, that movements in the heavens could be nothing but uniform and circular. Everywhere, everybody had always held this to be true *a priori*; Platonists and Aristotelians, Idealists and Nominalists, Copernicus and Galileo had accepted this dogma and Kepler himself was thoroughly convinced of its truth.

"Yet a difference of eight minutes between observation and calculation of the orbit of the planet Mars forced him, after a struggle of several years, to abandon this dogma of circularity and to postulate a non-uniform motion in elliptical orbits.

"He submitted to given facts rather than maintaining an age old prejudice; in his mind a

presented a system mathematically equivalent with that of Ptolemy and based on the Aristotelian, pre-Newtonian hypothesis of the circular movement of the planets without the substantial addition of new observations (experience). In describing the road to his discovery Copernicus mentions heliocentricity as an initial assumption which then, however, becomes conviction and certainty (*repperi!*), a claim improperly ignored by Osiander. Until hard proof had been ascertained by Galileo, Kepler, and Newton, Copernicus asked from his readers a faith in his intuition (*fides implicita*); from such faith the nominalists had wanted to free science in their crusade against metaphysics, against arguments drawn from a dimension of faith beyond the test of experience. Copernicus' discovery would not have been less, but more "modern," if he had highlighted the gap between his heliocentric "imagination" – as Oresme would have termed it – and the compound of experiment and experience interpreted by it. Such a procedure *might* have made Osiander's "fraud" redundant; it most *certainly* would have made early Copernicanism more difficult to combat. Whatever the differences in goals and methods, common to the natural sciences and the humanities is the accurate description of the credibility gap between conceived and sensed reality as a precondition for every advance in our different accesses to reality.

The most significant and lasting aspect of the Copernican discovery is that Copernicus crowned an era hungry for reality, groping for answers, and seeking to initiate change. By the very fact that the earth is launched as a planet into space, the macrocosm is drawn into the orbit of man: heliocentricity is the extension of creation in space and infinity. This projection into space is the part of the Copernican Revolution that has not yet been "received" and absorbed by modern man; it is the part that psychologically, i.e., effectively, is still ahead of us. At the historical beginnings of our conception of the universe the Greeks projected their *polis*, their city-state, into the skies as the model of the cosmos.[65] That was at the same time the beginning of a long process of demythologization of the divinized planets. Yet the older view proved to be virile, indomitable, time-and science-resistant: the gods jealously contested Man's access to space: "What is above you, man, is none of your business (*Quae supra vos nihil*

Christian empiricism gained the victory over platonic rationalism; a lonely man submitted to facts and broke away from a tradition of two thousand years. With full justice he could declare: 'These eight minutes paved the way for the reformation of the whole of astronomy', and it was with full justice, too, that in 1609 he gave to his book the title *New Astronomy*."

[65]Jaeger, op. cit. [note 1], p. 220.

ad vos)"! The Icarus complex – the hidden motive in the Icarus story, *space-angst* – is so fundamental a trait of man that faith, science, and superstition combined to stage the fundamental antithesis between Mother Earth and Father Cosmos. This is what was and is blocking the medieval emancipation of astral physics from cosmology and obscuring the distinction between *Weltbild* and *Weltanschauung*, between astronomy and astrology, and finally, between legitimate research and vain curiosity.

In this long drawn-out intellectual twilight Copernican heliocentricity is at the same time a manifesto proclaiming the *secular cosmos* and a call for the radical colonization of space: "*Quae circa nos tota ad nos,*" ["the cosmos around us is our immediate concern"].[66] Till this very day we modern men have not been existentially able to absorb this vision of reality, as is clear from the fact that the designation "cosmopolitan" has been reduced to the tourist badge for the well traveled on this very small globe.

I would like to conclude with an illusion to Paul Tillich's book *The Courage To Be* (1952) by saying that Copernicus is properly celebrated when in the name of the survival of man (Copernicus: "*propter nos*") the dedivinization of space finds its completion in the exorcism of our residual *space-angst*, thus freeing us to face the future with the courage to be in space.

5. APPENDIX: FROM COPERNICUS' DEDICATION TO POPE PAUL III

After I had pondered at length this lack of certainty in traditional mathematics concerning the movements of the spheres of the world, I became increasingly annoyed that the philosophers, who in other respects made such careful scrutiny of the smallest details of the world, had nothing better to offer to explain the workings of the machinery of the world – which is after all built for us by the Best and Most Orderly Workman of all. Hence I assigned myself the task of reading and rereading all the philosophers whose books I could lay my hands on, to see if anyone ever advanced the view that the movements of the spheres of the world are

---

[66]See Karl R. Popper: "Thus we live in an open universe. We could not make this discovery before there was human knowledge. But once we have made the discovery there is no reason to think that the openness depends exclusively upon the existence of human knowledge. It is much more reasonable to reject all views of a closed universe – that of a causally as well as that of a probabilistically closed universe; thus rejecting the closed universe envisaged by Laplace, as well as the one envisaged by quantum mechanics. Our universe is partly causal, partly probabilistic, and partly open: it is emergent." "Indeterminism is Not Enough," *Encounter*, vol. 40 (1973), pp. 20–26; esp. p. 26.

different from those postulated by the specialists in the field of mathematics.

As a matter of fact I first discovered in Cicero that Nicetas thought that the earth moved. Afterwards I also found in Plutarch that there were others of the same opinion. I shall quote his words here, so that they may be known to all:

"Whereas the others hold that the earth is immobile, Philolaus, the Pythagorean, claims that it moves around the fire with a nearly circular motion, not unlike the sun and the moon. Herakleides of Pontus and Ekphantus, the Pythagorean, do not assign to the earth any movement of locomotion. Instead they think in terms of a limited movement, rising and setting around its center, like a wheel."

This was reason enough so that I too began to think seriously about the mobility of the earth. And although this still seemed to me an absurd point of view, I knew that others before me had been granted the liberty of postulating whatever cycles they pleased in order to explain astral phenomena. Therefore, I thought that I too would be readily permitted to test, on the assumption that the earth has some movement, whether a more convincing explanation, less shaky than those of my predecessors, could be found for the revolutions of the celestial spheres.

Translated by the author from *Nicolai Copernici Thorunensis, De revolutionibus orbium libri sex*, vol. 2, edited by Franciscus Zeller and Carolus Zeller (Munich, 1949), pp. 5, 18–6, 3.

IX

DUNS SCOTUS, NOMINALISM, AND THE COUNCIL OF TRENT

In the *Collectio Judiciorum de Novis Erroribus*, published by the Parisian Doctor Carolus du Plessis d'Argentré, we find under the year 1315 a ten point "summary" of the thought of Johannes Duns Scotus. If its entry in a book "de Novis Erroribus" would still leave room for doubt, the heading chosen by d'Argentré for this section makes it unambiguously clear that key points in the doctrine of the great Franciscan theologian are regarded as deviating from Catholic truth: *Johannis Duns Scoti, O.F.M., temerariae opiniones, quas Doctorum Theologorum multitudo improbat*.[1]

Though perhaps an unusual way to open an article dedicated to the memory of the Doctor Subtilis, a description of these *temerariae opiniones* affords us in the first place the opportunity to point to a central fact; only since the turn of this century, due to a renewed, detailed, and empathetic analysis of the sources by both Roman Catholic and Protestant scholars,[2] is the cloud of suspicion so long obscuring the true stature of Duns Scotus now being increasingly removed, exactly with regard to those points called into question by du Plessis d'Argentré.

In the second place, we are here provided with a natural context within which decisive differences between the Scotist and Nominalist Schools of thought can be indicated – differences which will have to be borne in mind if one wants to understand the complexity and importance of the Franciscan

---

[1] *Collectio Judiciorum*, I, Paris, 1724, col. 285–290.

[2] We limit our reference to two works published at the beginning of this century and two representing more recent scholarship: Reinhold Seeberg, *Die Theologie des Johannes Duns Scotus: Eine dogmengeschichtliche Untersuchung*, Leipzig, 1900; Parthenius Minges, *Die Gnadenlehre des Johannes Duns Skotus auf ihren angeblichen Pelagianismus geprüft*, Münster i.W., 1906; Werner Dettloff, *Die Lehre von der Acceptatio Divina bei Johannes Duns Scotus mit besonderer Berücksichtigung der Rechtfertigungslehre*, Werl. Westf., 1954: Wolfhart Pannenberg, *Die Prädestinationslehre des Duns Skotus im Zusammenhang der Scholastischen Lehrentwicklung*, Göttingen, 1954. A reliable basis for future studies is now being provided in the critical, *Opera Omnia ... praeside P. Carolo Balić*, I –, Civ. Vat., 1950–. See further the excellent extensive bibliography by Odulf Schäfer, *Bibliographische Einführungen in das Studium der Philosophie*, XXII, *Johannes Duns Scotus*, Bern, 1953.

contribution to the final decisions of the Council of Trent.

1. JOHANNIS DUNS SCOTI: *TEMERARIAE*/ *OPINIONES*

1. It cannot surprise us that as the first of the "rash opinions rejected by most doctors of theology," the famous formal distinction is singled out for attack: "Scotus docet divinas virtutes et a se invicem et ab essentia Dei distingui ex natura rei, formali distinctione." After a few well chosen quotations[3] the conclusion follows: "Sed haec dicta Scoti effatis divinae Scripturae contraria sunt," followed by the *ad hominem* attack: "Captiosis autem ratiunculis Dialecticae abutitur Scotus in locis ante citatis." The formal distinction is said to imply exactly the same heretical position as that held by Gilbertus Porretanus, condemned by the Council of Reims (1148). It furthermore provides for the "instances theory" by which four stages are distinguished in the eternal counsel of God. To this crucial issue we shall return after a survey of the other nine points.

2. Scotus claims that *de potentia absoluta* God could have accepted human nature without the habit of grace *in puris naturalibus*.[4] Since d'Argentré does not permit the distinction between *potentia absoluta* and *potentia ordinata*, his conclusion is: "Haec opinio Scoti pugnat cum divinis oraculis et errori Pelagii admodum favet ... Quis enim, nisi Pelegianus, dicere audeat absolute fieri posse, ut noster animus natura sua Deum videat ita ut naturale donum sit aeterna vita, quae in aperta visione Dei posita sit?"[5]

3. Scotus claims that the necessity of infused faith cannot be established,[6] since man does not absolutely need the supernatural habit of faith to believe firmly in the articles of faith. Acquired faith suffices for such an act, since man by nature believes that God is true and since he has no reason to doubt the officially approved tradition of the Church, including Holy Scripture.[7] This opinion of Scotus is apparently so clearly contrary to orthodox truth that d'Argentré does not feel that an explicit censure is called for.

4. Scotus introduces a "new doctrine" when he argues that sanctifying

---

[3] *I Sent.* d 8 q 4 n 4; n 14; n 21; I *Sent.* d 2 q 7 n 41; n 42. All references are to the *Opus Oxoniense. Collectio*, col. 285.2.

[4] *I Sent.* 17 q 3 n 21; n 29. *Collectio*, col. 286.2.

[5] Adam Woodham, John of Ripa, and John of Mercuria (Mirecourt) are grouped together as followers of Scotus by adhering to "these absurd Scotist teachings." *Ibid.*

[6] *III Sent.* d 23 q 1 n 4.

[7] "Quia homo non dubitat de veracitate Dei, quia hoc cuilibet naturaliter inscribitur, scilicet Deum esse veracem; nec dubitatur de approbatione Ecclesiae, quae approbat dicta et scripta virorum praecedentium. Ideo non dubitatur de his quae in Scriptura revelantur, sed, fide acquisita ex auditu, firmiter eis adhaeret ..." *Ibid.*, n 5. *Collectio*, col. 287.1.

grace does not necessarily delete the guilt and stain of sin.[8] With a few biblical references – Rom. 3:24: "Justificati gratis per gratiam ipsius"; I Cor. 6, 11: "sed abluti estis, sed sanctificati estis, sed justificati estis," etc. – it is shown that Scotus' teaching runs contrary to the testimony of Holy Scripture: "Hac de re Sanctus Thomas recte disserit."[9]

5. Intimately connected with this point is the next accusation: Scotus holds that guilt can be forgiven without the infusion of grace since God can *de potentia absoluta* create a man without guilt and without grace *in puris naturalibus*. He can, therefore, also after the fall restore man by forgiving his guilt without the infusion of grace.[10] This thesis of Scotus and his followers contradicts the divine Scriptures. The conclusion is again: "doctrina Scoti erroribus Pelagii favet."[11]

6. The attack turns now to the doctrine of acceptation as such. Against the clear witness of Holy Scripture and the common teaching in the Schools, Scotus holds that no degree of love is sufficient for the justification of man:[12] "in scholis Theologorum multitudo cum S. Thoma docet. Quam sententiam ex divinis oraculis et sanctis Patribus accepimus."[13]

7. Scotus is said to argue that the character received in the Sacrament of Baptism is not an inherent imprint on man's soul but an extrinsic relation between the baptised and God.[14] This is obviously contrary to Scripture as documented e.g. by II Cor. 1,22: 'Et qui unxit nos Deus, et qui signavit nos?'[15]

8. Scotus undermines the Catholic doctrine of creation by claiming that *by nature* man loves himself more than God.[16] When man was created God called him good; but to love oneself more than God is not good. Furthermore, when Deuteronomy 6:4 commands "You shall love the Lord your God with all your heart," it formulates a natural law. This eighth point is the shortest and least documented of all.[17]

---

[8]". . . culpa et gratia non sunt formaliter opposita, nec formaliter oppugnantia." II *Sent.* d 16 q 2 n 4.

[9]*ST* I. II. 113. art. 6. *Collectio*, col. 287.2.

[10]II *Sent.* 16 q 2 n 4.

[11]*Collectio*, col. 287.2.

[12]III *Sent.* d 27 q 1.

[13]*Collectio*, col. 288.2.

[14]IV *Sent.* d 6 q 9 n 4.

[15]*Collectio*, col. 288.2. Cf. however the context as presented by Parthenius Minges, *Ioannes Duns Scoti Doctrina Philosophica et Theologica*, II, *Theologica Specialis*, Ad Claras Aquas, 1930, p. 555.

[16]*Collectio*, col. 289.1.

[17]In the *Opus. Ox.* we find exactly the opposite: "Diligere Deum super omnia est actus conformis rationi naturali rectae . . . Illud praeceptum 'Diliges Dominum Deum tuum' est de lege naturae et ita naturaliter notum est hunc actum esse rectum." III *Sent.* d 27 n 2.

9. Scotus is unbiblical and deviates from St. Augustine in his claim that some voluntary acts can be so neutral that they are neither good nor bad.[18] The critique of this point is not very revealing insofar as neither the historical[19] nor the systematic context of Scotus' discussion is taken into account.[20]

10. More significant, we feel, is the related charge that Scotus separates the wisdom and justice of God by separating the eternal law of God from the natural law as expressed in the second table of the Decalogue. Followed by Gabriel Biel and Jacob Almain, he holds that "res prohibitas in secunda tabula Decalogi (nec excepto mendacio) per se malos non esse. Item Gabriel censet et Almain."[21]

When one surveys this presentation of these *temerariae opiniones*, one realizes that the thought of Duns Scotus is not only measured on all ten points by the standard of adherence and subservience to the conclusions of Thomas Aquinas, but also that the critique tends to move from Scotus to his *sequaces* with which such Nominalists as Woodham and Biel are intended. It should furthermore be granted that almost every one of the Scotist theses presented here has found its way into the world of Nominalistic thought, to the point that some of them as e.g. the doctrine of acceptation and its corollaries (2–6), as well as the new understanding of the relation of eternal and natural law (10), have long been regarded as characteristically Nominalistic.

Before we can turn to an analysis of the Tridentine discussions of the doctrine of justification and the proper interpretation of such terms as *meritum de congruo, meritum de condigno, mereri,* and *promereri,* it is essential to emphasize the significance of the difference between Duns Scotus on the one side and Occam *cum suis* on the other side, with regard to the first point on the list of du Plessis d'Argentré. The formal distinction, posited there, forms the basis of Scotus' doctrine of predestination *ante praevisa merita*, since it allows for a formal distinction between four instances or stages in God's planning, his eternal counsel, applied to Peter and Judas as the traditional symbols of the elect and the reprobate. In the first two instances God is solely concerned with Peter: First, God predestines Peter to eternal glory;

---

[18]*Collectio*, col. 289.1; d'Argentré documents his charge with a quote which occurs in II *Sent.* d 41 q 1 n 3.

[19]See for this the question raised by St. Thomas, "utrum aliquis actus sit indifferens secundum individuum" in *ST* I. II. q. 18 art. 9.

[20]See Minges, *op cit.* I, pp. 400–403.

[21]*Collectio*, col. 289, 2–290.1: III *Sent.* d 39 n 3; For a discussion of this issue see my *Harvest of Medieval Theology*, Cambridge, Mass., 1963, pp. 105–111.

second, He wants to give Peter the means to this end, grace. In the third instance Judas appears for the first time as an object for God's will: God permits Peter and Judas to belong to the mass of perdition. Finally, Peter is saved and Judas rejected, according to justice, since Judas persevered in sin.

Along with the formal distinction, Occam and his followers reject the four "instances theory" and therefore the doctrine of predestination *ante praevisa merita*.[22] The weighty consequence is that the school of Occam does not merely reject the first of the ten *temerariae opiniones*, but that all the other articles which deal with justification (when taken in the narrow sense: 2–6) in which they seemed to agree with the Doctor Subtilis, are placed in a radically different context.

This decisive change can perhaps best be described by recalling the great advances in Scotus scholarship in this century. What had long been regarded as Pelagianism or semi-Pelagianism proved to be the freedom of man due to the elasticity of his lifeline which is at both ends, at the beginning by predestination *ante praevisa merita*, at the end by the *acceptatio divina*, firmly fastened in God's eternal counsel. Occam and his School, while rejecting Scotus' doctrine of predestination,[23] retained the latter's concern for the dignity of man and the sinner's responsibility for his own damnation. Whereas the same terminology is employed with regard to such issues as the habit of grace, merits *de congruo* and *de condigno* and more generally use is made of the paired terms *potentia absoluta* and *potentia ordinata*, the doctrine of predestination *post praevisa merita* changes the relation between the sovereign God and his *viator*. The *viator* still does not have a claim to the habit of grace or final acceptation, but he now has to take the decisive responsibility for

---

[22]Occam: ". . . non videtur bene dictum quod deus velit prius finem quam illud quod est ad finem; quia non est ibi talis prioritas actuum, nec sunt ibi talia instantia . . ." I *Sent.* d 41 q 1 F; Biel: ". . . falsum est quod prius vult finem et post ordinata in finem quia non est nisi unus actus divine voluntatis . . . quia ordo presupponit distinctionem ordinatorum . . . Nec tamen aliquod horum deus prius vult altero, sed quecunque vult, similiter et ab eterno vult." II *Sent.* d 20 q 1 art. 1 nota 3; cf. I *Sent.* d 41 q 1 art. 3 dub. 2. In the *Collectio Judiciorum*, col. 40, a number of statements by Gerson against the formal distinction are collected; on col. 286 Gerson is cited to support d'Argentré's exhortation to return not only to St. Bonaventure but also to St. Thomas. Cf. Gerson, *Opera Omnia*, ed. L. E. du Pin, I, Antwerpen, 1706, 91 D. Gerson's attack on the scholastic theology of his time should not be interpreted as an attack on Nominalism but rather seen as motivated by a Nominalistic ideal: to restore unity within the realm of theology: ". . . studeo eos quos Scotistas appellamus ad concordiam cum aliis doctoribus adducere . . ." *Opera* I, 101 C. As can be documented by Gerson's actual teaching *re* predestination and justification, it is more likely that he criticized the formal distinction from a Nominalistic rather than from a Thomistic vantage point. With regard to these central doctrines, we find no evidence for the development from Nominalist to Thomist as presented by André Combes in relation to mysticism. See his *Essai sur la critique de Ruysbroeck par Gerson*. III. I (Paris, 1959), p. 316f.

[23]Cf. my *Harvest of Medieval Theology*, p. 185–217.

reaching either the beatific vision or eternal damnation according to his use of the *facere quod in se est*.[24]

When we now turn to the *acta* of the Council of Trent, we are forwarned that many so-called Scotistic statements with regard to the doctrine of justification may actually have come from Council fathers deeply influenced by Nominalistic thought. Due to the fact that the doctrine of predestination was *de facto* dissociated from the doctrine of justification in the debates, and relatively only lightly touched upon and ultimately relegated to a separate chapter, the basis for distinguishing Scotistic and Nominalistic "interventiones" on this issue is *terra infirma*. For this reason we shall often have to refer to the joint impact of Scotistic and Nominalistic thought in terms of the "Franciscan contribution" to the Tridentine deliberations. But when finally at the end of this article we hope to have established that the "Franciscan contribution" has been far more penetrating than it usually has been given credit for, we are alerted to the importance of distinguishing between three rather than just two theological contexts for the Tridentine decree of justification: Scotism, Nominalism, and Thomism.

2. *PARTIM-PARTIM*

In recent years the Council of Trent has attracted a considerable amount of attention in popular books and learned journals alike. This concerns, however, not so much the doctrine of justification, in the sixteenth century the *articulus stantis et cadentis ecclesiae*,[24a] but rather the Tridentine decree on Scripture and the *sine scripto traditiones*. The phrase 'partim-partim' has acquired a new, almost symbolic, significance since its change into *et* in the final decree has been interpreted to indicate that the Fathers of Trent did not regard the time ripe for a definition of the relation of Scripture and Tradition.[25] It is argued that whereas what pertains to faith would be *totum in Scriptura, et iterum totum in Traditione*, the 'partim-partim' only applies to morals and observances.[26] A further study of the late medieval setting of the

---

[24]For documentation see *Harvest of Medieval Theology*, p. 208, note 58 and p. 209, note 60. For the opposite conclusion, see Paul Vignaux, *Justification et Prédestination*, Paris, 1934, p. 138f.

[24a]Hubert Jedin regards this same article as the pivot of Tridentine teaching. Cf. "Das vierhundertjährige Jubiläum der Eröffnung des Konzils von Trient und sein wissenschaftlicher Ertrag," in *Das Weltkonzil von Trient. Sein Werden und Wirken*, ed. Georg Schreiber [henceforth abbreviated as WT] I, Freiburg 1951, pp. 11–31; p. 23.

[25]J. R. Geiselmann, "Das Missverständnis über das Verhältnis von Schrift und Tradition und seine Überwindung in der katholischen Theologie," in *Una Sancta* II (1956), p. 139.

[26]Geiselmann, *Die heilige Schrift und die Tradition, Quaestiones disputatae*, Freiberg 1962, p. 284.

conciliar discussions might well be decisive in determining the historical intention of the Council fathers without thus necessarily settling the problem of theological interpretation.[27]

A similar issue and identical task awaits us with respect to the Tridentine decree on justification. Andreas de Vega (†1549), the Spanish Franciscan, significant author and influential participant in the Council,[28] reminds us that the doctrine of justification as discussed and defined by the Council fathers might also be understood in terms of the relation of 'partim-partim' and 'et.'[29]

So far as the relation of Scripture and Tradition is concerned, there can be little doubt how Vega interpreted the conciliar decree of which he had witnessed the makings. For him the 'sine scripto traditiones' are not the interpretations of Scripture nor observances in contrast to doctrines.[30] The unwritten traditions, which derived either directly from Christ or from the Apostles inspired by the Spirit, have explicitly doctrinal significance by containing such dogmata as the virginity of the Mother of God *post partum*, the dogma of the veneration of images and relics of the Saints, and of the total of seven sacraments, etc.[31] Though we have not found him to use the

---

[27]Cf. the presentation of the fifteenth-century discussion in my *Harvest of Medieval Theology*, pp. 371–412. On the problem of interpretation in connection with the different hermeneutics of Protestant and Roman Catholic historians see "Quo Vadis, Petre?" *Scottish Journal of Theology*, 16 (1963), pp. 252ff.

[28]Cf. B. Oromi, "Fr. Andreas de Vega O.F.M., theologus Concilii Tridentini," *Archivum Franc. Historicum*, 36 (1943), pp. 3–31.

[29]"Et ea tum raritas vel difficultas [facere bona opera sine gratia] partim proficiscitur ex parte nostra, partim ex parte Dei aut aliorum qui nos possent allicere et adiuvare ad operandum et non faciunt." *De iustificatione doctrina universa, Libris XV, absolute tradita et contra omnes omnium errores iuxta germanam sententiam Orthodoxae veritatis et sacri concilii Tridentini praeclare defensa.* Coloniae 1572. First ed. Venetiis 1548. XIII. 13. fol. 523.

[30]The interpretation of *traditiones* as *facienda* instead of *credenda* is suggested by Father Maurice Bevenot in "Traditiones in the Council of Trent," *The Heythrop Journal*, IV (1963), pp. 333–347: "... in the discussions themselves 'traditiones' referred always primarily to the various rites, observances, and practices of the Church and only indirectly to the fact that some of them (e.g., the sacraments) involved the faith too," *Ibid.*, pp. 341–342. Michael Hurley comes to the same conclusion in his interesting article "A Pre-Tridentine Theology of Tradition. Thomas Netter of Walden (†1430)," *The Heythrop Journal*, IV (1963), pp. 348–366; cf. p. 364.

[31]In an argument against John Calvin's holding the *verbum Dei* as the *optima interpres scripturarum*: "Sed te ista fugiunt, quia contemnis definita a Patribus in hoc concilio sessione 4 et fidem adeo vis pendere ab scripturis, ut nec illas traditiones quae sine scripto a christi ore vel ab Apostolis, Spiritu Sancto dictante, quasi per manus tradite ad nos usque pervenerunt, ad fidei doctrinam spectare credas ... Et huiusmodi sunt dogmata quae certa et indubitata tenet tota Ecclesia. Qualia sunt: Deiparam virginem fuisse perpetuo virginem, imagines et reliquias sanctorum esse reverendas, septem esse Ecclesiae sacramenta et multa alia huiusmodi ... Nunquid apud aliquem minoris est authoritatis verbum alterius quam scriptura ipsius?" *De iustificatione* XV. 6. fol. 686.

expression, it is clear that Vega interpreted 'et' in the sense of 'partim-partim'; in view of Vega's intimate involvement in the proceedings at the Council this conclusion should have significance for our interpretation of the Council's mind.

We shall return to Vega in reference to the second 'partim-partim' issue – the one taken up at the sixth session. This issue is at stake in the question, whether God is committed to give those who do their natural best – 'facientibus quod in se est' – first grace so that a *meritum de congruo* is constituted which is not a merit in the strict sense of the word, as is the *meritum de condigno*, but relates to that effort for which man is responsible before or while he is taken into the economy of grace.

3. *MERITUM DE CONGRUO*

In his important studies in early scholastic thought, Arthur Landgraf has shown that with respect to the relation of preparation and justification, a number of different solutions were advanced.[32] He points out that whereas some of them have a Pelagian ring for modern ears, nevertheless no one in that era posited an inner connection between nature and grace. Whenever such a connection is upheld, it is understood to depend on the merciful and faithful will of God; and whenever merits are admitted to precede grace, these merits are not understood to be merits in the full sense of the word but rather *merita interpretativa* or *de congruo*.[33]

There are also those who hold that no human merits whatsoever, even those that result from grace, are merits in a strict and full sense of the word. In a Lombardian commentary on St. Paul, we find that interesting combination of Romans 8:18 and Hebrews 13:16 which would be repeated time and again in the succeeding period. St. Paul's statement that there is no condignity between our sufferings of the present and the glory to come is interpreted to mean that man can not *promereri* his future glory in the full sense of the word.[34] The same point is made when, in a collection of

---

[32] *Dogmengeschichte der Frühscholastik* I. *Die Gnadenlehre*, Band I, Regensburg 1952, pp. 238–302.

[33] "Ausdrücklich sei noch einmal festgestellt, dass wir nirgends einen inneren Konnex zwischen Natur und Gnade angedeutet fanden. Wenn beide einmal mit Notwendigkeit verknüpft erscheinen, dann ist als Band der freie, erbarmende und getreue Wille Gottes eingefügt. Wo von einem Verdienst für die Gnade die Rede ist, baut entweder das Verdienst schon auf der Gnade selber auf, oder aber es handelt sich um ein Verdienst im uneigentlichen Sinn, wo Werk und Gnade wiederum nur äusserlich durch Gottes Willen verknüpft werden." Landgraf, *op. cit.*, p. 302.

[34] "Caritas, qua quis sustinet passiones, digna est future glorie. Ergo et ipse passiones, cum eiusdem sint meriti. Unde apostolus in epistola ad Corinthios: id quod in presenti est

Questiones which suggest Gilbertian influence, it is said that: "except for Christ, no one's merit suffices to earn (*promereri*) life eternal."[35]

How much influence the condemnation of this thesis at the Council of Reims (1148)[36] has exterted is difficult to establish. At the transition to high scholasticism, the question of the possibility of true merit has clearly shifted from life eternal to first grace. A considerable section of theological opinion in the thirteenth[37] and fourteenth centuries,[38] especially among the Franciscans, taught that one cannot earn first grace in a strict sense of the word, but that nevertheless God gives his grace to those who do what is in their power. The most sympathetic evaluation of this thesis is that it expresses a deep pastoral concern.[39] Between God's bestowal of grace and sinful man's best deeds there is no relation of condignity, but only one of congruity, resting in God's goodness. Grace is no reward but rather a gift on which man may count, since God has committed himself to give his grace "facientibus quod in se est."

Passionately Johannes Auer has defended the graciousness of God as the moving power behind the *meritum de congruo* against the critique of Adolf von Harnack who found here conclusive evidence for the total disintegration of the Augustinian concept of grace.[40] According to Auer, this critique is completely uncalled for; in the first place, man's activity is set in the context of grace and, in the second place, actual or prevenient grace has to incite

---

momentaneum et leve tribulationis nostre, supra modum in sublimitatem glorie eternum pondus operatur in nobis. Sic ergo accipe: non sunt condigne passiones ad futuram gloriam, scilicet ad tantam gloriam promerendam, quanta nobis dabitur. Semper enim plus dat de corona et minus de pena, quam homo mereatur. Vel potest dici, quod non sunt condigne quantum ad se, nisi ex Dei institutione, sicut si imperator statueret, ut qui citius campus percurreret, Xcem marcas acciperet. Et vere posset dici, quod cursus ille non esset dignus ad promerendas X marcas, utique ex se, tamen ex institutione imperatoris. Vel non sunt condigne, id est si districte ageretur, nullo modo ei comparari possent. Tribulatio namque est cum fine, merces erit sine fine, et multo maior erit ibi gloria quam hic labor." Cod. Bamberg. Bibl. 132, fol. 2v; quoted by Landgraf, *op. cit.*, p. 269, n. 4.

[35]"Nullius enim meritum sufficit ad vitam eternam promerendam, nisi solius Christi ..." *Questiones*, col. British Museum, Harley, lat. 1762, fol. 144v; quoted by Landgraf, *op. cit.*, p. 272.

[36]The condemned *sententia* is quoted by Otto of Freising as: "quod naturam humanam attenuando nullum mereri diceret praeter Christum," *Monumenta Germaniae Historica*. Script. XX (1868), p. 379. Since late medieval Nominalism is often said to show Pelagian tendencies, it is interesting to note that the Gilbertian heresy is regarded by Joh. Auer as "verbunden mit einer nominalistischen, rationalistischen Philosophie"! *Die Entwicklung der Gnadenlehre in der Hochscholastik.* II, *Das Wirken der Gnade*, Freiburg, 1951, p. 60.

[37]Landgraf, *op. cit.*, pp. 378ff.

[38]Auer, *op cit.*, pp. 84ff.

[39]"Es war das religiöse und vielleicht seelsorgliche Bedürfnis, aus der Güte Gottes die Möglichkeit einer wirksamen Vorbereitung auf die Gnade zu erweisen." Auer, *op. cit.*, p. 85.

[40]Harnack, *Lehrbuch der Dogmengeschichte*, III[5], Tübingen 1932, p. 636; 650ff.

man before he is able to dispose himself properly.[41]

Neither Harnack's attack nor Auer's defence takes account of the variety of ways in which the merit *de congruo* functioned. One is inclined to answer Harnack that the *meritum de congruo* is by all and always seen within the context of grace. The rule that God does not deny his grace to those who do their very best is a rule of grace. Turning now to Auer's second argument, it should be pointed out that it is by no means as clear as he suggests that this preparation for the reception of first grace is necessarily due to the influx of actual grace. In the case of the mature Aquinas there can indeed be little doubt, since for him the merit *de congruo* does not precede justification in time but is the meritorious action considered as the result of the action of free will, whereas the merit *de condigno* is that *same* action considered as proceeding from grace.[42]

The English Archbishop of Canterbury, Thomas Bradwardine (†1349), on the other hand, feels that the merit *de congruo*, as a merit preceding the gift of grace, is "propagated very much in our days, and many are blindly rushing into Pelagianism."[43] Gregory of Rimini (†1358) likewise opposes the opinion of some "modern doctors" that one can earn first grace *de congruo*.[44]

John Wyclif develops a theology of merits in the same line, but with a fresh radicality which reminds one of the twelfth century Gilbertian school. He does not reject the merit *de congruo*: on the contrary, this is the only kind of merit he admits. In his opinion one earns merit *de congruo* when God

---

[41]"Dass diese Lehre nichts mit den von Harnack aus tiefem inneren Unverständnis für die Hochscholastik geborenen Vorwürfen eines Neosemipelagianismus zu tun hat, ist ganz selbstverständlich, wenn man das ganz auf Gottes Barmherzigkeit gebaute interpretative Verdienst (das mit Harnacks menschlich-bürgerlichem Verdienstbegriff nichts zu tun hat) und die ganz in Gottes Gnade gesetzte Betätigung des Menschen überhaupt und die eigens vorausgesetzten aktuellen göttlichen Anregungen für diese Bereitung des Menschen für Gott ins Auge fasst. Im Gegenteil ist durch diese Lehre vielmehr die Heiligkeit und Liebe Gottes, die in so erhabener und zarter Weise um den Menschen wirbt, und der tiefe Ernst, der in diesem Anruf Gottes an den freien Menschen liegt, wie auch das Unaussprechliche des menschlichen Suchens und 'des Sich-begegnens, in seiner Zartheit wie in seiner ernsten Verpflichtung gesehen, über allen Vergleich wirklichkeitstreuer und erhabener und religiös tiefer und frommer, als es je ein aus verantwortungsloser Selbstpreisgabe oder verzweifelter Selbstbehauptung geborener Fiduzialglaube darstellen könnte." *Op. cit.* pp. 86–87.

[42]"... opus meritorium hominis dupliciter considerari potest: uno modo, secundum quod procedit ex libero arbitrio; alio modo, secundum quod procedit ex gratia Spiritus Sancti." *ST* I. II. q 114. art. 3. c.a. The footnote in the Marietti edition, Romae 1952, p. 567, n. 2 reads the young Thomas into this text when it states that a merit *de congruo* "non praesupponit statum gratiae, sed dispositionem quandam ad gratiam vel orationem ut est in peccatore." Cf. Aquinas as "sententiarius," II *Sent.*, d 28 q 1 art 40.

[43]"... dicunt enim homines ex solis propriis viribus gratiam Dei mereri de congruo, non autem de condigno." *De Causa Dei Contra Pelagium*, I, 39. 325ff.

[44]"... nemo potest mereri primam gratiam de condigno; nec etiam de congruo contra aliquorum sententiam modernorum." II *Sent.* d. 26, 27, 28 q 1 art 1; fol. 93 Q.

rewards *de pura gracia* those works which issue from his prevenient grace; *de condigno* one would earn merit when God rewards *de pura iustitia* those works which are completely man's own, in which God therefore does not *graciose* cooperate. This unusual definition of the merit *de condigno* forces Wyclif to reject merits *de condigno* altogether, since God always cooperates *graciose*: all merits are rewards *de pura gracia* and therefore always *de congruo*.[45]

In the pre-Wyclif tradition, the merit *de condigno* is also based on *iustitia*; but this *debitum iustitiae* is never understood as *pure* justice. Hus, who quotes Wyclif's definition of merit, tries to reconcile the two positions by pointing out that *pura iustitia* presupposes indeed an equality between work and reward, but that this equality can be taken either as an *equalitas quantitatis* or as an *equalitas proportionis*. One is right in rejecting the merit *de condigno* when condignity is understood in a quantitative sense; but it is quite defensible when understood only to indicate a proportionate equality.[46] It is nevertheless clear that Hus prefers Wyclif's rejection of the merit *de condigno* in favor of the merit *de congruo*.[47]

This position of the "late medieval Gilbertian school" remained the exception; a very different interpretation of the merit *de congruo* prevailed in the fifteenth century. In Scotistic and Nominalistic circles the merit *de congruo* refers to God's gracious acceptation of the sinner's *facere quod in se est*, which is not a merit in the strict sense of the word since it does not establish a *debitum iustitiae*.[48] So can the Dominican Durandus de St. Pourçain (†1334) regard the *meritum de congruo* as a *meritum ante gratiam*.[49] A detailed analysis of the thought of William of Occam (†1349), Robert Holcot (†1349), and Gabriel Biel (†1495) has led us to the conclusion that this gracious condescension of God is understood as a commitment by which God in

---

[45]"Et est duplex meritum, scilicet de congruo et de condigno: de congruo quando aliquis meretur de pura gracia premiantis, ut puta, quando premians prevenit cooperando omne meritum merentis. . .; de condigno autem dicitur quis mereri, quando meretur de pura iusticia ab alico premiante, quod fuit quando premians non graciose coagit cum illo . . . " *De Sciencia Dei*, fol. 61[va-vb]; quoted by J. A. Robson, *Wyclif and the Oxford Schools*, Cambridge 1961, p. 209, n. 1. We are unable to agree with Mr. Robson when he claims that Wyclif "makes the customary distinction between congruous and condign merit." Cf. his interpretation of this quotation, *op. cit.*, pp. 208f.

[46]"Qui eigo dicunt, quod non potest homo mereri vitam aeternam de condigno, attendunt equalitatem quantitatis; qui autem dicunt, quod homo potest mereri de condigno attendunt equalitatem proporcionis." II *Sent.* d 27 q 5; *Opera omnia*, II, ed. V. Flajshans, Prague 1905, p. 307. Cf. Thomas, III *Sent.* d 18 q 1 art. 2 C.

[47]". . . non potest pura creatura de condigno mereri vitam eternam." *Ibid.*, p. 308. ". . . impossibile est creaturam mereri a Deo . . . nisi a Deo mereatur illud premium de congruo, non de condigno." *Ibid.*, p. 309.

[48]Cf. Auer, *op. cit.*, pp. 81ff.

[49]II *Sent.* d 27 q 2; ed. Lugduni, 1562.

eternity obligated himself to impart to man's action a dignity which it would not have in itself. The golden rule of grace, "facientibus quod in se est Deus non denegat gratiam," can be designated by the symbol "partim-partim" insofar as it implies that if man goes halfway, God will meet him with the gift of grace. Without this gift of grace man is helpless; but it is just as true that without the full use of man's powers, the offer of grace is useless.[50] It is by no means always clear that this merit *de congruo* requires the prevenience of actual grace (*gratia gratis data*) or that this grace when posited is more than an exterior acquaintance with the law of God instead of an interior liberating power.[51]

Though the fifth chapter of the Tridentine decree on justification has retained the "partim-partim" structure,[52] it is more firmly embedded in the doctrine of the prevenience of grace than had been the case in large sections of late medieval thought.[53] But neither for the disciples of Bonaventure nor for those of Biel did this formulation necessarily imply a correction of their views. For the first in his *Breviloquium* had stated that nobody could sufficiently do what is in him to prepare himself for salvation without actual grace.[54] The second had taught in his popular commentary on the Mass, *Canonis Misse Expositio*, that the possibility of *facere quod in se est* was a gift of grace; for that very reason this disposition for sanctifying grace could not be regarded as constituting a merit *de condigno*, but rather a merit *de congruo*.[55]

Silvester Prierias, O.P. (†1523), friend of Cardinal Caietanus (†1534) and from 1515, as *Magister Sacri Palatii* in Rome, the advisor of Pope Leo X in the process against Reuchlin and Luther,[56] provides us with a clear example of the way in which a theologian of unquestioned orthodoxy can combine the

---

[50]Cf. my "Facientibus quod in se est Deus non denegat gratiam. Robert Holcot, O.P. and the Beginnings of Luther's Theology." *Harvard Theological Review*, 55 (1962), pp. 317–342.

[51]Cf. *The Harvest of Medieval Theology*, pp. 132ff.

[52]"...neque homo ipse nihil omnino agat, inspirationem illam recipiens, quippe qui illam et abicere potest, neque tamen sine gratia Dei movere se ad iustitiam coram illo libera sua voluntate possit." *Denz.* 797. *Concilium Tridentinum*, ed. Goerresiana, Friburgi Br. [henceforth cited as *CT*], V. 793.

[53]"... ipsius iustificationis exordium in adultis a Dei per Christum Iesum praeveniente gratia sumendum esse"; "... Dei nos gratia praeveniri confitemur." *Denz.* 797. *CT* V. 792, 793.

[54]"... et sine hac [gratia gratis data] nullus sufficienter facit quod in se est, ut se praeparat ad salutem." *Brevil.* 5.2.

[55]"... faciendo quod in se est non meretur primam gratiam que est gratia iustificans peccatorem de condigno, licet mereatur de congruo ... nullum enim donum gratie gratis date commensurabile est gratie gratum facienti." *Sacri Canonis Misse Expositio*, Basel 1510, Lect. 59 T. Edition Oberman-Courtenay, Wiesbaden 1965, p. 447.

[56]Cf. F. Laus s.v. *Prierias* in *RGG* V³, Tübingen 1961, col. 568; more extensive, Th. Kolde, s.v. *Prierias* in *RE* XVI, Leipzig 1905, cols. 30–32. A new study of Prierias' theological position is urgently needed.

facere quod in se est, as usually understood in the late middle ages, with the Tridentine emphasis on the prevenience of grace.[57] In his often reprinted *Aurea Rosa* of 1503,[58] he points out that without the aid of grace the sinner is able of his own free will to desire the gift of grace which God grants either instantaneously or over a period of time.[59] Moreover God will *never* grant his grace *unless* it is preceded by such a desire on the part of the sinner to receive it.[60] Since humility belongs to the *facere quod in se est*,[61] self-humiliation in the form of awareness of one's own sins is the basis for the infusion of grace, which in turn leads to eternal glory.[62]

Whereas we have found no evidence that Prierias would be willing to admit that the sinner can earn first grace or that God's vocation is a *reward* for good works preceding justification, this influential Inquisitor states unambiguously that God can nevertheless be relied on to respond with the *gift* of grace to the sinner's best efforts. And this is exactly what both Scotistic and Nominalistic schoolmen intended to express when they employed the term *meritum de congruo*.

4. THE PRESENT STATE OF SCHOLARSHIP

When we for the purposes of this article limit our investigation to that

---

[57]". . . vocatione, qua nullis eorum existentibus meritis vocantur . . ." *Denz.* 797. *CT* V. 792.

[58]*Aurea Rosa, R.P.F. Silvestri de Prierio Pedemontani Sacri ordinis Praedicatorum de Observantia, videlicet clarissima expositio super Euangelia totius anni, de Tempore et de Sanctis, tam secundum Ordinem Praedicatorum quam secundum Curiam, continens flores et rosas expositionum sanctorum Doctorum antiquorum*. We have used the edition published in Venice in 1582.

[59]". . . istud desiderium habendi donum Dei quod ex nostra libertate stante Dei generali influentia procedit, aliquando Deus statim mentibus infundit, vel ad illud movet, ut in Paulo. Aliquando paulatim nos ad illud provocat." *Aurea Rosa, Tractatus secundus*, Feria 6. post Domin. 3, in Quadrag., fol. 136 b^r.

[60]"Sed dicendum est, quod nunquam Deus homini suam gratiam infundit secundum modum consuetum iustificandi, nisi illam desideret habere, quod est petere donum Dei . . ." *Ibid*. This 'modum consuetum' allows for the exceptional cases of John the Baptist, the Virgin Mary, and St. Paul.

[61]The testimony of the Spirit is sufficiently clear *ad convertendos dispositos ad viam suae salutis*: ". . . Deus et natura non deficiunt in necessariis . . . unde cuilibet facienti, quod in se erat, istud testimonium erat sufficiens . . . unde bene ibi [Matt. 11:25, Lk. 10:21] 'parvulis,' id est humilibus et non superbis." *Aurea Rosa, Tractatus tertius*, Q. 44, fol. 323 a^r.

[62]"Et qui se humiliat per peccatorum cognitionem et praesentiam, exaltabitur in praesenti per gratiam et in futuro per gloriam." *Aurea Rosa, Tractatus secundus*, Dominica 11. post Trinitatem, fol. 263 bv. Luther must have had this position in mind when he affirms in his 1521 defense of the articles condemned by Pope Leo X that contrition has to precede awareness of sins as the tree precedes the fruits. With a jibe which might well be an allusion to Geiler of Keisersberg's *Ship of Fools* he adds that in the country of the Pope everything is topsy-turvy, since there the trees grow on the apples: "gleichwie sie auch auf den Ohren gehen" *W A* 7. 361. Cf. the Woodcut in the Strassburg 1510 edition of the *Navicula sive speculum fatuorum . . . a Jac. Othero collecta*, where the artist (Hans Burgmaier? Cf. Brunet, II. 1576) shows a fool walking on his head.

aspect of the justification of the sinner which deals with his preparation for the reception of sanctifying grace – usually called *gratia gratum faciens* or habitual grace – we note that presently there exists an interconfessional consensus that Trent opted for the Thomistic doctrine on this point. The Protestant church historian and influential Tübingen professor, Hanns Rückert, describes in a still authoritative study of Trent's doctrine of justification the development of the debate of the Council fathers on the problem of the disposition of the sinner. Whereas representatives of Nominalistic thought do not function in Rückert's account, he comes to the conclusion that the debates led to a clear victory of the Thomists over the Scotists. This victory is, in Rückert's opinion, clearly expressed in Trent's rejection of the meritorious nature of the disposition for justification. The Franciscan party after first having defended the *meritum de congruo* as God's liberal award for men's best efforts without the aid of sanctifying grace, finally had to yield to the Thomistic drive to have this concept stricken out of the final decree.[63]

In his impressive study on the relation of the Roman Catholic doctrine of justification to that of Karl Barth, Hans Küng argues that both can be characterized by *sola gratia* and by *sola fide*. He concludes by saying: "Man is therefore justified by God's grace alone. Man does not produce anything . . . he does not work, he believes."[64]

The key prooftext for Hans Küng seems to leave little doubt that this interpretation is completely justified and that Trent indeed rejected the doctrine of the *facere quod in se est* as the basis for a *meritum de congruo*:

"none of the acts which precede justification, whether faith or works, merits the grace of justification"[65]

---

[63]"In der Folgezeit ist dann die franziskanische Partei nicht mehr stark genug, um die Wiederaufrichtung des meritum de congruo durchzusetzen." *Die Rechtfertigungslehre auf dem Tridentinischen Konzil*, Bonn 1925, p. 185. Cf. Adolf von Harnack: "Das Decret über die Rechtfertigung, obgleich ein Kunstprodukt, ist in vieler Hinsicht vortrefflich gearbeitet; ja man kann zweifeln, ob die Reformation sich entwickelt hätte, wenn dieses Decret auf dem Lateranconcil am Anfang des Jahrhunderts erlassen worden und wirklich in Fleisch und Blut der Kirche übergegangen wäre." *DG* III⁵, Tübingen 1932, p. 711.

[64]"Gerechtfertigt wird der Mensch also durch Gottes Gnade allein. Der Mensch leistet nichts . . . er werkt nicht, er glaubt . . ." *Rechtfertigung. Die Lehre Karl Barths und eine Katholische Besinnung*, Einsiedeln 1957, p. 246; cf. p. 245 and p. 259. Cf. also Joseph Hefner: ". . . das menschliche Tun steht nur in einem konsekutiven, nicht aber in einem kausalen Verhältnis zur Rechtfertigung, und so bleibt einerseits die Würde des Menschen als sittlicher Persönlichkeit, wie anderseits die Freiheit Gottes im Werke der Rechfertigung unversehrt bestehen." *Die Entstehungsgeschichte des Trienter Rechtfertigungsdekretes*, Paderborn 1909, p. 206.

[65]". . . nihil eorum, quae iustificationem praecedunt, sive fides, sive opera, ipsam iustificationis gratiam promeretur." Concilium Tridentinum, Sessio VI, Caput 8; *CT* V, 794.

In the following, however, we want to show that the interpretation and translation of this passage is not so clear as generally assumed. The Latin verb used here and above translated as "to merit" is *promereri* and not *mereri*. On the strength of evidence drawn from late medieval sources and from the debates at the Council itself, we would rather suggest that *promereri* is to be distinguished from *mereri* and is to be translated as "to merit truly," "completely" or "fully". We would further suggest that whereas *mereri* is associated with the *meritum de congruo, promereri* refers to the *meritum de condigno*, i.e., full merit, which by definition can only be produced in a state of grace, *after* the reception of the *gratia gratum faciens*.[66]

If this is the case, the key prooftext in the Tridentine decree cited above has to be translated as:

". . . none of the acts which precede justification, whether faith or works, *fully* merits the grace of justification."

It is usually said that the Council of Trent in its definition of the truly Catholic doctrine of justification opted for the *via media*, steering away from both the Scylla of Lutheranism and the Charybdis of Nominalistic Pelagianism. If our interpretation is *e mente auctorum*, a true presentation of the mind of the Fathers of Trent, the nominalistic doctrine of justification has substantially contributed to the final formulation of the decree, and the Scotistic interest in the *meritum de congruo* has been fully validated, taken into account and safeguarded.

5. ANDREAS DE VEGA, O.F.M., AND THE PRE-CONCILIAR PERIOD

One of the most influential *periti* in the first stage of the Council of Trent is doubtlessly the Spanish Observant Franciscan Andreas de Vega (1498–1549). Realizing the central importance of the doctrine of justification in Reformation thought, he had the foresight to publish his *Opusculum de*

---

[66]Without giving an analysis of the history of *promereri*, J. Rivière seems to support this interpretation: "Ainsi, tout en évitant le terme technique mérite *de congruo*, qui soulevait des contestations, le concile en consacre manifestement l'idée." Mérite (au Concile de Trente), *DThC* X.1. col. 754. Cf. Eduard Stakemeier: "Damit war die Möglichkeit eines Billigkeitsverdienstes ausdrücklich ausgesprochen worden." *Glaube und Rechtfertigung*. Freiburg i. B. 1937, p. 120. Dr. Stakemeier nevertheless regards the decree as documenting a Thomistic victory. *Ibid.* In his interesting article "Trienter Lehrentscheidungen und Reformatorische Anliegen" he goes on to say: "Die Hauptanliegen der Protestanten sind in diesem Dekret erfüllt," *WT*1, p. 98. W. F. Dankbaar contends that Küng e.a. have overlooked that the *sola fide* and *sola gratia* aspect of the Tridentine decree applies only to the "first status" of justification: "This 'sola' applies only to the preparation, but is insufficient for justification itself" [my transl., H.A.O.]; "Calvijns cordeel over het Concilie van Trente, bepaaldelijk inzake het Rechtvaardigingsdecreet," in *NAK* 45 (1962), pp. 78–112; p. 102.

iustificatione, gratia et meritis in time to have it in the hands of the Council fathers before this subject matter was broached.[67] Vega is probably the co-author of the original draft for the decree on justification dated some seven months later, which formed the basis of the first discussions.[68] And again after the Fathers have had time for discussion and critique, it is Vega who writes a draft incorporating some of the more important observations made.

It is interesting to note that Vega, too, feels that the Council has to find the *media via*, but this time defining the Scylla and the Charybdis in terms different from the ones current in present-day Tridentine studies. According to Vega there are three schools of thought which constitute at the same time the three possible options as regards the problem of disposition. These are the Pelagians, the Thomists, and the followers of Gabriel Biel.

The *Pelagiani* are a dated school virulent around the time of St. Augustine, though, according to Thomas Bradwardine, this school later came to life again in Great Britain.[69] This school holds that justification is based on merits.[70]

---

[67]*Opusculum de iustificatione, gratia et meritis, autore F. Andrea Vega ordinis minorum regularis observantiae, ex alma provincia sancti Iacobi, Sacrae theologiae magistro Salmaticensi,* Venetiis 1546. The introduction is signed "Tridenti calendis Ianuarii anno Salutis 1546."

[68]The so-called *propositum a deputatis* or *prima forma* is dated July 24, 1546. See *CT* V, 384–391. According to the editors, St. Ehles and V. Schweitzer, from Vega's hand in view of the striking similarities with a draft published in *CT* XIII, 637–643, which Cardinal Cervini certifies as a work of Vega. Cf. *CT* XII, 637, n. 2. More recently Valens Heynck, O.F.M., has argued that *CT* XII, 637 ff. is only "eine nachträgliche Bearbeitung der 'prima forma' auf Grund der annotationes der Theologen und vielleicht auch der Zensuren der Väter." See his "Der Anteil des Konzilstheologen Andreas de Vega O.F.M. an dem ersten amtlichen Entwurf des Trienter Rechtfertigungsdekretes," *FS* 33 (1951) p. 59. His main argument for the dissimilarity between the *prima forma* and Vega's draft hinges, however, on the interpretation of *promereri*, which Heynck sharply distinguishes from *vere mereri*: "In der amtlichen Vorlage wird schlechthin ein 'promereri' der heiligmachenden Gnade durch die der Rechtfertigung vorausgehenden guten Werke zurückgewiesen; bei Vega bezeichnenderweise nur ein *'vere et proprie mereri,'* sodass dadurch ein meritum de congruo, das unser Theologe mit der ganzen mittelalterlichen Franziskanerschule für zulässig hält, . . . nicht ausgeschlossen ist." *Ibid.*, p. 57; cf. p. 75. If we are right in translating *promereri* with 'to merit fully,' at least one of Heyncks's more convincing arguments falls away. More important is that Vega himself can use *vere mereri* as a parallel expression for *promereri* in his *Opusculum* which antedates the *prima forma*! "Igitur *vere* potest quicunque peccator suam iustificationem *mereri*. Ea enim *promereri* possumus quae assequi per nostra opera possumus." *Opusculum*, Q VI, fol. 184. Though the authorship of the *prima forma* will always remain open to debate without further discoveries of sources, it seems of one piece with both the later *CT* XII, 637ff., draft and the earlier *Opusculum*. Luchesius Spätling is therefore too apodictic: "Vegas Autorschaft . . . steht unzweifelhaft fest," in "Der Anteil der Franziskaner am Konzil von Trient," *WT*, II, p. 517.

[69]"Revixit et postea in Scotia teste magistro Thoma Bradabaerdino decano Londoviarum, in Summa contra Pelagianos." *Opusculum*, Q VI, fol. 147.

[70]". . . iustificatio ex meritis." *Ib.*, fol. 146.

The second school is that of St. Thomas, which holds that no merits whatsoever precede the grace of justification.[71] To this school should be counted Nicolaus of Lyra (†1340), Thomas Netter (†1430), and that great defender of St. Augustine, Gregory of Rimini (†1358). Here both kinds of merit, *de condigno* and *de congruo*, are denied to the sinner.[72]

The third school can be identified by the names of the more recent theologians: Biel, Maior (†1550) and Almain (†1516). This is by no means, however, a new school since already at the time of Duns Scotus theirs was the *opinio communis* in the universities.[73]

This last school now is the *via media*, since it holds with the Thomists that man cannot acquire first justification by merits *de condigno* while it grants the Pelagians that the sinner can be justified on grounds of merits *de congruo*.[74]

In this venerable school, the *via media* of Gabriel Biel *cum suis*, Vega himself stands. He does not deny that one can merit first grace to a certain extent; what he denies is that one can merit this grace in an absolute sense of the word.[75] Merits *de congruo* have no claim on God's justice since they are committed in a state of sin. Nevertheless sinners still can perform acts of such moral quality that it is fitting for God to accept them in his goodness as "half" merits.[76]

---

[71] "... nulla prorsus merita antecedere gratiam iustificationis." *Ib.*, fol. 146.

[72] "... nullum esse in peccatore meritum suae iustificationis neque ex congruo, neque ex condigno. Et eadem sententiam tenent noster Nicolaus Lyranus super Ioannis primum, Thomas Waldensis in libro de sacramentalibus, et valens ille Gregorius Ariminensis, maximus et studiosissimus divi Augustini propugnator in II d. 26." *Ib.*, fol. 148.

[73] "... theologi recentiores Gabriel, Maioris, Almaynus et similes; et ante illos, ne adeo nova existemetur, videtur iam tempore doctoris subtilis fuisse haec opinio communis in scholis." *Ib.*, fol. 148.

[74] "... mediam quandam secuti sunt viam, concedentes cum posterioribus peccatores non iustificari ex meritis de condigno, sed interim dantes hoc prioribus quod tamen iustificentur ex meritis de congruo." *Ib.*, fol. 146. This surprising willingness to associate with the 'Pelagiani' even to a limited extent, a school of thought in which he obviously feels to stand himself, is due to the fact that so far as we can see for the first time a more historical and less 'dogmatic' picture of Pelagius' thought is given. Vega already saw that Augustine's presentation of Pelagianism, which had become the current medieval caricature, proves to be less than reliable if tested by Pelagius' actual statements: "Et quamvis ex nonnullis verbis divi Augustini contra Pelagianos ... aliquis colligere possit sic dixisse eos sufficere posse nobis liberum arbitrium ut sine gratia vel meritis Christi possimus remissionem peccatorum impetrare et beatitudinem consequi, tamen ... adduci non possum ut credam Pelagium sic sensisse." *Opusculum*, Q VI, fol. 154.

[75] "... absolute non possumus primam gratiam mereri." *Ib.*, fol. 171.

[76] "Alia vero sunt merita ex congruo quae in peccatoribus reperiuntur quae nullo praemio digna sunt quia fiunt ab hominibus Deo ingratis et exosis, sed tamen eiusmodi ex se sunt, ut congruum sit et divinam bonitatem condeceat ea ex liberalitate et benignitate sua acceptare, ut trahat peccatores ad suam gratiam. Et huiusmodi merita sic merita sunt ut tamen non necesse sit ea dicere merita absolute sed tantum merita ex congruo. Atque ideo quamvis fideles peccatores dicamus posse mereri ex congruo suam iustificationem, non est opus concedere absolute eos posse mereri suam iustificationem." *Opusculum*, Q VIII, fol. 211.

One can point to several weaknesses in Vega's historical presentation. One might argue that he is too optimistic in seeing "Pelagianism" contained to Great Britain; furthermore, he does not differentiate here between the positions of Thomas and Gregory.[77] The greatest flaw is perhaps one that contaminates even contemporary research: the crucial difference between the Scotistic and the Nominalistic support of the merit *de congruo* is overlooked. As we pointed out, Duns Scotus can allow for a great amount of freedom in man, even in man as a sinner, because the doctrine of justification is surrounded by the two clear and explicit doctrines of predestination and acceptation which safeguard God's sovereignty and eternal prevenience. The *homo peccator* can therefore do what is in him and thus produce merits *de congruo*, but he is never able to move himself into the operational sphere of God's predestination.[78] Since the Nominalistic theologian rejects Scotus' doctrine of predestination, while retaining the inner structure of Scotus' doctrine of justification, he has removed a central part of the outer safeguard or protecting wall. While he can make statements identical with the Scotists on such an issue as the merit *de congruo*, they are transferred into a new context in which divine acceptation alone has to perform the function which for Duns Scotus was performed by predestination and acceptation together.

Dominicus Soto (1495–1560)[79] the great Dominican *peritus*, learned opponent of Vega and specialist on this issue for the Thomistic party at the Council, is quick to point out this weakness and repeatedly claims Duns Scotus for his own position.

For Soto all those who defend the merit *de congruo* are obviously Pelagians since the relation between predestination and justification is so intimate that the claim to earn one's justification *de congruo* at once implies the claim to earn one's predestination *de congruo*. Thus he could drive a wedge between the Scotist and the Nominalist positions.[80]

In his presentation of the *via media* of Gabriel Biel, however, Vega has been accurate. It is in this school that we shall have to look for the beginnings

---

[77]Since Vega elsewhere proves to be very well aware of the differences between Thomas and Gregory – cf. Q V, fol. 133– he apparently generalizes for cataloguing purposes.

[78]See my *Harvest of Medieval Theology*, p. 212ff.

[79]On his life and works see the article by V. Beltram de Heredia in *DThC* XIV 2, col. 2423–2431. Most careful Friedrich Stegmüller, "Zur Gnadenlehre des Spanischen Konzilstheologen Domingo de Soto," in *WT*, I, pp. 169f.

[80]"Qui diceret quod iustificamur ex huiusmodi operibus quomodocumque seu tempore seu natura praecedentibus gratiam, publicus esset Pelagianus ... non consideraverunt unam eademque esse rationem et praedestinationis et iustificationis ... quapropter illi qui defendunt meritum de congruo antecedens gratiae, sequenter opinantur praedestinationis, puta de congruo ..." *In epistolam divi Pauli ad Romanos Commentarii*, Antwerpiae 1550, fol. 270.

of the distinction between *mereri* and *promereri* or *vere mereri* when we turn to the history of the word *promereri* at the Council itself.

6. SOME NOTES ON THE PRE-CONCILIAR HISTORY OF *PROMERERI*

A definitive history of the use of *promereri* by the Church fathers and medieval theologians must of course be a communal effort; only through team work can definite results be expected. The general presupposition has hitherto obviously been that *promereri* is nothing more than an embellished or rhetorical *mereri*. Only after we have been alerted to the possible importance of the distinction between *promereri* and *mereri* might we expect to collect extensive evidence. In every *Index verborum* to editions of Western theological texts which we have consulted, we have found the entry *promereri* wanting. A. Souter alerts us, however, to the fact that a disciple of Pelagius uses the verb three times to clarify the intention of his master.[81]

In an important article on the concept of merit in the writings of some early Latin Fathers, J. N. Bakhuizen van den Brink comes to the conclusion that 'merit' does not entail a claim on God's justice or an obligation on his part to reward. Throughout, the context suggests the minimal interpretation, so that e.g. "... *remissionem mereri* is just 'to receive forgiveness.'"[82] It is striking to note that the definition of the *meritum de congruo* in late medieval theology[83] describes precisely what in early Latin Fathers was meant by the concept of merit as such: "What both Tertullian and Cyprian had meant is nicely formulated by St. Augustine (*Sermo* 111.4.4): 'non debendo enim sed promittendo debitorem se Deus facit';"[84] "There is so little quality of merit in all this ... it is only the will of God...."[85] The controversy between Augustine and Pelagius, however, meant the end of an era, according to Bakhuizen van den Brink; it terminated "the ingenous use of *mereri* and *meritum.*"[86]

---

[81]See the Commentary on Rom. 9:2; II Cor. 5:9 and I Thes. 5:23 *Pelagius' Expositions of Thirteen Epistles of St. Paul: Pseudo Jerome interpolations.* Ed. A. Souter, Cambridge, Eng. 1931, p. 17, 46, 62. Cf. also Pelagius himself, commenting on Rom. 9:15: "Hoc recto sensu ita intelligitur: illius miserebor quem ita praescivi posse misericordiam promereri, ut iam tunc illius sim misertus," A. Souter, *Pelagius' Expositions of Thirteen Epistles of St. Paul: Text and Apparatus criticus.* Cambridge 1926, p. 75f.

[82]"Mereo(r) and *meritum* in some Latin Fathers," *Studia Patristica*, Vol. III. Part I, ed. F.L. Cross (Berlin 1961), pp. 333–340; p. 336. Cf. p. 335: "...*mereri* loses its strict notion of merit in proportion to the notion of grace which is inherent in its object."

[83]*Harvest of Medieval Theology*, p. 170ff.

[84]*Art. cit.*, p. 334.

[85]*Ib.*, p. 337.

[86]*Ib.*, p. 338.

Certainly by the time of the early Scholastics this simple use of *mereri* has given way to explicit considerations of God's obligations to those who do their very best before and after the reception of grace.[87] Due to the reception of Aristotle in the West, the problem of the relation of the natural to the supernatural, and of *materia* to *forma*, was posed in a new fashion. The most important scholastic distinction of grace as *gratia gratis data* or actual grace and *gratia gratum faciens* or habitual grace come to be paralleled by the distinction of *meritum de congruo* before the reception of habitual grace and *meritum de condigno* after the reception of habitual grace. It is therefore by no means surprising that different verbs should indicate the difference between acquiring merits *de congruo* and acquiring merits *de condigno*. Surprising is rather that it is so hard to establish that when *promereri* occurs it is consciously and intentionally chosen in contradistinction to *mereri*.

Thanks to Isidore of Seville (†636), we know that in the theological terminology antedating the seventh century, on the eve of early Scholasticism, *promereri* is understood in contrast to *mereri*. Whereas *mereri* is an ambiguous verb which can mean to merit punishment as well as to earn a reward, *promereri* can only have the positive connotation of earning a reward.[88]

This distinction may well have been in the mind of many theologians who in the following centuries made use of the verb *promereri*. As late as the beginning of the fifteenth century we find *promereri* used by John Hus in contrast to *demereri*.[89] The same author can say however that only Christ can in a fundamental way *promereri*,[90] and since he clearly admits man's ability to *mereri*, one is inclined to translate Hus' observation to mean that 'only Christ can merit in the full sense of the word.'

As we shall see, this development of a new contrast between *mereri* and *promereri* – different from the one known to Isidore – has become explicit by

---

[87]A.M. Landgraf, *Dogmengeschichte der Frühscholastik*, I. 1, Regensburg 1952, p. 260, n. 58; p. 269; p. 272; p. 280, n. 3.

[88]*Differentiae sive de proprietate sermonum. I, De differentiis verborum*; I. 361: "'meruit' commune est ad poenam et ad praemium, 'promeruit' tantum ad praemium." *Thesaurus linguae Latinae*, vol. VIII, Lipsiae 1952, p. 802. Whereas the positive connotation of *promereri* is clear and consistent, the ambiguity of the use of *mereri* appears from a reference drawn from Don. Ter. Hec. 487: "mereri bona dicimus, commereri mala," *Ibid. Commereri*, then, is synonymous with *demereri*.

[89]"... sicut in nulla materia quis compendiosius promereretur, sic nullibi facilius aut periculosius demeretur." III *Sent*. Inceptio. *Opera Omnia* II, ed. Wenzel Flajshans, Marie Kominkova, Prag 1905, p. 373, line 13.

[90]"...solum christus est homo fundamentaliter promerens." *Sent*. IV d 45 q 4; *ed cit*. p. 715, 1. 18/19; cf. *ibid*., p. 607: "Solus ille potuit capitaliter promereri." Cf. *De Ecclesia*, ed. Harrison Thomson, Cambr. 1956, p. 8, p. 82.

the time of the Council of Trent. In present day Mariology the term *promereri* can serve to define the association of the Virgin Mary in the Redemption through Christ and thus to further the *Coredemptrix* doctrine. Though there is no indication that the Mariologists involved are aware of the long pre-history of the words, the association of the Virgin Mary in the work of Christ is expressed by using the verb *promereri* for their joint work of redemption whereas the terms "*de condigno*" and "*de congruo*" indicate the different modes of participation in it.[91]

Between Isidore and Hus, however, evidence of a consciously intended distinction between *promereri* and *mereri* is exceedingly sparse. The medieval history of *promereri* is therefore so hard to trace because the burden of proof is on the one who claims that it means more than a "poetic" *mereri*. In early scholastic literature we find the verb *promereri* often enough used in the sense of *mereri de condigno*, but seldom explicitly contrasted with *mereri* in the sense of initial merit by the sinner who does his very best.[92] In both the treatise "On grace and free will" of Bernard of Clairvaux and Abelard's "Commentary on Romans" is the prefix *pro* employed; but in either case can its use very well have no more profound meaning than the wish of the author to vary the key terms of his argument.[93]

With the high scholastic Franciscan doctors such as Alexander of Hales and Bonaventure, the terms *meritum de condigno* and *meritum de congruo* are so prominent that we are inclined to suggest that for this reason no need is felt to apply consistently the parallel distinction between the verbs *promereri* and *mereri*. When Thomas Aquinas sometimes uses the verb *promereri*, there is nothing to prove that he intended to avoid *mereri*;[94] the very structure of his

---

[91]Cf. Pius X, *Ad diem illum*, Febr. 2, 1904, *AAS* 36 (1903–1904), p. 454: "... a Christo ascita in humanae salutis opus de congruo, ut aiunt, promeret nobis quae Christus de condigno promeruit." See René Laurentin, *La Question Mariale*, Paris, 1963, p. 164. Cf. for the present state of the debate Guilelmus Baraüna, O.F.M., *De Natura Corredemptionis Marianae in Theologia Hodierna (1921–1958)*, Romae 1960, esp. p. 173ff.

[92]The most notable exception here is Roland of Cremona: "Ad ultimum dicimus, quod nullo potest promereri gratiam ex condigno. Tamen dicitur, quod aliquis ex quadam congruitate potest mereri gratiam, quia si homo facit quod suum est, congruum est, ut Deus faciat, quod suum est," Summa, Coll. Paris MLat. 795 fol. 101; Landgraf, *op. cit.*, p. 279.

[93]Bernard: "Dei sunt proculdubio munera, tam nostra opera, quam eius praemia; et qui se fecit debitorem in illis, fecit et nos promeritores ex his." *Tractatus de gratia et libero arbitrio*, cap. 13. 43; *PL*. 182, 1026; 1029/1030. Abaelard: "Estne tanta illa haereditas, ut pro ea promerenda patiendum sit usque ad mortem sicut Christus passus est? Respondet ... Sola quippe charitas, quae nunquam excidit, vitam promeretur aeternam ..." *Expositio in epistolam Pauli ad Romanos*, cap. 9.15; *PL* 178. 903.

[94]One could of course regard 'advocari' in *Summa contra Gentiles* III, 159, as a synonym for 'mereri': "... licet aliquis per motum liberi arbitrii divinam gratiam nec promereri nec advocari possit, potest tamen seipsum impedire ne eam recipeat ..." *ST* I. II. q. 112 art. 3 corp. art.

mature doctrine of justification makes this highly unlikely. And when the great fourteenth century protagonist of St. Augustine *contra Pelagianos*, the Archbishop of Canterbury Thomas Bradwardine, insists that no one can *promereri* first grace, there is little reason to suspect that he wants there to safeguard the possibility of meriting (*mereri*) first grace in any sense![95] Elsewhere, however, Bradwardine, in speaking not merely about the *Pelagiani moderni*, but now about an even more modern (*recentissimus*) error, points to the latest 'trick' which consists in distinguishing between *promereri* and *impetrare*.[96]

Thus far our investigation has yielded no proof that in high scholasticism *promereri* is intentionally distinguished from *mereri*. Summarily stated one might say that the Thomistic school of thought would be in principle opposed to developing the doctrine of the *facere quod in se est*,[97] whereas the Franciscan theologians can say all they want by employing the distinction between *meritum de congruo* and *meritum de condigno*.

It is with the English Dominican and opponent of Thomas Bradwardine, Robert Holcot (†1349), that we find the first real evidence that early scholastic tendencies are reviving. In what seems to be a personal dialogue with Bradwardine the Nominalist Holcot states that of course no one can fully earn (*promereri*) sanctifying grace. But, he continues, this does not mean that the sinner would be unable to merit at all. He can indeed prepare himself *de congruo* for the infusion of grace.[98] A similar statement can be found with the Parisian Chancellor John Gerson (†1429), who had little sympathy

---

[95]Cf. my *Archbishop Thomas Bradwardine, A fourteenth century Augustinian*, Utrecht, 1958, p. 158. The same argument applies *a fortiori* to John Calvin: "Et accessus quidem nomine initium salutis a Christo esse docens, praeparationis excludit, quibus stulti homines Dei misericordiam se antevertere putant: ac si diceret, Christum nihil promeritis obviam venire manumque porrigere," J. Calvinus, *Commentarius in Epistolam Pauli ad Romanos*, cap. 5:2; *CR* 77 (Opera Calvini 49). Brunswigae 1892, col. 89. Cf. "Operantem vocat [Paulus] non quisquis bonis operibus addictus est, quod studium vigere debet in omnibus Dei filiis, sed qui suis meritis aliquid promeretur." Cf. "Si quis sit qui promereatur aliquid opere suo, res promerita non imputatur illi gratis, sed ut debita redditur." *Ibid.*, cap. 4:4; *ed. cit.*, col. 70. Erasmus uses *promereri* in reference to Scotus. LB (Leiden edition) X. 1327 DE. cf. LB X. 1457B; X. 1487A.

[96]Compare with: "Nullum posse primam gratiam promereri," *De Causa Dei*, II. 31. 606 E, Bradwardine's earlier statement: "Ex his autem clare convincitur error quidam recentissimus Pelagianorum fingentium quod licet homo nullo modo neque de condigno neque de congruo valeat gratiam promereri, potest tamen ipsam propriis tantum viribus impetrare." I. 39. 363 E.

[97]Cf. the development of Aquinas on this point: *Harvest of Medieval Theology*, p. 142f.

[98]". . . primam gratiam nullus potest promereri. Nam cum omne meritum sit ex gratia, si prima gratia caderet sub merito, primam gratiam precederet gratia. Et ideo deus sponte dat homini primam gratiam, homini, inquam, se ad gratiam disponenti dispositione naturali et non prebenti obicem gratie per malum usum liberi arbitrii. Licet autem ante primam gratiam requiratur dispositio conveniens, illa tamen non meretur gratiam merito condigni sed congrui tantum." *Super Libros Sapientiae*, Hagenau 1494, Lect. 116 A/B.

for Bradwardine. In his treatise on prayer Gerson denies that one who is not
in a state of grace can merit *de condigno*, since *promereri* is only possible for one
moved by charity.[99]

But in the school of Gabriel Biel we have as yet been unable to find
promereri used in the technical sense of the word.[100] Biel's younger friend and
theological ally, the influential Strassburg preacher John Geiler of
Kaisersburg (†1510), emphasizes the necessity of preparation for grace and
insists that it is to be believed with certain faith that God will turn to any
man who turns to him.[101] Whereas he is willing to admit this preparation as a
merit *de congruo* he denies the possibility of *promereri*.[102]

At the end of this summary of medieval data, we may conclude that the
distinction between *promereri* and *mereri* to differentiate between meriting in
the full sense in a state of grace after the reception of justifying grace, and
meriting *de congruo* in a state of sin, according to the evidence now before us,
cannot be said to have consistent school support. Whereas we had not
expected to encounter this distinction in the works of the Thomist school,
we have not found it generally used in the Franciscan tradition, either in its
Scotistic or Nominalistic varieties, where it would seem to be useful.

At the same time we may state that the distinction as we shall encounter it
in the *acta* of the Council of Trent is not without precedent in the preceding
medieval tradition. Only at a time when the expression *meritum de congruo*
came under the double attack of Luther[103] and a reviving Thomism did it

[99]"Porro si sit petitio per modum meritorie actionis, tunc nullus impetrat de condigno qui
caret charitate; qui vero charitatem habet, eo, ceteris paribus, est efficacior oratio sua pro
seipso quoad praemium essentiale beatificum promerendum quo fervor charitatis et conatus
fuerit maior." "De Oratione et eius Valore," *Opera Omnia*, Antwerpen 1706, ed. E. du Pin, III.
251 B. At the same time Gerson can repeatedly stress that God has committed himself to infuse
his grace in those who do their very best. Cf. *Opera* III. 7 D; III. 123 C. Cf. III. 86 C: "nulli
facienti quod est in se, hoc est bene utenti donis dei iam habitis, deest Deus in necessariis ad
salutem sive sint illa credenda sive operanda."

[100]At one place *promereri* is clearly related to meriting final acceptation rather than first grace:
". . . petitur bonum spiritualis gratie quo in via ad promerendam celestem gloriam preparamur.
Preparamur autem ad hanc promerendam per gratiam . . ." *Expositio Canonis Misse*, Lect. 68 A.
Cf. however, IV *Sent.* d 16. q 2. art. 3, dub. 4: ". . . opera bona moraliter et per consequens de
genere, nihil merentur de condigno, neque premium eternum, neque temporale. Cuius ratio:
quia inimicus nihil meretur de condigno (quod proprie est meritum) . . ."

[101]See the 1963 Harvard Ph. D. thesis, soon to be published, by E. J. Dempsey, *The Doctrine of
Justification in the Preaching of Doctor John Geiler of Keisersberg*.

[102]"Unde manifestissime probatur ne a domino quidem viam perfectionis quampiam
promereri [potest] . . .", "De vita veri christiani," in *Sermones et varii tractatus*, fol. 95ʳ2.

[103]Conclusio 30: "Ex parte autem hominis nihil nisi indispositio, immo rebellio gratiae
gratiam praecedit." "Contra scholasticam theologiam," *W A* I. 225. See further the important
study by Leif Grane, *Contra Gabrielem. Luthers Auseinandersetzung mit Gabriel Biel in der Disputatio
contra scholasticam Theologiam* 1517, Gyldendal 1962; esp. p. 336f; p. 372.

become important for theologians to look for a different terminology to safeguard human responsibility and initiative in the first stage of the road towards justification and final acceptation.

7. *PROMERERI* AT THE COUNCIL OF TRENT

Three times the verb *promereri* occurs in Trent's final decree on justification: once in connection with the disposition of the sinner[104] and twice in the statements dealing with man's ability in a state of grace to merit a growth of grace and eternal rewards.[105] It cannot surprise us that the *acta* only provide us with background information with regard to its first use. After all, Nominalists, Scotists, and Thomists had no difficulty in agreeing that man once justified can perform God-pleasing acts by which he is able in the fullest sense of the word to merit *de condigno*: he can therefore *promereri*.

A more elaborate documentation for the intention of the Council fathers we may expect to find in the discussion of the possibility of merit before the reception of the grace of justification.

The original proposal of July 1546 employs the verb *promereri* in a statement cast in the form of an anathema: Anathema on anyone saying that one can *promereri* the grace of justification with preceding works. It is immediately made clear that this only applies to *merita de condigno* and does not exclude *merita de congruo*: no such preceding works can entail a claim on God's justice.[106] Added to this anathema we find the explanatory comment: "In this justification the merits of man have to be silent, so that the *sola gratia* of Christ may reign."[107]

It may well have been this reference to *sola gratia* which led John Calvus of Corsica, the General of the Conventual Franciscans, to ask three weeks later, on August 17, for an explicit mention of the *meritum de congruo*. The original manuscript adds the observation that the decree actually does mention this merit. Though this last clause is later deleted, it allows for only one interpretation, namely that its author understood *promereri* to apply solely to *merita de condigno*.[108] That same day the bishop of the Canary Islands

---

[104]*Denz.* 801. *CT* v. 794.

[105]*Denz.* 809; 812. *CT* v. 797; *ibid.*

[106]"Si quis dixerit quod suis operibus hanc iustificationis gratiam praecedentibus eam infidelis valeat promereri, cum in illis, quantumlibet bonitate praepolleant, nihil sit iustitiae vel debiti, ut inquit et probat div. Paulus: anathema sit." *CT* V. 387.

[107]"In hac enim iustificatione merita hominis tacere debent, ut sola Christi gratia regnet." *CT* V. 387.

[108]"Gener. min. convert. cuperet fieri mentionem de meritis de congruo" [*Del*: 'quae tamen in decreto fit']. *CT* V. 410.

makes a similar request.[109]

Andreas de Vega, in an effort to incorporate the suggestions made, replaces *promereri* with the words *vere et proprie mereri*, its equivalent, as we believe, but less subject to misinterpretation. The words *nihil iustitiae vel debiti*, in an exact parallel, are replaced by the synonymous but more current phrase *nihil illis ex iustitia debetur*.[110] Whereas the future Cardinal Seripando (†1563) states in his draft of August 19, that merits as such are to be excluded before justification,[111] the so-called September draft significantly changes his phrasing so that only merits in the full sense of the word are excluded.[112]

Though it has been suggested that during the Sixth Session of the Council of Trent the Franciscan influence decreased with the progress of time, we find rather evidence for the contrary. In the beginning the representatives of the Franciscan mode of thought are far more defensive than proves to be the case later on. On October 7, 1546, the General of the Conventual Franciscans states in another intervention on the *meritum de congruo* that he stands over against "multi" or "nonnulli ex patribus" since they deny that justification follows the disposition with necessity, i.e. *de potentia ordinata*. This is the same interpretation of the *meritum de congruo* – a commitment of God to those who do their very best in preparation for justification – which we find with Gabriel Biel[113] and more generally with late medieval

---

[109]"In 9 canone placent omnia; si tamen aliqua fieret mentio de merito congrui, cum non ponat ius sed aequitatem, non esset inconveniens" *CT* V. 414.

[110]"Si quis dixerit quod infidelis suis operibus suam possit iustificationem vere et proprie mereri, anathema sit. Iustificamur enim gratis per gratiam Christi Iesu . . . Quantumlibet enim bonitate praecellunt opera praecedentia iustificationem nihil illis ex iustitia debetur; donatur namque magis quam comparatur; tribuitur, non retribuitur . . ." *CT* XII. 639.

[111]". . . et ea quoque, quae ante eam ipsam iustificationis gratiam cum fide aliqua fiunt, tamquam merita excludantur" *CT* V. 829. Though he is willing to admit formal differences, it is a denial of the importance of this issue when Luchesius Spätling states that Seripando's proposal "sich hinsichtlich der Lehre im Wesentlichen mit dem von A. de Vega deckte (ausgenommen die Frage der doppelten Gerechtigkeit) . . . ," *art. cit.*, p. 517. The same thesis underlies the dissertation of Bonaventura Oromi, *Los Franciscanos Españoles en el Concilio de Trento*, Madrid 1947, esp. p. 97ff.

[112]". . . et ea quoque quae post illuminationem Spiritus Sancti ante iustificationis gratiam cum fide aliqua fiunt, tamquam proprie merita excludantur" *CTV*. 423. In the Novmber draft (Nov. 5) this sentence reads: ". . . ea quoque quae post illuminationem Spiritus Sancti tamquam ad iustificationem necessaria et disponentia, cum fide aliqua fiunt tamquam merita, quibus gratia debeatur, ab ipsa iustificatione excludantur" *CT* V. 636. Ten Council fathers prefer *proprie merita* rather than *merita quibus gratia debeatur*. *CT* V. 681. The Dec. 10 proposal concedes to the Franciscan party even more than they asked: ". . . tamquam proprie merita, quibus gratia debeatur . . ." *CT* V. 696.

[113]Cf. ". . . peccator disponens se ad gratiam faciendo quod in se est, meretur gratiam primam qua iusticatur de congruo . . ." IV *Sent.*, d 16 q 2 art. 3 dub 4. For the status of Biel as *doctor catholicus* at Trent, see E. Stakemeier, "Die theologischen Schulen auf dem Trienter Konzil," *Theologische Quartalschrift.* 117 (1936), p. 343ff.

Nominalism.[114] The November draft mirrors the Franciscan concern even more clearly than did the September draft.

Since it is not our intention to follow the debates in all details, we turn now to the prelude to what we regard as the decisive discussion. Two days before Christmas 1546, Minoriensis and Bituntinus formulate the attack on the Nominalist–Scotist defense of the *meritum de congruo*. They suggest that the verb *mereri* should be employed, which in fact means a return to Seripando's suggestion that all merits are to be exlcluded.[115] This raises strong protests. Castellimaris wants at least the word *proprie* inserted[116] and the General of the Conventual Franciscans and the General of the Augustinians ask explicitly for a safeguard of the *merit de congruo*.[117]

On January 8, 1547, Cervini, the presiding Cardinal-legate, asks whether it is necessary to add to *promereri* the phrase "secundum debitum iustitiae" which would make it explicit that only *merita de condigno* are rejected before justification.[118]

On that same day the weighty consensus is reached that the clause "secundum debitum iustitiae" does not need to be added, since it is sufficiently understood that *promereri* envisages only the merits *de condigno* so that the *merits de congruo* can be upheld.[119] In the final form of the decree, this decision is then implemented.[120]

---

[114]"Nonnulli etiam ex patribus dixerunt dispositionem seu preparationem iustificationem ipsam non consequi; ego oppositum sentio inquiens, praeparationem ipsam ac dispositionem de necessitate sequi iustificationem, si particula ista 'regulariter' et 'de potentia ordinata' intelligatur et necessitas ista est immutabilitatis et infallibilitatis, ut disponentibus, praeparantibus se et facientibus quantum in se est Deus det gratiam, et est sententia Alexandri de Ales in 3. parte Summae q 69, art. 3 [vide: q. 64] cum quo est di. Thomas, Bonaventura, Ricardus et Scotus millies in eorum scriptis.
Multi sensurarunt particulam illam 'tanquam proprie merita excludantur' quos ego satis admiror, cum omnes theologi (excepto Gregorio Ariminensi ex ordine Eremitarum) ponant ista merita impropria, secundum quid, interpretativa, sive (ut uno verbo dicam) merita de congruo, distincta a meritis propriis, veris, gratuitis et de condigno. Ante ergo iustificationem nemo negat ex theologis, ut dixi, bona ista et merita impropria, licet quicumque excludat ea tanquam merita propria." *CT* V. 480. A few lines later, 1. 49, Biel is referred to.

[115]". . . gratis autem iustificari dicamur, quia nihil eorum quae iustificationem praecedunt, vel fides vel opera, iustificationis gratiam merentur." *CT* V. 737; cf. *CT* V. 829.

[116]"Magis placent verba decreti: sed si poneretur 'proprie,' placeret." *CT* V. 737. Cf. also Armacanus: ". . . et posset loco 'excluduntur' dici 'proprie merentur'." *CT* V. 737.

[117]"Placet si non destruitur meritum de congruo." *CT* V. 737.

[118]". . . an ibi 'iustificatione gratiam promerentur' sit addendum 'secundum debitum iustitiae' propter meritum de congruo," *CT* V. 764.

[119]"Et conclusum quod nihil additur, cum satis intelligatur meritum de congruo, ibi 'promerentur' scl. de condigno." *CT* V. 764. The further explanation added in a footnote refers to the discussion of Dec. 22, 1546: "Id est: 'Cum satis intelligatur non destrui meritum de congruo,' prout innuerant die 22. decembris generalis Convent, et S. Augustini." *Ibid.*, n. 3.

[120]". . . ipsam iustificationis gratiam promeretur." *CT* V. 794; Denz. 801.

Certain unclarities remain to be solved. We have no record for the debates on Chapter 16, *De fructu iustificationis*, and on its parallel in canon 32. Here both expressions occur: *vere promereri*[121] and *vere mereri*;[122] but it should be noted that here the Council is not directing itself to the Pelagian threat but rather to the Lutheran challenge of merits as such: on this point the Council could take a common stand.

The first three canons condemn a type of Pelagianism never taught by the Franciscan School, whether Nominalist or Scotist. Actually it condemns a Pelagianism never taught by *any* of the medieval doctors, including Pelagius himself. No Nominalist or Scotist ever taught that man could be justified before God without grace,[123] or that man could *promereri* life eternal.[124] And none even of the more Pelagianising Nominalists held that without prevenient grace one could fulfill the law *sicut oportet*, i.e., to use their terminology "in accordance with the intention of the Lawgiver, God" (*secundum intentionem praecipientis*). In short, the teachings condemned are those which the Franciscan Vega characterizes as Pelagian, not those which the Dominican Soto qualifies as such.

To summarize this section we may conclude:

1. It is the intention of the Council to exclude before the reception of justifying grace only the *merita de condigno*.

2. The verb *promereri* is intentionally differentiated from the verb *mereri* in such a fashion that the first is related only to *merita de condigno*, the latter to *merita de congruo*.

3. The Franciscan party, at the beginning of the debate on the defensive, has gained sufficiently in power to succeed in its stand for the *meritum de congruo*.

8. SOTO, O.P., AND VEGA, O.F.M.: EARLY INTERPRETERS OF THE DECREE

When we now by way of final postscript return to two early interpreters of the decree, chosen as leaders in opposing camps, we do this to have a final check on our conclusions. Was the use of *promereri* understood by its interpreters *e mente auctorum*?

In his *De natura et gratia libri tres* of 1547, Dominicus Soto attacks the *meritum de congruo* head on. According to him there is no *facere quod in se est* possible without prevenient grace. He stretches the literal interpretation of the

---

[121]*Denz.* 809. *CT* V. 797.

[122]*Denz.* 842. *CT* V. 799.

[123]Can. 1., *Denz.* 811, *CT* V. 797.

[124]And all the less merely 'facilius': can. 2; *Denz.* 812. *CT* V. 797. The words 'sicut oportet' are overlooked by Reinhold Seeberg when he concludes that the Nominalistic position is condemned in canon 3. See his *Dogmengeschichte* IV[4]. 2. Basel 1954, p. 775, n. 2.

phrase when he argues that man can never do what is in him unless it be a response to the inspiration of God: "... before justification through the infusion of sanctifying grace, there is no merit whatsoever in human works, neither *de condigno*, nor *de congruo*."[125]

It is clear that for the Dominican Soto the verb *promereri* is equivalent with *mereri*. It should be observed, however, that in the first place Soto likes to interpret in a Thomist sense even Tridentine formulations which are now generally held to avoid a decision favoring one school or another.[126] In the second place Soto regards the merit *de congruo* as a *causa praedestinationis*, a conclusion which Scotists and Nominalists, albeit in different fashions, had studiously avoided. With this presupposition in mind, Soto could argue in his 1550 *Commentary on Romans* that the merit *de congruo* could no longer be upheld by a Catholic, since in its decree on justification the Council of Trent had confirmed the decision of the Council of Orange (529), that no merits can precede the gift of faith active in love.[127]

For Soto good works preceding justification are not completely excluded but rather to be regarded as *effects* of predestination, and therefore never as *causes* of predestination.[128] Soto's completely different point of departure from e.g., the positions of Gabriel Biel, or of the General of the Conventual Franciscans – cf. his speech on Oct. 7 – or of Andreas de Vega, strikes one with new force, when one reads that the sinner can indeed fulfill the law *quoad substantiam*, but that this legal obedience has no significance whatsoever *coram Deo* and gets all its possible reward in praise from fellow human beings.[129]

---

[125]"... nimirum quod facere hominem quod in se est non intelligitur ante auxilium Dei, sed potius praeveniente Deo. Tunc enim homo facit quod in se est quando Deo inspiranti respondet cooperans et tunc certissima lege consequitur gratiam ... ante iustificationem quae fit per gratiam gratum facientem, nihil humanis operibus insit meriti, sive condigni sive congrui." First ed. Venetiis 1547. The ed. used here is the second ed., Antwerpiae 1550, fol. 96. Friedrich Stegmüller discusses the accusation of semi-pelagianism by Soto's contemporary and fellow-Dominican Pedro de Soto who based his criticism on *De natura et gratia*. We believe with Stegmüller that this accusation is not justified. Cf. *art. cit.*, p. 170, 193.

[126]"Igitur sapienter sancta nostra Synodus Tridentina sessione 5, can. 2 pronuntiavit Adam accepisse sanctitatem (id est gratiam) et iustitiam" *De natura et gratia*, fol. 16. Cf. *Denz.* 789.

[127]"... in Concilio Arausicano cap. 25: "Ipse Deus nobis nullis praecedentibus bonis meritis et fidem et amorem sui inspirat. Cui nunc decreto Concilium Tridentinum subscripsit." *In Epistolam divi Pauli ad Romanos Commentarii*, Antwerpiae 1550, fol. 270. Cf. *Denz.* 198.

[128]"Sed est praeterea argumentum efficax quod cum opera illa quatenus praeparatoria sunt ad gratiam effectus sint praedestinationis quia fiunt per auxilium speciale Dei moventis nos in praedestinationis finem, nequent vel esse vel dici causa ipsius." *Ibid.*, fol. 271.

[129]"... si faciunt [gentes] mandata quoad substantiam operum reportabunt humana laudem, si vero per Dei auxilium quoad intentionem praecipientis, reportabunt mercedem a Deo ... possit naturaliter homo legem implere quantum ad substantiam operum quae sint naturaliter bona, non tamen quantum ad intentionem praecipientis, ut sint coram Deo meritoria." *Ibid.*, fol. 85.

In this framework no place can be left for the merit *de congruo*, and *promereri* is by necessity identified with *mereri*.

Lastly we turn to a work of Andreas de Vega which he wrote immediately after the termination of the debates on justification at Trent.[130] We have discussed his preconciliar *Opusculum* and noted his participation in the conciliar discussions. This third study *De iustificatione* of 1547 is important for us because it claims to be an objective exposition of the matter as defined by Trent.[131] In the introduction to the Cologne 1572 edition, Petrus Canisius highlights Vega's authority as an eye-witness, as one who is able to interpret the Council from within.[132]

Vega lays the groundwork for his interpretation by pointing out that according to the majority opinion in the theological faculties, sinners are able to earn their justification *de congruo*.[133] It seems to him impossible to conceive how a Catholic can really doubt that all kinds of dispositions are in their own way causes of justification, regardless of whether they are prompted by prevenient grace or not.[134]

When he then turns to the crucial *promereri* clause he points out that this is to be understood as excluding only a *debitum iustitiae* and therefore only the merits *de condigno*.[135] As he had said two years before in his *Opusculum*, the fact that we cannot fully earn our justification means that we can not earn it in an absolute sense of the word. This now is asserted in the Tridentine *promereri*.[136]

---

[130]*De iustificatione doctrina universa. Libris XV absolute tradita et contra omnes omnium errores iuxta germanam sententiam Orthodoxae veritatis et sacri concilii Tridentini praeclare defensa*, Coloniae 1572. First ed. Venetiis 1547.

[131]Cf. *Praefatio ad Lectorem*.

[132]"Eoque charior in hoc opere Vega esse debet qui Tridenti doctissimos theologos et sapientissimos patres tunc disserentes audivit cum de iustificatione multis est mensibus acerrime disputatum, ipse que cum disputatibus aliis sua sensa studiossime contulit." *Ibid.*, Praefatio, B 5.

[133]"Porro haec sententia quod peccatores mereri possint ex congruo suam iustificationem communior nunc est in scholis theologorum." *De iustificatione*, VIII. 8. fol. 188.

[134]". . . non video posse a quoquam catholico verti in dubium quin causae sint suo modo nostrae iustificationis omnes dispositiones per quas venimus in Dei gratiam, sive illae sint ex solis viribus nostris naturalibus, sive etiam ex auxilio Dei speciali." *Ibid.*, VIII. 9. fol. 192.

[135]"Et ita hic Patres asseverant neque fidem neque aliqua opera bona praecedentia iustificationem promereri ipsam iustificationis gratiam. Nullus enim peccator iustificatur ex debito, nullus ex rigore iustitiae, nullus ex condignitate suorum operum, sed omnes qui iustificantur gratis a deo iustificantur et ex gratia et misericordia et absque meritis et condignitate suorum operum. Et nisi ita accepisset sancta Synodus verbum 'promereri' non recte exposuisset verbum 'gratis'." *Ibid.*, VIII. 10. fol. 192.

[136]"Sed quando Patres hoc loco tam diserte tradiderunt neque fidem neque alia opera praecedentia iustificationem promereri iustificationis gratiam, decet profecto filios Ecclesiae sic temperare sua verba ut nunquam sine additione aliqua commoda et idonea dicant vel scribant peccatores bonis suis dispositionibus gratiam promereri . . . Et sicut gratia iustificationis absolute neque dicitur neque potest dici merces nostrarum dispositionum, ita videntur neque illae vocandae esse absolute merita." *Ibid.*, VIII. 15. fol. 203. Cf. VI. 41, fol. 129.

"It is therefore completely clear that there is nothing in the edict of our Council that contradicts the opinion of those who assert the merit *de congruo.*"[137]

Though there can therefore be no question as to Vega's interpretation of *promereri,* two observations are in order. In the first place, the claim to objective explication of the decree from within cannot be documented from the argument reported above. We are surprised to find no mention of the decision of the Council fathers to regard *promereri* as solely related to merits *de condigno.* The basis of Vega's argument is rather that the majority opinion at his time requires this conclusion and that it is based on Scripture: "And if the Holy Synod would not have thus taken the word 'promereri,' it would not have rightly exegeted the word 'gratis.'"[138]

It is therefore more a theological argument *per analogiam fidei* than an historical analysis. In the second place we should note that Vega does not claim that the *meritum de congruo* is taught by the Council, but rather that such teaching does not run counter to the decree. With the records before us we are in the fortunate position to know that Vega's theological argument is, as we have seen, also historically sound.

We may therefore conclude not only that the Tridentine decree admits of such an interpretation which *allows for* the *meritum de congruo* in the same fashion in which the phrase "in qua constitutus fuerat"[139] admits of a Thomistic and a Scotistic interpretation of the decree on original sin. We may go a step further by concluding also that notwithstanding the Thomistic efforts, suggestions, and protests, it has been the decision of the Tridentine Fathers to safeguard the merit *de congruo* as a merit based on God's goodness and liberality rather than on God's justice.

Therefore we must point out that the fashionable presentation of the Tridentine decree on justification as the *via media* between the extremes of Pelagian Nominalism and Lutheran Augustinianism stands corrected. The Scotist-Nominalistic tradition is not only not touched by the *anathemata* in the *canones,* but had also a far more substantial part in the final formulations of the Council than hitherto has been supposed.

---

[137]"Manifesta igitur luce constat nihil repugnare opinionem asserentium meritum ex congruo verbis nostri Concilii." *Ibid.,* VIII. 10. fol. 194.

[138]*Ibid.,* VIII. 10. fol. 192.

[139]*Denz.* 788.

X

THE 'EXTRA' DIMENSION IN THE THEOLOGY OF CALVIN

If it is true that the built-in principle of radical self-criticism is one of the marks of the Reformation tradition, contemporary students of Reformation thought have a valid claim upon their place in its authentic succession. Though more slowly and with occasional relapses into an earlier stance of confessional apologetics, this applies increasingly also to studies dealing with the relation of the theology of Luther and Calvin.

When, in a recent attempt by a Lutheran scholar to assess the relevance of the Reformation for modern thought, the verdict is rendered that such an anticipation can be found 'in Luther alone',[1] this observation can definitely not be dismissed as a 'typically Lutheran' statement but it is to be read and weighed as one of the most challenging conclusions of decades of research of a scholar, who moved far beyond the confines of the *corpus* of Luther's works. There is no remnant of Protestant triumphalism in the statement that, either in the dissolution of the Middle Ages or in the birth of modern thought, 'the Reformation acted more as a retarding than as an accelerating force.'[2] Nor is there a trace of Lutheran apologetics in the thesis that, in contrast to the predominantly Lutheran regions, 'in Reformed lands the concept of the state has a distinctly progressive stamp'.[3]

Whatever the value of being 'progressive' may be, a reading of Calvin's important Sermons on II Samuel[4] shows more than any other part of his works the degree to which the concept of the State and of the *regnum Dei* is interrelated with an aspect of his thought, which is usually hardly regarded as 'modern', namely the so-called *extra calvinisticum*. In the following essay

---

[1]Hanns Rückert, 'Die geistesgeschichtliche Einordnung der Reformation', *Zeitschrift für Theologie und Kirche*, lii (1955), 55; English translation, 'Reformation – Medieval or Modern', in the *Journal for Theology and the Church*, ii (1965), II. The German version of this article appeared in the *Festschrift* Hanns Rückert, Berlin 1966, 323–56.

[2]Art. cit., 50; transl., 7.

[3]Ibid.

[4]*Supplementa Calviniana*, i: *Sermones de altero libro Regum*, ed. Hanns Rückert, Neukirchen 1936–61. (Hereafter abbreviated as *SC.*, i).

we want first to touch upon this interrelationship between the *extra calvinisticum* and the rule of God through the political and ecclesiastical order. From there we will be led to explore the 'extra' dimension of Calvin's thought in several contexts and to comment upon its original setting in the earlier strata of his works.

1. *ETIAM EXTRA ECCLESIAM*

The relatively more progressive element in the Reformed concept of the State can perhaps be explained in terms of Luther's attitude toward the socio-political realities of his time: 'Die Reformation war, soziologisch gesehen, eine Bewegung von Bürgern, was der fürstentreue Luther verhangnisvoll ubersehen, der Demokrat Zwingli klar erkannt und bewusst verwertet hat; der Jurist Calvin wiederum durchschaut mit Weitblick die kommende Entwicklung: er ist der erste, der "den Staat" und "die Kirche" zu trennen beginnt ...'.[5]

A more obvious direction of inquiry proceeds biographically. The two reformers of the first generation who would prove to be antipodes in Marburg (1529) differed both in schooling and office. Luther as sworn doctor of Scripture enjoyed – notwithstanding the interest and, at times, the concern of his Gönner, Federick the Wise – academic freedom and from his chair and presses in Wittenberg could appeal to the Church at large through pamphlets, treatises and open letters.

Zwingli, appointed by the town council of Zürich as preacher at the Grossmünster, charted the first plans for the Reformation in Zürich by means of *Ratschlägen*, guiding lines for city ordinances. Though Luther can say 'nihil aliud quaerimus quam salutem Germaniae',[6] for Zwingli *salus* has definitely the connotation of *iustitia civilis* when he indicates as motive for writing his *Ein gottlich Vermanung* (May 1522): 'Uss Forcht Gottes und Liebe einer *ersamen* Eyggnoschafft'.[7] From his first public appearance until his

---

[5]Gottfried W. Locher, 'Staat und Politik in der Lehre der Reformatoren', *Reformatio*, i (1952), 204; the best extant compact summary of Luther's 'Zweireichelehre' (206–8). In the light of Bernd Moeller's important study *Reichsstadt und Reformation*, Gütersloh 1962, there is good reason to emphasise the continuity with the medieval *corpus christianum* (*civitas christiana!*) in the reformed concept of the Christian (city) state (op. cit. 29, 33, 52; see especially the caveat on p. 48), and vice versa, the discontinuity with the Middle Ages in Luther's view of the relation between 'Church' and 'State': 'In der Konsequenz musste Luthers Anschauung die Stadtgemeinde zersprengen', 37. The question remains: (a) whether this 'musste' should not be read as 'sollte'; (b) whether the late medieval *civitas christiana* was not thus reduced to the earlier medieval stage of the *regio christiana*.

[6]*W A.*, 44, 346, 39.

[7]*Zwingli Hauptschriften*, Band 7: *Zwingli der Staatsmann*, ed. Rudolf Pfister, Zürich 1942, 6.

death at Kappel, the *res christiana* is for Zwingli *res publica christiana*. There may well be a strong element of humanism, with its (for the late medieval city so congenial) enthusiastic reappraisal of the republican era in Roman history, when Caspar Hedio is adorning Zwingli in 1519 not only with the epithet 'tuba evangelii' (traditionally reserved for one of the Evangelists!) but also with 'publica patriae salus'.[8]

In Calvin's sermons on the second book of Samuel, preached three years after the final Latin version of the *Institutio* and begun two years before his death on 27 May 1564, we see that the *episcopus* of Geneva, as the pastor of a congregation *in diaspora*, looks beyond the national boundaries and the particularities of local situations for his application of the reign of David to the reign of Christ. Speaking to his Geneva congregation, he deals with the responsibility of the State, magistrate and prince as a man who is obviously in touch with the situation elsewhere in Europe, in England, Poland and the Palatinate. Through the years Calvin's beloved refrain at the end of almost all post-sermon prayers suggests the universal scope of the majesty and grace of God: 'Que non seulement il nous face ceste grace, mais aussi a tous peuples et nations de la terre . . .'.

---

[8]Basel, 6 November 1519. *ZW.*, vii. 214, 10. We cannot deal here in detail with the claim of recent students of the left wing of the Reformation that there is a shift in Zwingli's position on the relation of State and Church in the fall of 1523. So Harold S. Bender, *Conrad Grebel c. 1498–1526: the Founder of the Swiss Brethren sometimes Called Anabaptists*, Goshen, Indiana 1950, 97ff.; John H. Yoder, 'The Turning Point in the Zwinglian Reformation', *Mennonite Quarterly Review*, xxxii (1958), 128–40, even discerns two shifts (136, 138). George H. Williams, *The Radical Reformation*, Philadelphia 1963, does not quote Bender but follows him *paene verbatim* on p. 90 (cf. Bender, op. cit., 253).

It should be noted that in Zwingli's letter of 29 December 1521 to Berchtold Haller (†1536), the reformer of Bern, it is clearly stated that the implementation and the timetable of reform should be adjusted to local situations: 'Nec apud tuos sic agere convenit, ut apud nostros . . .', *ZW.*, vii. 486, 29f. Here we also find a plea for tolerance with the weak, expressed in the idea of milk preceding and preparing for solid food (ibid. 487, 6; I Cor. iii. 2), which Yoder dates almost two years later in taking it to be a 1523 concession to civil authority (art. cit. 137). We should beware of describing as shifts of principle what are *de facto* differences in timing and assessment of opportunities for reform, always intended to avoid *tumultus*.

The contrast Williams creates between Zwingli's 'Erasmian pacifism' in July 1520, and Zwingli's view of the appropriate relation between congregation and town council in Zürich in October 1523, is artificial. The fallacy of his interpretation is partly due to the fact that Williams (op. cit., 89) has not noted that he quotes from a section of Zwingli's letter to Myconius of 24 July 1520 (the erroneous reference should be *ZW.*, vii. 343, 19–30; a composite of quotes is presented as one paragraph), which is clearly an answer to Myconius's letter of 10 June (*ZW.*, vii. 322, 9 ff.), '. . . admodum timeo Helvetiae nostrae'. More important for his whole book, insofar as it reveals the tendenciousness of his invention and use of the term 'Magisterial Reformation', is the fact that Zwingli, and not the impatient radical party in Zürich, opposes coercion of the doctrinally underprivileged, in 1523 as well as in 1520. Williams's modernising assumption that opposition to coercion presupposes the separation of Church and State precludes an understanding of what he calls the Magisterial Reformation.

The difference with Luther can be noticed at many points but at none so fundamentally as in Calvin's view of God as 'legislateur et roy', whereas one of the most perceptive Counter-Reformers, Ambrosius Catharinus Politus O.P., had indicated the heart of 'the Lutheran error' as the denial that Christ is both 'redemptor' *et* 'legislator'.[9] Calvin's theme throughout is the rule of God who has appointed Christ as King, as his Viceroy. Reformation is the re-ordering of the lives of the faithful. Confusion and dispersal is the undermining of the God-intended order by Satan and his evil instruments. By the grace and power of God this order is now here and there restored in local churches as well as in the public life of some cities and regions. The true restoration, re-assembling and final establishment of law and order, however, is to be awaited in patience by the faithful as the eschatological act of God.

In his sermon on II Sam. v. 4 – 'David reigned forty years' – Calvin notes that this was by no means an unchallenged or uninterrupted reign: 'ce n'a pas esté du premier coup en perfection'.[10] Then he proceeds ('c'est pour nous, que cecy est ecrit') to apply this text to the contemporary rule of God, giving here his religious testament, which is characteristically at the same time a political eschatology:

'. . . though we know that God rules, yet insofar as our Lord Jesus Christ is hidden in him and his very reign is hidden in this world, it has no splendour but it is little esteemed, indeed rejected by the majority. Therefore, we should find it not at all strange that our Lord Jesus Christ, though he has been established as King by God his Father, does not at all now have the authority among men which he is entitled to. Furthermore, today there is no certain time-limit ["terme" = kairos] indicated to us. When we see the rule of our Lord Jesus Christ is limited, since there is only a handful of people who have accepted him and since for every one city which has received the Gospel there are large countries where idolatry rules, – when we thus see that the rule of Jesus Christ is so small and despised according to the world, let us cast our eyes upon his figure which is given us here [in the rule of David], and let

---

[9]*Concilium Tridentinum*, v. 572. Cf. my article '"Iustitia Christi" and "Iustitia Dei": Luther and the scholastic doctrines of justification', *Harvard Theological Review*, lix (1966), 18.

[10]*SC.*, i. 104, 34 f. Cf. *Supplementa Calviniana*, v: *Sermones de libro Michaeae*, ed. Jean Daniel Benoît, Neukirchen 1964 (hereafter abbreviated as *SC.*, v), 120, 1–9; 121, 37–41. Cf. Simon van der Linde, *De leer van den Geest by Calvijn. Bijdrage tot de Kennis der reformatorische theologie*, Wageningen 1943, esp. 202f. Notwithstanding the fact that ultimately Christ is to hand over his *regnum* to the Father (for Calvin an example used to elucidate the communicatio idiomatum: *Inst.*, II. 14. 3; *Calvini Opera Selecta*, ed. Barth Niesel (hereafter abbreviated OS), iii. 461, 13; 462, 9), the bodily restoration is the final 'terme'; Cf. H. Quistorp, *Die letzten Dinge im Zeugnis Calvins*, Gütersloh 1941, 172 ff.

us await the end [terme], which God knows; for it is hidden to us. I say, let us await in patience, till his kingdom is established in perfection and God gathers those who are dispersed, restores what is dissipated and sets in order what is confused.'[11] '... let us not desist, as far as it is in us, from praying to God that he advances and enlarges [his Kingdom] and that each man apply to this with all his power; and let us allow ourselves to be governed by him in such a way that he is always glorified in us, both in life and in death.'[12]

We find here far more than the mere usage of political imagery: Calvin regards God as the *Dieu des armées*, the Christian essentially as a *homo politicus*, called into the service of God, to whom he is related as *commiles* rather than as a slave, through Christ the Mediator, in whose army he is enlisted through the Spirit of Christ the King. The function of the King extends beyond that of the Mediator insofar as the majesty and power of God extends beyond the *iustificatio impii*. God's concern is not only the rule of the hearts of the faithful, but also, in wider scope, the rule of the whole earth.[13] Here we have not only a political eschatology, but also a political programme, insofar as faith in God is confidence 'a ses promesses non seulement de la vie avenir, mais de la vie presente.'[14]

There is continuity between the 'small' kingdom established here and now and the future establishment 'in perfection'. But for our purposes the discontinuity between the 'small' and the perfect kingdom is more important. God 'advances' his Kingdom and 'makes it grow'; there is development. The climax, however, is not brought about only through intra-ecclesial evolution, but through God's extra-ecclesial intervention as well. We have to understand Calvin's call for patience and 'attention' in this light. In the ascension Christ as Mediator ascended to the royal throne and assumed the rule over his Church through Word and Spirit. Yet, as the Son of God, he had already ruled the world from the beginning of creation as the 'aeterna sapientia Dei, per quam reges regnant.'[15]

In his excellent monograph, *Das Wirken des heiligen Geistes nach Calvin*,

---

[11]*SC.*, i. 104, 42; 105, 10.

[12]Ibid., 105, 34–36. Cf. 113, 9–18.

[13]'... nous avons a retenir, ... quand il a pleue a Dieu de se manifester a nous en la personne de son filz unique, que c'est a fin qu'il soit glorifié ...': *SC.*, i. 685, 35 f. From the earliest times onward (Schol. Ps. i 1, *W A.*, 55 II. 3, 8, ed. Hanns Rückert and others, Weimer 1963), one could formulate the difference – to use Calvin's beloved expression, *forma docendi* – by saying that for Luther the *locus* of the *gloria dei* is the *iustificatio impii*, while for Calvin it is the *iustificatio iusti*. This is in my opinion the theological motivation for the different estimation of the function of the state.

[14]*SC.*, i. 127, 4f.

[15]*Corpus Reformatorum, Calvin Opera* (hereafter *CO*) xl. 592.

Werner Krusche quite appropriately emphasises that the *regnum Christi* is the rule of Christ over his Church; by way of documentation he refers to 'sicut in ecclesia regnat Christus, ita Satan extra ecclesiam'.[16] Yet, from the fall of Adam onwards, the eternal Son of God manipulates the kingdom of Satan as part of his hidden and incomprehensible reign: 'Nous voyons donc, comment Dieu a une facon secrete et qui nous est incomprehensible pour admener toutes ses oeuvres a fin, et qu'en cela il se sert des meschans et les applique a ce quil luy plaist'.[17] Calvin wants it to be clearly understood that in this sense the rule of Christ obtains *etiam extra ecclesiam*.

What in contemporary theological parlance is called the concern for Church *and* world is in Calvin's thought expressed by the complementary aspects of church history and universal history: 'Ie maintiendray', the inscription on the crest of the House of Orange, reads more fully 'Ie maintiendray vostre parti',[18] not only sustaining the faithful through Word and sacraments but also by bending the course of history to their immediate and ultimate benefit. It is this version of the universal action of the *Dieu des armées* 'etiam extra ecclesiam' which marks the difference with the *militia Christi* theme as elaborated by Thomas à Kempis in *De imitatione Christi*, by Jean Mombaer in his *Rosetum Exercitiorum*, by Erasmus in his *Enchiridion* and by Zwingli in his interest in Christ as *dux* or *Hauptmann*.[19]

2. *ETIAM EXTRA COENAM*

The two aspects of 'God's maintenance', reflected in the mutuality of Church and State and in the discontinuity between Church and Kingdom, have their christological or rather trinitarian basis in the so-called *extra calvinisticum*, the later name for the doctrine that the second person of the Trinity continues his rule during the Incarnation 'etiam extra carnem'. The fruitless and indeed frustrating *colloquia* of Maulbronn (1564) and

---

[16]Berlin 1957, 336, quoting from *CO.*, xlix, 381.

[17]*SC.*, i. 81, 15–17. The *duplex regnum* is systematically related to the *duplex voluntas* of God, *pro nobis* and *pro se*. The point of departure in each case remains the same: ... 'la volonté de Dieu est tousiours reiglee en toute perfection et droicture' (*SC.*, i. 605, 20f.). But this does not exclude God's will *etiam extra legem*: 'Or Dieu a deux facons de commander. Il y en a l'une qui est pour nostre reigle quant a nous et a nostre esgard, l'aultre pour executer ses iugemens secretz et pour accomplir ce quil a determiné en son conseil, et pour donner cours a sa providence. Quant est de la premiere facon de commander, elle est contenue en la Loy' (*SC.*, i. 473, 7–10).

[18]*SC.*, i. 437, 17.

[19]Cf. Gottfried W. Locher, 'Christus unser Hauptmann. Ein Stück der Verkündigung Huldrych Zwinglis in seinem kulturgeschichtlichen Zusammenhang', *Zwingliana*, ix (1950), 121–38; 125. This does not imply that Calvin never so refers to Christ; see *SC.*, v. 112, 24: '... nous ne demandions si non que d'etre enrollez par notre maistre et capitaine Jesus Christ'.

Montbéliard (1586) not only paved the way for the expression *extra calvinisticum*, but also associated it in the mind of contemporaries and later interpreters with the Nestorian heresy, with a spiritualising critique of certain elements in Luther's doctrine of the Eucharist (*manducatio oralis, manducatio indignorum, ubiquitas*), and with a peculiar, materialistic concept of heaven.

On this last point Calvin had already been taken to task by Joachim Westphal (†1574) in the wake of the Consensus Tigurinus (1549). Further reverberation is found in the accusation by the Lutheran Jacob Andreä (†1590) that Calvin's convert Caspar Olivian (†1587) and his associates from the Palatinate had a 'türkisches oder jüdisches' concept of heaven.[20] Modern interpreters have not dealt much more kindly with Calvin and his German followers, finding evidence of rationalism and biblicism. One can have hardly any quarrel with this evaluation of the form of the calvinistic *sessio* doctrine; it does not, however, provide for a satisfactory explanation of its function. As we saw above, the hiddenness of the rule of Christ in the world is associated by Calvin with the hiddenness of Christ in God, where he rules *ad dexteram dei*. The graphic realism of what we have called a political eschatology presents itself as a significant motif in the insistence upon 'the historical Jesus' in the doctrine of the *sessio*. The localisation of the historical Jesus in heaven has, indeed, all the marks of a mythological (whether rationalistic or biblicistic) furnishing of heaven according to earthly categories.[21] If one can evaluate a *causa formalis* only by grasping the related *causa finalis*, we have to take into consideration the way in which the *sessio* provides for the consistency between the two aeons, between this created order and the 'new heaven and the new earth'. The evolutional continuity

---

[20]Ernst Bizer, *Studien zur Geschichte des Abendmahlsstreits im 16. Jahrhundert,* Gütersloh 1940, 357.

[21]I am inclined to regard it as an apologetical or perhaps modernising inclination of Reformed historians to claim that '*ad dexteram Dei*' has no local implications for Calvin, but rather expresses the sovereign nature of Christ's rule and its transcendence above all earthly categories. See W. Niesel, *Calvins Lehre vom Abendmahl*, Munich 1935, 76 f; W. F. Dankbaar, *De Sacramentsleer van Calvijn*, Amsterdam 1941, 184 (cf. the statement of Dankbaar on page 194, where he not only defends Calvin against the charge of localisation, but even goes so far as to reproach Lutheran theology for the use of categories which are too spatial). Though Grass shows more sympathy for Luther than for Calvin and does not try to discover the function of the *sessio*, his evaluation of the *causa formalis* seems to me quite correct: 'die Vorstellung von einem lokal im Himmel befindlichen Leib, mit dem wir durch Vermittlung des Heiligen Geistes Verbindung bekommen, ist monströser als die lutherische Vorstellung der Multipräsenz des verklärten Leibes,' op. cit., 266; cf. Bizer, op. cit., 357. To be sure, we should bear in mind that Calvin attempted to tone down the emphasis on locality by writing in 1543 'spatio' instead of 'loco' in the central formulation of this issue: 'Atqui haec est propria corporis veritas, ut spatio contineatur': *Inst.*, IV. 17, 29; *OS.*, V. 386, 10. In the final version of the *Institutio*, the French translation of 1560, this entire sentence is omitted!

between the *regnum Christi in ecclesia* and its final perfection expressed in the advance of this kingdom '*magis et magis in dies*', reflected on the level of the individual Christian in the *iustificatio iusti* and his increasing sanctification, has its discontinuous counterpart in the termination [*terme*] and climax of the hidden rule *etiam extra ecclasiam*, reflected on the level of the individual Christian in his expectation: 'caro nostra particeps erit gloriae Dei ...'.[22] Though only the last day of the five days of the disputation at Maulbronn was dedicated to the Eucharist, this sacrament had been – and still is – pre-eminent in the confrontation of Calvin and Calvinism with Lutheranism. The relation between the *sessio* of Christ and his *praesentia realis* forces us to touch on the eucharistic controversy. This aspect of the doctrine of the *sessio* rather than its eschatological significance has continued to be of central interest to interpreters because of its obvious ecumenical importance. We will restrict ourselves to treating Calvin's sermons on II Samuel, since they have not yet functioned in research. Here, a year after the end of the debate with Westphal and Hesshus and two years before the disputation at Maulbronn, Calvin succinctly summarises his earlier position.

The 'Papist' position, according to which the Body of Christ is "enserré en une prison",[23] is quite explicitly rejected. At the same time it is asserted that the very *substance* of Christ is presented to the faithful in the Lord's Supper,[24] but without "the historical Jesus" in any way descending again to earth. "... though our Lord Jesus Christ dwells in [the place of] eternal glory, through baptism he has imprinted us with his mark, we know him through his Word ... and we are nourished by his own substance in the Eucharist; in short, he dwells in us [*habite en nous*] through faith ...'[25]

At one point, however, Calvin does more than summarise. He goes, we believe, beyond earlier positions (at least as generally understood today), in a direction which not only marks him off clearly from the position of Zwingli and Bullinger but also might have provided the Maulbronner disputation with a more auspicious point of departure, if not with a *formula concordiae*. Dealing with II Sam. vi. 2 ('Dieu des armées habitant entre les

[22]*CO.*, xlix. 560.

[23]*SC.*, i. 440, 15; 136, 37.

[24]'... pour monstrer que non seulement il est auec nous, mais qu'il habite en nous et que nous sommes vniz en luy, voire iusques a estre nourriz de sa propre substance': *SC*, i. 439, 42 f.

[25]*SC.*, i. 137, 28–31. For parallels, cf. Hans Grass, *Die Abendmahlslehre bei Luther und Calvin*, Gütersloh 1954, 246–54. Grass warns us that this 'substantialism' is to be taken *cum grano salis* (253). We give some weight to the fact that our source is a Genevan sermon and not one of the later treatises destined for international publication. This is important to note because it is customary to make the later treatises innocuous by maintaining that they were written 'pacificationis causa.'

cherubins'), Calvin applies the text to Baptism and the Eucharist: 'We should not take these signs as mere visible things, symbols to nourish our spiritual senses, but we are to know that God there unites his power and his truth: both the *res* and the *effectus* are there with the symbol; one must not separate what God has joined together.'[26] If we are right in concluding that with the symbol or sign (*sacramentum tantum*) not only the visible element[27] but also the *res sacramenti* or *effectus* is given,[28] a *manducatio oralis*[29] seems to be unavoidably implied. Christ 'habite en nous par foy'.[30] To receive him in bread and wine, however, is not the *effectus fidei* but the *effectus sacramenti*, inseparably attached to the sacrament by God. The demarcation line between the objective act of God and the subjective act of faith runs between *manducatio* and *inhabitatio*, not between *exhibitio* and *receptio* as the

---

[26]'Il ne faut pas donc que nous prenions ces signes comme choses visibiles et figures qui soyent pour paistre noz sens spirituelz, mais que nous sachions que Dieu y conioinct sa vertu et sa verité, et la chose et l'effect est avec la figure; il ne faut point separer ce que Dieu a conioinct': *SC.*, i. 137, 5–8. We attach some weight to the fact that our source is a sermon rather than one of the series of later treatises which have usually been written (too hastily, we believe) and published *pacificationis causa*.

[24]The obvious interpretation of 'la chose' is, in the light of the *Defensio de sacramentis*, published January 1555, 'res signata'. Here we find the reiteration of article 9 of the Consensus Tigurinus: '. . . nos inter signa et res signatas distinguendo, non tamen *disiungere* a signis veritatem . . .', *OS.*, ii. 272, 33f. In the context of our 1562 quote 'chose' follows the use of 'choses' explicitly identified as 'choses visibles'; hence we read 'la chose' as 'la chose visible', or the element of water, wine or bread, even though we realise that this interpretation can appeal to only a very limited textual basis and has, moreover, the weight of the entire remainder of Calvin's earlier testimony against it. See especially the *Defensio . . . de sacramentis*, *CO.*, ix. 30: 'Huius rei non fallacem oculis proponi figuram dicimus, sed pignus nobis porrigi, cui *res ipsa et veritas* coniuncta est: quod scilicet Christi carne et sanguine animae nostrae pascantur'. The issue is too important, however, not to reopen the discussion on this last stage in the formation of Calvin's doctrine of the Eucharist.

[28]'Sacramentum tantum' is the exterior visible aspect. As to our translation of the 'effect' as 'res sacramenti', cf. Joh. Altenstaig, *Vocabularius Theologie*, Hagenau 1517, fol. 224^{r-v}, s.v. 'sacramentum': 'Illud vero quod significatur, i.e. effectus ille quem deus invisibiliter operatur scl. gratia vel gratuitus effectus, dicitur res sacramenti sive effectus sacramentalis'. Cf. Thomas, *ST.*, iii q. 63 art. 6 ob. 3; ibid., q. 66 art. I c.a. Calvin is also terminologically well-informed about scholastic theology; cf. regarding confession: *Inst.*, IV. 19, 15; *OS.*, v. 449, 19–25.

[29]Cf. Helmut Gollwitzer, 'Hier wird die Beharrung beim Proprium des Sakraments sinnvoll;' 'Die spiritualis manducatio bezieht sich, sich gründend, auf die manducatio sacramentalis [i.e. oralis]: Damit ist das Verhältnis der beiden Empfangsarten beschrieben. Die geistliche Weise ist nur effectus, nicht causa des Sakraments': *Coena Domini*, Munich 1937, 212; 217. In view of Calvin's formulations a year before in his *Dilucida explicatio* against Tielmann Hesshus [See *CO.*, ix. 474. The immediate parallel for this paragraph in the sermons on II Sam, is in the appended tract, *Optima ineundae concordiae ratio* (1561); cf. *OS.*, ii. 291, 18: '. . . ideoque ex parte ipsius Dei non proponi vacua signa, sed veritatem et efficaciam simul coniunctam esse'], the 1562 version should rather be seen as a new 'dilucida explicatio' than as a shift. Calvin touches on this matter in his letter to Frederik III of 23 July 1563 without further elaboration: *CO.*, xx. 72–9. See W. Nijenhuis, *Calvinus Oecumenicus*, 's-Gravenhage 1959, 199.

[30]*SC.*, i. 137, 31.

younger Calvin, the Pfaltzer theologians at Maulbronn and – we may add – all those who later were to claim Calvin's authority have taught.

In the 1539 edition of the *Institutio*, Calvin had already cited the phrase 'vere et efficaciter exhiberi',[31] but according to Article 13 of the Consensus Tigurinus this is understood as qualified by God's good pleasure ('*ubi visum est*'[32]) and, therefore, not to be taken as a commitment of God or, in the Scotistic-nominalistic sense, as a *pactum Dei cum ecclesia*. Furthermore, Article 16 separates *sacramentum* and *res sacramenti* in such a way that all receive the first but only the *fideles*, i.e. the elect, receive the *res sacramenti*.[33] In the final version of the *Institutio* Calvin indeed asserted that the Body and Blood of Christ '*non minus vere dari indignis quam electis Dei fidelibus*'.[34] However, this statement does not deviate from the Consensus Tigurinus since it is to be understood in the light of what is said a few lines before: '*Aliud tamen est offerri, aliud recipi*',[35] with its implied separation of 'chose' and 'effect'.

It seems helpful to use here the traditional fourfold distinction:[36] (i) *manducare sacramentum et non sacramentaliter*, which applies to *anima bruta, infideles, heretici*, and hence can best be called *manducatio impiorum* (these *impii* receive the consecrated host and therefore Christ, but not the *res sacramenti*, the effect of grace); (ii) *manducare sacramentaliter*, which applies to the communion of all the faithful, who do not have to be *boni* but may well be *mali*, hence it may be called *manducatio indignorum*; (iii) *manducare sacramentum spiritualiter* which applies to all those who *digne accedunt* and *Christo adhaerunt fide, spe et caritate* (it is *the* characteristic of this spiritual eating, in contrast with the sacramental eating, that it is the effect of faith, not of the *fides informis* but of the *fides charitate formata*); (iv) *manducare corpus Christi*, which does not necessarily imply taking communion, although the effect is exactly the same as in the case of the spiritual eating, namely incorporation in Christ (here *credere* is *manducare*).

---

[31]*OS.*, i. 142, 41.

[32]'Organa quidem sunt, quibus efficaciter, ubi visum est, agit Deus . . .': *OS.*, ii. 250, 10 f. Cf. *OS.*, i. 142, 34 f.

[33]*OS.*, ii. 250, 24–29; cf. 251, 6: 'omnibus offeruntur Dei dona, fideles duntaxat percipiunt'.

[34]*Inst.*, IV. 17. 33; (*OS.*, v. 393, 37).

[35]Ibid., 393, 20.

[36]For the *veteri doctores* see Alex. *Summa*, IV q. II m. I art. 3, par 2 and 3; Thomas, IV *Sent.* d. 9 q. I art. 2 quaestiunc. 2–5; *S.T.*, III q. 80 art. 2–3; Scotus, *Oxon.* IV d. 8 q. 3 n. 2; (Vivès, xxvii. 75); *Rep.* IV d. 8 q. 3 n. 2 (Vivès, xxiv. 27 f.). For the *moderni* see the quotations in Altenstaig, op. cit., fol. 139ᵛ, 140ʳ, s.v. 'manducatio'. Since 1536, *Iust.*, IV. 19, 16 designates our categories ii and iii as 'manducatio duplex'. By using this formula as an argument against penance Calvin implicitly rejects the concept of duplex manducatio: 'Ut in Eucharistia duplicem manducationem statuunt, Sacramentalem, quae bonis aeque ac malis communis est: Spiritualem, quae bonorum tantum est propria: cur non et absolutionem bifaria percipi fingerent?': *OS.*, v. 450, 19–22.

When we survey the varying statements of Calvin on the Eucharist from 1536 through 1561, it is clear that his discussion remains centered on category (iii), the *manducatio spiritualis*. It marks the via media, repeatedly mentioned by Calvin, between the Lutheran position in category (ii) (from Calvin's point of view undistinguishable from category (i))[37] and the 'sacramentarian' position in category (iv).

We can also place in this context the conclusion of Krusche: 'Die eigentliche *Gabe* des Abendmahls: die Gemeinschaft mit Christus, ist bei ihm [Calvin] gerade keine spezifische Gabe des *Abendmahls*'.[38] The interpreter should be aware that the same term, *manducatio spiritualis*, applies to categories (iii) and (iv), and that both, according to the joint witness of all medieval doctors, yield the same effect, namely, the *inhabitatio Christi*. Otherwise he will necessarily overlook the difference between the two categories and wonder why the sacrament of the Eucharist is necessary at all.

Calvin always retained category (iv) in connexion with the preaching of the Word and the life of sanctification, as described in *Institutio*, III. It stands for the '*etiam extra coenam*', where God, *ubi visum est*, nourishes the soul of the faithful in the union with Christ.[39] In the context of categories (iii) and (iv), *manducatio* has the loaded meaning of *communio, inhabitatio, unio*. However, when in 1562 Calvin sees 'chose' and 'effect' as indissolubly united by God, category (iii) is extended to include category (ii) insofar as *manducatio* is no longer an *effectus fidei* but the result of God's commitment. Since the distinction of *fides informis* and *fides formata* is rejected,[40] the *manducatio* in category (ii), contrary to the medieval tradition, now implies that the *indignus* eats his own damnation. The decisive thing is that God has so

---

[37]*Inst.*, IV. xvii. 33 (*OS.*, v. 346, 25: 'Porro hic duo cavenda sunt vitia . . .'). Cf. *CO.*, ix. 162: 'Nos etiam in sacramento Christum non nisi spiritualiter manducari asserimus, quia ab illa crassa ingluvie, quam commenti sunt papistae, Wesphalus autem nimis cupide ab illis haurit, pietatis abhorret sensus. . . . Sacramentalis, ut dixi, nihil aliud est quam carnis Christi in ventrem ingurgitatio'. Cf. the Augustinian thesis of *credere* = *manducare* in Cornelius Hoen, *Epistola christiana, ZW.*, iv. 512, 21 f. and in Zwingli, *De vera et falsa religione commentarius, ZW.* iii. 818, 8. Zwingli rejects here the two kinds of faith, *informis* and *formata*, which determine the difference between (ii) and (iii): ibid., 819, 8–10. (This whole chapter in the *Commentarius* cannot be understood except in the light of the indicated categories). On the parallelism of *credere* = *manducare* and *est* (in *hoc est corpus meum*) = *significat*, see Walter Köhler, *Zwingli und Luther*, i. Leipzig 1924, 61 ff.; and ii. Gütersloh 1953, 92 ff.

[38]Op. cit., 272.

[39]Nevertheless, 'Et si autem extra sacramenti usum spiritualiter Christo communicant fideles, aperte tamen testamur, Christum, qui coenam instituit, efficaciter per eam operari': *CO.*, ix. 162.

[40]'. . . in scholis volitat nugatoria fidei formatae et informis distinctio': *Inst.*, III. xvii. 8 (*OS.*, iv. 16, 38–17, 1).

intimately put together '*chose*' and '*effect*' that the bond between *manducatio* and *inhabitatio* which obtained in category (iii) is loosened, so that the way is open for a *manducatio indignorum*. A strict parallel is thereby established between the effect of the Eucharist and of the preached word:[41] God's promise is so attached to it that it is never pronounced in vain: 'un glaive trenchant des deux costez'.[42]

3. *ETIAM EXTRA CARNEM*

Though the formula of 1562 could have gone a long way to assuage the Lutheran fear that the certainty of the reception of the Body and Blood of Christ would be made dependent upon the certainty of faith – the *contentio de fide*[43] – it would certainly not have provided for a *formula concordiae* at Maulbronn. The *sursum corda* remains Calvin's main theme till the end: '. . . so that we do not think for a moment that Jesus Christ comes down from heaven and that he leaves that glory behind in which he has once been received . . .'.[44] Though Calvin may be willing to go far in the direction of the *manducatio indignorum*, the real presence of Christ continues to be seen in the setting of the *sessio* doctrine, expressed in terms that reopen the whole *tropus*-debate.[45]

A typical example is Calvin's statement: 'When we receive the water of Baptism it is as if (*c'est autant comme si*) the Blood of our Lord Jesus Christ flows down from heaven . . .; when we receive the bread and wine in the Lord's Supper, it is as if (*c'est autant comme si*) Jesus Christ descends from heaven and becomes our food . . .'.[46] It can well be argued that this '*comme si*' is not to be regarded as a threat to Calvin's sacramental realism, since Christ as the true matter and the Spirit as the agent of salutary communion (the '*quis*' and the '*qua*' of sacramental communion) are not in competition. They

---

[41]Cf. my 'Reformation, Preaching and the *ex opere operato*', in *Christianity Divided*, ed. D. Callahan, New York 1960, 233. Though the *vocatio* is attached to the preaching of the Word, it can take place 'etiam extra praedicationem': '. . . Spiritus illuminatione, nulla intercedente praedicatione, vera sui cognitione donavit': *Inst.*, IV., xvi. 19 (*OS.*, v. 323, 13 f.).

[42]*SC.*, i. 684, 38. Cf. *SC.*, v. 163, 18 f.

[43]Bizer, op. cit., 59; cf. 127, 361.

[44]'. . . afin que nous ne pensions point que Iesus Christ descende du ciel et qu'il quicte cest gloire . . .': *SC.*, i. 181, 24 f.

[45]On the pre-history of the *tropus* concept see Hanns Rückert, 'Das Eindringen der Tropuslehre in die schweizerische Auffassung vom Abendmahl.' *Archiv für Reformationsgeschichte*, xxxvii (1940), 199–221.

[46]*SC.*, i. 137, 1–14. The same question of 'reality or meaning' occurs in connection with '*atque si*' in Melanchthon's *Loci* of 1521. *Melanchthons Werke*, ii. I, ed. Hans Engelland, Gütersloh 1952, *De Baptismo*, 145–6. See Ernst Bizer, *Theologie der Verheissung. Studien zur Theologie des Jungen Melanchthon, 1519–1524*, Neukirchen 1964, 72.

are to be seen as bound together in the light of a basic systematic principle which no one can ignore who wants to interpret Calvin *e mente auctoris*: 'nostrae tum purgationis tum regenerationis in Patre causam, in Filio materiam, in Spiritu effectum consequimur'.[47] Yet, if the *'comme si'* suggests that Christ can be on earth according to his divinity while remaining in heaven according to his humanity, can Calvin teach a real Incarnation; is not his Christology Nestorian? The Latin equivalent, *quasi*, occurs in the center of Calvin's christological exposition: he states that Christ 'in seipsum recepit' the characteristics of human nature, 'quasi mediatoris personae coveniant'.[48] Historically and systematically the discussion about the real presence ushers in questions of Christology. It is in this context that the expression *extra calvinisticum* developed.[49]

The charge of Nestorianism dates from the first stages in the debate between Lutheran and Calvinist theologians, and it is already presupposed by Question 48 of Sunday 18 in the Heidelberg Catechism, with which the *extra calvinisticum* is traditionally associated.[50] Not until considerably later and in response (as I believe) to the Calvinistic inclination to characterise the Lutheran Christology and especially its interpretation of the *communicatio idiomatum* as 'Roman',[51] have Roman Catholic theologians also paid attention to the *extra calvinisticum* and its relation to Nestorianism. In our time this is usually stated in quite a nuanced fashion. Thus A. Hulsbosch, O.E.S.A., writing in 1953: 'It is clear that Calvin wanted definitely to preserve the personal unity of Christ ... Yet a closer investigation of the controversy Cyrillus-Nestorius would show that the Reformed theologian, notwith-

---

[47]*Inst.*, IV. xv. 6 (*OS.*, v. 289, 28–30, dating from 1539).

[48]*Inst.*, II. xiv. 2 (*OS.*, iii. 460, 9 f.).

[49]For a description of the pre-history of this term since the *Consensus Tigurinus, via* the *Colloquia* of Maulbronn and Montbéliard, to the 'extra calvinianum' (1621) of Balthazar Mentzer (Sr., †1627), see the excellent Harvard dissertation (1962) of Edward D. Willis, *Calvin's Catholic Christology*, Leiden 1966, 8–23.

[50]Indicated as Sunday 17 in the edition of Wilhelm Niesel, *Bekenntnisschriften und Kirchenordnungen der nach Gottes Wort reformierten Kirche*, Zürich 1954, 160. Question and Answer 48 read according to the Latin text: 'An vero isto pacto duae naturae in Christo non divelluntur, si non sit natura humana, ubicunque est divina? Minime: Nam cum divinitas comprehendi non queat, et omni loco praesens sit, necessario consequitur, esse eam quidem extra [!] naturam humanam, quam assumsit, sed nihilominus tamen esse in eadem, eique personaliter unitam permanere': *Collectio Confessionum in Ecclesiis Reformatis Publicatarum*, ed. Hermann A. Niemeyer, Leipzig 1840, 440. Cf. *The School of Faith*, ed. Thomas F. Torrance, New York 1959, 77.

[51]Cf. H. Bavinck: 'Beide, Luthersche en Roomsche Christologie, bergen hierdoor in zich een docetisch element ...': *Gereformeerde Dogmatiek*, iii. 3rd ed. Kampen 1918, 337. We note that the same accusation has been made by Max Thurian against Calvin: 'Calvin n'est pas toujours exempt d'un certain docetisme ...': *L'Eucharistie Memorial du Seigneur*, Neuchâtel 1959, 262. More accurate is Jan Koopmans in his *Das altkirchliche Dogma in der Reformation*, Munich 1955, 127.

standing his own protest, finds himself on the side of Nestorius'.[52] Even more restrained is the formulation of Johannes L. Witte, S.J.: 'Calvin hat einige wertvolle antiochenische Elemente der Christologie betont, welche zum "depositum fidei" gehören ... Dies tat er in einer Weise, dass er mit den anderseitigen Bestimmungen der chalkedonischen Definition wenigstens formell [!] nicht in Widerspruch geriet'.[53] This evaluation by Witte is all the more striking when compared with the conclusion of the Reformed systematician F.W.A. Korff, who fervently criticises the 'extra' as 'a conclusion drawn from the doctrine of the immutability of God' and who proceeds to accuse Calvin of Nestorianism, the reformed Christology of Ebionitism, and the Lutheran Christology of Docetism.[54]

Turning now to the *extra Calvinisticum* – the doctrine of the operation of the second person of the Trinity *'etiam extra carnem'* – as it functions in Calvin's works, we should note first that the preferred designation of Christ is *'deus manifestatus in carne'* (I Tim. iii. 16).[55] One of the most revealing illustrations of the setting of the 'extra' dimension in Calvin's theology can be found in the *Responsum ad Fratres Polonos* [1560] drawn up by Calvin and other Genevan ministers: The eternal Word of God is the mediator and reconciler, not only since the Incarnation but already from the beginnings of creation, 'quia semper fuit caput ecclesiae et primatum tenuit etiam super angelos primogenitus fuit omnis creaturae'.[56] This 'first-born of all creation' (Col. i. 15) should be especially noted, since the 'deus manifestatus in carne' has enhanced a super-naturalistic Christ-image in the Reformed tradition, as well as in the pens of its critics.[57]

---

[52]'De Genade in het Nieuwe Testament', in *Genade en Kerk*, ed. A. van Straaten, Utrecht 1953, 24 f.

[53]'Die Christologie Calvins', in *Das Konzil von Chalkedon*, ed. Aloys Grillmeier, S.J. und Heinrich Bacht, S.J., iii: *Chalkedon Heute*, Würzburg 1954, 529.

[54]*Christologie. De leer van het Komen Gods*, Nijkerk 1940, i. 257, 262, 265.

[55]'Non potuit magis proprie de Christi persona loqui, quam his verbis: Deus manifestatus in carne': *CO.*, xviii. 289 f.; Calvin retained this emphasis throughout his life; cf. *SC.*, i. 193, 9–12: 'Voila nostre Seigneur Iesus Christ qui est une avec son Pere car il est d'une mesme essence; mais oultre cela encores, il est ung, entant qu'en son humanité, il est appellé d'une costé Dieu et d'autre costé homme, mais en une seule personne, il est Dieu manifesté en chair'. Cf. ibid., 155, 9; 181, 13.

[56]'Unde colligimus non modo post Adae lapsum fungi coepisse mediatoris officio, sed quatenus aeternus Dei sermo est, eius gratia coniunctos fuisse Deo tam angelos quam homines, et integri perstarent': *CO.*, ix. 338. Cf. *SC.*, v. 156, 36f. See E. Emmen, *De Christologie van Calvijn*, Amsterdam 1935, 30 and H. Schroten, *Christus de Middelaar bij Calvijn*, Utrecht 1948, 109. Cf. Alexandre Ganoczy, *Calvin Théologien de l'Église et du ministère*, Paris 1964, 146 ff.

[57]Cf. J.A.T. Robinson. *Honest to God*, London 1963, 66: 'God Almighty walking about on earth, dressed up as a man. Jesus was not a man born and bred – he was God for a limited period taking part in a charade. He looked like a man, he talked like a man, he felt like a man, but underneath he was God dressed up – like Father Christmas'.

Of the two classical *loci* for the *extra Calvinisticum* in the *Institutio* (II. xiii. 4 and IV. xvii. 30) the first appears in the final edition of 1559 with the rejection of Manichaeism, which goes back to the first edition of 1536, enlarged in 1543 to include a parallel rejection of the Marcionites.[58] Calvin wants to reject the teaching that Christ had merely assumed a celestial body in the Incarnation. He is responding to the argument that a real incarnation would imply a staining of the body of Christ and imprison God within the limitations of a given place: 'descendit Filius Dei, et caelum tamen non relinqueret ... ut semper mundum impleret, sicut ab initio'.[59]

The second *locus classicus* is *in nuce* already in the edition of 1536 and is similarly characterised by its emphasis on the reality of the Incarnation, that Christ is flesh of our flesh. When one analyses how, in 1543, Calvin divides the material of 1536 over two chapters, adds new sections and elaborates earlier paragraphs, one sees that the Marcionite Docetism is rejected because it defends the *vere deus* at the expense of the *vere homo*; and, as Calvin puts it in 1539, this leads to a 'corpus phantasticum'. In 1543 the explicit motivation for the *extra calvinisticum* is given: 'Cavendum est enim, ne ita divinitatem astruamus hominis, ut veritatem corporis auferamus'.[60] In 1559 the *extra calvinisticum* is further unfolded through one of the very rare positive references to the '*Scholastici*' (in the French edition of 1560 explicitly referred to as 'les Théologiens Sorbonniques'): 'C'est que Jesus Christ est partout en son entier [*totus*], mais que tout ce qu'il a en soy n'est point par tout [*totum*]'.[61]

It is of extreme importance to realise that the *scopus* of the *extra calvinisticum* is not a rejection of Cyril with possible Nestorian results. Indeed, it is not at all to be placed in the dimension of the alternatives Cyril-Nestorius, but in an earlier stage in the history of Christian thought, the period in which adoptionism and docetism were the decisive alternatives. Parallel to the history of the development of early Christian thought, Calvin has to make clear in the later editions of the *Institutio* that his primary opposition to Docetism does not open doors to Nestorianism.[62] The Genevan reformer and his first disciples did this over against Lutheran criticism. We see the reverberation of this controversy in the formulation of Question 48 of the Heidelberg Catechism, where the accusation of

---

[58]Cf. *OS.*, i. 80f. with *CO.*, i. 519. For the following see Willis, op. cit., 26–31.

[59]*OS.*, iii. 458, 10–13.

[60]Cf. *OS.*, i. 140 with *CO.*, i. 1006.

[61]*Inst.*, IV. xvii. 30. Ed. Jean Daniel Benoît, *Institution de la Réligion Chréstienne*, Paris 1957, iv. 419. Cf. *OS.*, v. 389, 16–19.

[62]See Inst. II, xiv. 4, where Calvin inserted in 1539 a warning against both Nestorius and Eutyches: *OS.*, iii. 463, 18–25.

Nestorianism is presupposed, and rejected on the grounds of the unity of the person of Christ, not threatened but expressed in the *extra calvinisticum*.

The second *locus classicus* for the *extra calvinisticum* must have been understood by the first generation of readers of the *Institutio* in connexion with developments in medieval Mariology, and should, therefore, be interpreted by us in that light. The context of the passage is found in the edition of 1536 in chapter iv, 'De Sacramentis', to be later elaborated into Book IV of the *Institutio*. The discussion is about the way the body of Christ is offered to us in the Lord's Supper. As we have seen, the answer is 'vere et efficaciter'.[63] Then follows a passage, set forth as a *summa*, the reiterated 'vera' emphasising the reality of the Incarnation as the basis for hope in our own bodily resurrection: 'Christus, ut veram nostram carnem induit, cum e virgine natus est, in vera carne nostra passus est, cum pro nobis satisfecit; ita eandem veram carnem et resurgendo recepit et in coelum sustulit. Haec enim nobis nostrae resurrectionis et in coelum ascensionis spes est, quod Christus resurrexit et ascendit. Porro, quam infirma et fragilis spes foret ista, nisi ipsa nostra caro in Christo vere suscitata et in regnum coelorum ingressa esset? Atque haec est perpetua corporis veritas, ut loco contineatur, ut suis dimensionibus constet, ut suam faciem habeat.'[64]

The point of Calvin's fear is that room is left for a doctrine of ubiquity, undermining the 'flesh of our flesh', through the *communicatio idiomatum*, according to which the characteristics of the two natures are exchanged directly[65] – in contrast with his own interpretation, according to which this exchange occurs indirectly by attribution to the one Person. The *extra calvinisticum* serves to relate the eternal Son to the historical Jesus, the Mediator at the right hand to the sacramental Christ, in such a way that the 'flesh of our flesh' is safeguarded. Rather than hiding secret divine resources, which mark a divide between the incarnate Christ and fallen man, the *extra calvinisticum* is meant to express both the reality of the *kenosis* and the reality of the Ascension. The theological motive is the *caro vera*, the religious motive is the *spes resurrectionis*.[66]

In the medieval development of Mariology there are two theses which

---

[63]*OS.*, i. 140; cf. i. 142: '... dicimus vere et efficaciter exhiberi, non autem naturaliter.'
[64]*CO.*, ii. 1030; cf. *OS.*, v. 386, I-II.

[65]The so-called *genus auchematicum* or *majestaticum*. From 1536 onwards Calvin says that the *coniunctio* between the two natures – the *tropus* which the *veteri* call *communicatio idiomatum* – is by the Scriptures expressed 'tanta religione ... ut eas quandoque inter se communicent': *Inst.*, II. xiv. I; *OS.*, v. 459, 8 f.

[66]I believe that the reason why this has not been clearly seen in Calvin scholarship is the misleading smoke curtain of the adage *'finitum non capax infiniti'*. For the following section see 'Infinitum capax infiniti' in *Vox Theologica* xxxv (1965), 165–74.

the reformers especially and quite emphatically rejected.[67] The first, which we mention here only in passing, holds that at the time of Mary's Assumption, the Kingdom of God was divided in such a way that the Virgin Mary as *mater misericordiae* assumed responsibility for the *regnum misericordiae* and Christ as *iudex* became responsible for the *regnum iustitiae*. It is this understanding of *iustitia* which is described by Luther as the *iustitia Dei activa*, and rejected as such.[68] While this first thesis played a role especially in the devotional literature and the graphic arts of the period, the second thesis, which concerns us here, played a more refined dogmatic role. The concern here was to describe the Virgin Mary as *purus homo* or *pura creatura*, not *'purus'* in the sense of 'free from sin' but in the sense of 'with only one nature'. In a fascinating and much quoted sermon, Bernard of Clairvaux formulated this point explicitly, 'But perhaps you fear also in him [Christ] the divine majesty, because though he became man, he remained, nevertheless, God. If you want to have someone who pleads for you with him, then turn to Mary. After all, in Mary is pure humanity, not just 'pure' as 'free from all stains' but also 'pure' in the sense of a person with only one nature'.[69]

Calvin's concern to preserve the *purus homo* status of Christ, not only in the Incarnation but also in the session, and in the interrelation of these two concerns, can be understood in the light of a second quotation. The influential late medieval theologian Gabriel Biel (†1495) pursued the Bernardine theme in various ways and quoted it explicitly and discussed it at length in his much-read and often-printed *Canonis misse Expositio*.[70] In its most concise form he once put it thus: 'Christ reigns at the right hand of the Almighty Father not as pure man (*homo purus*) but as God-man (*deus homo*). How would man, being earth and dust, and thrown out of his earthly paradise, dare to aspire to the heavenly paradise, if he did not know that in someone else [the Virgin Mary] his own simple nature had preceded him?'[71]

---

[67]For documentation see my *Spätscholastik und Reformation*, Zürich 1965, i, 291 ff. and my article 'Schrift und Gottesdienst: Die Jungfrau Maria in evangelische Sicht', in *Kerygma und Dogma*, xix (1964), 245 ff. Cf. G.C. Berkouwer, *Vatikaans Concilie en nieuwe theologie*, Kampen 1964, 309 ff.

[68]That this is not merely a late medieval *Fehlentwicklung*, but of contemporary relevance, may appear from the encyclical 'Menso Maio' of Pope Pius VI, 30, April 1965. *See Katholeik Archief*, xx (1965), 586; *Herder-Korrespondenz*, xix (1965), 411.

[69]'Sed forte et in ipso maiestatem vereare divinam, quod, licet factus sit homo, mansit tamen deus. Advocatum habere vis et ad ipsum, ad Mariam recurre. Pura siquidem humanitas in Maria, non modo pura ab omni contaminatione, set et pura singularitate nature': *Sermo in Nativitate B.V.M.*, in P.L., clxxxiii. 441. For the parallel definition of 'pura creatura', see St. Antonius of Florence, *Summa Theologica*, IV, xv. 20.

[70]Lectio 32 B: ed. Oberman-Courtenay, Wiesbaden 1963, i. 329.

[71]'Neque Christus enim homo purus, sed homo deus ad dexteram patris regnat omnipotentis. Quomodo enim homo, terra et pulvis, de terrestri paradiso extrusus, ad celestem adspirare auderet, si non in aliquo suam naturam puram precessisse cognosceret?': *Sermones de Festivitatibus B.V.M.*, Hagenau 1510, Sermo 25 A.

Another time he applies the contrast between Mary and Christ to the bodily Resurrection: because of the hypostatic union between the two natures in Christ, we do not derive from the Resurrection of Christ 'such great hope and trust (*spei fiducia*) for our own Resurrection as we do from the Resurrection of the Virgin who possessed a purely human nature, not hypostatically united with the divine'.[72]

As is well-known, Calvin used in re-working the 1559 edition of *Institutio* IV. xvii. 20–34 passages derived from his treatises defending the *Consensus Tigurinus* against Lutheran attacks, especially those of Joachim Westphal.[73] The first draft of our passage, however, was published thirteen (!) years before this *Consensus* was developed. It was directed not against Luther and his followers, but against the medieval scholastic tradition. Though Calvin does not pursue Mariological problems here, he implicitly rejects in 1536 the contrast between 'purus homo' and 'deus homo', and that in a two fold way: 'The same real [that is, our own human] flesh he had not only retained in the Resurrection but also carried to heaven. This now is the hope for our own resurrection and our ascension to heaven, that Christ is risen and ascended ...'.[74]

Just as we have to understand Calvin's concern for Christ as *purus homo* in the light of the preceeding medieval tradition, so we have to understand the *extra calvinisticum* itself. In this respect Calvin scholarship lags behind the study of the *initia Lutheri*. Scholarly research has been primarily concerned with Calvin's relation to Augustine, Luther, Humanism, and, to a lesser extent, Zwingli. Yet Calvin shows himself to be acquainted with Anselm, Lombard and Aquinas, and well read in Bernard. In the Collège de

---

[72]'Quamvis enim scimus corpus domini corruptionem videre non poruisse, quia unitum est deitati, quod in nullo alio homine invenitur, idcirco nequaquam tantam spei summimus fiduciam nostre resurrectionis future, quantam ex resurrectione virginis, que puram habuit humanam naturam, i.e. deitati hypostatice non unitam': op. cit., Sermo 18 I. See also the popular, often-printed Wisdom Commentary of Robert Holcot, Lectura 35 C.

Eustachius van Zichem O.P. (†1538), the first Dutch opponent of Luther, whom we will have to classify as a theologian of the *via antiqua*, provides us with an interesting parallel for the interrelation of Christology, Mariology and Eucharist with the *vera caro*. In his *Sacramentorum Brevis Elucidatio*, Lovanii 1523, G4ᵛ, he proves the necessity of transsubstantiation: since Christ cannot leave heaven, therefore these substances have to be changed into Christ. '... Sane non migrat e coelo Christus, qui non deserit patris dexteram [up to this point Eustachius agrees with his fellow countryman, Hoen!], igitur nihil erit, quo iisce sub rebus claudi posset, nisi transmutata in se panis et vini substantia'. [Hoen completed the thrust of the argument by not terminating the elevation of the substances halfway, but placing them in heaven itself]. Eustachius gives, then, as a further example the Incarnation: Christ was indeed born *utero clauso* from the Virgin Mary and, though he is her issue, 'non tamen nisi commutato virginis sanguine'. Text in F. Pijper, *Primitiae Pontificiae Theologorum Neerlandicorum Disputationes contra Lutherum, inde ab A. 1519 usque ad A. 1526 promulgatae*, Hagae-Comitis 1905, 331 ff.

[73]Cf. W.F. Dankbaar, *De Sacramentsleer van Calvijn*, Amsterdam 1941, 170f.

[74]Loc. cit., *OS* v. 386, 2–5; cf. 7–9.

Montaigu he may have studied for several years – until 1528 or 1529 – under the learned Johannes Major (†1550), a nominalist with strong Scotist sympathies, and French editor of Gabriel Biel.[75] Through his knowledge of these authorities, Calvin was in a position to establish that the so-called '*extra calvinisticum*' was at least an '*extra scholasticum*', and, after inquiry into the Greek and Latin fathers, even an '*extra Christianum*'. As usual, in his *Institutio* Calvin does not refer to authorities by name. But in is *Ultima Admonitio ad Ioachimum Westphalum* (1557), Calvin appeals to Peter Lombard 'and the sophists who followed him'. A moment later he adds: 'Ac mirum est homines istos [Westphal, c.s.] tam proterve contra veteris ecclesiae consensum ferri'.[76]

In a concise survey of the state of scholarship, Karl Barth shows, with quotations from Athanasius, Gregory of Nyssa, John of Damascus, Augustine and Thomas, 'dass die Reformierten dies nicht etwa als eine theologische Neuerung, sondern in Fortsetzung der Tradition der ganzen älteren Christologie (mit Einschluss der griechischen) gesagt haben'.[77] We should explicitly add here: auch in Fortsetzung der neueren, d.h. scholastischen Christologie! For Calvin the appeal to the consensus of the early church is of course of more fundamental importance. His reference to the medieval commentators of Lombard's *Libri quattuor sententiarum* has all the marks of a debating manoeuvre, by which Westphal and his Lutheran following are alerted to the fact that even the 'sophists' had still insight enough to preserve this part of the Christian heritage.

For the understanding of Luther's relation to scholasticism it is important to highlight this crucial point of discontinuity. On the other hand, we should realise that it would be an over-simplification to place Calvin together with

---

[75]In a recent article, typical of the state of contemporary research, it is claimed in a somewhat contradictory fashion that Calvin is at once the victim of a 'mangelhaften scholastischen Bildung' *and* of 'der Erstarrung des scholastischen Denkens seiner Zeit,' Johannes L. Witte, art. cit., 527. The observations by François Wendel on Calvin's relation to Duns Scotus, *Calvin: sources et évolution de sa pensée religieuse*, Paris 1950, 99 ff., may well provide an encouragement for pursuit of more extensive research.

[76]CO., ix. 194f. This quotation I owe to a kind indication by Dr. Willis. See exactly the same emphasis on the authority of the *ecclesia vetus* in Melanchthon, *Loci communes*, 'De Filio', with an accurate definition of the *communicatio idiomatum* as the 'praedicationem in qua proprietates naturarum personae recte attribuuntur …'; in the 1559 edition op. cit., 200, 1–5, explicitly entitled, 'forma loquendi in concreto'; see 152 n. i. For documentation as regards Calvin's 'sophists', see my *Spätscholastik und Reformation*, i. 247. One should add at that point the quotations and discussion by Biel in his *Canonis Misse Expositio*, Lectio 65 A–D (ed. Oberman-Courtenay, iii. Wiesbaden 1966, 70–3).

[77]*Die kirchliche Dogmatik*, i. 2, p. 184. Willis summarises his detailed investigation of the prehistory of the '*extra calvinisticum*' with the designation '*extra catholicum*', op. cit. 60.

the scholastic tradition over against Luther. Calvin's indirect communicatio idiomatum – communicatio in concreto,[78] rejected by Luther, deviates at an important point from the medieval tradition. According to the notorious thesis of Thomas, Scotus, Occam, and others, God could have – *de potentia absoluta* – 'incarnated' himself into a *creatura irrationalis* (Thomas), into a stone (Scotus), yes, even into an ass (Occam). Scotus writes in defence of this thesis, in a passage often copied verbatim by later theologians, that the fact that an irrational creature has no personality is no problem, since there is, in any case, a *hypostasis* or *suppositum*: 'The *unio* does not just take place in the person, but especially in the *hypostasis* and *suppositum*'.[79] Calvin sharply rejected this kind of question, partly because he regarded it as 'perverse curiosity', and partly because the joining of the two natures in Christ takes place exactly in the Person.[80] The Incarnation is not the assumption of a *suppositum*, but the action of the Mediator who '*Adae personam induit*', in order that '*communem naturam pignus esse nostrae cum Filio Dei societatis.*'[81] Although the *extra scholasticum* and the *extra calvinisticum* may appear to be identical in form, their application to the Lord's Supper leads to quite divergent conclusions, completely in accordance with Calvin's shift of accent from a natures-Christology to an offices-Christology, converging towards a Mediator-theology.[82]

Not until now have we touched upon the axiom '*finitum non capax infiniti*'. There was no reason to explore this formula before, for the simple reason that it does not occur in the works of Calvin.[83] Yet it has become habitual to connect the *extra calvinisticum* with this axiom, either to establish its value and truth or to prove its indefensibility. A Reformed historian of Christian thought, Alexander Schweizer, describes the '*finitum non capax infiniti*' in a

---

[78]The best survey of late medieval opinions can be found in Joh. Altenstaig, op. cit., *s.v.* 'Communicatio', and even more explicitly, *s.v.* 'Idioma', fol. 44^r, fol. 104^v – 105^v. Universally, the communication of *abstracta*, i.e., of the two natures, is rejected; communication *in concreto*, i.e. through the Person, is alone accepted.

[79]*Opus Oxoniense*, III. d 2. q. I art. I Cf. *Spätscholastik und Reformation*, i. 239.

[80]*Inst.*, II. xii. 5 (*OS.*, iii. 443, 24, 36).

[81]*Inst.*, II. xii. 3 (*OS.*, ii. 439, 25; 440, 14 f).

[82]Cf. *Inst.*, II. xiv. 3 (*OS.*, iii. 462, 6–9).

[83]As a mathematical thesis the '*non capax*' is accepted in scholasticism as a matter of course: that which is limited [circumscriptum], cannot possibly contain the unlimited [infinitum]. This cannot, however, be applied to anthropology. Thus, Biel defines man as *creatura rationalis* '*dei capax*', Lectio 77 T; ed. cit., iii. 293. Wyclif refers to this thesis, '*infiniti ad finitum nulla est proporcio*', as an epistemological axiom, but he does not regard it as applicable to the relation between God and the soul 'cum inter deum et animam sit optima proporcio creata, quia finita ad duo bona extrema': *De Trinitate*, x (ed. A. Dupont Breck, University of Colorado 1962, 117). Cf. Thomas, *Exp. in 8 libros Physicorum*, 3 c; *de Veritate*, 2. 9 c.

positive sense as one of the five characteristics of calvinistic doctrine.[84] Friedrich Loofs draws upon Schweizer for his own exposition, but believes that this characteristic forms the basis for the Nestorian tendencies in Calvin and Calvinistic theology.[85] Werner Elert goes a step further by relating this Reformed, 'unbiblical principle' which 'nur einem naiven Denken einleuchten kann' to Nestorius himself.[86] Even more common is the criticism that the theology of Calvin and his disciples has at this point fallen victim to philosophical prolegomena. As far as I can see this is not a malicious Lutheran caricature, since the Reformed tradition itself is responsible for the idea that the 'non capax' is genuinely Calvinistic. Even quite recently, a respected Reformed theologian could defend the relevance of Sunday 18 of the Heidelberg Catechism by claiming that the 'finitum non capax infiniti' is 'the very best basis of Reformed Christology, until this day under assault by sectarian and humanising Christians'![87]

This 'very best basis' is not only absent in a literal sense from Calvin's *corpus*, but it is completely alien to the intentions of the 'extra calvinisticum', with which it is so often connected. If it were merely a rational *philosophicum* which was at stake, one would not have to hesitate one moment before opting for Luther's confession: '. . . ego nullum, nec in coelo neque in terra, Deum habeo aut scio extra hanc carnem, quae fovetur in gremio Mariae Virginis'.[88] If we are right in our conclusion that in the *extra calvinisticum* Calvin is concerned with the *caro vera* and, behind that, with the *spes resurrectionis*, we not only cannot be satisfied with a sharp rejection of the 'non capax' thesis, we also have to go much further, coming to a complete inversion: 'infinitum capax finiti'. The eternal Son, appointed as Mediator

---

[84]*Die Glaubenslehre der evangelisch-reformierten Kirche*, Zürich 1847, ii. 291 ff.

[85]*Realencyklopädie für protestantische Theologie und Kirche*, 3rd. ed. Leipzig 1898–1908, iv. 54.

[86]'Über die Herkunft des Satzes "Finitum infiniti non capax",' Festschrift Carl Stange, *Zeitschrift für systematische Theologie*, xvi (1939), 503. The only quotation, taken from a translation by Mercator, is not convincing.

[87]Th. L. Haitjema, *De Heidelbergse Catechismus als klankboden en inhoud van het actuele belijden onzer kerk*, Wageningen 1962, 124; cf. 122.

[88]Scholion in Esaiam, iv. 6; *WA.*, 25, 107. The theological motive is the exclusion of 'Schwärmerei'; the religious motive is the *certitudo salutis*. Luther formulates the intention of his '*non extra carnem*' in 1537 in a few words: 'Periculosum est sine Christo mediatore nudam divinitatem velle humana ratione scrutari et apprehendere . . .', *WA.*, 39, i. 389. Karl Barth is, if possible, even more radical in his criticism of the '*extra*': 'Post Christum aber, in Rückblick auf die Inkarnation, kann diese Aussage nur eine Aussage des Unglaubens sein', *Die christliche Lehre nach dem Heidelberger Katechismus*, Munich 1949, 71. Though Calvin's order of battle is different, he combats, together with Luther, a *theologia gloriae*. L.G.M. Alting von Geusau appropriately refers to 'der Bundestheologie, . . . die in ihrer Dynamik ein Gegengift gegen einseitige Tendenzen zugunsten einer "theologia gloriae" bedeutet . . .', *Die Lehre von der Kindertaufe bei Calvin*, Bilthoven/Mainz 1963, 199.

before the beginning of the world, has in the Incarnation not diluted or compromised the reality of our humanity; he has identified himself with it by becoming 'flesh of our flesh'. Already in 1536 Calvin expressed the idea in the short formula: 'Ea conditione carnem induit Christus, cui incorruptionem quidem et gloriam dedit, naturam et veritatem non abstulit'.[89] Whereas in medieval theology a symbiosis proved to be possible between the *extra scholasticum* and the dangerous contrast between *purus homo* and *deus homo*, the *extra calvinisticum* threw up a barricade between the two, not by a philosophical negation, but by a theological assertion: 'infinitum capax finiti'.

4. *ETIAM EXTRA LEGEM*

Looking back over the road we have travelled, we can see that the *extra calvinisticum* is not a peculiar Calvinistic idiosyncrasy in christological matters. In the first place, the *etiam extra carnem* is not an 'extra' peculiar to Calvin's theology, but had been taught by the *doctores veteri* and *moderni* (the 'sophists') alike. Contrary to the usual assumptions, Calvin is on this point not 'less medieval' than Luther and the Lutheran spokesmen for the *ubiquitas* doctrine. In the second place, and of more concern, the *extra calvinisticum* is not an isolated phenomenon but rather, like the top of an iceberg, only the most controversial aspect of a whole 'extra' dimension in Calvin's theology: *extra ecclesiam, extra coenam, extra carnem, extra legem, extra praedicationem*.[90] The word 'etiam' is important because it underscores the fact that the primary and basic concern is the very *ecclesia, coena, caro, lex* and *praedicatio* itself. To these means of revelation and redemption God has committed himself, since he has attached his *promissio* to them. Here again Calvin stands in a scholastic tradition which, rooted in St. Augustine, was unfolded by Johannes Duns Scotus and became the central theme in late medieval theology, expressed as God's commitment to the established order, *de potentia ordinata*.[91] It would, after Calvin, find its way as Federal theology *via* the Netherlands and Britain to Puritan New England.

---

[89]*OS.*, i. 142.

[90]Because of the necessity for an extensive discussion of medieval sources, we cannot here extend our scope to Calvin's interpretation of the *concursus* or *influxus generalis*. Whereas the whole cosmos is seen by him as a *machina* (cf. *Inst.*, I. xvi. I; *OS.*, iii. 188, 4; *Inst.*, I. xvii. 2; *OS.*, iii. 204, 34 etc.) created and sustained by God, Calvin's *concursus*, unlike that of Thomas, Scotus or the nominalists, implies a sustaining action, a '*providentia in actu*' (*Inst.*, I. xvi. 4; *OS.*, iii. 192, 20 f.), '*etiam extra machinam*': '... puerile cavillum est eam [gubernationem] includere in naturae influxu ... Deum sua gloria fraudant ... qui Dei providentiam coarctant tam angustis finibus ...,' *Inst.*, I. xvi. 3 (*OS.*, iii. 190, 31–192, 3).

[91]Cf. my *Spätscholastik und Reformation*, i. 163 ff., and passim.

Here we should note, however, the vital differnce between God as '*exlex*' and as ruling '*etiam extra legem*'. In late medieval theology the *potentia ordinata* is the (for natural reason unaided by grace) unpredictable, but reliable (because of God's fidelity to his commitments!) expression of God's very being, the compound of his will, justice and goodness. In contrast, the *potentia absoluta* covers the whole range of possibilities which God has not chosen to realise, the realm in which God is *exlex*, because its limits are not defined by his will, justice and goodness, but by the law of non-contradiction, accessible to, and indeed the basic axiom of, human reason.

Though deviating on points of content, e.g. election, justification, sanctification – and on all these points much closer than Luther to Gregory of Rimini – Calvin has retained the structure of the *potentia ordinata* as the realm of God's free but dependable commitment. It is in the understanding of the *potentia absoluta* that we discern a radical difference. Whereas the *potentia absoluta* served in late medieval theology to show that there is no *necessitas rei* and hence no *necessitas dei* for commitments *de potentia ordinata*, with Calvin the *potentia absoluta* does not indicate what God could have done but what he actually does.[92] For Calvin the *potentia* (or *voluntas*) *absoluta* is not the realm of the *Deus exlex* but of God's rule *etiam extra legem*; it is the *ius mundi regendi nobis incognitum*'.[93] Calvin asserts a rule of God which is absolute and inscrutable: 'Non illa quidem absoluta voluntas de qua garriunt sophistae, impio profanoque dissidio separantes eius iustitiam a potentia'.[94] God's rule *per legem* and the rule *etiam extra legem* are both to the same extent an expression of his very being, his power and his justice: 'The will of God is always "reiglee en toute perfection et droicture"'.[95] Furthermore, the realm of *extra legem* is characterised exactly by the fact that it is not accessible to human reason and hence not at all defined by the law of non-contradiction:

---

[92]*Inst.*, I. xvii. 2 (*OS.*, iii. 205, 12–19).

[93]*Inst.*, I. xvii. 2 (*OS.*, iii. 205, 12f.); cf. '. . . quamvis nobis absconditae sint rationes' (ibid., 205, 19). 'Vray est qu'il ne fait pas cela d'une puissance absolue, comme disent les Papistes': *SC.*, i. 605, 19 f. 'Deum enim exlegem qui facit, maxima eum gloriae sua parte spoliat, quia rectitudinem eius ac iustitiam sepelit. Non quod legi subiectus sit Deus, nisi quatenus ipse sibi lex est. Talis enim inter potentiam eius ac iustitiam symmetria et consensus, ut nihil ab ipso nisi moderatum, legitimum et regulare prodeat': *CO.*, viii. 361; cf. sermon on Job xxxii. 2: *CO.*, xxxiv. 339.

[94]*OS.*, iii. 205, 15–17. Calvin gives here a fair description of the *exlex* character of the late medieval *potentia absoluta*. I disagree here with the interpretation of Wendel (op. cit., 93), who claims that the Scotist *potentia absoluta* 'est limitée . . . par la nature même de Dieu, c'est-à-dire par sa bonté'. This limitation, however, applies to the *potentia ordinata*. The principle of non-contradiction abstracts from what God actually decided to do. It is, therefore, not this principle which 'empêche Dieu de décider le contraire de ce qu'il avait décrété précedément', but the reliability of God's covenant *promissiones, decreta, pacta*.

[95]*SC.*, i. 605, 20; cf. ibid., 473, 5.

'How could we honour God [through reliance upon him] if he would reveal to us all his secrets and if we would know more than the angels in paradise.'[96]

Although it is clear that much research remains to be done before the exact relation of Calvin to the preceding theological tradition can be established with a sufficient degree of certainty and precision, the above has indicated the positive and negative relation of Calvin to one central theme in late medieval theology. Calvin's 'extra' dimension also provides a basis of comparison and contrast with Zwingli and Luther. Though beyond the scope of this Calvin-orientated article, one way to pursue such a line of investigation would be to inquire whether Zwingli's usage of the same 'etiam' categories might be distinctive in view of the absence of Calvin's emphasis on the inscrutable character of God's 'extra' operation – an emphasis that comes through in Zwingli's doctrine of providence, his view of the election of great heathen, and his less 'demonic' and, hence, more optimistic notion of the State.

Comparing Calvin with Luther, one would have to pursue each 'etiam' separately to come to an approximately valid non-partisan conclusion. The most basic observation to be made is that Luther so radically breaks with the two orders of late medieval theology that, in so far as Calvin continues this tradition in his 'extra' dimension, Luther is 'less medieval' than Calvin. In regard to the *etiam extra legem*, the contrast might be defined in some such way that the inscrutable 'extra' dimensions of Calvin are regarded by Luther as the very heart of God's order *de potentia ordinata*, where God reveals himself in Christ *'sub contrario'*.

In the *etiam extra ecclesiam* we find it is Calvin who has the more 'progressive' or modern vision of God's rule thrusting beyond the heart of the justified sinner and beyond the boundaries of the Church, to encompass the State, Society and the whole created order. In so far as this view is ultimately concerned with the doctrine of the *sessio* and the *etiam extra carnem*, it is obvious that it does have repercussions for a Catholic understanding of the Incarnation. We have tried to point out that the *etiam extra carnem* is not related to Nestorianism and it is not a threat to the reality of the Incarnation, but actually functions to emphasise that the eternal Son of God became 'flesh of our flesh'. Yet, with Luther the Christmas joy is more abundant, because in Christ God has fulfilled all his promises and revealed his last word and his very being. With Calvin we encounter the medieval theme that in Christ the *umbra* of the Old Testament has been replaced by the *veritas* of the New Testament. Part of God's promises have been fulfilled, but much more is still

---

[96]*SC.*, i. 605, 22–4.

in store. God has revealed himself, but certain 'secrets' are not to be shared till the final manifestation of Christ in glory.

The impressive universal scope of the 'extra' dimension of Calvin's theology presents such a challenge to contemporary thought that it cannot afford either simply to ignore it or to reject it out of hand. To those who seek for the Catholicity of Christian thought 'etiam extra Calvini opera' – hence *secundum mentem Calvini*! – Calvin's political testament, formulated less than two years before his death and expressed in his search for God's 'etiam extra' path in history, offers a 'theology of patient resistance' as a viable alternative to a utopian 'theology of revolution', utopian in that it disregards 'the establishment' – of God.

XI

CALVIN'S CRITIQUE OF CALVINISM

The theme of our conference as it was originally announced reads: "Reformed Higher Educational Institutions as a Bulwark for the Kingdom of God – Present and Future". And here I am, representing a professedly neutral institution, intended as a bulwark for progress, not for the Kingdom of God, a university soon to celebrate its 500th birthday, and an Institute which does not deal with the present or future, but with the Middle Ages and the Reformation.

1. SCHOOLS OF CALVIN INTERPRETATION

In approaching our theme it is important to realize in advance that we hail from different worlds, not merely from different continents. Our common bond, however, is that all of us regard this theme as rich – and perhaps even loaded. Let us tax and test this bond to the utmost in challenging each others' presuppositions with the same fearless openness for truth which characterized the Genevan Reformer. The shortest procedure for flushing out these presuppositions may well be a sketch of the history of Calvin research which can then be used as a compass to reveal where each of us stands. Such a sketch is of necessity tendentious; it must ignore the more subtle variations and nuances. Furthermore, this task is a baffling one because of the large number of publications to be taken into account. Dr Kempff's impressive *Bibliography of Calviniana: 1959–1974*, which has recently been published simultaneously in Potchefstroom and Leiden, gives eloquent testimony to the present state of affairs. Since Professor Nauta of the Free University prepared a more comprehensive discussion of recent Calvin research, for the last Calvin Research Congress in Amsterdam, I can limit myself here to what interests us most, the prevailing schools of Calvin interpretation. Enumerated as concisely as possible, I discern six basic types of schools.[1] In the second part of this paper I shall indicate six issues in recent

---

[1]For a more elaborate discussion of the first three schools I refer to Henry Van der Goot: "A typology of 'Schools' of Calvin interpretation in 19th and 20th century theology", prepared for the University of Toronto.

scholarship which I regard as relevant to our theme of Calvin's challenge today.

1. *The classical interpretation.* Even today we can admire the excellent and comprehensive grasp of Calvin's dogmatic treatises and of the *Institutes* which was demonstrated by this school. Yet, not unlike the German phenomenon in the field of theology when a reference to Scripture is replaced by a quotation from Martin Luther, the classical school interprets Calvin with the pretence of presenting the Word of God itself. Valid theology is the reiteration of the positions described – and hence prescribed! – by Calvin.

2. *The confessional interpretation.* Calvin is here viewed through the eyes of the Westminster Confession and the Heidelberg Catechism: Scripture and predestination are seen to be the foci of his thought.

3. *The neo-orthodox school:* God's revelation is only grasped in Christ, *through* Scripture, *reflected* in predestination as the covenant of grace ("Gnadenwahl").

4. *The Dutch school* (Abraham Kuyper and Herman Bavinck) stresses the sovereignty of God over all cultural manifestations of life; hence it includes a theology of society, of the state, of politics, yet not in the strict sense of the word 'theocratic'. In his assessment of "Kuypers idee eener christelijke cultuur" Arnold A. van Ruler – a true theocrat, the first to design a theology of hope – concludes that "de gemeene gratie uitsluitend de functie van een leer van het aanknopingspunt in het groot heeft".[2] For Kuyper common grace has the sole purpose of keeping the machine of creation running and of preparing for the conversion and rebirth of individuals, and not, as Van Ruler sees it, of sanctifying creation as the one and single eschatological (= now) purpose of God. We shall return to this point in our discussion of decisive points in contemporary Calvin research.

5. *The anti-orthodox interpretation.* Not characteristic of any particular group, this view builds upon some mythical and some historical elements. Calvin is described as the enemy of culture and of research; as the murderer of Servetus, and the manager of police-controlled Geneva.

---

[2]Nijkerk, s.a. (1943), p. 147.

6. *The historical school.* Originally in reaction against all forms of 'theological' interpretation, this school has made giant strides by trying to abstain from taking sides in the debate around the right 'use' of Calvin. It thus has little patience with any form of confessional interpretation, be it orthodox or neo-orthodox; yet, *de facto*, it has done the most to answer the theses implied in the anti-orthodox view. The humanist Calvin, the editor of Seneca's *De Clementia*, is shown not to be a passing stage but to determine: 1. his interests in education; 2. his concern with affairs of state – and both with a wide ecumenical horizon.

Although all six 'types' or 'schools' are represented in this country, I expect that most will recognize themselves as belonging to the position I have described as II, III or IV. Yet the most substantial and lasting contribution in the last type described has been made by a South African, André Malan Hugo (†1975) who not only provided us with a fine study entitled *Calvijn en Seneca*[3] (Groningen, Djakarta, 1957), but also – together with the English translator of the *Institutes*, Ford Lewis Battles – an exemplary critical edition of *De Clementia* (Leiden 1969).

We mention André Hugo at the end of our presentation of the six types partly so that we may honour a scholar who died too young, leaving a sizable gap which will not be readily filled in the ranks of international scholarship; and partly because his work shows in a nutshell the extent to which the historical method can help us to demythologize long-venerated Calvin images and allow us ultimately to bridge the divide between the dogmatic and the anti-dogmatic types, orthodox. veneration and anti-orthodox iconoclasm.

2. EMBATTLED FRONTS

In the second part of this presentation I intend to touch upon some six key issues which deserve our renewed attention in view of new developments in the field.

Their common scope can perhaps best be designated as "Calvin's critique of Calvinism". As a minority group in a divided world Calvinism is understandably inclined to assume an apologetic attitude, to defend the status quo and to point proudly to the achievements of Calvinistic principles and institutions. An assessment of these from the perspective of Calvin may

---

[3]*Calvijn en Seneca. Een inleidende studie van Calvijn's Commentaar op Seneca, De Clementia, anno 1532* (Groningen-Djakarta, 1957).

well provide us with a platform for reorientation, renewal and reform. At the same time, recent research may show us the limits of Calvin himself, the respects in which he was a product of circumstances that do not apply to us to the same extent.

1. *Calvin the Humanist.* Calvin as the twenty-three year old commentator on Seneca is not yet the reformer; as a matter of fact he does not yet see how reform can be possible without detriment to the Church Catholic. Indeed, as Hugo has pointed out, the writing of this commentary may well have "served him as a temporary means of escape from the inner conflict occasioned by that problem".[4] But in 1532, in this year before his conversion – and that means before his discovery that the Church Catholic is a community of believers obedient to the Word of God rather than to the Church of Rome – Calvin placed himself within the ranks of those who were called the *humanistae theologizantes*. In a decree of 22 August 1523 the Sorbonne had decided "that all new translations of the Bible made from Hebrew or Greek into Latin are of no value to the Church, but are pernicious", a decree confirmed by the Council of Trent in 1546. In 1532 Calvin opted for the 'resourcement', the renewal, of the human spirit through a return to the classical sources; in 1533 he found that 'resourcement' in the Scriptures as providing access to the life of the Spirit. For us it is important to realize that it would be a mistake to play off Calvin the Christian against Calvin the humanist scholar. From the very beginning stages of Calvinism these two, the campaign against obscurantism and the struggle for reform of the Church, belong together. Where they are separated an orthodoxy is bound to emerge which is blind to the needs of the mind and the body alike, and which isolates the Church from society.

2. *Renewal and the unity of the Church.* Calvin could very well have become a 'Nicodemian' or an Erasmian Christian, avoiding confrontation (*tumultus!*) and trusting that the new culture of the mind would suffice for the reform of the Church. But Calvin, the student of law – even in that last year of 1532–1533 in Orleans – carried his legal interests over into his study of theology and continued to be concerned with structures, organizations, and politics as the *Ordonnances Ecclésiastiques*, as well as Book IV of the *Institutes*, document.

In a very bold and – to use an epithet seldom applied in a scholarly presentation – a wise chapter in the volume honouring Paul Oskar Kristeller

---

[4]Ed. cit., p. 16*

on his 70th birthday, William Bouwsma discusses the tension between two thrusts in humanism, between two spirits in one breast, the 'Stoic' and the 'Augustinian' elements: on the one hand, Stoic consolation and on the other, the Augustinian call for social engagement and political action.[5] Writing on "The Two faces of Humanism," he observes: "Humanists of more Stoic tendencies, like Erasmus, seem to have been less likely to become Protestants than those of the more Augustinian kind. But the more Augustinian humanist might end up in either the Protestant or Catholic camp".[6]

Why then did the 'Augustinian' Calvin end up becoming a Protestant? As the letter to Cardinal Sadoleto (1539) indicates, it was the doctrine of the Church which proved to be the decisive locus in Calvin's conversion. Augustinianism, Biblical studies and the freedom-hungry protest against tyranny as voiced in his commentary on Seneca were all factors in this event. Yet most importantly in this combination the possibility of opting out of reality and sublimating the longing for the renewal of the Church through the escape hatch of the invisible Church was excluded. For the whole Reformed tradition it was to be of lasting importance that for Calvin it is impossible to participate in the Church Catholic of the Creed without also participating in the local, visible church. At times in Calvinism this had led to an overemphasis on the completeness of the *ecclesia loci*. But Calvin's vision blocks that kind of cheap ecumenism which transcends and escapes the hardships of urgent Church reform by reference to the invisible Church universal. Within this context, Calvinism has striven from its very beginning for Church unity in faith and order. But it should be added that at the same time Calvinism has suffered most from splinter groups which absolutized their own local traditions. Here I discern the greatest threat resulting from the presently disrupted relations between the churches in this country and the World Council of Churches. Withdrawal can be the necessary attitude over against a political organization, but in the Church of Christ the truly Calvinist course of action is to hang on, to seek communion and to provide for communication – till the partner-churches proceed with *de facto* excommunication ... much to their own detriment.

3. *Conversion and the Eucharist.* A point of seemingly less immediate interest

---

[5]*Itinerarium Italicum. The Profile of the Italian Renaissance in the Mirror of its European Transformations.* Dedicated to Paul Oskar Kristeller, H.A. Oberman with Th. A. Brady, Jr., eds. (Leiden, 1975), pp. 3–60; 56.
[6]*Ibid.*, p. 57.

concerns the two short Latin words "subita conversio". Calvin himself uses
these words in his Psalms Commentary of 1559 to describe his conversion.[7]
Taken literally, the phrase means "sudden conversion" and it has been
understood in this sense by those inside and outside of the Reformed family
who have seen in Calvin the divinely ordained prototype of conversion.
True conversion has to be sudden, datable; yes, indeed, 'clockable', and those
who could not pass this test could not be part of the fold.

Much research has been directed toward understanding this reference to
conversion. As a matter of fact, the right understanding of the even smaller
word 'subita' could have helped decisively in this effort. Throughout the
Middle Ages "subita" marks the work of God in contrast to the time-
consuming achievements of man. "Subita" does not refer to a time-unit but
to the divine agent, to the vertical in contrast to the horizontal dimension.

Conversion is, as Calvin likes to emphasize, penance, which in turn is the
work of the Holy Spirit and which lasts as long as life itself. Conversion
cannot be made into an emotional proof of one's belonging to the elect.

The gravest danger, however, proved ultimately not to lurk in a
Calvinistic pietism – which I am prepared to defend as the precious core of
the Reformed tradition – but in an elitest doctrine of the Eucharist. The
"Half-Way Covenant" of the New England Puritans documents[8] how this
central sacrament and focal point of Calvin's theology is debased into a sign
of progress by the Saints, instead of being regarded as the necessary food for
faith – essential for survival on the trek towards the Kingdom.

4. *Scripture and Science.* In 1973 when the 500th anniversary of the birth of
Nicolaus Copernicus was celebrated, numerous articles utilized the occasion
in order to associate Calvin – as well as the other reformers – with
obscurantism. The words of Thomas S. Kuhn were readily quoted:
"Protestant leaders like Luther, Calvin and Melanchthon led in citing
Scripture against Copernicus and in urging the repression of Copernicans".[9]

R. Hooykaas has eloquently opposed the myth that Calvin mentioned and
rejected Copernicus in his works: "There is no lie so good as the precise and
well-detailed one and this one has been repeated again and again, quotation
marks included, by writers on the history of science, who evidently did not

---

[7] "... subita conversione ad docilitatem subiget". *Opera Calvini* 31, 22 f. Cf. most recently A.
Ganoczy: *Le jeune Calvin, Genèse et Evolution de sa vocation réformatrice* (Wiesbaden, 1966), pp.
272–304; 298.

[8] Cf. E. Brooks Holifield: *The Covenant Sealed: The Development of Puritan Sacramental Theology in
Old and New England, 1570–1720* (New Haven, 1974).

[9] *The Copernican Revolution* (Cambridge, Mass., 1957), p. 196.

make the effort to verify the statement. For fifteen years, I have pointed out in several periodicals concerned with the history of science that the 'quotation' from Calvin is imaginary and that Calvin never mentioned Copernicus; but the legend dies hard".[10]

The reason why the voices of historians were not heeded is no mystery: it was not Calvin, but some of his followers who construed a division between faith and science which tragically forced many a Christian to choose between the two. Hence Calvinists themselves gave credence to this distortion of Calvin.

As far as Calvin himself is concerned, in his commentary on Genesis he points out that the story of creation does not compete with "the great art of astronomy", but that it accommodates and speaks in terms of the unlettered *idiota*, the man in the street.[11]

In the name of Calvin much damage has been done in later times and stores of faith and piety have been sacrificed on the altar of rigid inspiration theories. Calvin's exegetical methods were far ahead of his own time; it is our task not to fall behind him today.

5. *Piety between Theology and Moralism.* My fifth point concerns that elusive entity best called the spirituality of Calvin. It has often been argued that the influence of the *Devotio moderna* (Collège de Montaigu and its principal since 1483, John Standonck!) extends through Calvin far into the Reformation period. And indeed, it is remarkable that a strong Calvinism flourished most easily in those areas which had been centers of the *Devotio moderna:* the Low Countries and the Rhine valley.

However, the more we are able to grasp what it is that characterizes this late medieval reform movement, the better we are able to see some of the unique characteristics in Calvin's spirituality. While *devotio* stood for the fundamental disposition toward God as well as for an attitude of contempt toward the world, *pietas*, Calvin's key word, represents the life of sanctification through intensive involvement in this world. It is another sign of ecumenical openness in Reformation studies[12] that it was a Jesuit, Father Lucien Richard, who made a major advance at this point.[13] He argued that

---

[10]*Religion and the Rise of Modern Science* (Edinburgh-London, 1972), p. 121.

[11]*Calvini Opera* 23, 20–22.

[12]Cf. R. Bäumer: 'Das katholische Calvinbild" in H. Jedin, R. Bäumer: *Die Erforschung der kirchlichen Reformationsgeschichte seit 1876 und 1931* (Darmstadt, 1975), pp. 99–102. This survey omits the significant contribution by L.G.M. Alting van Geusau: *Die Lehre von der Kindertaufe bei Calvin* (Bilthoven-Mainz, 1962).

[13]*The Spirituality of John Calvin* (Atlanta, 1974).

Calvin's *pietas* stands for a new spirituality which is grounded in his understanding of the knowledge of God. Piety is derived simultaneously from the Word of God and the internal testimony of the Spirit. "Simultaneously" is to be underlined since the Spirit provides that inwardness and personalism which are also to be found in the *Devotio moderna*. But at the same time this form of spiritual communication is set in the objective context of theological knowledge of the Word of God. Thus, Calvin's spirituality differs radically from that of the *Devotio moderna* on three essential points. First, it is a spirituality of service to the world; second, it is based on a new Word-directed religious epistemology; and third, it stresses the inner unity of Christian life and theology.[14] In those instances where Calvin's spirituality has given way to Calvinist morality, it has relapsed into the ethics of the *Devotio moderna*. We have a clear task of reform ahead of us here.

6. *Calvinism and the democratic ideal.* Our last point concerns the most highly sensitive issue of the relation of Calvin to democracy.[15] I begin here with some quotations which document the radically opposing interpretations which have been applied to Calvin: "Calvin was as much in favor of the democratic form as he was opposed to the monarchical one".

"Calvin was a great propagator of democracy, but he energetically tried to ward off its abuses and excesses". – Emile Doumergue.

"From considering only his political ideas, one would certainly be entitled to conclude that Calvin was not a precursor of modern democracy". – Charles Mercier.

"If Calvin mixes democratic elements with aristocratic constitutions, he nevertheless remains completely foreign to the dogmas of modern democracy ... he does not believe either in popular sovereignty or in individual rights". – Marc-Edouard Chenevière.

"'Democracy' is not a term in favor with Calvin. He does not advocate democracy in and of itself: he fears its deterioration into anarchy. Nevertheless, his notion of 'aristocracy tempered by democracy' approaches our conception of representative democracy. It becomes unmistakably clear in his later writings that the ideal basis of government is election by the citizens". – John T. McNeill.

---

[14]Cf. the appreciative review by Joseph N. Tylenda, S.J. in *Theological Studies* 36 (1975), pp. 356–358.

[15]For literature see the excellent workbook by Robert M. Kingdon and Robert D. Linder: *Calvin and Calvinism. Sources of Democracy?* (Lexington, 1970). The following quotations here on p. XIII f.

The key to this apparent mystery of these many interpretations is held once again by the historian who is prepared to place Calvin in the context of his time. In this respect I find most validity in the conclusion of Hans Baron: "Calvinist political thought helped more than any other tendency of the time to prevent a full victory of absolutism, and to prepare the way for constitutional and even republican ideas".[16] Michael Walzer has demonstrated the transition from the sixteenth to the seventeenth and following centuries: "What Calvinists said of the saint, other men would later say of the citizen: the same sense of civic virtue, of discipline and duty lies behind the two names".[17]

Yet, in working through the sources I have come to the conclusion that Calvin's own ideal of state government is best described in terms of a form of aristocracy. This is marginally tempered by group interests to which we may validly assign the name 'democratic expressions'. To put it crudely, either reiterating Calvin or using his political views as a blueprint for contemporary society would spell sheer tyranny,[18] the very state of affairs he had challenged as a young humanist. As was the case in each of the previous five aspects I have discussed, this shows us once again that to reiterate is the surest path to distortion.

Allow me to conclude with a quotation from Calvin himself, a statement which bears reiteration because it reveals the living centre of his piety and faith. In his sermon on II Sam. v. 4 – 'David reigned forty years' – Calvin notes that this was by no means an unchallenged or uninterrupted reign: 'ce n'a pas esté du premier coup en perfection'. Then he proceeds ('c'es pour nous, que cecy est ecrit') to apply this text to the contemporary rule of God, giving here his religious testament, which is characteristically at the same time a political eschatology:[19]

"... though we know that God rules, yet insofar as our Lord Jesus Christ is hidden in him and his very reign is hidden in this world, it has no splendour but it is little esteemed, indeed rejected by the majority. Therefore, we should find it not at all strange that our Lord Jesus Christ, though he has been established as King by God his Father, does not at all have the authority among men which He is entitled to. Furthermore, today there is no certain

[16]"Calvinist republicanism and its historical roots", *Church History* 8 (1939), pp. 30–41; 41.
[17]*The Revolution of the Saints* (Cambridge, Mass., 1965), p. 2.
[18]Basil Hall's words of caution – à propos W. Fred Graham: *The Constructive Revolutionary: John Calvin and his Socio-Economic Impact* (Richmond, Va., 1971) – are to the point: "... he (Calvin) was a party to reducing the small amount of democratic procedure allowed". "A sixteenth-century miscellany", *The Journal of Ecclesiastical History* 26 (1975), pp. 309–321; 318.
[19]*Supplementa Calvinia* I, 105, 34–36. Cf. my "The 'Extra' Dimension in the Theology of Calvin", *The Journal of Ecclesiastical History* 21 (1970), pp. 43–64; 46. See above Chapter 10.

time limit ('terme' = kairos) indicated to us. When we see the rule of our Lord Jesus Christ is limited, since there is only a handful of people who have accepted him, and since for every one city which has received the Gospel there are large countries where idolatry rules, – when we thus see that the rule of Jesus Christ is so small and despised according to the world, let us cast our eyes upon this figure which is given us here (in the rule of David), and let us await the end (terme), which God knows, for it is hidden to us. I say, let us await in patience, till his Kingdom is established in perfection and God gathers those who are dispersed, restores what is dissipated and sets in order what is confused."

"... let us not desist, as far as it is in us, from praying to God that he advances and enlarges (his Kingdom) and that each man apply to this with all his power; and let us allow ourselves to be governed by him in such a way that he is always glorified in us, both in life and in death."

This text stems from Calvin's last sermons which were not published till recently and hence virtually 'lost'. Yet with this testament of faith and piety in hand, we are in a position to answer the question raised in the theme of this conference quoted at the beginning of this paper.

Whenever and wherever Calvinism did not 'await in patience' but rather sought to establish its own 'kingdom' by force, repression and domination, it did not serve the kingdom of God but its own cultural and political achievements. Calvin's vision of perseverance 'amidst idolatry' is at once critique of and encouragement for the reformed community around the world: ecclesia reformanda quia reformata.

XII

QUO VADIS, PETRE?
TRADITION FROM
IRENAEUS TO HUMANI GENERIS[1]

This year's topic for the Dudleian Lecture is designated as 'Roman Catholicism and Protestantism', or, in the words of the statutes, this lecture is intended: 'For the detecting and convicting and exposing the idolatry of the Romish church, their tyranny, usurpations, damnable heresies, fatal errors, abominable superstitions and other crying wickednesses in their high places; and finally, that the Church of Rome is that mystical Babylon, that man of sin, that apostate church, spoken of in the New Testament.'

Although this latter description is longer in form it is not for that reason less clear. Though the 'damnable heresies' and 'crying wickednesses' may seem to many in this era of 'brotherhood' and 'dialogue' anachronistic, they serve to remind us that Rome and Reformation confront each other with the claim to divine truth and the charge of heresy. This consideration does not lead us to ridicule the intensified conversations between Protestant and Roman Catholic theologians and laymen in our time. On the contrary, we are thus forced to acknowledge the dimension of ultimate seriousness in the presuppositions, form and progress of this dialogue.

Secondly, from all corners of the *oikoumenè* there is abundant evidence of the acute awareness that Holy Scripture can only be properly interpreted in fellowship with the Brethren and in communion with the Fathers. Protestants have not lost the vision that this includes the Roman Catholic denomination. Though indeed they have to be regarded as heretics, heresies have throughout the ages been the major stimulants to call the Church to its task of timely and true, that is, catholic interpretation of the Revelation witnessed to in Holy Scripture.[2]

Therefore when we take up today the issue of the relation of Scripture and tradition, we are not only interested in establishing the demarcation line

---

[1]The Dudleian Lecture for 1961–2, given at Harvard University on 3rd May 1962.

[2]Tertullian, *De Praescriptione Haereticorum* 4.7; ed. Scriptores christiani primaevi (Hagae Comitis, 1956), p. 11.

between Rome and Reformation on this point, as if this were an apologetic rearguard action. We see this discussion as subordinated to and instrumental for a clarification of what from the vantage point of the Reformation tradition can and has to be said regarding the authority of Holy Scripture, its inspiration, canon and its relation to the tradition of the Church.

We have selected the issue of tradition since this by its very nature presupposes that bond between history of Christian thought and systematic theology which allows us to learn from the past the true dimensions of our present division. We shall in a first part try to sketch the development of the relation of Scripture and tradition by singling out some of the more crucial junctures in this history. This will afford us the opportunity to touch on the lively contemporary discussion on the relation of Scripture and tradition in the early Church, the Middle Ages, the Reformation, and Counter-Reformation. In a second part we shall deal with some systematic questions arising out of the historical material.

The sixteenth century witnessed bitter polemics concerning the source and norm of the Church's knowledge of God's revelation. Traditionally this is described as the clash of the *sola scriptura*-principle with the Scripture *and* tradition-principle. Ironically enough both groups, the Reformers and those who would soon come to be known as Roman Catholics, accused each other of undermining the purity and authority of the Word of God. The Reformers pointed to the 'ecclesiastical' or 'human traditions' as accretions and distortions of the Gospel preserved in Holy Scripture. Spokesmen for the Counter-Reformation accused the Reformers of arbitrary interpretation of Scripture and of a break with the tradition of the Church. In both cases reliance on human authority is said to interfere with the rule of obedience to Holy Scripture.

It is our contention that this confusing clamour of rival claims can only be unravelled if we abandon the time-honoured assumption that the issue before us is that of 'Scripture *or* tradition'. What we are confronted with is rather the clash between two concepts of tradition. To discover the precise content and connotations of these two concepts, we shall have to start our investigation in the early Church at the time of gradual reception of the canon.

1. THE EARLY CHURCH

(1) There is in our time a convergence of scholarly opinion that Scripture and tradition are for the early Church fathers in no sense mutually exclusive: kerygma, Scripture and tradition coincide entirely. Let us mention some

significant characteristics of what has been called the coinherence of Church and Scripture.

(a) It is in the living, visible Body of Christ, inspired and vivified by the operation of the Holy Spirit that Scripture and tradition coinhere. This is not merely to be understood in the one-level sense of the coinherence of source and interpretation. That is certainly also the case. But this coinherence is first of all the result of the understanding that both Scripture and tradition issue from the same source: the Word of God, Revelation.

(b) They find, therefore, their common basis in the operation of the Holy Spirit through whom the content of the Christian faith, and the act of participation, translation and thus interpretation by the Apostolic Church, the *fides quae creditur* and *fides qua creditur*, are held together.

(c) Tradition is not understood as an addition to the kerygma contained in Scripture, but either as the handing down of that same kerygma in living form, or as Revelation itself. This implies for the Fathers the explicit denial of extra-scriptural tradition. 'To appeal to revelatory truth apart from Scripture is [for Irenaeus] heretical gnosticism',[3] and only within the Church can this kerygma be handed down undefiled. While Clement of Alexandria acknowledged a charismatic apostolic succession independent of the official episcopal line,[4] Irenaeus seems to identify the transmission of the truth with episcopal succession[5]; yet inasmuch as the Apostles did not institute other Apostles but bishops, however, the episcopal witness is a *derived* witness,[6] and its function is to preserve the integrity and totality of the original Apostolic witness. To this end the canon was formed.

Though Scripture and Church coinhere, they do not form an amorphous organism; that which differentiates the Church is its instrumental task of receiving and conserving the writings of the Apostles which were

---

[3]E. Flesseman van Leer, *Tradition and Scripture in the Early Church* (Assen, 1953), p. 191. See further J. N. Bakhuizen van den Brink, 'Traditio im theologischen Sinne', *Vigiliae Christianae* 13 (1959), pp. 65–86. O. Cullmann, '"Kyrios" as Designation for Oral Tradition concerning Jesus', *Scottish Journal of Theology* [*S.J.T.*] 3 (1950), pp. 180–97.

[4]*Strom.* VI.63; VI.106. It has been suggested that Clement would here betray gnostic influences; G. Bardy, *La théologie de l'Eglise. I. De St. Clément de Rome à St. Irénée* (Paris, 1945), p. 176.

[5]'... qui cum episcopatus successione charisma veritatis certum secundum placitum Patris acceperunt.' *Adv. Haereses* 4.26; ed. W. Wigan Harvey (Cantabrigiae, 1857), II, p. 236. Damien van den Eynde points out that this *charisma* is not 'une grâce distincte de la vérité, sorte d'infaillibilité'. It is the truth of revelation itself. *Les normes de l'enseignement crétien dans la littérature patristique des trois premiers siècles* (Gembloux, 1933), p. 187.

[6]Oscar Cullmann, 'Scripture and Tradition', in *S.J.T.*, 6 (1953), p. 116. Also in *Christianity Divided*, ed. Callahan, Oberman, O'Hanlon (New York, 1961), pp. 7–33.

understood to contain the original kerygma *in toto*.[7] We should therefore beware of an emphasis on the creative contribution of the post-apostolic Church in accepting certain writings as apostolic.[8]

(*d*) In the fourth place we should mention the relation of oral and written tradition. Form criticism has made us more aware than ever that the Scriptures received by the Church as canonical are the product of a geographically differentiated and complex interplay of oral and, later, written traditions. From a modern Roman Catholic point of view two observations have been made: (1) The canon constitutes a snapshot of a multidimensional living tradition. (2) This document from the early Church has the drawback of being only two dimensional. A petrified part of the living tradition can by its very nature convey only the teaching and not the fulness of the life of the Church. The distinction current in contemporary Roman Catholic theology between *real* and *verbal* tradition makes this observation explicit.[9]

(2) Let us turn with these questions in mind to the two earliest 'Latin' Fathers writing towards the end of the second century, Irenaeus and Tertullian. Irenaeus insists that the rule of faith or the rule of truth (*regula fidei* or *regula veritatis*) is faithfully preserved by the apostolic Church and has found multiform expression in the canonical books.[10] There is an unbroken continuation of the preached kerygma into Holy Scripture. One may speak here of an 'inscripturisation' of the apostolic proclamation which in this written form constitutes *the* foundation and cornerstone of the faith.[11]

Irenaeus' enumeration of Rome's oldest bishops' list is usually cited in discussions of early Church polity as evidence of episcopal authority in this

---

[7] J. N. Bakhuizen van den Brink, 'Tradition und Heilige Schrift am Anfang des dritten Jahrhunderts', in *Studia Catholica* 9 (1953), p. 109. Cf. J. R. Geiselmann: 'Dass in der Heiligen Schrift nur ein Teil des apostolischen Kerygmas niedergelegt sei, davon weiss wohl die gegen die Reformation gerichtete Kontrovers-Theologie, davon weiss aber die Theologie der Vaeterzeit nicht.' 'Die Tradition', ed. Feiner, Truetsch, Boeckle, *Fragen der Theologie heute* (Einsiedeln, 1957), p. 97.

[8] cf. the statement of Ives Congar: 'Il [Tavard] semble en effet leur attribuer une position très proche de celle de certains apologistes catholiques du XVIe siècle, e.g. pour lesquels c'est *l'Eglise* qui a discerné les livres inspirés. Mais les Pères anciens faisaient du Canon une tradition *apostolique* que l'Eglise gardait et transmettait seulement.' 'Sainte Ecriture et sainte Eglise', in *Rev. Sc. Ph. et Theol.* 44 (1960), p. 82, n. 8.

[9] Peter Lengsfeld, *Ueberlieferung. Tradition und Schrift in der evangelischen und katholischen Theologie der Gegenwart* (Paderborn, 1960), esp. p. 70.

[10] *Adv. Haeres.* II.41.4; *ed. cit.*, I, p. 352.

[11] 'Non enim per alios dispositionem salutis nostrae cognovimus, quam per eos per quos Evangelium pervenit ad nos: quod quidem tunc praeccnaverunt, postea vero per Dei voluntatem in Scripturis nobis tradiderunt, fundamentum et columnam fidei nostrae futurum.' *Adv. Haeres.* III.1.1, ed. cit. II, p. 1.

period.[12] In our context it is important to note that episcopal succession does not for Irenaeus constitute a channel of oral tradition which would stand alongside Scripture as a second source of revelation. The successors of the Apostles were given rather the task of preserving the rule of faith in the interval between the first public preaching of the kerygma till the time that this truth, which can be traced back through them to the Apostles, is available 'for all openly and without ambiguity'.[13] In other words Irenaeus uses his list of episcopal succession to insist on the complete identity of the rule of faith received by the Apostles from Christ himself and the rule of faith received in his own day in the apostolic writings, transmitted by these bishops.

It has recently been shown that this *regula fidei*, this rule of faith, as used by Irenaeus, Tertullian and Clement of Alexandria is not to be understood as the rule *for* faith as it would later be interpreted to mean in the phrase: 'The Church is the rule for (of) faith.' The *regula fidei* is the rule constituted *by* faith or truth: the historical facts of God's action in creation and redemption.[14]

This rule of faith is not to be regarded as authoritative interpretation of Holy Scripture nor to be identified with the Creed. The Creed is a confession of the historical reality of the acts of God in creation and redemption; and instead of being interpretation of Scripture, the rule of faith is revelation itself, the backbone and structure of Holy Scripture.

The differentiation of verbal and real tradition cannot be maintained here since Irenaeus, true to the Johannine tradition, identifies truth and reality. The reality which we perceive with our eyes is the same as the reality to which the kerygma pertains.[15]

The antimontanistic thrust as well as the antignostic thrust is obvious. Inspiration is not to be regarded as new revelation. The operation of the Holy Spirit does not create a new 'internal word' but guarantees the participation of the canonical books in the *ephapax* character of God's unique action in creation and redemption.

Furthermore, revelation is not regarded as a secret doctrine meant to initiate its believers into timeless truths transcending secular history. The acts of God contained in the rule of faith are a group of clearly indicated historical facts in the most secular sense of the word. Truth is reality; not an

---

[12]ibid., III.3.1ff; *ed. cit.*, II, pp. 8ff.

[13]*Adv. Haeres.* II.27.2; *ed. cit.*, I, p. 348.

[14]Bengt Haegglund, 'Die Bedeutung der "regula fidei" als Grundlage theologischer Aussagen', *Studia Theologica* 12 (1958), pp. 1–44.

[15]Haegglund, op. cit., p. 15.

other-worldly reality but the right understanding and illumination of man's own reality.

Finally one may add that in Irenaeus' understanding of the relation of Christ, the Apostles and the canonical writings, there is no place for a so-called 'creation' of the canon by the Church. The act of the Church is an act of acknowledgment, of 'conserving' and 'receiving' of the rule of faith which now in manifold form expresses a series of historical acts of God.

One comes perhaps closest to the understanding of those involved in the defence of the (developing) canon if one describes the formation of the canon as the corporate re-enactment of the action of the individual Christian who received the Christian Creed at his baptism: the canon is entrusted to the custody of the Church.

(3) With Tertullian and Cyprian we find a marked insistence on the decisive difference between the tradition of God, preserved in the canon and the traditions of man (*consuetudines*). Tertullian became well known for his contrasting of Athens and Jerusalem, Academy and Church, heretics and Christians.[16] This statement has usually been understood as expressing an anti-philosophical and anti-intellectualistic bias on Tertullian's part. Etienne Gilson goes even so far as to construct from among the Fathers and Doctors a 'Tertullian family' which he characterises as suspicious of natural reason and philosophy.

It is Gilson's contention that these Tertullians hold that 'Revelation had been given to men as a substitute for all other knowledge, including science, ethics and metaphysics'.[17] Gilson finds here 'the crude statement of an absolute opposition between religious faith in the word of God and the use of natural reason in matters pertaining to Revelation'.[18] In conclusion Gilson shows his disenchantment when he exclaims: 'Had the Middle Ages produced men of this type only, the period would fully deserve the title of Dark Ages....'[19]

Indeed it is true that Tertullian calls Aristotle 'miserable' and regards Aristotle's works as the arsenal of the heretics.[20] But if we take a closer look at Tertullian's medical prescription against the fever of heresy it proves not to be directed against 'the use of natural reason in matters pertaining to

---

[16]'Quid ergo Athenis et Hierosolymis? quid academiae et ecclesiae? quid haereticis et christianis? nostra institutio de porticu Solomonis est...' *De Praescript. Haer*, 7.9; *ed. cit.*, p. 14.

[17]*Reason and Revelation in the Middle Ages* (New York, 1938), p. 5.

[18]op. cit., p. 11.

[19]op. cit., p. 15.

[20]'miserum Aristotelen! qui illis dialecticam instituit, artificem struendi et destruendi...' *De Praescript. Haer*. 7.6; *ed. cit.*, p. 13.

Revelation' but against that kind of philosophy which forms a second source of revelation in addition to the writings of the Apostles, and which would thus undercut the sufficiency of Holy Scripture. No, Tertullian insists, without adding any of their own inventions, the apostolic authors have faithfully recorded what they received from Christ. Nothing is to be added to this deposit of faith. Anathema, therefore, even on the angel from heaven who would bring another Gospel![21]

Tertullian does not attack the secular sciences as such but the diabolical perversion of the mysteries of faith by knowledge of God which relies on extra-scriptural sources.[22] Such a perversion takes place when reason is employed to exegete God's nature and action directly, by-passing Holy Scripture, and this actually means a reliance on human invention. Thus used, reason is *temerarius*, rash, undisciplined.[23]

Proper use of reason is the adequate exegesis and interpretation of Holy Scripture. A disciplined use of reason will show that the text in Math. 7.7 'Seek and you will find' is not an injunction to find more and other truths than those received from the churches, the Apostles, from Christ and ultimately from God.[24]

For this period it is not relevant to insist on the usual distinction between active tradition, the act of handing down, and passive tradition, the content of what is handed down. Tradition corresponds at once with *fides quae*, the articles of faith and *fides qua*, the act of faith. Tradition is not only divine in content and origin but also in its providential path through history. This can be stressed to the degree that we are forced to translate *traditio* with 'revelation' and *tradere* with 'to reveal'.[25]

---

[21]'nobis vero nihil ex nostro arbitrio inducere licet sed nec eligere quod aliquis de arbitrio suo induxerit. apostolos Domini habemus auctores qui nec ipsi quicquam ex suo arbitrio quod inducerent elegerunt sed acceptam a Christo disciplinam fideliter nationibus adsignaverunt. itaque etiamsi angelus de caelis aliter evangelizaret anahema diceretur a nobis.' *De Praescript. Haer.* 6.3–5; *ed. cit.*, p. 12. Cf. ibid., 24.5–25.9; *ed. cit.*, p. 29f; ibid., 29.6; *ed. cit.*, p. 33.

[22]*De Praescript. Haer.* 4.1; *ed. cit.*, p. 44.

[23]'Hae sunt doctrinae hominum et daemoniorum prurientibus auribus notae de ingenio sapientiae saecularis quam Dominus stultitiam vocans stulta mundi in confusionem etiam philosophiae ipsius elegit; ea est enim materia sapientiae saecularis, *temeraria interpres* divinae naturae et dispositionis.' *De Praescript. Haer.* 7.1–2; *ed cit.*, p. 13.

[24]'interim ex fiducia probationis praevenio admonens quosdam nihil esse quaerendum ultra quod crediderunt, id esse quod quaerere debuerunt ne 'quaerite et invenietis' *sine disciplina rationis* interpretentur.' *De Praescript. Haer,* 9.6; *ed. cit.*, p. 17. Cf. the expression *ratio verborum* in 9.2.

[25]In connexion with the 'Traditionskette' retraced to God himself, Bakhuizen van den Brink observes: 'Gott kann also das Subjekt von *tradere* sein: das Verbum bedeutet dann offenbaren und das Substantiv *traditio*: goettliche Offenbarung.' *Art. cit.*, p. 71. Cf. *De Praescript. Haer.* 21.4; *ed. cit.*, p. 25 and 37.1; *ed. cit.*, p. 41.

2. THE PERIOD OF TRANSITION

(1) Moving now into the fourth and fifth centuries, we should remember at least two points which are typical of the pre-augustinian concept of tradition. (i) The immediate divine origin of tradition together with the insistence on a clearly circumscribed series of historical acts of God in the rule of faith or the rule of truth; (ii) The rejection of extra-scriptural tradition.

It has been the thesis of Father George Tavard in his widely hailed book, *Holy Writ or Holy Church*,[26] that there is an unbroken continuity between patristic and medieval theology, at least till the early decades of the fourteenth century. At that time, however, an organic understanding of the relation of Scripture and Church is undermined by two new currents of thought: (*a*) one which opposes the Scriptures to the Church in admitting the possibility that only a remnant in the visible Church would be obedient to Scripture; (*b*) one which introduces the concept of post-apostolic and oral traditions and raises the Holy See to the dignity of judge of post-apostolic revelation. 'The breaking asunder of that synthesis [the coinherence of Scripture and Church] in the fourteenth century not only made the Church subservient to Scripture or the Scripture ancillary to the Church. It furthermore threw open a door, by way of a supposed superiority of the Church over Holy Writ, to the idea that the Church had her own revelation, independent of that which the Apostles recorded in their writings.'[27]

The curialistic extremists under the canon lawyers mark, according to Tavard, a departure 'from medieval classicism. Living authority replaces both Scripture and its traditional interpretation.'[28]

The opposing group, however, is equally responsible for destroying the classic patristic and medieval vision. Those who make the canon of Scripture the sole criterion of catholic truth accept a cleavage in the economy of salvation. They stand by a restrictive notion of Scripture and thus pave the way for a complete denial of the Church. 'From this to the doctrines of the Reformation there is only a difference of degree.'[29]

The Council of Trent, according to Tavard, rejected both deviations from the classical view.

While presently we shall come back to the problem of the proper interpretation of Trent's understanding of the sufficiency of Holy Scripture,

---

[26]New York, 1959.
[27]op. cit., p. 36.
[28]op. cit., p. 39.
[29]op. cit., p. 40.

we have first to point out that the shift which Tavard locates in the later Middle Ages can be traced back at least to the very beginning of the Middle Ages.

A new concept of tradition is formulated in the East by Basil the Great (c. 330–370) and is propagated half a century later also in the West by Augustine. In Basil's treatise *On the Holy Spirit* the relation of Scripture and tradition is discussed in connexion with certain liturgical traditions of the Church. We meet here for the first time the idea that the Christian owes equal respect and obedience to the written *and* to the unwritten ecclesiastical traditions, whether they are contained in the canonical writings or in the secret oral tradition handed down by the Apostles through succession.[30]

We find this Basilian passage quoted by canonists of the early Middle Ages. The great expert in canon law, Ivo of Chartres (d. 1116), refers to it to insist on equal reverence for scriptural and for extra-scriptural oral traditions.[31] Most important is that Gratian of Bologna (d. 1158) copied this passage from Ivo, and incorporated it into his highly influential *Decretum* from where it found its way to the textbooks of both canon lawyers and theologians.[32]

(2) For the canon lawyer, then, the two-sources theory is established: canon law stands on the two pillars of Scripture and tradition. The same does not seem to apply to the medieval doctor of theology. For him theology is the science of Holy Scripture. Notwithstanding the constant and growing temptation to comment on the comments, Holy Scripture is understood as the authoritative source which stands in judgment over the interpretation of later commentators.[33] The term 'sacred page' for theology is indicative for this close relationship.

Nevertheless there is in the history of medieval theology a development which corresponds with the one originating with Basil the Great. Due to a lack of an extensive monographic literature we are not yet in a position to draw the lines of development without some hesitation. But the medieval understanding of the famous words of Augustine on the relation of Scripture and Church presents an excellent key to the history of this relationship.

---

[30]*De spiritu sancto* 66; *P.G.* 32.188. Basil's *ta men . . . ta de* is rendered here as *alia . . . alia*.

[31]*P.L.* 161.283; here instead of *alia . . . alia: quasdam . . . quasdam*.

[32]*C.I.C.*, Decreti I d. XI, c. V; ed. E. Friedberg, *Corpus Iuris canonici* (Leipzig, 1879), p. 23. Gratian follows Ivo in the use of *quasdam . . . quasdam*.

[33]'Innititur enim fides nostra revelationi apostolis et prophetis factae qui canonicos libros scripserunt, non autem revelationi si qua fuit aliis doctoribus facta.' Thomas Aquinas, *Summa Theologica* I, q. 1, art. 8, ad 2.

While repeatedly asserting the primacy of Scripture,[34] Augustine himself does not contrast this at all with the authority of the Catholic Church: '. . . I would not believe the Gospel, unless the authority of the Catholic Church moved me.'[35] The Church has a practical priority; her authority as expressed in the direction-giving meaning of *commovere*, to move, is an instrumental authority, the door which leads to the fulness of the Word itself.[36]

Towards the end of the Middle Ages the Church came to understand Augustine's statement of the practical authority of the Church as though it implied a metaphysical priority. The moving authority of the Church becomes in late medieval versions the Church's approval or creation of Holy Scripture.[37] Until our own time, Augustine's words have even been taken to imply that Holy Scripture is a contingent product of the life of the Church.[38]

The lonely voice of the fourteenth-century Augustinian Gregory of Rimini (d. 1358), protesting that Augustine meant merely a practical priority of the Church over Scripture, went unheard. For him the authority of the Church should be compared with the function of the miracles of Jesus to prompt His contemporaries to heed His words.[39]

If it were only for this passage, we would not hold Augustine to be the western counterpart of St. Basil. He himself, however, has to shoulder some of the responsibility for later misunderstandings of the passage which we discussed. Whereas Irenaeus and Tertullian taught the sufficiency of Scripture, with Augustine we meet with an authoritative extra-scriptural oral tradition. While on the one hand the Church 'moves' the faithful to discover the authority of Scripture, Scripture on the other hand refers the

---

[34]'. . . deferens ei [Holy Scripture] culmen auctoritatis.' *De serm. dom.* I.ii.32; *P.L.* 34.1245.

[35]'. . . ego vero evangelio non crederem, nisi me catholicae ecclesiae commoveret auctoritas', *Contra ep. fund.*, 5; *C.S.E.L.* 25.197, 22.

[36]'. . . credamus divinae auctoritate quam voluit esse in scripturis sanctis de filio suo', *De agone christiano* 10.11; *C.S.E.L.* 41.113, 6.

[37]cf. Gerson, '. . . nulla auctoritas cuiuscunque scripturae aut doctoris habit efficaciam ad aliquid probandam . . . nisi inquantum doctrinae ecclesiasticae congrueret aut ab ecclesia approbaretur. . . . Non solum doctrinae doctoris sed etiam ipsi canonice praefert [Augustinus] ecclesiam.' *Opera Omnia*, ed. E. Du Pin (Antwerpiae, 1706), I. 463A. For a more extensive documentation see my discussion in *The Harvest of Medieval Theology* (Harvard University Press, 1963), p. 378–412.

[38]Adhemar d'Ales interprets Augustine's 'ego vero evangelio non crederem. . .' as implying that '. . . la foi et la religion pourraient subsister sans l'Ecriture', 'La tradition chrétienne dans l'histoire', *Etudes par des Pères de la Compagnie de Jésus* 44, (1907) p. 12.

[39]'. . . non tamen aliquod principium primum cuius fides causa esset ut evangelio crederetur.' Prol. I *Sent.* q 1, art 2; fol 3 F; ed. Venice 1522. Compare with this the observation of one of the participants at the Trentine Council, Petrus de Soto: '. . . magis traditione agendum esse quam scriptura, quae traditio in cordibus hominum servatur, quaeve habetur ex ore apostolorum: neque Scripturis crederemus, nisi ecclesiae auctoritas id nobis praeciperet. . .' *C.T.* VIII. 743f.

faithful back to the authority of the Church with regard to a series of issues with which the Apostles did not deal in writing.[40] Augustine refers here to the validity of baptism by heretics, Abelard later to mariology, Bonaventure to the *filoque*, Aquinas to the form of the sacrament of confirmation and the veneration of images.[41]

One cannot claim here a neat distinction between doctrinal truths and liturgical practices: the *lex orandi* proves also here to be the *lex credendi*. The fourteenth-century theologians who believed the immaculate conception of the Virgin Mary to be among the catholic truths based one of their main arguments on the celebration of the feast of the conception of Mary.

(3) One may wonder whether the *Commonitorium* of Vincent of Lerins, written in the early part of the fifth century, has perhaps influenced the spread of this concept of tradition. His thesis is that the Catholic Church must hold to that which has been believed everywhere, always and by everyone.[42] This seems to allow for an authoritative extra-biblical tradition.

When we read this statement in its context we find that Vincent does not reject the material sufficiency but the formal sufficiency of Holy Scripture. He insists that Holy Scripture needs to be interpreted by the Church since the heretics from Novation to Nestorius all advanced their own exegeses of biblical passages.[43] But the sole purpose of interpretation is preservation: the faith once declared to the Apostles has to be protected against change, which represents for him perversion.[44] He does not find the guarantee of proper biblical exegesis in a secret oral tradition traceable to the Apostles themselves, but in the explicit consensus of the Fathers which provides a safeguard against arbitrary interpretation. Vincent echoes the words of

---

[40]'Apostoli autem nihil quidem exinde praeceperunt: sed consuetudo illa ... ab eorum traditione exordium sumpsisse credenda est, sicut sunt multa quae universa tenet ecclesia, et ob hoc ab apostolis praecepta bene creduntur, quamquam scripta non reperiantur.' *De Bapt.* 22.36; *P.L.* 43.192.

[41]For references see Paul de Vooght, *Les sources de la doctrine chrétienne* ... (Bruges, 1954), pp. 13–32. De Vooght does not indicate that the appeal to the *sine scripto traditiones* does not merely go back to Abelard (d. 1142), but all the way to Augustine.

[42]'In ipsa item catholica ecclesia magnopere curandum est ut id teneamus quod ubique, quod semper, quod ab omnibus creditum est...' *Commonitorium* II.3; ed. by Reginald S. Moxon (Cambridge, England, 1915), p. 10.

[43]'Hic forsitan requirat aliquis: Cum sit perfectus scripturarum canon sibique ad omnia satis superque sufficiat, quid opus est ut ei ecclesiasticae intelligentiae iungatur auctoritas? Quia videlicet scripturam sanctam pro ipsa sui altitudine non uno eodemque sensu universi accipiunt, sed eiusdem eloquia aliter atque aliter alius atque alius interpretatur, ut paene quot homines sunt, tot illinc sententiae erui posse videantur. Aliter namque illam Novatianus ...' *Commonitorium* II.2; *ed. cit.*, p. 7f.

[44]'... quisquis ille traditam semel fidem mutare temptaverit, anathema sit.' *Commonitorium* VIII.13; *ed. cit.*, p. 33.

Tertullian[45] when he warns against rashness and lack of disciplined reason on the part of the biblical exegete.[46]

It is important to note that Vincent does not want the interpretation of the Church, which one may call the exegetical tradition, to become a second tradition or source apart from Holy Scripture. Even the truly catholic Fathers are in principle *magistri probabiles*, teachers whose utterances are probable but do not yet constitute proof.

Their opinion does not represent the deposit of faith till five requirements have been met: (1) not one or two but all Fathers must hold it (*non unus aut duo tantum sed omnes pariter*); (2) the consensus has to be exactly the same (*uno eodemque consensu*); (3) their opinion should be openly and explicitly formulated (*aperte*); (4) repeatedly advanced (*frequenter*); and (5) continuously held, written and taught (*perseveranter tenuisse, scripsisse, docuisse*).[47]

It has often been suggested that Vincent directs his *Commonitorium* against the sharp edges of Augustine's doctrine of grace and predestination.[48] This may indeed have been Vincent's ulterior motive. But one does not tax the sources too heavily when one concludes that Vincent here directs his concept of authoritative exegetical tradition primarily against a two-sources theory. And this one can trace back not only to St. Basil but also to St. Augustine.

3. MIDDLE AGES – REFORMATION – COUNTER REFORMATION

(1) If for clarity's sake we call the single exegetical tradition of interpreted scripture 'Tradition I' and the two-sources theory which allows for an extra-biblical oral tradition 'Tradition II', we may say that both Tradition I and Tradition II find their medieval partisans. It is hard to say whether the conscious elaboration of Tradition II is to be understood as a reaction against the further development of Tradition I, in the sense in which the decisions of the Council of Trent are often claimed to be a mere reaction

---

[45]Notwithstanding Tertullian's defection Vincent calls him 'apud Latinos nostrorum omnium facile princeps'. *Commonitorium* XVIII.24; *ed. cit.*, p. 75.

[46]'... paucorum temeritati vel inscitiae,' *Commonitorium* III.4; *et. cit.*, p. 12.

[47]'Tunc operam dabit, ut conlatas inter se maiorum consulat interrogetque sententias, eorum dumtaxat, qui diversis licet temporibus et locis, in unius tamen ecclesiae catholicae communione et fide permanentes, magistri probabiles exstiterunt; et quicquid non unus aut duo tantum sed omnes pariter uno eodemque consensu aperte frequenter perseveranter tenuisse scripsisse docuisse cognoverit, id sibi quoque intellegat absque ulla dubitatione credendum.' *Commonitorium* III.4; *ed. cit.*, p. 13.

[48]*Commonitorium* X.15 refers to 'excellentes quaedam personae in ecclesia constitutae res novas catholicis adnuntiare [sinuntur]'; cf. Berthold Altaner, *Patrologie* (Freiburg, 1958), 5th edition, p. 418.

to the writings of the Reformers. One can make a good claim that the reaction worked rather the other way around.

In the fourteenth century, at the time of the Western Schism and the final phase of the struggle between Pope and Emperor, the canon lawyer is in high demand and, if we may believe the many bitter comments by doctors of theology, he not only equals but surpasses the theologian in status both at the papal *curia* and the royal courts.[49] Though with varying degrees of happiness, both curialists and conciliarists necessarily draw extensively on the decretes and decretals. Under these circumstances, it is not surprising that the canon-law tradition starts to feed into the major theological stream and that the Basilean passage can become a truly theological argument. Gabriel Biel, 'the last of the scholastics' (d. 1495), finds in St. Basil the warrant for investing the unwritten traditions with the same apostolic authority as the Scriptures.[50]

In the development from Augustine to Aquinas and into the later Middle Ages, theologians find an increasing number of doctrinal points on which Holy Scripture is silent.[51] The last verse of the Fourth Gospel provides the explanation for the 'silence' or material insufficiency of the Scriptures: 'But there are many other things which Jesus did; were every one of them written, I suppose that the world itself could not contain the books that would be written' (John 21.25, RSV).

Whereas the canon lawyer in the Basilean line is straightforward in positing two sources requiring equal respect, it appears that the scholastic doctors of Scripture develop the oral tradition in a more subtle way. In theory the material sufficiency of Holy Scripture is upheld long after it has

---

[49]Without any doubt this growth in status has a financial basis. Cf. Astrik L. Gabriel, *The College System in the Fourteenth-Century Universities*, Baltimore s.a. [1962], p. 3. Myron P. Gilmore calls attention to the bitter criticism of the canon lawyers – the 'Bartolist position' – on the part of early humanists, e.g. on the part of Lorenzo Valla in 1433. 'The Lawyers and the Church in the Italian Renaissance', *The Rice Institute Pamphlet* 46 (1960), pp. 136–54; p. 139f. An investigation of the relation between the attack on the Basilean position and on the Bartolist position may lead us to the basis of the – temporary – alliance between Humanism and Reformation.

[50]Gabriel Biel, *Expositio* [1488] (Basel, 1515), *Lect.* 2B; 'In libro de sancto spiritu, capite XXIX affirmat [Basilius] apostolicum esse etiam non scriptis traditionibus inhaerere . . .'; John Driedo, *De ecclesiasticis scripturis et dogmatibus libri quatuor* (Louvain, 1533), fol. 259r C; see John L. Murphy, *The Notion of Tradition in John Driedo* (Milwaukee, 1959), p. 60. Cf. my review in *Theologische Zeitschrift* 17 (1961), pp. 231–4.

[51]'Si aliqua veritas est catholica aut est dicenda catholica quia a deo revelata, vel quia in scripturis divinis contenta vel quia ab universali ecclesia recepta vel sequitur ex illis vel aliquo illorum quae sunt divinitus revelata et in scripturis divinis inventa et ab ecclesia universali recepta vel quia a summo pontifice approbata.' *Dialogus* I.2.12; ed. Goldast, *Monarchia romani imperii* II (Frankfurt, 1614), p. 419.

been given up in actuality. The key term of this development is the word 'implicit' and the history of this term is one of increasing loss in content. When then finally the two propositions – 'Holy Scripture implicitly says' and 'Holy Scripture silently says' – are equated, the exegetical concept of Tradition I has fully developed into what we called Tradition II. The Basilean passage borrowed from canon law then provides the rational and patristic authority.

We have to keep this history in mind if we want to understand the Council of Trent and contemporary Roman Catholic theology on this point since they stand both historically and systematically in the line of Tradition II.

(2) When we turn now to the medieval history of Tradition I, it is self-evident that it is impossible to trace this concept in the early part of the Middle Ages. In this period Tradition I and Tradition II cannot be clearly separated for the simple reason that those who *de facto* hold Tradition II, continue to declare themselves for the material sufficiency of Holy Scripture.[52] But once such nominalists as Occam, Gerson, d'Ailly and Biel had prepared the way for Trent's reception of Tradition II, the historian is in a better position to discern the contrasts. So long as his eyes are still blinded, however, by the traditional contrast of Scripture versus tradition, he is bound to err in his interpretation of the sources.[53]

Fourteenth- and fifteenth-century theologians like John Wyclif, John Hus and Wessel Gansfort do not defend Scripture against tradition, but they pose Tradition I against Tradition II. True to Vincent's five restrictive requirements for an authoritative tradition, they defend along with the material sufficiency of Holy Scripture the authority of the exegetical tradition whenever there is a common and explicit witness of the Fathers, in particular of the four great doctors of the Church: Augustine, Jerome, Ambrose and Gregory.

By way of summary of this position it may be said that these representatives of Tradition I do not deny the importance and validity of episcopal succession for the preservation of the truth. They indeed regard

---

[52]Josef Finkenzeller regards Duns Scotus as the turning point: 'Die Tradition als urspruengliche und unabhaengige Quelle der christlichen Lehre ist in der Zeit, in der Skotus die Sentenzen kommentiert, unbekannt.' 'In der Betonung der apostolischen Tradition im Sinne einer ueber die Hl. Schrift hinausgehenden Ueberlieferung hat unter den Theologen der Hochscholastik Duns Skotus den entscheidenden Durchbruch gewagt ...' *Offenbarung und Theologie nach der Lehre des Johannes Duns Skotus,* (Muenster i. W., 1960), p. 74f.

[53]The most recent example is the well-documented essay by Michael Hurley, S.J., 'Scriptura sola: Wyclif and his Critics', *Traditio* 16 (1960), pp. 275–352, who fails to understand Wyclif because he presses Wyclif under the yoke of the either-or of Scripture or Tradition. See esp. op. cit., p. 278f.

tradition as the execution of the custodian's task of the Church. But in contrast to those holding to Tradition II, the emphasis falls rather on the *successio doctorum* than on the *successio episcoporum*.

Understandably, their attack is especially directed against the canon lawyers, the most conspicuous bearers of Tradition II. But they also sharply react against the theologians' practice of building tradition into the 'silent places' of Holy Scripture. In its strongest forms this criticism may lead to the deformation of Tradition I. Here perhaps we stand at the cradle of what is usually called biblicism, which *via* some branches of the Radical Reformation and of seventeenth-century orthodoxy comes down to us in the form of fundamentalism.

On the other hand Wessel's emphasis on the operation of the Holy Spirit and his clear distinction of Gospel and Law brings him closer, indeed remarkably close to the positions of Luther, Melanchthon and Calvin. Though the positions of these Reformers should be differentiated, their consensus appears in its contrasts with Tradition II.

(3) With these few words we have already suggested that as much as Trent represents Tradition II, the Reformers represent Tradition I. And our observation concerning the later Middle Ages can be applied to the period of Reformation and Counter-Reformation: We are here not confronted with the alternatives of Scripture and tradition but with the clash of two radically different concepts of tradition: Tradition I and Tradition II. After a sketch of the concept of tradition in its Lutheran and Tridentine formulation we hope to have reached a vantage point which allows us to make a few observations bearing on the contemporary scene.

There can be no doubt that one of the most essential aspects, even the very foundation of Luther's theology is the *sola scriptura* principle. We have seen that this principle as such does not necessarily imply a rejection of the so-called coinherence of Church and Scripture. It indicates, however, that Luther's theological enterprise does not move within the context of Tradition II, but in that of Tradition I.

How Luther himself understood and applied this principle, however, is not easy to define in a few words.[54] One thing is clear: even if one is not willing to distinguish between a 'young Luther' and an 'old Luther', one has

---

[54] A few of the most important secondary sources are: Otto Scheel, *Luthers Stellung zur Heiligen Schrift* (Tuebingen, 1902); Paul Althaus, 'Gehorsam und Freiheit in Luthers Stellung zur Bibel', in *Luther* 9 (1927), pp. 74ff; Heinrich Bornkamm, *Das Wort Gottes bei Luther* (Berlin, 1933); J. M. Reu, *Luther and the Scriptures* (Columbus, Ohio, 1944), Ragnar Bring, *Luthers Anschauung von der Bibel* (Berlin, 1951); Regin Prenter, *Spiritus Creator* (Munich, 1954); H. Oestergaard-Nielsen, *Scriptura sacra et viva vox: Eine Lutherstudie* (Berlin, 1957).

to concede that it is misleading to rely primarily on evidence drawn from the pre-1522 period. Luther is one of the most striking examples of a 'contextual' theologian. Especially in his letters and treatises, he does not write in a well-balanced, scholarly *summa*-style by reasoning from principle to application. His writing is in the pastoral sense of the word 'opportunistic', *situationsbedingt*, and the interpreter therefore has to take the relevant situation into serious consideration to discover the underlying principles.

One does not need therefore to fall back on a development-hypothesis to point out that in the first five years Luther's primary purpose was to contrast the teachings of Holy Scripture with papal decisions. In the first period Luther emphasises the authority of Scripture over against 'human additions'. Though in 1518 – at the time of his Augsburg debate with Cajetan – he is still willing to accept papal decrees as secondary sources, he has already rejected the Tradition II concept.[55] The burning of the books of canon law at the Elster Gate at Wittenberg, 10th December 1520, is the eloquent symbol and seal of the rejection of a tradition which we found indeed to have been carried by canon lawyers.

Shortly afterwards he says: '. . . Christ's teaching and the pope's teaching will not and cannot rule jointly; for Christ wants to be sole Master, as he says in Matthew 23.8'[56] This would be a consistent theme in Luther's theology throughout his life. But faced with the rising tide of the Radical Reformation, he expressed more clearly what the *sola scriptura* principle positively stands for.

It is in this context that we have to search for an answer to the question as to whether he does not go so far as to reject along with Tradition II also

---

[55]J. N. Bakhuizen van den Brink has noted – and criticised – that the editors of the *Konkordienbuch* (Goettingen, 1930), refer in the index from 'Tradition' to 'Menschensatzungen'. 'La tradition dans l'Eglise primitive et au XVIᵉ siècle', in *Revue d'Histoire et de Philosophie religieuses* 36 (1956), pp. 271–81; p. 272f. Cf. the same in *The Book of Concord* (Phila., 1959), *sub voce*. When one checks the references it appears that not 'tradition' but 'traditions' are meant, which are identified with 'observances': 'We gladly keep the old traditions set up in the Church because they are useful and promote tranquility, and we interpret them in an evangelical way [by] excluding the opinion that holds that they justify.' *Apology of the Augsburg Confession*, art. XV; *ed. cit.*, p. 220. As proved to be the case with Gabriel Biel, these traditions are understood to be rites and observances. They are rejected as the work of 'summists and canonists', who neglected 'more important things such as faith, consolation in severe trials, and the like'. *Augsburg Confession*, XXVI; *ed. cit.*, p. 66. These statements do not refer to what we termed Tradition I. J. T. Mueller's *Die symbolischen Buecher der evangelisch-lutherischen Kirche* (Stuttgart, 1860), p. 971, accurately refers to 'traditiones'. Cf. for the same use *The Little Catechism*, of 1556 'approved by . . . John Calvin', answer 4 in *The School of Faith*, ed. T. F. Torrance (New York, 1959), p. 239. This plural 'traditiones' cannot surprise us in view of the fact that – except at two places in the *Acta* – this was the disputed term at the Council of Trent.

[56]*Evangelium von den zehn Aussaetzigen*, 1521; *W.A.* 8, 341.

Tradition I; whether he does not reject along with the authority of the Pope, the authority of the Church as the only realm within which the Scriptures are properly understood.[57]

The scepticism to which the private right to interpret the Bible may lead is well worded by Caspar Schwenckfeld circa 1530: '... the Papists damn the Lutherans; the Lutherans damn the Zwinglians ...; the Zwinglians damn the Anabaptists and the Anabaptists damn all others.'[58]

Luther is keenly aware of the threat of individualism; he protests that the hermeneutical principle should not be found in the individual listener or reader, but in Scripture itself: 'Therein God is most interested that his Holy Word is purely preserved from additional teaching by man. But this Word cannot survive unless one sees Christ as the sole *Bauherr* (Master builder) and acknowledges him as such. If that is missing, unity is absent and Babel the necessary result.'[59]

Two years later Luther stresses that this understanding of Christ as *Bauherr* is handed down by the Church – and for Luther that means by the visible Church: 'It [the Christian Church] is the Mother that begets and bears every Christian through the Word of God...; where Christ is not preached, there is no Holy Spirit to create, call, and gather the Christian Church, and outside it no one can come to the Lord Christ.'[60]

In 1528 in a treatise on rebaptism, Luther makes very clear that his interpretation of the *sola-scriptura* principle does *not exclude, but includes* a high regard for Tradition I: 'We do not act as fanatically as the sectarian spirits. We do not reject everything that is under the dominion of the Pope. For in that event we should also reject the Christian Church. ... Much Christian good, nay, all Christian good, is to be found in the papacy and from there it descended to us.'[61]

---

[57]It is Tavard's contention that Luther replaced the authority of the Church with an arbitrary principle of his own liking. He would even boast in 'my own doctrine' as Tavard repeats five times. Op. cit., pp. 81–96. Joseph Lortz defines Luther's position as 'ein starker Dogmatismus im Subjektivismus, ein subjektiver Dogmatismus'; *Die Reformation in Deutschland* (Freiburg, 1941[2]), I, p. 401. Albert Ebneter mentions the first passages where Luther comments on Augustine's 'Ego non crederem ...': *W.A.* 2.430; 2.429–432; 2.288; cf. 2.263. 'Luther und das Konzil', *Zeitschrift fuer Katholische Theologie* 84 (1962), pp. 1–48; p. 19, note 122. Tavard's conclusion should be compared with the statement: 'Das Urteil ueber die Wahrheit steht bei den Theologen, die in der Schrift ihr Fundament haben', ibid., p. 13.

[58]*Corpus Schwenckfeldianorum* (Leipzig, 1907ff), IV.818; quoted by Paul L. Maier, *Caspar Schwenckfeld on the Person and the Work of Christ* (Assen, 1959), p. 29.

[59]1527. *W.A.* 24.233.

[60]1529. *Large Catechism*, II.3. *Book of Concord*, ed. Th. G. Tappert (Philadelphia, 1959), p. 416. One wonders how Tavard could feel that it is typical only for Calvinism that 'in an inseparable diptych the Word guarantees the Spirit, and the Spirit is the criterion of the Word'. Op. cit., p. 99.

[61]*W.A.* 26.146f.

This 'descent' is the tradition of the living Word, of the same Word which is contained in Holy Scripture, yet in a different mode. There are not two sources for the Christian faith, but two modes in which it reaches the Church in every generation: Holy Scripture and the *viva vox evangelii*. This position would not be restricted to that of Luther, but would form a constitutive part of the 'heritage of the Reformation'. The Calvinistic *Confessio Helvetica posterior* (1562) would succinctly formulate this with the words: 'praedicatio verbi dei est verbum dei':[62] The preaching of the word of God is *the* word of God.

(4) While the Reformation understood the coinherence of Scripture and Church in terms of Tradition I, the Council of Trent in its fourth session gave its sanction to the coinherence of Scripture and Church in terms of Tradition II. Herewith it finalised a development which we sketched above. The Christian faith reaches the Church in every generation through two sources, the written and unwritten tradition. The extra-scriptural apostolic tradition should be regarded with 'equal esteem and loving respect' as the canonised written tradition, Holy Scripture. This implies not only that the *successio fidei* coincides with the *successio episcoporum*, but also an elevation of the authority of the Church above the authority of the canonised apostolic kerygma. Due to the restrictive localisation of the *testimonium internum* of the Holy Spirit in the teaching office of the Church, Holy Scripture can only have a mute authority.[63]

Here we should mention Joseph Geiselmann's effort to reinterpret this decision of the Council of Trent in such a sense that it really would have abstained from a decision in favour of Tradition II.[64] Father Tavard has

---

[62]Cap. I.1; in E. F. K. Mueller, *Die Bekenntisschriften der reformierten Kirche* (Leipzig, 1903), p. 171. For the understanding of tradition in the sixteenth century see J. N. Bakhuizen van den Brink, *Traditio in de Reformatie en het Katholicisme in de zestiende eeuw* (Amsterdam, 1952). For Melanchthon see the very important dissertation by Peter Fraenkel, *Testimonia patrum. The Function of the Patristic Argument in the Theology of Philip Melanchthon* (Genève, 1961). For Chemnitz and early Lutheranism see Jaroslav Pelikan, 'Die Tradition im konfessionellen Luthertum', *Lutherische Rundschau* 6 (1956–7), pp. 228ff; *Lutheran World* 3 (1956), pp. 214–22. See my 'Reformation, Preaching and Ex Opere Operato', *Christianity Divided: Protestant and Roman Catholic Theological Issues* (New York, 1961), pp. 223–41.

[63]The Reformation position is most succinctly stated by the reformed theologian, Johannes Wollebius: 'Testimonium hoc duplex est, principale et ministeriale. Principale est testimonium spiritus sancti, – ministeriale vero testimonium est testimonium ecclesiae.' *Christianae theologiae compendium* (Basilae 1626) p. 3; quoted by Heinrich Heppe (– Ernst Bizer), *Die Dogmatik der evangelisch-reformierten Kirche* (Neukirchen, 1958²), p. 23.

[64]'Das Konzil von Trient ueber das Verhaeltnis der Heiligen Schrift und der nicht geschriebenen Traditionen', in *Die Muendliche Ueberlieferung* (Muenchen, 1957), pp. 125–206; esp. pp. 148ff. For a more detailed presentation of the 'Roman View', cf. J. K. S. Reid, *The Authority of Scripture* (New York, no year), pp. 121–44. Mr Reid omits, however, a discussion of the position of the 'new-theology' group.

followed suit: the two-sources theory results from the fact 'that the main post-Tridentine theologians misinterpreted the formula of the Council'.[65] The Council itself implicitly accepted the sufficiency of Holy Writ and understood tradition as the *viva vox evangelii*. 'For the opposite conception, that the Gospel is only partly in Scripture and partly in the traditions, was explicitly excluded.'[66]

Though Geiselmann's interpretation has not remained uncontested,[67] it has been generally well received by Roman Catholic historians and theologians.[68]

We shall simply enumerate a series of considerations which make it impossible to accept Geiselmann's thesis.

(a) The partly-partly (*partim-partim*) formula of the original draft of the Tridentine decree on the respective authorities of Scripture and tradition cannot be explained away as a product of nominalistic philosophy as Geiselmann suggests.[69] Though one has to cede to the nominalistic theologians the honour of having made the two-sources theory ripe for its official reception at Trent, the formulation 'partly-partly' as such is rare and has not yet been traced to a nominalist theologian. The more current translation of the Basilean passage, 'some – and others' (*quasdam – quasdam*), is used by Gabriel Biel but can be traced back to the early medieval canonists. In view of this textual history, one would be well advised not to give too much weight to the change of the initial 'partly-partly' to the copulative

---

[65]op. cit., p. 244.

[66]op. cit., p. 208.

[67]cf. H. Lennertz, 'Scriptura sola', in *Gregorianum* 40 (1959), pp. 38–53; 'Sine scripto traditiones', ibid., pp. 624–35; Johannes Beumer, 'Die Frage nach Schrift und Tradition bei Robert Bellarmin', in *Scholastik* 34 (1959), pp. 1–22; esp. important excursus on pp. 20ff. Alois Spindeler, 'Pari pietatis affectu. Das Tridentinum ueber Heilige Schrift und apostolische Ueberlieferungen', *Theologie und Glaube* 51 (1961), pp. 161–80. See also Hubert Jedin, a scholar who is without doubt the greatest living authority on the Council of Trent: 'Es kann nicht zweifelhaft sein, dass die Mehrzahl der in Trient anwesenden Theologen wenn nicht den Ausdruck partim-partim, so doch die Sache billigten, naemlich *dass die dogmatische Tradition einen die Schrift ergaenzenden Offenbarungsstrom beinhalte.*' *Geschichte des Konzils von Trient.* II (Freiburg, 1957), p. 61.

[68]See *Herder Korrespondenz* 8 (1959), p. 351: '. . . nach den Prinzipien katholischer Theologie und Kanonistik [wuerde] derjenigen Auffassung der Vorzug zu geben sein, die weniger in das Trienter Glaubensgesetz hineinlegt, und das ist die von Geiselmann.' Cf. Peter Lengsfeld, op. cit., p. 126, who tries to reconcile the points of view of Geiselmann, Lennertz and Beumer. See, however, Lennertz, 'Scriptura et traditio in decreto 4. sessionis Concilii Tridentini', *Gregorianum* 42 (1961), pp. 517–22. On grounds of the continued debate regarding the choice between 'simili' and 'pari' as adjectives for 'affectu', Lennertz concludes: '. . . manifestat Concilium mentem suam non mutavisse.' *Art. cit.*, p. 521. Critical of Lennertz and favouring Geiselmann is Karl Rahner, *Ueber Schriftinspiration* (Freiburg, 1959), pp. 42ff; pp. 80ff.

[69]op. cit., p. 148; p. 177.

'and' (*et*). All three formulations render satisfactory St. Basil's own choice of words (*ta men, ta de*).

(*b*) This conclusion is borne out by the statement of the cardinal legate Cervini who announces on 6th April 1546 after a night spent on the revision of the original draft that the final version is 'in substance' the same.[70] This would hardly seem compatible with the idea that the Council changed its mind.

(*c*) The energetic protest against the 'partly-partly' formulation which Geiselmann cites as the cause for the alleged change proves to be limited to two representatives, Bonacci and Nacchianti, of which the first stands under suspicion of heresy on points related to Scripture and tradition and the second was once called 'avid for novelties'.[71]

(*d*) The *Catechismus Romanus* (1566) quite clearly interprets 'and' (*et*) as 'partly-partly' (*partim-partim*) when it states that the Word of God is *distributed* over scripture and tradition.[72]

In short, the Council of Trent clearly admits that not all doctrinal truths are to be found in Holy Scripture. Tradition is seen as a second doctrinal source which does not 'simply' unfold the contents of Scripture, as in Tradition I but adding its own substance complements Holy Scripture contentwise. The gradually eroded connexion between explicit and implicit truths has been snapped; the exegetical tradition has been transformed into Tradition II.

We have gone into some detail to present the historical background and setting of the doctrinal decision taken at the Council of Trent not merely to refute Geiselmann's interpretation. However important it may be to try to set the historical record straight, we have to take Geiselmann's effort seriously as a theological expression representing a large and influential section of contemporary Roman Catholic theology. The position of this group can perhaps be best characterised by the adage: 'The total [kerygma] is in Holy Scripture and at the same time in the unwritten traditions.'[73]

---

[70]Changes have been made, 'non tamen in substantia', *C.T.* V.76.

[71]*C.T.* I.535; *C.T.* I.494. Cf. Alois Spindeler, 'Pari pietatis affectu ...', p. 171f.

[72]'Omnis autem doctrinae ratio, quae fidelibus tradenda sit, verbo Dei continetur, quod in scripturam, traditionesque distributum est.' *Praefatio*, Sectio 12, p. 7f; *Catechismus Romanus ex decreto sacrosancti Concilii Tridentini iussu S. Pii V Pontifici Maximi editus* (Romae, 1796). This *partim-partim* is of course compatible with *et* whenever one speaks about Scripture and Tradition as two sources of proof and confirmation. 'Ac de huius quidem doctrinae veritate [ignis purgatorius], quam et Scripturarum testimoniis, et Apostolica traditione confirmatam esse sancta Concilia declarant ...' De quinto articulo, Caput VI.3, p. 59: cf. De Ordinis Sacramento, Caput VII.29, p. 325.

[73]'... totum in sacra scriptura et iterum totum in sine scripto traditionibus ...', Geiselmann, op. cit., p. 206.

Geiselmann is seriously concerned to show the fallacy of the two-sources theory. But, as we shall see, this does not mean that he comes closer to an understanding of tradition in terms of Tradition I.

4. TOWARDS CONTEMPORARY THEOLOGY

Let us now indicate a few landmarks which help us to find our way in the history of Roman Catholic thought on the relation of Scripture and tradition from Trent to our own day. This is of course largely a history of the effort to interpret the mind of the Council on this point.

The authority of the Roman catechism and the wide influence of Peter Canisius and Robert Bellarmin have preserved into our own time the Tradition II concept which we found to be the intention of the participants at the Council of Trent.[74]

The Tübingen School of the first part of the nineteenth century, indebted as it is to Romanticism with its emphasis on the organic and universalistic nature of society, has become identified with the notion of 'living tradition'. Johann Adam Möhler in his *Symbolik* of 1832 presents tradition as the Gospel living in the Church, not simply as a conservation of the original deposit of faith, but as a development of it.[75] Holy Scripture is for Möhler the matter, the Church, the life-giving form.[76]

As we follow the course of the last century we should note that the Vatican Council quotes the Tridentine formulation and implies that Trent taught two parallel sources of revelation.[77] In the same year in which papal infallibility is declared, J. B. Franzelin publishes his *De Divina Traditione et Scriptura* (1870), emphasising the concept of active tradition and the importance of the succession of the doctors.[78]

The two notions of living development and binding authority of the teaching office of the Church to which Cardinal Newman and systematic theologian Jos. Scheeben (d. 1888) contributed in the same century, together

---

[74]For the post-Tridentine period see: J. R. Geiselmann, op. cit., III. 'Die Ueberwindung des Missverstaendnisses der nachtridentinischen Kontrovers-Theologie', pp. 178–206; *Die lebendige Ueberlieferung als Norm des christlichen Glaubens dargestellt im Geiste der Traditionslehre Johannes Ev. Kuhns* (Freiburg, 1959); Ives M.-J. Congar, O.P., *La Tradition et les Traditions* (Paris, 1960), pp. 233–63. Henri Holstein, *La Tradition dans l'Eglise* (Paris, 1960), pp. 103–40.

[75]*Symbolik oder Darstellung der dogmatischen Gegensaetze der Katholiken und Protestanten* (Koeln, 1958²), Par. 38–42; pp. 412–48.

[76]'Hiernach lautet der Grundsatz der Katholiken: Du wirst dich der vollen und ungeteilten christlichen Religion nur in Verbindung mit ihrer wesentlichen Form, welche da ist die Kirche, bemaechtigen', Par. 39, p. 426.

[77]*Denz.*, 1787.

[78]Congar, op. cit., p. 251; Franzelin's work has 'largement déterminé la théologie moderne', ibid.; cf. Holstein, op. cit., pp. 125ff.

with the declaration of the dogmas (1854) of the immaculate conception of the Virgin Mary, of (1870) the definition of papal infallibility and of (1950) the pronouncement of the bodily assumption of the immaculate Virgin, have led in our time to a reconsideration of the relation of the *Magisterium* as active tradition to the so-called sources of Revelation as the objective tradition. Notwithstanding appearances the debate on the relation of Scripture and extra-biblical tradition has lost some of its former urgency. A Tradition III concept is in the process of being developed by those who tend to find in the teaching office of the Church the one and only source for revelation. Scripture and tradition are then not much more than historical monuments of the past. In any case the papal encyclical *Humani Generis* of 12th August 1950 can still be understood in terms of Tradition II. According to this authoritative document, the teaching office of the Church is the *regula proxima* or immediate rule for faith.[79]

On this point, however, where we cross over into the area of present day events, we have to terminate our historical survey.

5. *QUO VADIS, PETRE?*

We want to select three systematic observations, which transcend the level of pure historical investigation but which seem to us to be implied in the foregoing: (1) The significance of Tradition I for the Protestant understanding of canon and canonicity; (2) The basic contrast between Protestant and Roman Catholic scholarship; (3) The implications of the development from Tradition II to Tradition III in Roman Catholic theology.

(1) It is important for Protestants who want to participate seriously in the present-day dialogue on the point of Scripture and tradition to know that they have to handle the traditional battle cry of *sola scriptura* with care and precision.

'Scripture alone' stands for the sufficiency of Holy Scripture. This sufficiency expresses not only a doctrinal quantitative perfection but also a spiritual qualitative perfection. This corresponds to a twofold response of the Church, the articles of faith (*fides quae*) and the act of faith (*fides qua*). It is this correspondence which is taken seriously in the concept of Tradition I.

The Reformers were more aware than their predecessors in Tradition I that a distinction between material and formal sufficiency of Holy Scripture may carry the dangerous connotation of contrast between the dead matter of Holy Scripture and the life-giving form of the Church. But they have always

---

[79]'regula proxima veritatis', *Acta apostolicae sedis* 42 (1950), p. 567.

emphasised that the sufficiency of Holy Scripture in both its material and formal aspects can only function when Scripture is opened, that is, when Scripture is seen as the Book given to the Church, which is gathered and guided by the Holy Spirit. The Holy Spirit as the principal Doctor uses the Church to lead the faithful into all truth, that is, from implicit to explicit truth, to open the Scriptures by his internal testimony; by the drawing up of confessions; but primarily and centrally by the preaching of the *kerygma*, which is the very Word of God. Since we have demonstrated the mutual interdependence of *sola scriptura* and Tradition I we are in a position to reject two claims concerning the role of Scripture, one of Protestant and one of Roman Catholic origin.

The first claim is the current Protestant insistence that the canon should be regarded, at least in principle, as open and subject to growth since the concept of a closed canon would imply the infallibility of the early Church.[80] Is it not clear, however, that the concept of an open canon to which other truths can be added is exactly that concept of tradition which we have been sketching in its development to Trent and the Vatican Council? Not Tradition I, but Tradition II operates with an open canon, open towards the overflow of revelation in tradition.

It seems equally indefensible to sacrifice the concept of a closed canon for fear of a theory of verbal inspiration of the Mormon-like Holy Book. The closing of the canon is a historical process, subject to historical investigation.

Whereas from the standpoint of Tradition II the formation of the canon is to be regarded as an approval or *creation* by the Church, Tradition I speaks in terms of *reception* of the canon by the Church. Oscar Cullmann has called the Church's acknowledgment of the canonical books an act of humility.[81] Indeed the Church thus acknowledged the necessity of an unambiguous authority amidst the confusing claims of pseudepigraphic literature and oral traditions. Those writings which we now know as the canonical books were received as sharing in the uniqueness of God's revelation in Jesus Christ. It is this unique character which is expressed and respected in the concept of the closed canon.

The second claim to which we referred comes from the Roman Catholic side. Protestantism has been accused of undermining the authority of the

---

[80]Karl Barth, *K.D.* I.2.532; recently Gerhard Ebeling, *Die Geschichtlichkeit der Kirche und ihrer Verkuendigung als theologisches Problem* (Tuebingen, 1954), p. 51.

[81]*Die Tradition als exegetisches und historisches und theologisches Problem*, (Zuerich, 1954), p. 45. Cf. his *The Early Church* (London, 1956), pp. 87–98.

canon by carving out after the example of Luther a canon within the canon.[82] To answer this claim we should first say that it is less polemical and more appropriate to speak of a living centre of Holy Scripture than of the canon within the canon.

There are at least four ways in which the idea of a canon within the canon can be shown to function without undermining the authority of Scripture. (1) Irenaeus[83] and Tertullian see Holy Scripture as the receptacle of the rule of truth or the rule of faith and mean with these expressions a series of historical acts of God which are in manifold ways reflected in Holy Scripture. (2) This nucleus is not only the historical kernel but also and at the same time the hermeneutical centre of Holy Scripture from which the lines of interpretation are drawn. (3) An historical investigation would indicate that each era and generation has and lives with its own canon even in those communions where through the centuries the same lectionary is followed. The very choice of these lections constitutes a canon within the canon. (4) Luther's hermeneutical principle 'Was Christum treibet' allows every generation in its unique historical situation to discover new treasures in Holy Scripture and to add these to those already handed down to her in the exegetical tradition of the Church.

(2) In the second place the contrast between Tradition I and Tradition II has far-reaching consequences for Protestant and Roman Catholic biblical interpretation and the exploration of the history of Christian thought. Co-operation in these fields can be fruitful, but only when the differing doctrinal bases are understood; and this basis for Roman Catholicism is of course the latest concept of the relation of Scripture and tradition.

A Roman Catholic theologian wrote in 1950 as a comment on the dogmatisation of the bodily assumption of the Virgin Mary: 'The theological discussion of mariological questions is indicative of the contemporary state of Catholic systematic theology. Since the definition of the immaculate conception, it employs a method which was before that time not usual. The weakness of proofs from Scripture and tradition gave the teaching office of the Church as the *regula proxima fidei*, a primary position which had of course its repercussion on the concept of dogma as such. Not upheld by the certainty of graspable evidence it has again been more strongly placed in the realm of irrational faith.'[84] This seems to me not an extreme statement: it points to another important contribution of nominalistic theology which first in the later Middle Ages prepared the Church for the reception of Tradition II, and now again for this new development of Roman Catholic doctrine.

Humani generis declared in 1950 that it is the task of theology to show in what way a doctrine defined by the Church is contained in the sources of faith: Scripture and tradition.[85] The task of the doctor, be he biblical scholar or Church historian, is to read the latest doctrinal decisions back into his sources. From the vantage point of medieval history, we may say that what first was the vital teaching office of the Doctor of Scripture, standing together with the Bishop as custodian of the deposit of faith, has now been transformed into the office of the Apologete of the Teaching Office of the Church; the Doctor has become the *ancilla papae*!

Scheeben, perhaps guided by the 1854 definition of the immaculate conception, had at the end of the nineteenth century granted that, though all problem areas are touched upon in Holy Scripture, not all catholic truths are contained in Holy Scripture. For the future it was even more significant that the development from 'explicit', to 'implicit', and finally to 'silent' is reflected in his thought in the distinction between analytic and synthetic interpretation.[86]

Between analytic and synthetic interpretation of the biblical and ecclesiastical sources runs the demarcation line dividing Protestant and Roman Catholic scholarship. The 'secular' codes of historical inquiry will retain an importance for the Protestant theologian which it has not for his Roman Catholic colleague. The interpretation of the decision of the Council of Trent may serve as an example.

We have argued on strictly analytical grounds that Geiselmann's interpretation of Trent is untenable. We should, however, not overrate the importance of this historical conclusion for our Roman Catholic partner. For

---

[82]Tavard, op. cit., p. 85. '. . . eine Grenze, die innerhalb eines Rahmens verschiebbar ist, bleibt auch dann nur eine verschiebbare Grenze; und mit ihrer normativen Kraft ist es aus.' Peter Lengsfeld, *Ueberlieferung* . . ., p. 94.

[83]Damien van den Eynde, op. cit., p. 187.

[84]Th. A. Sartory, *Benediktinische Monatsschrift* 1950, p. 276, note 17; quoted by Hans Grass, 'Die katholische Lehre von der Heiligen Schrift und der Tradition', *Quellen zur Konfessionskunde*, A 1 (Lueneburg, 1954), p. 63, note 29.

[85]*A.A.S.* 42.568.

[86]'. . . sie [die Tradition] kann und soll *ebensowenig* wie die Heilige Schrift eine *materiell adequate* Quelle und eine formell vollkommene Regel des Glaubens sein.' *Handbuch der katholischen Theologie*. I. *Theologische Erkenntnislehre* (Freiburg, 1959), 3 ed., n. 353, p. 171. 'In der Tat enthaelt die Schrift *die meisten und wichtigsten* Lehren der Tradition . . . in der Schrift [sind] alle Gebiete der offenbarten Wahrheiten wenigstens beruehrt, und weitaus die meisten einzelnen Wahrheiten virtuell ausgesprochen oder doch angedeutet so dass es *keine* offenbarte Wahrheit gibt, die nicht analytisch oder synthetisch als naehere Bestimmung oder Entwicklung der in der Schrift enthaltenen Wahrheiten sich darstellte und in dieser einen Anknuepfungspunkt finden koennte.' ibid., n. 298, p. 149. Peter Lengsfeld's study on tradition is an example of this new apologetic task of the doctor which should not be confused with historical inquiry. Omitting sections of the above quotations, he claims that Scheeben belongs to those who hold 'das Enthaltensein aller Heilswahrheiten in der Schrift', op. cit., p. 122, n. 140.

him it is the prerogative of his Church to interpret its own sources; the documents of the past are to be interpreted by the Teaching Office since this is the authoritative centre of the living tradition.[87] By adding now to the traditional analytic method the synthetic method of interpretation, the Tridentine decree cannot constitute for the Church an obstacle for accepting officially the thesis that everything is simultaneously contained in Scripture and in tradition.

Once such a doctrine would be officially defined which is not, or at least not yet, the case, it would instantly become the task of the Roman Catholic theologian to support Geiselmann's interpretation of the Tridentine decrees. An understanding of this basic difference as regards historical standards and method of interpretation between Roman Catholic and Protestant is a necessary condition for a realistic dialogue.

(3) Let us finally ask ourselves whether this new emphasis on the fact that everything is contained in Holy Scripture signifies a rapprochement to the Protestant position. It seems to me that the theological vision which stands behind Geiselmann's historical inquiry suggests rather that Tradition II has developed into a Tradition III concept than that it is in the process of being transformed into Tradition I, however 'open' the discussion of this matter at Vatican II may appear.

Tradition II developed, as we have said, out of Tradition I when the theologians and canon lawyers discovered that all the truths actually held by the Church could not be found explicitly or implicitly in Holy Scripture. Especially due to the mariological dogmas of 1854 and 1950, theologians have concluded once again, that not only Scripture, but now also Scripture and tradition taken together are materially insufficient to support by simple explication these authoritative definitions. Scripture and tradition are still held to be the *sources*, and the Teaching office of the Church, the *norm* which preserves and interprets the sources.[88] But in as much as this interpretation is synthetic, the norm takes on the function of the source. The Apostolic Constitution in which the bodily assumption of the Virgin Mary is defined refers to the unique consensus, not of the Church of all ages, but of the present-day Church. Not as an *argument for*, but as *part of* this authoritative definition it is announced that this divine truth is contained in the deposit of faith.

Whereas in Tradition I truth is grasped and held through reflection on

---

[87]'Totum depositum fidei ... et custodiendum et tuendum et interpretandum concrederit [Magisterio]' *A.A.S.* 42 (1950), p. 567.
[88]Apostolic Constitution *Munificentissimus Deus.* Nov. 1, 1950, *A.A.S.* 42 (1950), p. 757.

Holy Scripture and in Tradition II through reflection[89] on Scripture and Tradition, in this last stage, the stage of Tradition III, truth is grasped and held by introspection and self-analysis on the part of the Church focused in the Teaching Office.

The validity of our interpretation can perhaps be best documented by the words of the influential Roman Catholic theologian, Walter Burghardt: 'A valid argument for a dogmatic tradition, for the Church's teaching in the past can be constructed from her teaching in the present. And that is actually the approach theology took to the definability of the assumption before 1st November 1950. It began with a fact: the current consensus, in the Church teaching and in the Church taught, that the Corporeal Assumption was revealed by God. If that is true, if that is the teaching of the magisterium of the moment, if that *is* the Church's tradition, then it was always part and parcel of the Church's teaching, part and parcel of tradition.'[90]

This state of affairs is certainly not promising for the Protestant-Roman Catholic dialogue. It would be unrealistic to deny this. Oscar Cullmann could end his important essay on tradition with the encouraging observation that there is within Roman Catholicism a rising tide of interest in biblical studies proved by valuable Roman Catholic contributions to the understanding of Holy Scripture.[91] And, indeed, in the encyclical *Divino Afflante Spiritu* of 30th September 1943, a new era of Roman Catholic biblical studies has been initiated.

But in the light of the foregoing, we have to add that this upsurge of biblical research, welcome as it is to us, has to be realistically regarded as due to the movement away from the sources of revelation to the norm of revelation or in other words as due to the transformation of Scripture into a monument of the 'living tradition'.

Nevertheless, so long as the Roman Catholic Church was committed to Tradition II, it stood under the authority of its past decisions among which the Council of Trent formed a major barrier in the ecumenical dialogue. The Tradition III concept gives the Church a new and a large measure of freedom, not only over against Holy Scripture but also over against its own doctrinal past. Although therefore Tradition III does not imply a rapprochement to the Protestant position, it leaves room for the age-old dream so powerfully described by Friedrich Heiler, the dream of yearning

---

[89] cf. Barth, *K.D.* I.2.651.

[90] 'The Catholic Concept of Tradition in the Light of Modern Theological Thought', *Proceedings of the Catholic Theological Society of America* (Washington, 1951), p. 74.

[91] *The Early Church* ... p. 98.

296 THE DAWN OF THE REFORMATION

for the 'Evangelical Pope'[92] who would be able to break the bonds of tradition and guide the Roman communion back into obedience to the rule of faith and full possession of the charism of truth.

---

[92]Friedrich Heiler, *Der Katholizismus, seine Idee und seine Erscheinung*, 2nd edition (München, 1923), p. 334.

BIBLIOGRAPHICAL INFORMATION

1. "Fourteenth-Century Religious Thought: A Premature Profile," *Speculum*, 53 (January, 1978), 80–93.
   Paper read on the occasion of the Fiftieth Anniversary Meeting of the Mediaeval Academy of America on 18 April 1975, Cambridge, Mass.
2. "The Shape of Late Medieval Thought: The Birthpangs of the Modern Era," *Archiv für Reformationsgeschichte* 64 (1973), 13–33; also in *The Pursuit of Holiness in Late Medieval and Renaissance Religion*, Studies in Medieval and Reformation Thought, vol. 10, ed. Charles Trinkaus with H.A. Oberman (Leiden, 1974), 3–25.
3. "Headwaters of the Reformation. *Initia Lutheri – Initia Reformationis,*" in *Luther and the Dawn of the Modern Era. Papers for the Fourth International Congress for Luther Research*, Studies in the History of Christian Thought, vol. 8, ed. H.A. Oberman (Leiden, 1974), 40–88.
4. "Facientibus quod in se est Deus non denegat gratiam. Robert Holcot, O.P. and the Beginnings of Luther's Theology," in *The Harvard Theological Review* 55 (October, 1962), 317–342 and in *The Reformation in Medieval Perspective*, ed. Steven E. Ozment (Chicago, 1971), 119–141.
5. "'Iustitia Christi' and 'Iustitia Dei'. Luther and the Scholastic Doctrines of Justification," *The Harvard Theological Review* 59 (January, 1966), 1–26.
6. "Simul gemitus et raptus: Luther and Mysticism," in *The Reformation in Medieval Perspective*, ed. Steven E. Ozment, Chicago, 1971, 219–251, and in *Kirche, Mystik, Heiligung und das Natürliche bei Luther*, Vorträge des Dritten Internationalen Kongresses für Lutherforschung, ed. I. Asheim, (Göttingen, 1967), 20–59.
7. "The Gospel of Social Unrest: 450 Years after the so-called 'German Peasants' War' of 1525," *Harvard Theological Review* 69 (1976), 103–129.
   Also in *The German Peasant War of 1525 – New Viewpoints*, eds. B. Scribner, G. Benecke (London, 1979), 39–51.
8. "Reformation and Revolution: Copernicus' Discovery in an Era of Change," in *The Nature of Scientific Discovery*, ed. Owen Gingerich (Washington, D.C., 1975), 134–169; expanded version in *The Cultural Context of Medieval Learning*, eds. J.E. Murdoch, E.D. Sylla (Dordrecht, 1975), 397–435.
9. "Duns Scotus, Nominalism, and the Council of Trent," in *John Duns Scotus, 1265–1965*, eds. J.K. Ryan, B.M. Bonansea (Washington, D.C., 1965), 311–344.
10. "The 'Extra' Dimension in the Theology of Calvin," *The Journal of Ecclesiastical History* 21 (January, 1970), 43–64. Originally in German, "Die 'Extra'-Dimension in der Theologie Calvins," in *Geist und Geschichte der Reformation*, Festgabe Hanns Rückert, eds. Heinz Liebing, Klaus Scholder (Berlin, 1966), 323–356.

11. "Calvin's Critique of Calvinism," in *Christian Higher Education. The Contemporary Challenge*, Proceedings of the First International Conference of Reformed Institutions for Christian Scholarship, Potchefstroom, 1975; published by the Institute for the Advancement of Calvinism (Potchefstroom, 1976), 372–381.

12. "Quo vadis, Petre? Tradition from Irenaeus to Humani generis", in *Scottish Journal of Theology* 16 (1963), 225–255.

INDEX OF NAMES & PLACES

Étaples, Lefèvre d' – see Faber
   Stapulensis
Euclid 68
Europe 1, 8, 19, 25, 26, 155, 172, 173,
   188, 236
Eustachius van Zichem 251
Eutyches 248
Eynde, Damien van den 292

Faber Stapulensis 57, 79, 133, 146, 147,
   150
Favaroni, Augustinus 68, 69, 70, 73, 74,
   83
Ferguson, Wallace K. 19
Festugière, A.J. 84
Fevyn, Joh. de 167
Ficino, Marsilio 9, 33, 37
Ficker, Joh. 126
Fidati, Simon 73
Fife, Robert H. 94
Finkenzeller, Josef 282
Finsler, Georg, II 48
Fischer, Robert H. 71
Fitzralph, Richard 111
Flajshans, Wenzel 214, 223
Flanders 165
Fleischlin, Bernhard 170
Flesseman, E., van Leer 271
Florence 22
Forster, Anselm 118
Fraenkel, Peter 286
France 12, 21, 39, 155, 192
Francis, St. 4, 23, 24
Franz, Günther 21, 46, 156, 177
Franz, Marie Louise von 129
Franzelin, J.B. 289
Frederick the Wise 235
Freising, Otto of 212
French, Peter J. 199
Friedberg, E. 25, 277
Friedensburg, Walter 75
Friemel, Salesius 69
Fuchs, Walther Peter 156

Gabriel, Astrik L. 56, 281
Gaismair, Michael 156, 163, 164
Galileo 28, 181, 182, 183, 188, 200, 201
Ganoczy, Alexandre 247, 264
Gansfort, Wessel 56, 57, 139, 152, 282,
   283
Geiler, John, of Kaiserberg 56, 137, 143,
   152, 216, 226
Geiling, Joh. 41

Geiselmann, J.R. 209, 272, 286-289,
   293, 294
Geneva 39, 163, 172, 236, 260
George, St. 177
Gerlach, Horst 157,161
Germany 21, 52, 57, 104, 165, 166, 167,
   170, 176, 192
Gerrish, Brian A. 63, 65
Gerson, Jean 25, 31, 32, 33, 34, 36, 37,
   43, 54, 57, 111, 113, 126, 130, 131,
   133, 135, 136, 137, 138, 143, 145,
   151, 152, 185, 186, 192, 196, 208,
   225, 226, 278, 282
Ghellinck, J. de 85
Giese, Bishop Tideman 189
Giles of Rome 48, 73
Giles of Viterbo 66
Gilmore, Myron P. 49, 281
Gilson, Etienne 2, 3, 89, 92, 133, 274
Gingerich, Owen 181
Giotto 4
Goldast 282
Gollwitzer, Helmut 242
Goot, Henry van der 259
Gorcum, Heinrich of 4
Grabmann, Martin 2, 3
Graham, W. Fred 267
Grane, Leif 10, 59, 60, 62, 64, 75, 104,
   226
Grass, Hans 240, 241, 292
Gratian of Bologna 277
Graus, Frantisek 22, 25
Great Britain 13, 219, 221, 255
Grebel, Conrad 236
Gregory of Rimini 7, 8, 10, 11, 45, 54,
   56, 61, 67, 68, 69, 73, 74, 75, 76, 77,
   82, 83, 86, 91, 107, 131, 213, 220,
   221, 229, 256, 278, 282
Gregory the Great 136
Greschat, Martin 51
Grey, Hanna 37
Grillmeier, Aloys 247
Grimm, Harold J. 116
Grisar, H. 59
Groote, Geert 15, 137, 140
Grossmann, Maria 74
Grossmünster 235
Grottaferrata 12
Grunenberg, Joh. 143
Grünewald, Kate 141

Hägglund, Bengt 59, 95, 96, 148, 273
Haitjema, Th. L. 254